The United Nations in the 21st Century

Dilemmas in World Politics

Series Editor: Jennifer Sterling-Folker, University of Connecticut

Why is it difficult to achieve the universal protection of human rights? How can democratization be achieved so that it is equitable and lasting? Why does agreement on global environmental protection seem so elusive? How does the concept of gender play a role in the shocking inequalities of women throughout the globe? Why do horrific events such as genocide or ethnic conflicts recur or persist? These are the sorts of questions that confront policymakers and students of contemporary international politics alike. They are dilemmas because they are enduring problems in world affairs that are difficult to resolve.

These are the types of dilemmas at the heart of the Dilemmas in World Politics series. Each book in the Dilemmas in World Politics series addresses a challenge or problem in world politics that is topical, recurrent, and not easily solved. Each is structured to cover the historical and theoretical aspects of the dilemma, as well as the policy alternatives for and future direction of the problem. The books are designed as supplements to introductory and intermediate courses in international relations. The books in the Dilemmas in World Politics series encourage students to engage in informed discussion of current policy issues.

Books in This Series

The United Nations in the 21st Century, Fifth Edition
Karen A. Mingst, Margaret P. Karns, and Alynna J. Lyon

Global Environmental Politics, Seventh Edition
Pamela S. Chasek, David L. Downie, and Janet Welsh Brown

Global Gender Issues in the New Millennium, Fourth Edition
V. Spike Peterson and Anne Sisson Runyan

United States Foreign Policy in the 21st Century: Gulliver's Travails
J. Martin Rochester

Democracy and Democratization in a Changing World, Third Edition
Georg Sørensen

International Human Rights, Fourth Edition
Jack Donnelly

Southern Africa in World Politics
Janice Love

Ethnic Conflict in World Politics, Second Edition
Barbara Harff and Ted Robert Gurr

Dilemmas of International Trade, Second Edition
Bruce E. Moon

Humanitarian Challenges and Intervention, Second Edition
Thomas G. Weiss and Cindy Collins

The European Union: Dilemmas of Regional Integration
James A. Caporaso

International Futures, Third Edition
Barry B. Hughes

Revolution and Transition in East-Central Europe, Second Edition
David S. Mason

One Land, Two Peoples, Second Edition
Deborah Gerner

Dilemmas of Development Assistance
Sarah J. Tisch and Michael B. Wallace

East Asian Dynamism, Second Edition
Steven Chan

FIFTH EDITION

The United Nations in the 21st Century

KAREN A. MINGST,

MARGARET P. KARNS,

AND

ALYNNA J. LYON

WESTVIEW
PRESS

Westview Press was founded in 1975 in Boulder, Colorado, by notable publisher and intellectual Fred Praeger. Westview Press continues to publish scholarly titles and high-quality undergraduate- and graduate-level textbooks in core social science disciplines. With books developed, written, and edited with the needs of serious nonfiction readers, professors, and students in mind, Westview Press honors its long history of publishing books that matter.

Copyright © 2017 by Westview Press

Published by Westview Press,
An imprint of Perseus Books
A Hachette Book Group company
2465 Central Avenue
Boulder, CO 80301

www.westviewpress.com

Every effort has been made to secure required permissions for all text, images, maps, and other art reprinted in this volume.

Westview Press books are available at special discounts for bulk purchases in the United States by corporations, institutions, and other organizations. For more information, please contact the Special Markets Department at 2300 Chestnut Street, Suite 200, Philadelphia, PA 19103, or call (800) 810-4145, ext. 5000, or e-mail special.markets@perseusbooks.com.

A CIP catalog record for the print version of this book is available from the Library of Congress.

PB ISBN: 978-0-8133-4964-0
EBOOK ISBN: 978-0-8133-5048-6

10 9 8 7 6 5 4 3 2 1

Contents

Illustrations

Tables

Boxes

Figures

Photographs

Cartoons

Preface

More than twenty years have passed since we first wrote this book. With each successive edition, we have endeavored to keep it fresh while preserving elements that seem to work well. We are reminded this time, once again, how much we live in a world of rapid change, and of the challenge of not allowing the length of the book to grow too much. The twenty-first century is more than a decade and a half old now and the Cold War's end, which inspired the first edition, seems ever more distant. Even more than when we did the fourth edition, the dynamics of world politics are being reshaped by rising powers, particularly China, and by both Russia's and China's greater assertiveness. The threat of transnational terrorism seems to grow rather than diminish, particularly with the emergence of ISIS. The UN continues to take on ever more ambitious peace operations, blurring the boundary between peacekeeping and enforcement, with more peacekeepers in the field than at any other time in its seventy years. Even as it launches a second major development initiative, the Sustainable Development Goals, its role in international economic relations more broadly is further diminished as the IMF, World Bank, World Trade Organization, G-20, and other bodies play more important roles in dealing with financial crises, trade, and development. The effects of climate change are now more apparent than ever, and the agreement reached at the 2015 Paris conference finally promises concrete, if still inadequate, steps to address it. And, despite the seeming consensus on the responsibility to protect civilians at risk in armed conflicts, humanitarian crises, and natural disasters, the reality continues to be a very selective will to act, as the 2015 refugee and migration crisis has shown.

This new edition adds a fourth dilemma—the need for inclusiveness, such as by appointing more women to senior positions within the UN, advocating for other marginalized groups, and providing more access for civil society—which can be in conflict with deep-seated prejudices, cultural practices, and inequalities. In addition to general updates, readers will find new case studies of the 2015 Paris climate change conference, the refugee and migration crisis, WHO and Ebola, failed statebuilding efforts in South Sudan, complex peacekeeping in Mali, and the debate over why the Security Council authorized humanitarian intervention in Libya in 2011 but not in Syria since then. We also examine China's growing role as a major power within the UN system, the effects of China and Russia's greater assertiveness in the use of the veto, and recent analyses of targeted sanctions and of the International Criminal Court.

In updating the book, we have welcomed Alynna Lyon as a third coauthor. We wish to thank Charla Burnett, a doctoral student at the University of Massachusetts Boston, for her assistance with the new case study on the refugee and migration crisis. We also thank Lynne Rienner for allowing us to use material on the United Nations from the third edition of our book *International Organizations: The Politics and Processes of Global Governance* (2015). We dedicate this fifth edition to our children and grandchildren, Ginger, Brett, Paul, McKayla, Madelyn, Quintin, and Anna, whose generations must sustain the United Nations in the twenty-first century. And we wish to thank our husbands, Robert Stauffer, Ralph Johnston, and Daniel Hartman, whose patience, support, and encouragement have enabled us to bring this work to fruition.

Karen A. Mingst
Margaret P. Karns
Alynna J. Lyon

Acronyms

AfDB	African Development Bank
AFISMA	African-led International Support Mission to Mali
AI	Amnesty International
AIIB	Asian Infrastructure Investment Bank
AMISOM	African Union Mission to Somalia
ANC	African National Congress
ASEAN	Association of Southeast Asian Nations
AU	African Union
BRICS	Brazil, Russia, India, China, South Africa (emerging powers)
CACM	Central American Common Market
CAR	Central African Republic
CARE	Cooperative for Assistance and Relief Everywhere
CEDAW	Convention on the Elimination of All Forms of Discrimination Against Women
CFCs	chlorofluorocarbons
CGIAR	Consultative Group on International Agricultural Research
CoNGO	Conference of Non-Governmental Organisations in Consultative Status with UN ECOSOC
COP	Conference of Parties
CSD	Commission on Sustainable Development
CSO	civil society organization
CSW	Commission on the Status of Women
CTC	Counter-Terrorism Committee
CTED	Counter-Terrorism Executive Directorate
CTITF	Counter-Terrorism Implementation Task Force
CWC	Chemical Weapons Convention
DPKO	UN Department of Peacekeeping Operations
DRC	Democratic Republic of the Congo
ECA	Economic Commission for Africa
ECE	Economic Commission for Europe

ECLA	Economic Commission for Latin America
ECOSOC	United Nations Economic and Social Council
ECOWAS	Economic Community of West African States
EPTA	Expanded Programme of Technical Assistance
ESCAP	Economic and Social Commission for Asia and the Pacific
EU	European Union (previously referred to as the European Community [EC] or the European Economic Community [EEC])
FAO	Food and Agriculture Organization
G-4	Group of Four
G-7	Group of Seven
G-8	Group of Eight
G-20	Group of Twenty
G-77	Group of 77
GATT	General Agreement on Tariffs and Trade
GCC	Gulf Cooperation Council
GDP	gross domestic product
GEF	Global Environmental Facility
GNP	gross national product
GONGOs	government-organized nongovernmental organizations
GSP	Generalized System of Preferences
HDI	Human Development Index
HIPC	Heavily Indebted Poor Countries Initiative
HIV/AIDS	human immunodeficiency virus/acquired immune deficiency syndrome
HRC	Human Rights Council
HRW	Human Rights Watch
IAEA	International Atomic Energy Agency
IATA	International Association of Transport Airlines
IBRD	International Bank for Reconstruction and Development (also known as the World Bank)
ICAO	International Civil Aviation Organization
ICC	International Criminal Court
ICJ	International Court of Justice
ICRC	International Committee of the Red Cross
ICSID	International Centre for Settlement of Investment Disputes
ICTR	International Criminal Tribunal for Rwanda
ICTY	International Criminal Tribunal for the Former Yugoslavia
IDA	International Development Association
IDB	Inter-American Development Bank
IDP	internally displaced persons

IFAD   International Fund for Agricultural Development
IFC   International Finance Corporation
IFOR   Implementation Force (NATO force in the former Yugoslavia)
IGO   international intergovernmental organization
IHR   International Health Regulations
ILGA   International Lesbian, Gay, Bisexual, Trans, and Intersex Association
ILO   International Labour Organization
IMF   International Monetary Fund
IMO   International Maritime Organization
INGO   international nongovernmental organization
INSTRAW   International Research and Training Institute for the Advancement of Women
IO   international organization
IOM   International Organization for Migration
IPCC   Intergovernmental Panel on Climate Change
IR   international relations
ISAF   International Security Assistance Force
ISIS   Islamic State of Iraq and Syria
ITU   International Telecommunication Union
KFOR   Kosovo Force (NATO)
LDCs   less developed countries (also referred to as "the South")
LGBT   lesbian, gay, bisexual, and transgender persons
MDGs   Millennium Development Goals
MIGA   Multilateral Investment Guarantee Agency
MINUSMA   Multidimensional Integrated Stabilization Mission in Mali
MNCs   multinational corporations
MONUC   UN Organization Mission in the Democratic Republic of the Congo
MONUSCO   UN Organization Stabilization Mission in the Democratic Republic of the Congo
MSF   Médecins Sans Frontières (Doctors Without Borders)
MSLR   mean sea-level rise
NAM   Nonaligned Movement
NATO   North Atlantic Treaty Organization
NEPAD   New Partnership for Africa's Development
NGO   nongovernmental organization
NIEO   New International Economic Order
NNWS   non-nuclear-weapon states
NPT   Treaty on the Non-Proliferation of Nuclear Weapons

NWS nuclear-weapon states
OAS Organization of American States
OAU Organization of African Unity
OCHA Office for the Coordination of Humanitarian Affairs
OFFP Oil-for-Food Programme
OHCHR Office of the High Commissioner for Human Rights
OIC Organisation of Islamic Cooperation
OIHP Office International d'Hygiène Publique
OPCW Organisation for the Prohibition of Chemical Weapons
OPEC Organization of Petroleum Exporting Countries
OSCE Organization for Security and Cooperation in Europe
P-5 permanent members of the UN Security Council
PBC Peacebuilding Commission
PBSO Peacebuilding Source Office
PCA Permanent Court of Arbitration
PLO Palestine Liberation Organization
POC protection of civilians
PRC People's Republic of China
PRSP Poverty Reduction Strategy Papers
R2P responsibility to protect (also RtoP)
ROC Republic of China (Taiwan)
RPF Rwandan Patriotic Front
SADC Southern African Development Community
SARS severe acute respiratory syndrome
SDGs Sustainable Development Goals
SRSG Special Representative of the Secretary-General
SWAPO South West Africa People's Organization
UN United Nations
UNAIDS United Nations Joint Programme on HIV/AIDS
UNAMID AU-UN Mission in Darfur
UNAMIR United Nations Assistance Mission in Rwanda
UNCED United Nations Conference on the Environment and Development
UNCHE United Nations Conference on the Human Environment
UNCLOS United Nations Conference on the Law of the Sea
UNCTAD United Nations Conference on Trade and Development
UNDP United Nations Development Programme
UNEF I, II United Nations Emergency Force (in Egypt)
UNEP United Nations Environment Programme

UNESCO United Nations Educational, Scientific and Cultural
Organization
UNFCCC United Nations Framework Convention on Climate Change
UNFICYP United Nations Force in Cyprus
UNFPA United Nations Fund for Population Activities
UN.GIFT United Nations Global Initiative to Fight Human
Trafficking
UNHCR United Nations High Commissioner for Refugees
UNICEF United Nations Children's Fund
UNIDO United Nations Industrial Development Organization
UNIFEM United Nations Development Fund for Women
UNIFIL United Nations Interim Force in Lebanon
UNIHP United Nations Intellectual History Project
UNIKOM United Nations Iraq-Kuwait Observer Mission
UNITA National Union for the Total Independence of Angola
UNITAF Unified Task Force on Somalia (also known as Operation
Restore Hope)
UNMEER United Nations Mission for Ebola Emergency Response
UNMIK United Nations Mission in Kosovo
UNMIL United Nations Mission in Liberia
UNMISS UN Mission in South Sudan
UNMIT UN Integrated Mission in Timor
UNMOVIC United Nations Monitoring, Verification, and Inspection
Commission (in Iraq)
UN-NGLS United Nations Non-Governmental Liaison Services
UNOCI United Nations Operation in Côte d'Ivoire
UNODC United Nations Office of Drugs and Crime
UNOSOM I, II United Nations Operation in Somalia
UNPROFOR United Nations Protection Force (in the former Yugoslavia)
UNRWA United Nations Relief and Works Agency
UNSCOM United Nations Special Commission for the Disarmament
of Iraq
UNSG United Nations Secretary-General
UNTAC United Nations Transitional Authority in Cambodia
UNTAET United Nations Transitional Administration in East Timor
UNTAG United Nations Transition Assistance Group (in Namibia)
UPR Universal Periodic Review
UPU Universal Postal Union
WCED World Commission on Environment and Development

WFP World Food Programme
WHA World Health Assembly
WHO World Health Organization
WIPO World Intellectual Property Organization
WMD weapons of mass destruction
WTO World Trade Organization

1

The United Nations in World Politics

For more than seventy years, the United Nations has played a key role in shaping the world as we know it. It is consistently called upon to respond to both human and natural disasters, and to coordinate global efforts on the challenges of poverty, health security, women's empowerment, and climate change. As the UN marked its seventieth anniversary in 2015, it was hard to imagine the world without it despite its many ups and downs over the years. It has embodied humankind's hopes for a better world through the prevention of conflict. It has promoted a culture of legality and rule of law. It has raised awareness of the plight of the world's poor, and it has boosted development by providing **technical assistance**. It has promoted concern for human rights, including the status of women, the rights of the child, and the unique needs of indigenous peoples. It has been the source of numerous concepts and ideas over its history, including **peacekeeping**, human development, and sustainable development. It contributed immensely to making **multilateral diplomacy** the primary way in which international norms, public policies, and law are established. It has served as a catalyst for global policy networks and partnerships with other actors. It plays a central role in **global governance**. Along the way, the UN has earned several Nobel Peace Prizes, including a 2005 award to the International Atomic Energy Agency (IAEA); the 2001 prize to the UN and Secretary-General Kofi Annan; the 1988 award to UN peacekeepers; and the 1969 honor to the International Labour Organization (ILO).

In the many areas of UN activity, we can point to the UN's accomplishments and also to its shortcomings and failures. More than seventy years after its creation, the UN continues to be the only **international organization (IO)** or, more correctly, **international intergovernmental organization (IGO)** of global scope and nearly universal membership that has an agenda encompassing the broadest range of governance issues. It is a complex system that serves as the central site for multilateral diplomacy, with the UN's General Assembly as center stage. Three weeks of general debate at the opening of each fall assembly session draw foreign ministers and heads of state from small and large states to take advantage of the opportunity to address the nations of the world and to engage in intensive diplomacy. Diplomats are joined by activists, **nongovernmental organizations (NGOs)**, international corporations, and civil society groups for discussions both within and around the UN to address the growing demands of a complex and globalized world. As one member of the UN staff describes it, "The whole world comes to New York in September, and the UN provides great value in bringing everyone together, even if they are not working through the UN."[1]

As an IGO, however, the UN is the creation of its member states; it is they who decide what that they will allow this organization to do and what resources—financial and otherwise—they will provide. In this regard, the UN is very much subject to the winds of world politics and the whims of member governments. To understand the UN today, it is useful to look back at some of the major changes in world politics and how they affected the UN.

THE UNITED NATIONS IN WORLD POLITICS: VISION AND REALITY

The establishment of the United Nations in the closing days of World War II was an affirmation of the desire of war-weary nations for an organization that could help them avoid future conflicts and promote international economic and social cooperation. As we discuss further in Chapter 2, the UN's Charter built on lessons learned from the failed League of Nations created at the end of World War I and earlier experiments with international unions, conference diplomacy, and dispute settlement mechanisms. It represented an expression of hope for the possibilities of a new global security arrangement and for fostering the social and economic conditions necessary for peace to prevail.

The United Nations and Politics in the Cold War World
The World War II coalition of great powers (the United States, the Soviet Union, Great Britain, France, and China), whose unity had been key to the UN's founding, was nevertheless a victim of rising tensions almost before the first General Assembly session in 1946. Developments in Europe and Asia between 1946 and 1950 soon made it clear that the emerging Cold War would have fundamental effects on the UN. How could a **collective security** system operate when there was no unity among the great powers on whose cooperation it depended? Even

the admission of new members was affected between 1950 and 1955 because each side vetoed applications from states that were allied with the other.

The Cold War made Security Council actions on threats to peace and security extremely problematic, with repeated sharp exchanges and frequent deadlock. Some conflicts, such as the French and American wars in Vietnam and the Soviet interventions in Czechoslovakia and Hungary, were never brought to the UN at all. The UN was able to respond to the North Korean invasion of South Korea in 1950 only because the Soviet Union was boycotting the Security Council at the time.

In order to deal with a number of regional conflicts, the UN developed something never mentioned in its charter, namely, peacekeeping; this has involved the prevention, containment, and moderation of hostilities between or within states through the use of lightly armed multinational forces of soldiers, police, and civilians. UN peacekeeping forces were used extensively in the Middle East and in conflicts arising out of the decolonization process during the Cold War period. Thirteen operations were deployed from 1948 to 1988. The innovation of peacekeeping illustrates what the Cold War did to the UN: "It had repealed the proposition that the organization should undertake to promote order by bringing the great powers into troubled situations. . . . Henceforward, the task of the United Nations was to be defined as that of keeping the great powers out of such situations."[2]

The Effects of the Nuclear Revolution. The UN Charter had just been signed when the use of two atomic bombs on Japan on August 6 and 10, 1945, began a scientific and technological revolution in warfare that would have a far-reaching impact on the post–World War II world. The earliest and most obvious effect of nuclear weapons was to restore the issue of disarmament to the UN's agenda. Disarmament as an approach to peace had been discredited during the interwar era, but the UN almost from its inception in early 1946 became a forum for discussions and negotiations on **arms control and disarmament**. Hence, the nuclear threat not only transformed world politics but also made the UN the key place where world leaders sought to persuade each other that war had become excessively dangerous, that disarmament and arms control were imperative, and that they were devoted to peace and restraint.

The Role of the United Nations in Decolonization and the Emergence of New States. At the close of World War II, few would have predicted the end of colonial rule in Africa and Asia. Yet twenty-five years after the UN Charter was signed, at the height of the Cold War, most of the former colonies had achieved independence with relatively little threat to international peace and security. Membership in the UN more than doubled from 51 states in 1945 to 118 in 1965

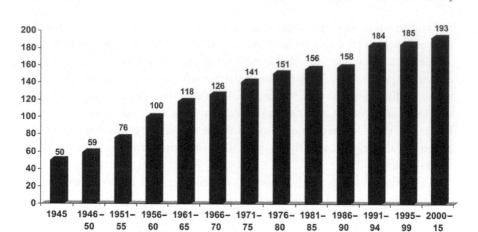

FIGURE 1.1. Growth in UN Membership, 1945–2015

Sources: Compiled from Robert E. Riggs and Jack C. Plano, *The United Nations: International Organization of World Politics*, 2nd ed. (Belmont, CA: Wadsworth, 1994), 45, and updated.

and had tripled by 1980 (see Figure 1.1), the vast majority of these new members being newly independent states. Twenty-six new states were later seated in the UN after the Cold War's end, mostly as a result of the dissolution of the Soviet Union and Yugoslavia.

The UN played a significant role in this remarkably peaceful transformation. The UN Charter endorsed the principle of **self-determination**. Already independent former colonies, such as India, Egypt, Indonesia, and the Latin American states, used the UN as a forum to advocate an end to colonialism and independence for territories ruled by Great Britain, France, the Netherlands, Belgium, Spain, and Portugal. Success added new votes to the growing anticolonial coalition, so by 1960 a majority of the UN's members favored decolonization. General Assembly Resolution 1514 that year condemned the continuation of colonial rule and preconditions for granting independence (such as a lack of preparation for self-rule) and called for annual reports on progress toward independence for all remaining colonial territories. In short, the UN was an important forum for the **collective legitimation** of a change in international norms (that is, colonialism and imperialism were no longer acceptable patterns of state behavior, and colonial peoples had a right to self-determination).

The consequences of decolonization and the expanded number of independent states were manifold. The less developed states of Africa, Asia, and Latin America formed a strong coalition within the UN known as the **Group of 77 (G-77)** and commanded a majority of votes on a broad range of issues after 1960. Whereas the Cold War had shaped politics in the UN until 1960, the G-77, and what became known as the North-South conflict between the developed countries of the industrial North and the less developed countries (LDCs) of the South, shaped much of the politics thereafter. The two conflicts became entwined in complex ways. For example, the Soviet Union and many Western European states often sided with the G-77, and the United States frequently found itself in a small minority.

Beginning in the 1960s, new issues, especially issues of economic and social development, proliferated on the UN's agenda, many at the urging of the G-77. For example, in 1967, Arvid Pardo, the representative from Malta, argued on behalf of newly independent states that the resources found on the deep seabed were the "common heritage of mankind," not the property of any specific nation. This subsequently had an impact on emerging environmental issues as well as on the law of the sea. Of all the issues pushed by the G-77, however, none received more attention than the drive for economic and social development.

The North-South Conflict. The ideological leaning of the G-77 in the 1960s and 1970s toward a heavy government role in economic development and re-distribution of wealth shaped many UN programs and activities. In the 1970s the G-77 pushed for a **New International Economic Order (NIEO)**, marshaling support in the UN General Assembly for "A Declaration on the Establishment of a New International Economic Order" and "A Charter of Economic Rights and Duties of States." For most of the decade, the NIEO debates dominated and polarized the UN system, with the deep divide between North and South at times making agreement on both economic and security issues impossible to achieve.

The North-South conflict continues to be a central feature of world politics, and hence of the UN, although the rhetoric and issues of the NIEO sharply diminished in the late 1980s and 1990s. For example, the UN's treatment of environmental issues, which began with the Stockholm Conference on the Human Environment in 1972, has been permeated by North-South differences. The 1997 Kyoto Conference on Climate Change heard echoes of the North-South conflict when developing countries insisted that industrial countries make the first reductions in carbon dioxide emissions. Those echoes still persist in the negotiations on climate change. The G-77, however, is no longer as cohesive a group; its members' interests increasingly diverged in the 1980s when some states, especially in Southeast Asia, achieved rapid economic growth and as many developing countries shifted from statist-oriented economic policies to neoliberal ones, calling for open markets and privatization. Chapter 5 discusses these shifts further as well as the increased emphasis on poverty alleviation that accompanied the now concluded **Millennium Development Goals (MDGs)** and the **Sustainable Development Goals (SDGs)** approved in 2015.

World Politics Since the Cold War's End

The Cold War's end in 1990 meant not only new cooperation among the five permanent members of the Security Council but also a resurgence of nationalism, civil wars, and ethnic conflicts; the new phenomenon of failed states; and a related series of humanitarian crises. The consequence was greater demands than ever before on the United Nations to deal with threats to peace and security as well as environmental and developmental issues, democratization, population growth, humanitarian crises, and other problems. UN peacekeepers were called on to rebuild Cambodia; create peace in Bosnia; organize and monitor postconflict elections in Nicaragua, Namibia, and many other places; monitor human rights violations in El Salvador; and oversee humanitarian relief in Bosnia, Somalia, Rwanda, Kosovo, the Democratic Republic of the Congo (DRC), East Timor, and Afghanistan. Since Iraq's invasion of Kuwait in 1990, the UN's enforcement powers have been used more in the post–Cold War era than at any previous time.

In the late 1980s and 1990s, **democratization** spread to all regions of the globe, from Latin America, Eastern Europe, and states created from the former Soviet Union to Africa and Asia. Many authoritarian governments were forced to open their political processes to competing political parties, adopt more stringent human rights standards, and hold free elections. Since 1990 the UN has been in heavy demand to provide observers for elections in countries around the world. UN-sanctioned intervention in Haiti in 1993 marked the first time the UN took action to restore a democratically elected government. In Namibia, Kosovo, Bosnia, East Timor, and, most recently, South Sudan, the UN was called upon to assist with organizing the elements of newly independent states, including the provision of transitional administrations, writing of constitutions, training of police and judges, and organization of elections. The trend toward more democratization has regressed in recent years, however.

By 1995, the early post–Cold War optimism about the United Nations had faded. The peacekeepers in Somalia, Bosnia, and Rwanda found little peace to be kept, although their presence did alleviate much human suffering. Despite almost continuous meetings of the UN Security Council and numerous resolutions, the UN's members lacked the political will to provide the military, logistical, and financial resources needed to deal adequately with these and other complex situations. In addition, the UN faced a deep financial crisis in the late 1990s caused by the increased cost of peacekeeping and other activities and the failure of many members, including the United States, to pay their assessed contributions. The organization clearly needed significant reforms to meet the increased demands and address weaknesses in its structures and operations, but member states failed to use either the occasion of the UN's fiftieth anniversary in 1995 or the sixtieth anniversary in 2005 to approve many of the necessary changes. Some changes could be and were made without member states' approval, however. And, in its responses to many complex conflicts, humanitarian crises, new threats to peace posed by nuclear weapons proliferation and terrorism, and persistent global poverty, the UN demonstrated that it was still central to many aspects of global governance, as discussed in subsequent chapters.

Beginning in the 1970s, well before the Cold War's end, the UN began to play an important role on a nexus of **interdependence** issues by convening global conferences and summits on topics ranging from the environment, food, housing, the law of the sea, disarmament, women, and water to human rights, population and development, and social development. These conferences articulated new international norms; expanded international law; set agendas for governments and the UN itself, through programs of action; and promoted linkages among the growing communities of NGOs active on different issues, the UN, and member states' governments.

The UN has never played a central role in international economic relations, however. Although economic topics appear on the agendas of the General Assembly and the United Nations Economic and Social Council (ECOSOC), much of the decisionmaking has always taken place in institutions that have never really been part of the UN system. The **Bretton Woods institutions**—the World Bank, the International Monetary Fund (IMF), and the former General Agreement on Tariffs and Trade (GATT)—while technically part of the system, have operated quite independently. The World Trade Organization (WTO, established in 1995 as the successor to GATT), the **Group of 7 (G-7)**, the **Group of 20 (G-20)**, major corporations, and banks are all outside the UN system. The UN has, however, been active from its earliest years in efforts to promote economic and social development, introducing the ideas of development aid in the 1950s, sustainable development in the 1980s, human development in the 1990s, the MDGs in the 2000s, and now the SDGs. Many of the global conferences reinforced understanding of the way development overlaps with the status of women, population, food, and other problems. UN Secretary-General Kofi Annan used the occasion of the new millennium to convene a Millennium Summit in 2000, hoping "to harness the symbolic power of the millennium to the real and urgent needs of people everywhere."[3] His special report, *We the Peoples*, provided his views of the state of the world, the major global challenges, and the need for structural reform of the UN itself. Annan's successor, Secretary-General Ban Ki-moon, convened the Climate Summit in 2014, bringing together more than one hundred heads of state or government and leaders from the private sector and civil society to marshal support for efforts to address the central environmental challenge of the twenty-first century.

Over the last thirty years, what had initially appeared to be simply growing interdependence among states and peoples has become something much more fundamental—a complex multidimensional process of economic, cultural, and social change. **Globalization** is the process of increasing worldwide integration of politics, economics, social relations, and culture that often appears to undermine state **sovereignty**. Particularly noticeable is the rapid pace of change, the compression of time and space, and the scale and scope of interconnectedness. In its contemporary form, globalization has linked economic markets, cultures, peoples, and states to an unprecedented degree. This is thanks to improvements in transportation and communications that speed the movement of ideas, goods, news, capital, technology, and people, and to the deregulation and privatization of businesses, finance, and services in many countries.

Many regard globalization as desirable because it has fueled greater prosperity and higher standards of living in many parts of the world. Others, however, point to the growing inequality among and within nations and the ways in which globalization creates both winners and losers, such as those whose jobs in developed countries are lost to workers in developing countries who are paid lower wages. There is also the dark side of globalization, which has facilitated the growth of trafficking in drugs and persons, transnational terrorism, and other criminal enterprises. Finally, as globalization promotes industrialization and consumption, it has increasing ecological and environmental impacts. Many are concerned that the regulations and incentives that could mitigate the damages associated with globalization are still lacking.

The UN itself and various **specialized agencies** within the UN system have struggled to address globalization issues. Although the International Labour Organization, World Health Organization (WHO), and World Intellectual Property Organization (WIPO) are very much involved in globalization-related issues of labor, health, and intellectual property rights, the fact that the targets of anti-globalization protesters have been the World Bank, IMF, G-7, and WTO has underscored the UN's marginal role in international economic relations. Yet globalization has fueled the growth of NGOs. Subsequent chapters illustrate how the UN and NGOs, which represent what some have called global **civil society** and still others refer to as part of the "third UN," are involved in new partnerships that make each more responsive to globalization issues.

The emergence of the United States as the world's sole superpower was another aspect of post–Cold War world politics, the era of globalization, and the early twenty-first century. The economic and military capabilities of the United States far exceeded those of any other state, and with the collapse of the Soviet Union, the United States had no serious rival. Many worried that this development would result in the UN's marginalization, particularly if, or when, the United States chose to act unilaterally. This view was borne out when the United

States invaded Iraq in 2003 in defiance of international opposition and vigorous Security Council debate. An alternative view was that the UN could become a puppet of the sole superpower, dependent upon its goodwill for funding and subservient in authorizing US actions. Yet in the late 1990s and first decade of the twenty-first century, we saw groups of states and NGOs push ahead with policy initiatives opposed by the United States, examples being the International Criminal Court and the convention banning land mines. Although its support has fluctuated, in fact, the United States has always been important to the United Nations, as discussed further in Chapter 3.

Now, with the rapid rise of China in particular, as well as of India, South Africa, Brazil, and other emerging powers, and the reassertiveness of Russia (a group collectively known as the **BRICS**), world politics is again shifting, and the years ahead will likely see significant changes in how these shifts play out within the UN. Already in international economic relations, the G-7 has been partially replaced by the Group of 20 (G-20), and the emerging powers have pushed for changes in their voting shares within the World Bank and IMF. China has taken the lead in creating new institutions such as the Asian Infrastructure Investment Bank (AIIB), drawing many developed as well as developing countries to become charter members in 2015, despite the opposition of the United States. US power and influence are noticeably declining in what, for lack of a better phrase, one might call the post-post–Cold War era. The reform of UN Security Council membership is likely to gain new attention and urgency with these power shifts.

To understand the links between world politics and the United Nations, it is also important to examine the major international relations theories to see how they explain global changes and the roles of IGOs such as the UN.

CONTENDING INTERNATIONAL RELATIONS THEORIES

For much of the post–World War II era, **realist theory**, or **realism**, provided the dominant explanation for international politics. Realists see states as the most important actors in the international system and as unitary actors that define their national interests in terms of maximizing power and security. Sovereign states coexist in an anarchic international system and, therefore, must rely primarily on themselves to manage their own insecurity through balance of power, alliances, and deterrence. International rules (law) and norms, as well as international organizations, do not carry much weight with realists because they lack enforcement power. In realists' view, IGOs and NGOs are marginal actors. IGOs, in particular, do not enjoy autonomy or capability for independent action on the world stage. Rather, they reflect the interests of their members, especially the most powerful ones. In this view, the UN is constrained by its members' willingness to work through it in dealing with specific problems, to comply with and support its actions, to provide peacekeeping contingents (military or civilian), and to pay for its regular operations and special programs. In realist theory, co-operation among states is not impossible, but states have little incentive to enter into international arrangements, and they are always free to exit from them.[4]

For many international relations scholars, however, realist theory is an inadequate theoretical framework for analyzing world politics, and especially the rapid changes since the Cold War's end as well as the expanded practice of **multilateralism**, the activities of the UN and other IGOs among the elements of global governance. One major alternative is **liberalism**.[5]

Liberals regard states as important actors, but they place importance on a variety of other actors in the international system, including IGOs, NGOs, **multinational corporations (MNCs)**, and even individuals. States, in their view, are pluralistic, not unitary, actors. Moral and ethical principles, power relations, and bargaining among different domestic and transnational groups amid changing international conditions shape states' interests and actions. There is no single definition of national interest; rather, states vary in their goals, and their interests change. Liberal theorists characterize the international system as an interdependent one in which there is both cooperation and conflict and where actors' mutual interests tend to increase over time. State power matters, but it is exercised within a framework of international rules and institutions that help to make cooperation possible.

Neoliberal institutionalists have provided a somewhat different explanation for why cooperation occurs. For classical liberals, cooperation emerges from establishing and reforming institutions that permit cooperative interactions and prohibit coercive actions. For neoliberal institutionalists, cooperation emerges when actors have continuous interactions with each other. Institutions help prevent cheating; they reduce transaction and opportunity costs for those who seek gains from cooperation within them. Institutions are essential; they build upon common interests. They help to shape state interests and state preferences. IGOs such as the United Nations make a difference in world politics by altering state preferences and establishing rules that constrain states. They are not merely pawns of the dominant powers but actually modify state behavior by creating habits of cooperation and serving as arenas for negotiation and policy coordination.

For some liberal theorists, the growth of multilateralism, IGOs, and international law is indicative of a nascent international society in which actors consent to common rules and institutions and recognize common interests as well as a common identity or sense of "we-ness." Within this emerging society, international institutions change the way states and other actors interact with each other. Many scholars argue that the growing role of nongovernmental actors represents an emerging global civil society.[6]

A third and relatively recent approach to international relations is **constructivism**, which has become important for studying various aspects of global governance, particularly the role of norms and institutions. Constructivism has several variants, and questions have arisen about whether it is a theory of politics. Yet it offers a valuable way of studying how shared beliefs, rules, organizations, and cultural practices shape the behavior of states and other actors as well as their identities and interests. Among the key norms affecting state behavior in constructivists' view is multilateralism. Several studies have examined the impact of norms and principled beliefs on international outcomes such as the evolution of the international human rights **regime**, bans on certain types of weapons, and humanitarian interventions in which the UN and other IGOs have played a role. They have found that international organizations can be not only "teachers" but also "creators" of norms; as such, they can socialize states into accepting certain political goals and values.[7]

Constructivists tend to see IGOs as actors that can have independent effects on international relations and as arenas in which discussions, persuasion, education, and argument take place that influence government leaders', businesspeople's, and NGO activists' understandings of their interests and of the world in which they live. The consequences are not always positive, however, because IGOs can also stimulate conflicts, their actions may not necessarily be in the interests of their member states, and IGO bureaucracies such as the UN Secretariat may develop agendas of their own, be dysfunctional, lack accountability, tolerate inefficient practices, and compete for turf, budgets, and staff.[8]

There are also critical theories that challenge realism's focus on the primacy of states' power and liberalism's optimism about the value of international law and institutions for promoting cooperation. Among the most prominent are Marxist and neo-Marxist theories and their derivative, **dependency theory**, with their focus on exploitative structures in economic, political, and social systems. Even with the demise of the Soviet Union, Marxism and its variants did not disappear. They had significant influence on many LDCs from the 1950s to the 1980s. Some aspects of these critical theories have resurfaced in the debates over globalization, particularly among opponents of globalization, including those who oppose corporate control over the economy and those who are trying to strengthen protection for workers, small farmers, poor people, and women.

There are several feminist perspectives that build on both the liberal and critical traditions and bring attention to the role of women in and around the UN. Liberal feminists call for an increased focus on the role of women as international leaders, staffers, and lobbyists. Historically women have been poorly represented in the halls of power; only recently have they held senior positions at the United Nations. Liberals also call for increased attention to developing organizational policies that affect women, especially the role of women in economic

development, women as victims of crime and discrimination, and women in situations of armed conflict. For too long these issues have been neglected. Critical
feminists argue that studying gender involves more than just counting women
in elite positions or cataloging programs targeting women. They see women as
particularly vulnerable to exploitation when the public sector fails to provide
essential services or is adversely affected by globalization. They point, for example, to the fact that the overwhelming majority of trafficked persons are women
who experience a double exploitation by virtue of the way the world economy
is defined and managed. Critics, including other feminists, have challenged the
misandrogynistic tone of some critical feminist writing, arguing that the exploitative structures they describe are not automatically the fault of men, but that
both women and men are part of the problem and part of the solution. The UN
has become a battleground for these feminist perspectives.

Realism, liberalism, constructivism, critical theories, and feminism, then, are
different lenses through which scholars view world politics and the United Nations. No matter which theory one finds most valuable, understanding the role
of the UN in the twenty-first century requires the exploration of four dilemmas.

DILEMMAS THE UN FACES IN THE
TWENTY-FIRST CENTURY

Dilemma 1: Expanding Needs for Governance
Versus the UN's Limited Capacity

The United Nations has faced increasing demands that it provide peacekeeping
and peacebuilding operations, initiate international regulation to halt environmental degradation and alleviate poverty and inequality in the world, promote
greater human economic and social well-being, provide humanitarian relief to
victims of natural disasters and violence, and protect human rights for various
groups. These are demands for global governance, not world government—that
is, demands for rules, norms, and organizational structures to manage trans-
boundary and interdependence problems that states acting alone cannot solve,
such as terrorism, crime, drugs, environmental degradation, pandemics, and
human rights violations.[9]

These governance demands test the capacity and the willingness of states to
commit themselves to international cooperation and the capacity of the UN
and other IGOs to function effectively. Can they meet these new demands without simply adding more programs? How can the initiatives be funded? Can
the UN be more effective in coordinating the related activities of various institutions, states, and NGOs? Can it improve its own management and personnel practices? Can it adapt to deal with the changing nature of conflicts and
persistent poverty and inequality? The most important issues concerning the

global economy are discussed and decided outside the UN system. The UN Charter's provisions are designed for interstate conflicts, yet most conflicts since 1990 have been intrastate civil wars. Many have involved nonstate actors such as militias, paramilitary groups, or terrorist groups such as Al Qaeda or the Islamic State of Iraq and Syria (ISIS), on the one hand, and regional IGOs collaborating with the UN in mounting various types of peace operations, on the other. The UN's membership has grown from 50 to 193 states. The Security Council was structured to reflect power realities in 1945, not the twenty-first century, and efforts to update its membership structure have so far failed despite wide agreement on the importance of reform.

Clearly, the UN needs to increase its capacity to meet new demands, to mobilize resources, to reflect the changing distribution of power and authority, and to strengthen its links with nonstate actors and regional IGOs. One of the UN's strengths to date has been its flexibility in response to new issues and a membership more than three times the size of the original membership. Its weaknesses are the rigidity of its central structures, its slowness to accommodate nonstate actors and the changing realities of geopolitics, and the continuing inability of member states to agree about major reforms. It has also been weakened by states' failure to meet their commitments for funding and their reluctance to grant too much power to the UN Secretariat. Yet the current demands for global governance require the commitment of states and enhanced institutional capacity in the UN; they therefore also require that states give up more of their sovereignty. This leads to the second dilemma.

Dilemma 2: Sovereignty Versus Challenges to Sovereignty

The UN Charter affirms the long-standing principles of state sovereignty and nonintervention in states' domestic affairs, yet sovereignty has eroded on many fronts and is continually challenged by issues and problems that cross states' borders and that states cannot solve alone. Historically, sovereignty empowered each state to govern all matters within its territorial jurisdiction. **Nonintervention** is the related principle that obliges other states and international organizations not to intervene in matters within the internal or domestic jurisdiction of a sovereign state. Global telecommunications, including the Internet and social media, economic interdependencies such as global financial markets, international human rights norms, international election monitoring, and environmental regulation are among the many developments that infringe on states' sovereignty and traditional areas of domestic jurisdiction.

The growing activities of IGOs, NGOs, corporations, and private foundations have eroded the centrality of states as the primary actors in world politics. For example, Amnesty International (AI) and the International Commission of Jurists have been key actors in promoting human rights, sometimes exerting more influence than states themselves. The Gates Foundation provides a large proportion of funding for international health programs. NGOs can influence legislators and government officials both from within countries and from outside through transnational networks and access to the media. To be sure, some governments have increasingly worked to maintain control by using firewalls and restrictions on the activities of NGOs. MNCs with operations in several countries and industry groups such as oil, steel, automobiles, insurance, and shipping are important players in trade and climate change negotiations, a number of them having more resources than some states. Partnerships between the UN and the private sector, including MNCs, have become increasingly important for addressing a variety of governance challenges.

International norms and rules, such as those on nuclear nonproliferation, trade, the seas, intellectual property rights, ozone-depleting chlorofluorocarbons (CFCs), and women's rights, have been established through UN-sponsored negotiations. They set standards for states and relevant industries as well as for consumers and citizens. When states themselves accept commitments to uphold these standards (by signing and ratifying international treaties and conventions), they are simultaneously exercising their sovereignty (by making the commitment) and accepting a diminution of that sovereignty (by agreeing to international standards that will then be open to international monitoring). Establishing rules to address climate change poses particularly daunting challenges for both global governance and state sovereignty.

Although multilateral institutions in theory take actions that constitute intervention in states' domestic affairs only with their consent, there has been a push since 2000 to accept a new norm of **responsibility to protect (R2P)** to justify **humanitarian intervention** to alleviate human suffering during violent conflicts when states fail to protect their citizens. It was first invoked to provide food relief and reestablish civil order in Somalia in 1993–1994, and later to call for international action against genocide in the Darfur region of Sudan in 2005–2006. The 2005 UN World Summit endorsed the R2P norm, but many states, particularly developing countries, continue to fear its consequences for the norms of nonintervention and sovereignty. The Security Council's approval of humanitarian intervention in Libya in 2011 is discussed in Chapter 4 along with the Council's failure to act in the case of Syria's civil war and humanitarian crisis.

The reality remains that "the capacity to mobilize the resources necessary to tackle global problems also remains vested in states, therefore effectively incapacitating many international institutions."[10] That includes the United Nations. Thus, the dilemma associated with state sovereignty links also to the third dilemma: the need for leadership.

Dilemma 3: The Need for Leadership

World politics in the twenty-first century was marked initially by the dominance of the United States as the sole superpower and a diffusion of power among many other states, the European Union (EU), and a wide variety of nonstate actors that exercise influence in different ways. As noted earlier, however, even before the end of the first decade, it was apparent that the rise of emerging nations such as Brazil, India, and China as well as constraints on the United States were leading to shifting patterns of power and leadership. This was underscored by both Russia and China's greater assertiveness since 2014. Yet traditional measures of power in international politics do not necessarily dictate who will provide leadership or be influential within the UN.

Multilateral institutions such as the UN create opportunities for small and middle powers as well as for NGOs, groups of states, and IGOs' executive heads to exercise initiative and leadership. UN secretaries-general, in fact, have often been important figures in the international arena depending on their personality and willingness to take initiatives such as mediating conflicts or proposing responses to international problems that may or may not prove acceptable to member states. Both Boutros Boutros-Ghali and Kofi Annan, for example, were noted for their leadership both within and outside the UN, while Ban Ki-moon has been less assertive. Prominent individuals, such as former Australian prime minister Gareth Evans and Mohamed Sahnoun of Algeria, who chaired the independent International Commission on Intervention and State Sovereignty that in 2001 proposed the new norm of responsibility to protect as an obligation of states, can exercise leadership through technical expertise and diplomatic skill. Middle powers such as Australia, Canada, Brazil, and India have been influential in international trade negotiations on agricultural issues, as they have long been in peacekeeping and development. Canada provided leadership for the effort in the late 1990s to ban antipersonnel land mines, while Norway led a similar effort on cluster munitions that culminated in a treaty in 2008. Brazil, Japan, and India led the effort in 2005 to secure Security Council reform and renewed their push ahead of the UN's seventieth anniversary in 2015.

NGOs can also provide leadership along with states, UN secretaries-general, and other prominent individuals. The success of both the land mine and cluster munitions efforts owed much to the leadership of coalitions of NGOs. The Intergovernmental Panel on Climate Change (IPCC) has been a lead actor in international efforts since the late 1980s to analyze data on climate and to promote efforts to address the problem. In 2015, two NGO coalitions pushed for change in the process for selecting a new UN secretary-general: the campaign called 1for7Billion sought to build support through social media for transparent selection criteria and a more formal application process; Equality Now, a network of women's rights groups, pushed for a woman to be selected and posted a list of fourteen potential female candidates.[11]

Still, states matter, and leadership from major powers with resources and influence matters. Hence the dilemma. As we have seen, with the demise of the Soviet Union in 1991 the United States became the sole remaining super-power—the only state with intervention capabilities and interests in many parts of the globe. The United States remains a clear military superpower, as American military expenditures equal those of its nearest fourteen competitors combined, although both Russia and China have rapidly increased their defense budgets. By most accounts, the United States is still the world's largest economy, but Chi-na's GDP is predicted to overtake it by 2020.

A dominant power can rely on its sheer weight to play hardball and get its way—up to a point. The prolonged insurgency and failures in Iraq following US military intervention in 2003 demonstrated the limits of hard power. Lead-ership depends on the inspiration and cultivation of soft power as well as on followers. In the late 1990s, US opposition to the creation of the International Criminal Court (ICC), the convention banning antipersonnel land mines, the Comprehensive Test Ban Treaty, and the Kyoto Protocol on Climate Change signaled a "go-it-alone" pattern that continued in the early years of the twen-ty-first century with the Bush administration's opposition to international treaties and invasion of Iraq.[12] This made many countries less willing to accept US dominance.[13] It also fueled anti-Americanism in many parts of the world. Consequently, the United States lost a good deal of its soft power and ability to lead. President Obama initially reversed some of that loss and has been more inclined to forge international consensus, as in NATO's intervention in Libya and limited US intervention in Syria, mindful of the constraints of the US bud-get deficit and lack of good military options. Still, the history of US engagement with the UN is one of mixed messages and considerable variation. As discussed further in Chapter 3, Congress blocked full payment of US dues to the UN from the mid-1980s until 2000; in 2011 it defunded the UN Educational, Scientific and Cultural Organization (UNESCO) and decreased the funding levels of sev-eral other UN agencies. The perception of domestic political dysfunction in the United States and its reluctance to use force (especially in the Middle East) have raised questions about the US ability and willingness to lead, build coali-tions, and create consensus through multilateralism. The decline in US power also creates uncertainty about the UN's future and about whether emerging powers such as China will find the UN a valuable venue. China has begun to create alternative organizations, as noted earlier in this chapter. Yet there are also indications that the Chinese see a strong future for the UN. In 2014 one senior UN official remarked, "The Chinese want as many people as possible funneling through the UN to gain the experience, while the Americans in the

State Department actually don't like the New York assignment."[14] In a world of emerging powers, the likelihood that the United States can lead, even when it chooses to, is inevitably diminished. Yet those rising powers may not be willing or able to assume leadership either. And the nature of the norms and rules they may promote may be very different from those the United States and other Western nations have promoted since the 1940s.

Dilemma 4: The Need for Inclusiveness

The first three words in the UN Charter proclaim "We the People," and Articles 1, 8, and 101 (3) recognize the dignity and worth of all people. For more than seventy years, the UN has served as a leading advocate against discrimination. Despite progress, inequality and exclusion persist, and in many parts of the world are actually increasing.[15] Recently the UN began recognizing that respecting all people as a moral imperative is not enough. In order for the UN to address many key issues including poverty, climate change, conflict resolution, and global health, it must address inequality and include the marginalized. Reversing social exclusion is now viewed as part of fostering both human security and development. Lack of participation and voice often translate into lack of education, employment, and social services, which contributes to poverty, discrimination, political instability, and even violence.

The need for inclusiveness presents several dilemmas for the UN. First, there is a renewed focus not only on advocating for excluded groups but also on including them. Here the UN faces challenges in combating deep-seated prejudices, cultural practices, and inequalities that may be entrenched in states' political and economic systems. Can the UN be effective in setting robust standards as well as in establishing accountability for those states and societies where discriminatory practices persist?

Women's issues, in particular, intersect with poverty, development, education, political equality, migration, and refugees. In this regard, there is increased awareness that women are essential stakeholders in the peacebuilding process and a key part of promoting human rights and sustainable development. In 2006, former Secretary-General Kofi Annan wrote, "It is impossible to realize our goals while discriminating against half the human race."[16]

The UN has spearheaded many efforts to ensure equal opportunities, beginning with its long history of setting international human rights standards, as discussed in Chapter 6. This emphasis was expanded at the 1995 World Summit for Social Development, which proclaimed that "no human being should be condemned to endure a brief or miserable life as a result of his or her class, country, religious affiliation, ethnic background or gender." The MDGs and the SDGs also promote the need for inclusiveness by striving to achieve universal education, promote gender equality, reduce child mortality, and improve maternal health. Over many years and with the creation of UN Women in 2011, the UN has made significant strides in gender mainstreaming. As critics of the SDGs point out, however, trying to include too many people and concerns among the goals may create a list that is too broad, unattainable, and unfocused. The UN's focus on inclusiveness has expanded to include people living in poverty, persons with disabilities, children, older persons, and recent migrants. More recently, the list extended to incorporate persons with diverse gender identities as well as socially excluded groups with distinct ethnic, religious, and cultural backgrounds.

The UN also faces challenges of inclusiveness in terms of its own management and personnel. As discussed further in Chapter 2, it is only since the late 1980s that any women have held high-level posts in UN agencies, and their numbers are still quite small. Only 20 percent of the 193 member states are represented by women. This inequity within the UN system triggered the push for a female secretary-general to succeed Ban Ki-moon, as discussed earlier in this chapter and in Chapter 2. For the UN to remain relevant and legitimate, it must widen its own net.

Different groups with different interpretations of feminism, as discussed above, come to the UN with diverse views of inclusiveness and the remedies needed. The demand for inclusion tests the capacity of the UN and the level of member state commitment to address social and economic inequalities, including providing sufficient funding to meet goals for inclusiveness. While the UN itself may promote inclusiveness, there are also member states and groups within those member states that use the UN as a forum to push back and even block such initiatives.

STRUCTURE OF THE BOOK

Subsequent chapters explore these dilemmas in the context of different areas of UN activity. Chapter 2 outlines the historical foundations of the United Nations and describes the various structures, politics, and processes within it as well as efforts at reform. Chapter 3 considers the major actors in the UN system, including NGOs, coalitions and blocs, small states and middle powers, and the United States and other emerging powers, as well as the UN secretary-general and the Secretariat. Chapter 4 deals with the UN's role in peace and security issues, including peacekeeping, enforcement, peacebuilding, statebuilding, humanitarian intervention, counterterrorism, and nuclear proliferation, with case studies of Somalia, Bosnia, Democratic Republic of the Congo, Kosovo, Timor-Leste, Mali, and South Sudan. In Chapter 5, which covers the role of the UN system in promoting development, we explore case studies of women and development, the MDGs and SDGs, and poverty alleviation. Chapter 6 analyzes the role of the UN in the evolution of international human rights norms with case studies of the antiapartheid movement, the women's rights agenda, human trafficking, and genocide, crimes against humanity, and war crimes. Chapter 7, on human security, deals with environmental degradation and health issues, including case studies of ozone, climate change, the Ebola epidemic, and the refugee/migration crisis. Chapter 8 explores the questions of what the UN has done best, where it has fallen short, and whether and how it can make a difference in the world of the twenty-first century.

NOTES

1. Staff member, United Nations Peacebuilding Commission, personal interview with author, New York, March 30, 2012.

2. Inis L. Claude Jr., *The Changing United Nations* (New York: Random House, 1965), 32.

3. Christopher S. Wren, "Annan Says All Nations Must Cooperate," *New York Times,* September 6, 2000.

4. See, for example, Hans Morgenthau, *Politics Among Nations,* 4th ed. (New York: Alfred A. Knopf, 1967), and John J. Mearsheimer, "The False Promise of International Institutions," *International Security* 13, no. 3 (1994–1995): 5–49.

5. See, for example, Michael W. Doyle, "Liberalism and World Politics," *American Political Science Review* 80, no. 4 (December 1986): 1151–1169; Hedley Bull, *The Anarchical Society: A Study of Order in World Politics* (New York: Columbia University Press, 1977); Robert O. Keohane and Joseph S. Nye, *Power and Interdependence,* 3rd ed. (New York: Longman, 2001); and Robert O. Keohane and Lisa L. Martin, "The Promise of Institutionalist Theory," *International Security* 20, no. 1 (1995): 39–51.

6. See, for example, Ronnie Lipschutz, "Reconstructing World Politics: The Emergence of Global Civil Society," *Millennium: Journal of International Studies* 21, no. 3 (1992): 398–399, and Craig Warkentin, *Reshaping World Politics: NGOs, the Internet, and Global Civil Society* (Lanham, MD: Rowman and Littlefield, 2001).

7. See, for example, John Gerard Ruggie, "Multilateralism: The Anatomy of an Institution," in *Multilateralism Matters: The Theory and Praxis of an Institutional Form,* ed. John Gerard Ruggie (New York: Columbia University Press, 1993), 3–47; Martha Finnemore, *National Interests in International Society* (Ithaca, NY: Cornell University Press, 1996); and Martha Finnemore and Kathryn Sikkink, "Taking Stock: The Constructivist Research Program in International Relations and Comparative Politics," *Annual Review of Political Science* 4 (2001): 391–416.

8. Michael Barnett and Martha Finnemore, *Rules for the World: International Organizations in Global Politics* (Ithaca, NY: Cornell University Press, 2004).

9. Margaret P. Karns, Karen A. Mingst, and Kendall W. Stiles, *International Organizations: The Politics and Processes of Global Governance,* 3rd ed. (Boulder, CO: Lynne Rienner, 2015).

10. Thomas G. Weiss and Ramesh Thakur, *Global Governance and the UN: An Unfinished Journey* (Bloomington: Indiana University Press, 2010).

11. Somini Sengupta, "After 70 Years of Men, Some Say It Is 'High Time' a Woman Led the U.N.," *New York Times,* August 22, 2015.

12. Stewart Patrick and Shepard Forman, eds., *Multilateralism and U.S. Foreign Policy: Ambivalent Engagement* (Boulder, CO: Lynne Rienner, 2002).

13. David M. Malone and Yuen Foong Khong, eds., *Unilateralism and U.S. Foreign Policy: International Perspectives* (Boulder, CO: Lynne Rienner, 2003).

14. Staff member, *Security Council Report*, personal interview with author, New York, April 14, 2014.

15. See UN Department of Economic and Social Affairs, "Analysing and Measuring Social Inclusion in a Global Context," ST/ESA/325, 2010, www.un.org/esa/socdev/publications /measuring-social-inclusion.pdf.

16. Kofi Annan, "Message from the Secretary-General of the United Nations," in *The State of the World's Children 2007: Women and Children* (UNICEF, 2006), vi.

2

⁓

The Evolution of the
United Nations System

The United Nations was established at the end of World War II, but its roots can be traced to sixteenth-century European ideas about international law and organization, a series of developments in the nineteenth century, and the League of Nations, established after World War I. In 1815, the European states established the **Concert of Europe**. Under the Concert system, the leaders of the major European powers came together in multilateral meetings to settle problems and coordinate actions. Meeting more than thirty times between 1815 and 1878, the major powers legitimized the independence of new European states such as Belgium and Greece. At the last meeting in Berlin in 1878, they extended the reach of European imperialism by dividing up the previously uncolonized parts of Africa. These Concert meetings solidified some important practices that persist today in the UN, including multilateral consultation, collective diplomacy, and special status for "great powers" in the Security Council.

Also in the nineteenth century, a number of public international unions were established among European states to deal with problems stemming from the expanding commerce, communications, and technological innovation of the Industrial Revolution: for example, health standards for travelers, shipping rules on the Rhine River, increased mail volume, and the cross-boundary usage of the newly invented telegraph. These practical problems of expanding international relations led to the creation of the International Telegraph Union in 1865 and the Universal Postal Union in 1874. Thus, the public international unions gave rise to **functionalism**—the theory that IGOs can help states deal with practical problems in their international relations—and many are now specialized agencies within the UN system.

The public international unions spawned several procedural innovations; among them were international secretariats, that is, permanent bureaucrats hired from a variety of countries to perform specific tasks. They also developed the practice of involving specialists from outside ministries of foreign affairs as well as private interest groups in their work. Multilateral diplomacy was no longer the exclusive domain of traditional diplomats. In addition, the public unions began to develop techniques for multilateral conventions—law- or rule-making treaties. Many additional such organizations were established in the twentieth century, including the International Maritime Organization (IMO) and the International Civil Aviation Organization (ICAO).

In addition, a pair of conferences of European and non-European states convened in The Hague (Netherlands) in 1899 and 1907 by Czar Nicholas II of Russia set a number of precedents that also shaped the UN as we know it today. The conferences were intended to consider techniques that would prevent war and the conditions under which arbitration, negotiation, and legal recourse would be appropriate. Exploring such issues in the absence of a crisis was a novelty. They led to the Convention for the Pacific Settlement of International Disputes, ad hoc international commissions of inquiry, and the Permanent Court of Arbitration, which still exists. Among its most recent cases is the Philippines' complaint that China's activities in the South China Sea violate the UN Convention on the Law of the Sea.

The Hague conferences also produced several major procedural innovations. This was the first time that participants included both small and non-European states. The Latin American states, China, and Japan were given an equal voice, an advance that not only established the principle of universality but also bolstered legal equality. Thus, what had been largely a European state system until the end of the nineteenth century became a truly international system at the beginning of the twentieth. For the first time, multilateral diplomacy employed such techniques as the election of chairs, the organization of committees, and roll call votes, all of which became permanent features of twentieth-century organizations, including the UN. The Hague conferences also advanced the codification of international law and promoted the novel idea that humankind has common interests.

The institutional developments of the nineteenth century, however, did not prevent war among the major European powers. The Concert system broke into two competing military alliances at the turn of the twentieth century. Cooperation in other areas of interest proved insufficient to prevent war when national security was at stake. Hence, the outbreak of World War I pointed vividly to the weaknesses of the nineteenth-century arrangements. The war had hardly begun when private groups and prominent individuals in Europe and the United States began to plan for the postwar era. Nongovernmental groups such as the League to Enforce Peace in the United States and the League of Nations in Great Britain were eager to develop more permanent frameworks for preventing future wars. President Woodrow Wilson's proposal to create a permanent international organization in the Versailles Peace Treaty was based on these plans. Because the League of Nations had a significant influence on its successor, the United Nations, we examine it in more detail.

THE LEAGUE OF NATIONS

The League of Nations reflected the environment in which it was conceived.[1] Almost half of the League Covenant's twenty-six provisions focused on preventing war. Two basic principles were paramount: member states agreed to respect and preserve the territorial integrity and political independence of states and to try different methods of dispute settlement. If they failed, the League had the power under Article 16 to enforce settlements through sanctions. The second principle was firmly embedded in the proposition of collective security, namely, that aggression by one state should be countered by all members acting together as a "league of nations" with economic sanctions and force if necessary.

The League Covenant established an assembly and a council, the latter recognizing the special prerogative of great powers, a lasting remnant of the European Concert system, and the former giving pride of place to universality of membership (about sixty states at that time). Authority rested with the council, composed of four permanent and four elected members. The council was to be the settler of disputes, the enforcer of sanctions, and the implementer of peaceful settlements. The requirement of unanimity, however, made action difficult.

The League did enjoy a number of successes, many of them on territorial issues. It conducted plebiscites in Silesia and the Saar and then demarcated the German-Polish border. It settled territorial disputes between Lithuania and Poland, Finland and Russia, and Bulgaria and Greece, and it guaranteed Albanian territorial integrity against encroachments by Italy, Greece, and Yugoslavia.

Despite these successes, the League's council failed to act decisively against the aggression of Italy and Japan in the 1930s. Collective security failed as Britain and France pursued their national interests. Voluntary sanctions approved after Italy's invasion of Ethiopia in 1935 carried little effect. The absence of great-power support for the League was particularly evident in the failure of the United States, as a result of congressional opposition and a resurgence of isolationism, to join the organization.

The League could not prevent the outbreak of World War II, yet it represented an important step forward in the process of international organization. Planning for the post–World War II peace began even before the United States entered the war and involved several high-level meetings of the Allied leaders—Roosevelt,

Churchill, and Stalin—as well as other officials in Allied governments. Most important, this planning built on the lessons of the League in laying the ground-work for its successor, the United Nations. Despite the League's shortcomings, there was consensus on the importance of such an international organization, albeit one whose scope would be far greater than the League's. President Roosevelt, a firm believer in the importance of such an organization, early on sought to ensure domestic support for US participation.

THE ORIGINS OF THE UNITED NATIONS

The Atlantic Charter of August 14, 1941—a joint declaration by US president Franklin Roosevelt and British prime minister Winston Churchill calling for collaboration on economic issues and a permanent system of security—was the foundation for the Declaration by the United Nations in January 1942. Twenty-six nations affirmed the principles of the Atlantic Charter and agreed to create a new universal organization to replace the League of Nations. The UN Charter was then drafted in two sets of meetings between August and October 1944 at Dumbarton Oaks in Washington, DC. The participants agreed that the organization would be based on the principle of the sovereign equality of members and that all "peace-loving" states would be eligible for membership, thereby excluding the Axis powers—Germany, Italy, Japan, and Spain. It was also agreed that decisions on security issues would require unanimity of the permanent members of the Security Council, the great powers.

When the United Nations Conference on International Organization convened in San Francisco on April 25, 1945, delegates from the fifty participating states modified and finalized what had already been negotiated among the great powers. On July 28, 1945, with Senate approval, the United States became the first country to ratify the Charter, and it would take only three more months to obtain a sufficient number of ratifications (legal consents) from other countries. (An abridged and amended version of the UN Charter can be found in the Appendix.)

One conference participant made the following comments after the Charter was signed:

> One of the most significant features was the demonstration of the large area of agreement which existed from the start among the 50 nations. . . . Everyone exhibited a serious minded determination to reach agreement on an organization which would be more effective than the League of Nations. . . . Not a single reservation was made to the Charter when it was adopted. . . . The conference will long stand as one of the landmarks in international diplomacy. . . . [Nonetheless,] one wonders—will the conversations of men

prove powerful enough to curb the might of military power or to harness it to more orderly uses?[2]

THE ORGANIZATION OF THE UNITED NATIONS

Basic Principles

Several principles undergird the structure and operation of the UN and represent fundamental legal obligations of all members. These are contained in Article 2 of the Charter as well as in other Charter provisions.

The most fundamental principle is the sovereign equality of member states. Since the Peace of Westphalia of 1648, states as political units do not recognize any higher governing authority. "Equality" refers to the legal status of states, not to their size, military power, or wealth; Russia, Lithuania, China, and Singapore, for instance, are equals. Sovereign equality is the basis for each state having one vote in the General Assembly. Yet inequality is also part of the UN framework, embodied in the permanent membership and **veto** power of five states in the Security Council: the United States, Russia, China, Great Britain, and France.

Closely related to the UN's primary goal of maintaining peace and security are the twin principles that all member states shall refrain from threatening or using force against the territorial integrity or political independence of any state, refrain from acting in any manner inconsistent with UN purposes, and settle their international disputes by peaceful means. Many times over the years, states have failed to honor these principles, often failing even to submit their disputes to the UN for settlement. Yet the UN's members continue to demonstrate strong support for these core principles, as evidenced by their firm response to Iraq's occupation of Kuwait in 1990.

Members also accept the obligation to support **enforcement actions**, such as economic sanctions, and to refrain from giving assistance to states that are the objects of UN preventive or enforcement action. They have the collective responsibility to ensure that nonmember states act in accordance with these principles as necessary for the maintenance of international peace and security.

A further key principle is the requirement that member states fulfill in good faith all the obligations assumed by them under the Charter. This affirms a fundamental norm of all international law and treaties, *pacta sunt servanda*—treaties must be carried out. Those obligations include payment of assessed annual contributions (dues) to the organization, compliance with sanctions, and provision of troops for peacekeeping operations.

Finally, Article 2(7) asserts that "nothing in the present Charter shall authorize the United Nations to intervene in matters which are essentially within the domestic jurisdiction of any state or shall require the Members to submit such matters to settlement under the present Charter . . . [although] this principle shall not prejudice the application of enforcement measures under Chapter VII." This provision underscores the long-standing norm of nonintervention in the domestic affairs of states. But who decides what is an international problem and what is a domestic one? Since the UN's founding in 1945, the scope of what is considered international has broadened, with UN involvement in human rights, development, and humanitarian intervention. Since the Cold War's end, most UN peacekeeping operations have involved intrastate rather than interstate conflicts, that is, conflicts within rather than between states, as well as intrusive peacebuilding efforts. The UN's founders recognized the tension between the commitment to act collectively against a member state and the affirmation of state sovereignty represented in the nonintervention principle. They could not foresee the dilemmas that changing definitions of security, new issues, and ethnic conflicts would pose, let alone shifting interpretations of sovereignty itself.

The Preamble and Article 1 of the UN Charter both contain references to human rights and obligate states to show "respect for the principle of equal rights and self-determination of peoples." Hence, discussions about human rights have always been regarded as a legitimate international activity rather than solely a domestic concern. Actions to promote or enforce human rights have been more controversial. Since the late 1990s, there have been extensive debates over "sovereignty as responsibility" and the responsibility to protect peoples at risk in situations of humanitarian crisis.

In Article 51, the Charter affirms states' "right of individual or collective self-defence" against armed attack. Thus, states are not required to wait for the UN to act before undertaking measures in their own (and others') defense. They are obligated to report their responses, and they may create regional defense and other arrangements. This "self-defence" principle, not surprisingly, has led to many debates over who initiated hostilities and who was the victim of aggression.

Structure of the United Nations

The structure of the United Nations as outlined in the Charter includes six major bodies: the General Assembly, the Security Council, the Economic and Social Council (ECOSOC), the Secretariat, the International Court of Justice (ICJ), and the Trusteeship Council. Each has changed during the life of the organization in response to external realities, internal pressures, and interactions with other organs.[3]

In reality, it is more accurate to speak of the **United Nations system**, because the UN has evolved into far more than these six organs.[4] Articles 57 and 63 of the Charter called for the affiliation with the UN of various specialized agencies established by separate international agreements to deal with particular issues, as discussed later in this chapter. The General Assembly, the Security Council, and ECOSOC have also used their powers to create separate and subsidiary bodies; in doing so, they have illustrated the phenomenon of "IGOs creating other IGOs."[5] For example, in 1964, developing countries, with their large majority in the General Assembly, created the United Nations Conference on Trade and Development (UNCTAD) to focus more attention on the trade and development problems of newly independent and developing states. UN Women was established by the General Assembly in 2010 through a merger of various parts of the UN, as discussed further in Chapter 5. Figure 2.1 shows the complexity of the UN system.

In the sections that follow, we discuss how the six major UN organs have evolved in practice and some of their political dynamics. We also provide brief discussions of one specialized agency and of UN-sponsored global conferences. Subsequent chapters will illustrate the relationships among different parts of the UN system.

The General Assembly. The General Assembly, like the League of Nations assembly, was designed as the general debate arena where all members would be equally represented according to a one-state/one-vote formula. It is the organization's hub, with a diverse agenda and the responsibility for coordinating and supervising subsidiary bodies but with power only to make recommendations to members, except on internal matters such as elections and the budget. It has exclusive competence over the latter, giving it a measure of surveillance and control over all UN programs and subsidiary bodies. The assembly has important elective functions: electing the nonpermanent members of the Security Council, ECOSOC, and the Trusteeship Council; appointing judges to the International Court of Justice; and, upon the recommendation of the Security Council, admitting states to UN membership and appointing the secretary-general. In many ways, the General Assembly comes closer than any other international body to embodying what is often called the "international community." It is a "forum where 'the masses' can rally to counterbalance 'the aristocracy' of the permanent five."[6] To paraphrase Shakespeare, if all the world's a stage, the UN General Assembly is center stage—particularly for small states such as Fiji, Malta, and Burundi.

The General Assembly can consider any matter within the purview of the UN Charter (Article 10) and make nonbinding recommendations. Over time, the number of items on the assembly's agenda has continually grown, from 46 in 1946 to more than 150 in recent years. Many items, however, are repeated year after year, because they either constitute routine UN business or represent efforts by member states to reiterate support for some cause. The issues range from conflict situations such as the Israeli-Palestinian conflict to arms control, development, global resource management, human rights, legal issues, and the UN's

The United Nations System

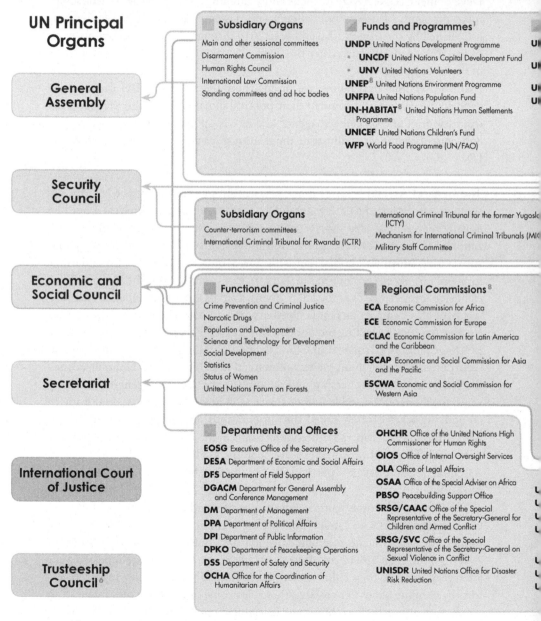

UN Principal Organs

General Assembly

Security Council

Economic and Social Council

Secretariat

International Court of Justice

Trusteeship Council[6]

Subsidiary Organs

Main and other sessional committees
Disarmament Commission
Human Rights Council
International Law Commission
Standing committees and ad hoc bodies

Funds and Programmes[1]

UNDP United Nations Development Programme
　• **UNCDF** United Nations Capital Development Fund
　• **UNV** United Nations Volunteers
UNEP[8] United Nations Environment Programme
UNFPA United Nations Population Fund
UN-HABITAT[8] United Nations Human Settlements Programme
UNICEF United Nations Children's Fund
WFP World Food Programme (UN/FAO)

Subsidiary Organs

Counter-terrorism committees
International Criminal Tribunal for Rwanda (ICTR)

International Criminal Tribunal for the former Yugoslavia (ICTY)
Mechanism for International Criminal Tribunals (MICT)
Military Staff Committee

Functional Commissions

Crime Prevention and Criminal Justice
Narcotic Drugs
Population and Development
Science and Technology for Development
Social Development
Statistics
Status of Women
United Nations Forum on Forests

Regional Commissions[8]

ECA Economic Commission for Africa
ECE Economic Commission for Europe
ECLAC Economic Commission for Latin America and the Caribbean
ESCAP Economic and Social Commission for Asia and the Pacific
ESCWA Economic and Social Commission for Western Asia

Departments and Offices

EOSG Executive Office of the Secretary-General
DESA Department of Economic and Social Affairs
DFS Department of Field Support
DGACM Department for General Assembly and Conference Management
DM Department of Management
DPA Department of Political Affairs
DPI Department of Public Information
DPKO Department of Peacekeeping Operations
DSS Department of Safety and Security
OCHA Office for the Coordination of Humanitarian Affairs

OHCHR Office of the United Nations High Commissioner for Human Rights
OIOS Office of Internal Oversight Services
OLA Office of Legal Affairs
OSAA Office of the Special Adviser on Africa
PBSO Peacebuilding Support Office
SRSG/CAAC Office of the Special Representative of the Secretary-General for Children and Armed Conflict
SRSG/SVC Office of the Special Representative of the Secretary-General on Sexual Violence in Conflict
UNISDR United Nations Office for Disaster Risk Reduction

FIGURE 2.1. The United Nations System

SOURCE: United Nations, 2015.

Strong
UN.
Better
World.

Research and Training

IIDIR United Nations Institute for Disarmament Research

ITAR United Nations Institute for Training and Research

SSC United Nations System Staff College

U United Nations University

Other Entities

ITC International Trade Centre (UN/WTO)

UNCTAD[1,8] United Nations Conference on Trade and Development

UNHCR[1] Office of the United Nations High Commissioner for Refugees

UNOPS United Nations Office for Project Services

UNRWA[1] United Nations Relief and Works Agency for Palestine Refugees in the Near East

UN Women[1] United Nations Entity for Gender Equality and the Empowerment of Women

Related Organizations

CTBTO Preparatory Commission Preparatory Commission for the Comprehensive Nuclear-Test-Ban Treaty Organization

IAEA[1,3] International Atomic Energy Agency

ICC International Criminal Court

ISA International Seabed Authority

ITLOS International Tribunal for the Law of the Sea

OPCW[3] Organisation for the Prohibition of Chemical Weapons

WTO[1,4] World Trade Organization

via   Peacekeeping operations and political missions

           Sanctions committees (ad hoc)

T)   Standing committees and ad hoc bodies

Advisory Subsidiary Body

Peacebuilding Commission

HLPF High-level Political Forum on sustainable development

Other Bodies

Committee for Development Policy

Committee of Experts on Public Administration

Committee on Non-Governmental Organizations

Permanent Forum on Indigenous Issues

UNAIDS Joint United Nations Programme on HIV/AIDS

UNGEGN United Nations Group of Experts on Geographical Names

Research and Training

UNICRI United Nations Interregional Crime and Justice Research Institute

UNRISD United Nations Research Institute for Social Development

Specialized Agencies[1,5]

FAO Food and Agriculture Organization of the United Nations

ICAO International Civil Aviation Organization

IFAD International Fund for Agricultural Development

ILO International Labour Organization

IMF International Monetary Fund

IMO International Maritime Organization

ITU International Telecommunication Union

UNESCO United Nations Educational, Scientific and Cultural Organization

UNIDO United Nations Industrial Development Organization

UNWTO World Tourism Organization

UPU Universal Postal Union

WHO World Health Organization

WIPO World Intellectual Property Organization

WMO World Meteorological Organization

World Bank Group[7]

• **IBRD** International Bank for Reconstruction and Development

• **IDA** International Development Association

• **IFC** International Finance Corporation

NODA United Nations Office for Disarmament Affairs

NODC[1] United Nations Office on Drugs and Crime

NOG United Nations Office at Geneva

N-OHRLLS Office of the High Representative for the Least Developed Countries, Landlocked Developing Countries and Small Island Developing States

NON United Nations Office at Nairobi

NOP[2] United Nations Office for Partnerships

NOV United Nations Office at Vienna

Notes:

[1] All members of the United Nations System Chief Executives Board for Coordination (CEB).

[2] UN Office for Partnerships (UNOP) is the UN's focal point vis-a-vis the United Nations Foundation, Inc.

[3] IAEA and OPCW report to the Security Council and the GA.

[4] WTO has no reporting obligation to the GA, but contributes on an ad hoc basis to GA and Economic and Social Council (ECOSOC) work on, inter alia, finance and development issues.

[5] Specialized agencies are autonomous organizations whose work is coordinated through ECOSOC (intergovernmental level) and CEB (inter-secretariat level).

[6] The Trusteeship Council suspended operation on 1 November 1994, as on 1 October 1994, Palau, the last United Nations Trust Territory, became independent.

[7] International Centre for Settlement of Investment Disputes (ICSID) and Multilateral Investment Guarantee Agency (MIGA) are not specialized agencies but are part of the World Bank Group in accordance with Articles 57 and 63 of the Charter.

[8] The secretariats of these organs are part of the UN Secretariat.

This Chart is a reflection of the functional organization of the United Nations System and for informational purposes only. It does not include all offices or entities of the United Nations System.

Published by the United Nations Department of Public Information   DPI/2470 rev.4 — 15-00040 — July 2015 finances. Resolutions may be aimed at individual member states, nonmembers, the Security Council or other organs, the secretary-general, or even the assembly itself.

Although the Security Council is the primary organ for dealing with threats to international peace and security, the assembly can make inquiries and studies with respect to conflicts (Articles 13, 14), it may discuss a situation and make recommendations if the council is not exercising its functions (Articles 11, 12), and it has the right to be kept informed by the Security Council and the secretary-general (Articles 10, 11, 12). The **Uniting for Peace Resolution**, passed during the Korean War in 1950, however, ignited controversy over the respective roles of the two bodies. Under the resolution, the General Assembly claimed authority to recommend collective measures when the Security Council was deadlocked by a veto. It was subsequently used to deal with crises in Suez and Hungary (1956), the Middle East (1958, 1967, 1980, 1982), the Congo (1960), and Palestine-Israel (1997). In all, ten emergency special sessions of the General Assembly have dealt with threats to international peace when the Security Council was deadlocked. Since the early 1990s, however, the permanent members of the Security Council have tacitly agreed that only the Security Council should authorize the use of armed force, and this authority is discussed further below. In any case, the General Assembly is a cumbersome body for dealing with delicate situations concerning peace and security. It is a far better organ for the symbolic politics of agenda setting and for mustering large majorities in support of resolutions.

The UN Charter also gave the General Assembly an important role in the development of international law (Article 13). Although it is not a world legislature, its resolutions may lay the basis for new international law by articulating new principles, such as one that called the seas the "common heritage of mankind," and new concepts, such as sustainable development. When reiterated in resolutions over several years, these can become the basis for "soft law"—norms that represent a widespread international consensus. This norm-creating role is now recognized as one of the UN's major contributions. In some instances, new norms may be subsequently incorporated in "hard law"—creating treaties and conventions drafted under General Assembly authorization. For example, the "common heritage" principle was incorporated into the 1967 Treaty on Outer Space and 1982 Convention on the Law of the Sea.

Over time, the General Assembly has produced a large number of multilateral lawmaking treaties, including the 1961 Vienna Convention on Diplomatic Relations, the 1969 Vienna Convention on the Law of Treaties, the 1968 Treaty on the Nonproliferation of Nuclear Weapons, the 1994 Convention on the Safety of United Nations and Associated Personnel, and the 2013 Arms Trade Treaty. Assembly resolutions have also approved all the major conventions on international human rights, although most were drafted in the former Commission on Human Rights that functioned under ECOSOC, as discussed in Chapter 6.

The Security Council and General Assembly share responsibilities for Charter revision. The assembly can propose amendments with a two-thirds majority; two-thirds of the member states, including all the permanent members of the Security Council, must then ratify the changes. The General Assembly and Security Council together may also call a general conference for the purpose of Charter review. There have been only two instances to date, however, of Charter amendment, both enlarging the membership of the Security Council (1965) and ECOSOC (1965 and 1973).

How the General Assembly Functions. Regular annual meetings of the General Assembly are held for three months (or longer) each fall; they begin with a "general debate" period when heads of state, prime ministers, and foreign ministers speak before the assembly. Each year, the General Assembly elects a president and seventeen vice presidents who serve for that year's session. By tradition, presidents come from small and middle-power states. Only on three occasions (in 1953, 1969, and 2006) has a woman been elected. The president's powers come largely from personal influence and political skills in guiding the assembly's work, averting crises, bringing parties to agreement, ensuring that procedures are respected, and accelerating the large agenda. In addition to regular sessions, there have been twenty-eight special sessions called to deal with specific problems (for example, with HIV/AIDS in 2001, with children in 2002, and to follow up on the International Conference on Population and Development in 2014). These special sessions should not be confused with the assembly's emergency special sessions convened under a Uniting for Peace Resolution or with the global conferences the UN has sponsored since the 1970s.

The bulk of the General Assembly's work is done in six functional committees on which all members sit: the First, or Disarmament and International Security Committee; the Second, or Economic and Financial Committee; the Third, or Social, Humanitarian, and Cultural Committee; the Fourth, or Special Political and Decolonization Committee; the Fifth, or Administrative and Budgetary Committee; and the Sixth, or Legal Committee. The assembly also has created other, smaller committees to carry out specific tasks, such as studying a question (the ad hoc Committee on International Terrorism) or framing proposals and monitoring (the Committee on Peaceful Uses of Outer Space and the Disarmament Commission).

Member states' delegations are key to the assembly's functioning. The Charter provides that each member can have no more than five representatives in the assembly, but alternates and advisers are permitted. Delegates are organized in permanent missions, a practice begun with the League of Nations. Missions vary in size from about 120 (the United States) to one or two persons of diplomatic rank. Small and poor states often combine their UN mission with their embassy in Washington, DC, to save money; most states' missions grow significantly during the fall assembly sessions, sometimes including a few parliamentarians or legislators. (The US House and Senate alternate in having representatives on the US delegation each year.) Ties between UN missions and home governments vary from loose to tight. Some delegations have considerable autonomy in dealing with the various issues on assembly agendas and determining how best to represent their countries' interests. Others operate on a tighter leash and must seek instructions from their capitals on what strategies to use and how to vote on given resolutions.

Delegates attend assembly and committee sessions, participate in efforts to shape agendas and debate, and represent national interests. Expertise matters and enables some delegates to be more influential than others. Because almost all states of the world are represented at the annual assembly sessions, there are many opportunities for informal bilateral and multilateral contacts, which countries may use to deal with issues outside the assembly's agenda. Multilateral diplomacy requires different skills, more akin to those of a parliamentary body than to traditional bilateral diplomacy.

Politics and Decisionmaking in the General Assembly. Politics within the General Assembly has mirrored world politics; it is the place to set the agendas of world politics, to get ideas endorsed or condemned, to have actions taken or rejected. Any state can propose an agenda item, and the assembly has been an especially valued tool of small and developing states. Under the one-state/one-vote system, it takes a simple majority of member states present and voting (50 percent plus one) to approve most resolutions. For those items determined to be "important questions," such as resolutions dealing with the maintenance of peace and security, admission of new members, suspension or expulsion of a member, and budgetary questions, a two-thirds majority is required.

Since the General Assembly often mirrors world politics, it is not surprising that member states have formed **voting blocs** to coordinate positions on particular issues and build support for them. As discussed further in Chapter 3, there emerged during the Cold War two competing coalitions aligned with either the United States or the Soviet Union; later, the North-South coalitions tended to dominate assembly discussions and voting patterns, although those coalitions were never completely unified and changed over time. Thus, while the assembly's agenda was dominated by Cold War and decolonization issues in the 1950s, from the 1960s to the 1980s developing countries used their voting power to push a number of Third World goals, as discussed in Chapter 5. The lopsided voting and frequent condemnations of US policies led the United

States, in particular, to regard the General Assembly as a "hostile place" by the mid-1970s. In the mid-1970s, issues regarding the Middle East, particularly the Israeli-Palestinian conflict and issues of human rights, surpassed the focus on colonialism and development.[7] Assembly agendas still largely reflect developing countries' interests in self-determination, economic development, global inequalities, and neocolonialism, but since the late 1980s, differences in social and economic conditions among Asian, African, and Latin American countries have made common policy positions difficult to forge. The South is splintered between a number of more developed countries such as Brazil, China, India, South Africa, Mexico, and Malaysia; a large number of very poor countries; and others in between. The developed countries have never been as cohesive as the South.

Today, the North-South divide persists around issues of economic inequality and development, self-determination (particularly for Palestine), and great-power military capabilities. But **human security** issues, including human rights, development, international security, global inequalities, and the environment, are often very divisive, as are questions of political rights, state sovereignty, and UN intervention. On these issues, while the North-South divide is still salient, there are more crosscutting currents. Chapter 3 explores further the phenomenon of blocs and coalitions.

Although coalitions and blocs emerged in response to the Charter's provisions for "equitable geographical distribution" in elections and voting, more General Assembly decisionmaking in recent years has been done by consensus, that is, by acclamation or acquiescence without any formal vote. In this case, the assembly president consults with delegations and then announces that a resolution is adopted. Consensus, therefore, refers to a decision "supported by, or at least not objectionable to, all parties involved."[8] When the assembly does vote, Article 18, paragraph 2, specifies that it use a simple majority of those states "present and voting" to decide all questions other than "important questions" dealing with peace and security, elections, budget, and admission or suspension of members. Only one-third of Assembly decisions between the first and sixty-fourth sessions involved recorded votes, however, with the highest percentage of these occurring in the 1980s on Middle East issues.[9] Coalitions and blocs are as active in trying to forge consensus as in marshaling votes, but the outcome is less divisive because states' individual positions are not revealed as in a roll call vote.

Criticisms directed at the UN are often criticisms of the General Assembly. Many resolutions are "ritual resolutions"—their texts repeated almost verbatim year after year on agenda items such as the right to development and the situation in the Palestinian territories. Many are also drafted in very general terms, thus masking dissent that would be evident if the wording were more specific. And many are passed with little concern for implementation. The number of resolutions passed in the General Assembly has ranged from about 117 annually during the first five years to a peak of 360 in 2001–2002. The 69th Assembly in 2014 approved 327 resolutions. This situation has led to arguments that there are too many resolutions with redundant or watered-down content, calling for too many reports, with delegates showing too little concern about commitments made. There has been some progress since the mid-1980s in reducing the agenda and number of resolutions as well as requiring explicit renewal of programs or funds based on continuing relevance and effectiveness. Changes, however, require the concurrence of a majority of states.

Since 1990, the General Assembly has been marginalized as the epicenter of UN activity shifted to the Security Council and Secretariat, much to the dismay of the South, which would like more consultation between the General Assembly and the Security Council on peace and security issues. However, with the council stymied by Russian and Chinese vetoes over the Syrian civil war since 2011, as well as Russia's takeover of Crimea and actions in Ukraine in 2014, the General Assembly demonstrated its availability as an alternative forum with its resolution affirming Ukraine's sovereignty and territorial integrity. Still, there is no doubt that the General Assembly needs reform and revitalization.

The Security Council. Under Article 24 of the Charter, the Security Council has primary responsibility for maintaining international peace and security and the authority to act on behalf of all members of the UN. Chapter VI deals with the peaceful settlement of disputes and provides a wide range of techniques for investigating disputes and helping parties achieve resolution without using force. Chapter VII specifies the Security Council's authority to identify aggressors and to commit all UN members to take enforcement measures, such as economic sanctions, or to provide military forces for joint action. Prior to 1990, the Security Council used its enforcement powers under Chapter VII on only two occasions. During the Cold War years, it relied on the peaceful settlement mechanisms under Chapter VI to respond to the many conflicts on its agenda; hence, prior to 1992, all UN peacekeeping forces were authorized under Chapter VI. Since then, the Security Council's use of Chapter VII, including its provisions for economic sanctions and military enforcement action, has increased dramatically, and most peacekeeping operations now carry Chapter VII authority, as discussed in Chapter 4 of this book. Article 25 of the Charter under which UN members agree to accept and carry out council decisions gives the council effective lawmaking power, which it has exercised in a number of ways since 1990, as discussed below. The Security Council is also the designated enforcer of the treaties on nuclear, chemical, and biological weapons.

The Security Council was deliberately designed to be small so that it could facilitate swifter and more efficient decisionmaking in dealing with threats to international peace and security. It is also the only UN body that has permanent

PHOTOGRAPH 2.1. Security Council adopts resolution establishing a monitoring system for Iran's nuclear program, July 20, 2015
Source: UN Photo 638482, July 20, 2015.

and nonpermanent members. The five permanent members (P-5) the United States, Great Britain, France, Russia (successor state to the seat of the Soviet Union in 1992), and the People's Republic of China (PRC, replacing the Republic of China [ROC] in 1971)—are key to Security Council decisionmaking because each has veto power. The nonpermanent members, originally six in number and expanded to ten in 1965, are nominated by one of the five regional groups and elected for two-year terms. At least four nonpermanent members must vote in favor of a resolution for it to pass. Under current rules, no country may serve successive terms as a nonpermanent member. Five of the nonpermanent seats go to Africa and Asia, two each to Latin America and Western Europe, and one to Eastern Europe.

The designation of permanent members reflected the distribution of military power in 1945 and the desire to ensure the UN's ability to respond quickly and decisively to aggression. Their veto power reflected the unwillingness of either the United States or the Soviet Union to accept UN membership without such a provision. It also reflected a realistic acceptance by others that the UN could not undertake enforcement action against its strongest members. The veto, however, has always been controversial among small states and middle powers. Today, with the many changes in world politics and the reality that other states contribute more financially than three of the permanent members, there are serious questions about the legitimacy and effectiveness of the composition of permanent membership. The issue of reforming the makeup of the Security Council is discussed later in this chapter.

The Security Council differs from the General Assembly and ECOSOC in that it has no regular schedule of meetings or agenda; historically, it has met and acted only in response to specific conflicts and crises. Any state, including those that are not UN members, has the right to bring issues before the Security Council, although there is no guarantee of action. The secretary-general can also bring a matter to the council's attention. Beginning in 2000, the Security Council initiated so-called thematic meetings to address broader issues such as HIV/AIDS as a threat to peace, child soldiers, women, peace and security, and cooperation between the UN and regional organizations under Chapter VIII of the Charter.

Nonmembers may attend formal meetings and address the council upon request when they have an interest in a particular issue. In practice, nonmembers are often invited to private and informal meetings as well. Also, states contributing peacekeeping troops now regularly participate in informal consultation with the council, as do the heads of the International Committee of the Red Cross (ICRC), other NGOs, and other individuals with relevant expertise under what is known as the Arria formula, named for Venezuelan ambassador Diego Arria, who first applied it in 1992 in connection with the war in Bosnia. The purpose is to give Security Council members real-time information from the field. The council members have also visited countries and conflict areas for fact-finding, supporting peace agreements, and mediation efforts, although, not surprisingly, such field trips are subject to criticism of their cost, agendas, and destinations. In short, despite how it may appear at times, "the Security Council is not a sealed chamber, deaf to voices and immune to pressure from beyond its walls."[10]

Much of the diplomacy and negotiation relating to the council's work takes place in informal consultations such as those of the P-5, who have come to dominate much of the council's work. This frustrates the nonpermanent members (sometimes referred to as the E-10), particularly other powerful members such as India and Germany. The P-5's dominance, however, has also been shown to be the result of the deference of other UN members and the failure of E-10 members to maximize their influence.[11] Still, the P-5's informal consultations are closed to non–council members and most Secretariat staff, and there are no public records kept.[12] Little, if any, of the bloc or coalition-building activity so common in the General Assembly takes place in the Security Council. None of the P-5 can necessarily count on the support of other permanent or nonpermanent members, although there have been patterns of joint exercise of vetoes such as Britain and France together and, most recently, Russia and China. The council presidency rotates monthly among the fifteen members, and presidents play an active role in facilitating discussions and consensus-building, determining when the members are ready to reach a decision and, hence, to convene a formal meeting. The president also confers regularly with the secretary-general, relevant states, and other actors that are not represented on the council.

In addition to its responsibilities under the Charter for maintaining international security, the council participates in the election of the secretary-general, justices to the International Court of Justice, and new UN members in collaboration with the General Assembly. The Cold War limited its use; in 1959, for example, only five meetings were held. Between 1946 and 1989, it adopted just 646 resolutions. Since 1990, the frequency of formal and informal meetings has steadily risen and the number of resolutions between 1990 and 2015 soared to 1,598. In addition, the council issued hundreds of presidential statements summarizing the outcomes of meetings where no resolutions were acted upon.

The permanent members' veto power has always been controversial, yet represents the recognition that the UN cannot act against the wishes of the major powers. During the Cold War, the Soviet Union employed its veto frequently not only to block action on many peace and security issues but also to block admission of Western-supported new members and nominees for secretary-general. The United States did not exercise its veto until the 1970s, reflecting its early dominance and many friends, particularly Britain and France. Since then, however, the United States has used its veto more than any other permanent member, most frequently on resolutions relating to the Arab-Israeli-Palestinian conflict and in defense of Israel. China took advantage of the early precedent that allowed abstentions not to be counted as negative votes (i.e., vetoes) to abstain a total of twenty-seven times between 1990 and 1996 on a series of enforcement measures (including those against Iraq), thus registering its disagreement but not blocking action. Since 2007, China's dramatic economic rise and growing assertiveness (discussed further in Chapter 3) have altered that pattern. Russia and China worked in tandem in jointly vetoing six resolutions on Syria and other issues between 2007 and 2014, reflecting their shared concerns regarding sovereignty, nonintervention, and US dominance. (See Table 2.1 for a summary of vetoes cast and note how the pattern has changed over time.) It is also important to recognize that vetoes are exercised only when other council members insist on a vote on a draft resolution that they know a P-5 member objects to and will likely veto.[13]

Since the late 1980s, the Security Council has taken action on more armed conflicts, made more decisions under Chapter VII of the UN Charter, authorized more peacekeeping operations, and imposed more types of sanctions in more situations than ever before. Since 1990, some of its actions have amounted to lawmaking. It authorized the use of "all necessary means" to protect civilians during Libya's 2011 uprising, an Intervention Force Brigade in the Democratic Republic of Congo in 2013, and a stabilization mission in Mali also in 2013.

TABLE 2.1. Changing Patterns in the Use of the Veto in the Security Council, 1946–2015

Period	China[a]	France	Britain	US	USSR/Russia	Total
1946–1955	1	2	—	—	80	83
1956–1965	0	2	3	—	26	31
1966–1975	2	2	10	12	7	33
1976–1985	0	9	11	34	6	60
1986–1995	0	3	8	24	2	37
1996–2005	2	0	0	10	1	13
2006–2011	2	0	0	3	3	8
2012–2015	3	0	0	0	6	9
Total	10	18	32	83	131	274

[a]Between 1946 and 1971, the Chinese seat on the Security Council was occupied by the Republic of China (Taiwan), which used the veto only once (to block Mongolia's application for membership in 1955). The first veto exercised by the present occupant, the People's Republic of China, was therefore not until August 25, 1972.

SOURCES: www.globalpolicy.org/images/pdfs/Z/Tables_and_Charts/useofveto.pdf; www.un.org/Depts /dhl/resguide/scact2011.htm; http://research.un.org/en/docs/sc/quick.

It passed a 2014 resolution aimed at preventing the flow of "foreign fighters" to terrorist groups in Syria and Iraq. It took the unprecedented step of creating war crimes tribunals to prosecute individuals responsible for genocide and war crimes in Rwanda, the former Yugoslavia, and Sierra Leone and required all states to cooperate with these tribunals. It authorized NATO bombing against Bosnian Serb forces in Bosnia in 1995 and African Union (AU) peace enforcement in Somalia. It authorized UN-administered protectorates in Kosovo and East Timor. It expanded definitions of threats to peace to include terrorism even before the 9/11 attacks and thereafter approved Resolution 1373, which requires all member states to adopt antiterrorism measures in the International Convention for the Suppression of the Financing of Terrorism, which came into effect in 2002. Since 2000, as the very concept of security has expanded to encompass issues of human security, the council has taken up a number of so-called thematic issues, ranging from HIV/AIDS to child soldiers, the role of women in peace and security, and protection of civilians. Nonpermanent members of the council have often provided impetus for these debates, which are discussed in more detail in subsequent chapters. It is important to note here that the Security Council's attention and resolve with regard to various threats to peace and security have been highly inconsistent. The council has never established criteria for its involvement, and opposition from one or more P-5 members can keep a conflict off the council's agenda.[14]

The Security Council has also created a number of monitoring bodies since 1990. These include sanctions committees, the Counter-Terrorism Committee (CTC), and the 1540 Committee, established following the passage in 2004 of Resolution 1540, which obligates states to establish domestic controls to prevent proliferation of weapons of mass destruction (WMD) to state or nonstate actors. The use of such authority *over* UN members constitutes what former Canadian diplomat David Malone called "a movement toward a regulatory approach to international peace and security."[15]

Although the Charter gives the council enormous formal power, it does not give it control over the means to use that power. For that the council must depend upon the voluntary cooperation of states willing to provide military and civilian personnel for peacekeeping missions, to enforce sanctions, to pay their dues, and to support enforcement actions either under UN command, by a coalition of the willing, or by a regional organization such as the African Union. Yet many council Chapter VII decisions since 1990 have proved more ambitious than either the member states were willing to support with resources and troops or the Secretariat could effectively manage. Thus, critics have charged that the extensive use of Chapter VII damages the council's credibility, as the Chapter VII language may be intended primarily to convey resolve where there is disagreement on real action.[16]

The Security Council's activism since 1990 and US decisions in 1999 (Kosovo) and 2003 (Iraq) to undertake military actions without explicit council authorization provoked vigorous debate among scholars and policymakers about the council's power, authority, and legitimacy.[17] Clearly, the Charter endows the Security Council with a great deal of formal power and authority. In the case of the 2003 Iraq War, for example, it was recognition of the council's authority that led both supporters and opponents of the US-led invasion to seek approval or to block it. And despite concerns at the time that the council was a "failed" and "debilitated" body, both sides clearly saw the legitimacy of the council's authority at stake.[18] Searching for evidence of the council's authority for the post-9/11 antiterrorism actions mandated in Resolution 1373, for example, Bruce Cronin and Ian Hurd note, "It is not the act of issuing these mandatory declarations that offers evidence of increased authority, but, rather, the fact that most member states accepted the *right* of the Council to do so."[19] Still, as former British ambassador Jeremy Greenstock notes, "As instances of failure on hard issues (Palestine, Kashmir, Sri Lanka, Cyprus, the former Yugoslavia, Darfur, Iraq, Afghanistan, Libya, Syria) pile up over the decades, criticism of the Council accumulates."[20] Even Secretary-General Ban Ki-moon was heard to scold the major powers in late 2015, saying, "You're not doing much at all . . . you need to fix the way you operate."[21] We return to the issues of the council's legitimacy and ability to function effectively below, when we examine reforms.

The Economic and Social Council. ECOSOC, with its fifty-four members, is the UN's central forum for addressing international economic and social issues, and its purposes range from promoting higher standards of living to identifying solutions to economic, social, and health problems and "encouraging universal respect for human rights and fundamental freedoms." The activities it oversees encompass a majority of the UN system's human and financial resources. The founders of the UN envisaged that the various specialized agencies, ranging from the ILO and WHO to the World Bank and the IMF, would play primary roles in operational activities devoted to economic and social advancement, with ECOSOC responsible for coordinating those activities. Hence, the Charter speaks of ECOSOC's functions in terms of that coordination and also charges it with undertaking research and preparing reports on economic and social issues, making recommendations, preparing conventions, and convening conferences. Of those tasks, coordination has been the most problematic because so many activities lie outside the effective jurisdiction of ECOSOC. It is through consultative status with ECOSOC that many NGOs have official relationships with the UN and its activities. (See Chapter 3 for further discussion.)

ECOSOC's membership has been expanded through two Charter amendments. The original membership of eighteen was increased to twenty-seven in 1965 and to fifty-four in 1973. Members are elected by the General Assembly to three-year terms based on nominations by the regional blocs. Motivated by recognition that states with the ability to pay should be continuously represented, four of the five permanent members of the Security Council (all but China) and major developed countries have been regularly reelected. ECOSOC acts through decisions and resolutions, many of which are approved by consensus or simple majority votes. None are binding on member states or on the specialized agencies, however. Recommendations and multilateral conventions drafted by ECOSOC require General Assembly approval (and, in the case of conventions, ratification by member states).

ECOSOC holds one 4-week substantive meeting each year, alternating between UN headquarters in New York and Geneva, where several of the specialized agencies and other programs are headquartered. It also holds many short sessions and preparatory meetings. In 2007 and 2008, respectively, ECOSOC launched two new types of meetings. The first is the Annual Ministerial Review, initiated in 2005 to assess progress toward the Millennium Development Goals. The second is the biennial Development Cooperation Forum, intended to bring together all relevant actors for dialogue on policy issues affecting development cooperation. Both sets of meetings include member states, all relevant UN institutions, civil society, and the private sector.

The economic and social activities that ECOSOC is expected to coordinate are spread among subsidiary bodies (such as expert and working groups), nine functional commissions, five regional commissions, and the nineteen special-ized agencies. (See Figure 2.1.) A number of entities created by the General Assembly, such as the UN Development Programme (UNDP), UN Fund for Population Activities (UNFPA), UN Children's Fund (UNICEF), and World Food Programme (WFP), report to both the General Assembly and ECOSOC, compounding the complexity and confusion. The scope of ECOSOC's agenda includes widely diverse topics, from housing to narcotic drug control, from lit-eracy to refugees, from the environment to rights of indigenous peoples. Devel-opment is the largest subject area.

Functional and Regional Commissions. Part of ECOSOC's work is done in a set of eight functional commissions: Social Development, Narcotic Drugs, Status of Women, Science and Technology for Development, Population and Devel-opment, Crime Prevention and Criminal Justice, Statistics, and Forests. The Statistical Commission reflects the importance of statistical studies and anal-ysis for analyzing problems and making national and international social and economic policies. The wide range of data on social and economic conditions that has been gathered over the years is vital to dealing with various world problems.

Two of the most active commissions are the Commission on the Status of Women (CSW), established in 1946 to prepare recommendations and reports concerning women's political, economic, social, and educational rights, and (un-til 2006) the Commission on Human Rights. All of the UN-initiated declara-tions and conventions on human rights up to then were products of this body's work. Both of these are discussed further in Chapter 6.

Beginning in 1947, ECOSOC also created five regional commissions to stim-ulate regional approaches to development, with studies and initiatives to pro-mote regional projects based on the rationale that cooperation among countries within a geographic region would benefit all. A 1950 report of the Economic Commission for Latin America, for example, highlighted data on the declining terms of trade of developing countries and influenced many countries to adopt import-substitution policies to reduce their dependence on trade. In the 1960s, the Economic Commission for Africa pioneered the study of population growth and the role of women in development. The regional commissions are discussed further in Chapter 5.

Coordination is inherently difficult within any complex organization, and na-tional governments have their own problems in this regard. Indeed, one analyst argues that ECOSOC's problems are attributable in part to "the absence of coordi-nation at the national level in regard to international policies and programmes."[22] The steady expansion of UN economic and social activities over more than sixty-five years has made ECOSOC's mandate for coordination almost impossible to fulfill. This has led to persistent, but largely unsuccessful, calls for reform since the late 1940s, described below.

The Secretariat. The UN Secretariat is composed of approximately 41,000 professional and support staff based in New York, Geneva, Vienna, Nairobi, Bangkok, and other UN offices around the world. They are individuals who, though nationals of member countries, serve the international community. Early IGO secretariats were established by the Universal Postal Union and International Telegraph Union in the 1860s and 1870s, but their members were not independent of national governments. The League of Nations set the first precedents for a truly international secretariat of individuals who were expected to be impartial in serving the organization as a whole and dedicated to its principles. A complementary principle of an international civil service is for member states to respect the international character and responsibilities of the staff, regardless of their nationality. This practice carried over to the UN and its specialized agencies (which have their own secretariats), with personnel for all but the most senior posts recruited from a broad geographic base and advanced over time on the basis of merit and seniority. Top-level posts do not, however, conform to this civil service model but are appointed by the secretary-general based on nominations and political pressures from member governments. Secretariat members are not expected to give up their national loyalty, but are expected to refrain from promoting national interests—a sometimes difficult task at times in a world of strong nationalisms. Articles 100 and 101 deal with the Secretariat's internationalism and independence.

The Secretary-General. The UN secretary-general's position has been termed "one of the most ill-defined: a combination of chief administrative officer of the United Nations and global diplomat with a fat portfolio whose pages are blank."[23] The secretary-general is the manager of the organization, responsible for providing leadership to the Secretariat, preparing the UN's budget, submitting an annual report to the General Assembly, and overseeing studies conducted at the request of the other major organs. Article 99 of the Charter also authorizes the secretary-general "to bring to the attention of the Security Council any matter which in his opinion may threaten the maintenance of international peace and security." This provides a basis for the secretary-general's authority and ability to be an independent actor.

Over time, secretaries-general have often, but not always, come to play significant political roles as spokespersons for the organization; as conveners of expert groups, commissions, and panels to frame issues, marshal research, and outline choices; and as mediators drawing on the Charter's spirit as the basis for taking initiatives. Yet the secretary-general is simultaneously subject to the demands of two constituencies—member states and the Secretariat itself. States elect the UN's chief administrator and do not want to be either upstaged or publicly opposed by the person in that position. The secretary-general also has to answer to the Secretariat personnel working in programs and agencies across the UN system. The balancing act is not always easy. As chief executive officer, the secretary-general also has to have good personnel management and budgetary skills.

The secretary-general holds office for a five-year renewable term on the recommendation of the Security Council and election by two-thirds of the General Assembly. The process of nomination is intensely political and secretive, with the P-5 having primary input because of their veto power. For example, when the United States opposed the reelection of Boutros Boutros-Ghali in 1996, it forced members to agree on an alternative candidate, Kofi Annan. Efforts to establish a better means of selecting this global leader have thus far not been successful, but in 2015 the General Assembly took the unusual step of unanimously passing a resolution (A/RES/69/321) calling for a more open and transparent selection process, one that would allow all member states to review information on candidates and to meet and question them. The push to name a woman to the post got a boost with language that referred to the need for "gender and geographical balance while meeting the highest possible requirements." The 1for7Billion civil society campaign to open the selection process even placed an ad in *The Economist* for the position of UN secretary-general! Not surprisingly, past secretary-generals have all come from relatively small states, and none have been heads of state or government (see Box 2.1). Still, there is no rule that the post must rotate among geographic groups. As Simon Chesterman notes, "In the past two appointments . . . it was widely accepted that the Secretary-General would be African and then Asian." The Eastern European group made it clear in 2015 that theirs was the only group never to have had a secretary-general; hence, speculation was widespread that the next selection would likely be a woman from Eastern Europe. Chesterman adds, however, that the P-5 have shown a distinct preference for an individual accustomed "to taking orders rather than giving them—someone who will be more 'secretary' than 'general.'"[24]

Because of differences in personality and skills as well as in the challenges faced, each secretary-general has undertaken his tasks in a different way, with varying consequences for the organization. Their personalities and interpretations of the Charter, as well as world events, have combined to increase the power, resources, and importance of the position. More than just a senior civil servant, the UN secretary-general has become an international political figure and even the UN's moral voice, and a key factor in the emergence of the UN as an independent actor in world politics. We explore the secretary-general's role more fully in Chapter 3.

BOX 2.1. **UN Secretaries-General (1946–2016)**

Secretary-General	Nationality	Dates of Service
Trygve Lie	Norway	1946–1953
Dag Hammarskjöld	Sweden	1953–1961
U Thant	Burma	1961–1971
Kurt Waldheim	Austria	1972–1981
Javier Pérez de Cuéllar	Peru	1982–1991
Boutros Boutros-Ghali	Egypt	1992–1996
Kofi Annan	Ghana	1997–2006
Ban Ki-moon	Republic of Korea	2007–2016

Functions of the Secretariat. The UN Secretariat is organized into a series of offices and departments as shown in Figure 2.1, including the Executive Office of the Secretary-General; the Office of Legal Affairs; the Departments of Political Affairs, Peacekeeping Operations, Field Support, Disarmament Affairs, and Economic and Social Affairs; and the Office for the Coordination of Humanitarian Affairs. Each of these is headed by an undersecretary or assistant secretary-general, division head, or high commissioner. In 1997, the post of deputy secretary-general was created and a more cabinet-like style of management was adopted in 2005. The Senior Management Group, chaired by the secretary-general, brings together leaders of UN departments, offices, funds, and programs in regular meetings, including video conferences with UN offices around the world. In addition, there is the Chief Executives Board, which includes the executive heads of twenty-nine UN specialized agencies and programs and meets twice a year to facilitate coordination across the entire UN system.

Only about one-third of Secretariat personnel are based at headquarters in New York or Geneva; others are posted in more than 140 countries. Their work often has little to do with the symbolic politics of the General Assembly, or even with the highly political debates of the Security Council, but it may contribute ideas for addressing specific problems drawn from outside consultants, NGOs, and expert groups. Most Secretariat staff are involved in implementing the economic, humanitarian, and social programs that represent much of the UN's tangible contribution to fulfilling the Charter promises to "save succeeding generations from the scourge of war . . . promoting social progress and better standards of life in larger freedom." Others support UN peace operations. The Secretariat is also responsible for gathering statistical data, issuing studies and reports, servicing meetings, preparing documentation, and translating speeches, debates, and documents into the UN's six official languages. Service in the UN Secretariat is not without risk. More than 350 civilian staff members have died while in UN service, including Sergio Vieira de Mello, the secretary-general's special representative to Iraq, and twenty-one others in the August 2003 bombing of UN offices in Baghdad as well as UN Secretary-General Dag Hammarskjöld in a plane crash in the Congo in 1961.

The UN Secretariat staff and the secretariats of the specialized agencies share a number of the characteristics of bureaucracies more generally. They derive authority from their rational-legal character and from their expertise; they derive legitimacy from the moral purposes of the organization and from their claims to neutrality, impartiality, and objectivity; and they derive power from their missions of serving others.[25] Many Secretariat staff are technocrats—individuals with specialized training and knowledge, such as the neoliberal economists in the World Bank and IMF and the public health experts in WHO. How they see a problem and how the organizational culture frames an issue may determine what solutions are discussed and the actions taken.

Women have rarely occupied key positions in the UN Secretariat. As one scholar comments, "One might have expected the UN to lead in integrating women into work compared with other institutions. The pace has been glacial."[26] From 2003 to 2013 the total percentage of female staff in the UN Secretariat rose from 36.7 to 40.5 percent.[27] However, when it comes to women in leadership positions within the UN, progress has been slow. The chair of the first World Conference on Women, held in Mexico City in 1975, was a man. Nafis Sadik of Pakistan was the first woman to head a major UN agency when she was appointed head of the UN Fund for Population Activities in 1987. Louise Frechette of Canada was appointed as the first deputy secretary-general in 1998. Today, about one-third of the professional and higher ranks of the UN Secretariat's professional staff are women; only at the entry levels has gender balance been achieved. As another scholar writes, "The UN has not always led by example where gender equality and women's rights are concerned."[28] No women have been among the top candidates for secretary-general in the past, but in 2015 several campaigns were launched advocating that a woman serve as the ninth secretary-general. Women accounted for only seven of the forty-four special representatives to the secretary-general in 2015 and, as of that year, five women had headed UN agencies.

The UN Secretariat has been criticized not only for its failure to hire women but also for lapses in its neutrality, duplication of tasks, and poor administrative practices. It was particularly tarnished by the scandal over UN mismanagement of the Oil-for-Food Programme (OFFP). Initiated in 1996, this program permitted limited sales of Iraqi oil to finance food supplies and medicine as humanitarian relief. An independent investigation found that private companies, European politicians, the Palestine Liberation Organization (PLO), and a handful of UN administrators, including the director of the OFFP, had also received kickbacks. Although the secretary-general was not found guilty, his son was implicated, and others at the UN resigned or were fired. The scandal provided plenty of fuel for UN critics in the United States and elsewhere. The UN has also been tarnished by allegations of sexual misconduct by UN peacekeepers that raised questions of integrity and oversight.

Member states share blame with UN secretaries-general and staff for many of the administrative problems, however. General Assembly and Security Council resolutions may be vague and unrealistic; objectives often depend on member governments' actions, funding commitments, and other factors to be fulfilled; and since the UN is a political organization, the Secretariat is subject to interference and pressure from member states. Key positions in the secretary-general's cabinet are, in fact, reserved for nationals nominated by P-5 governments, and other member states have demanded a share of senior posts as well. Although there have been numerous criticisms of Secretariat inefficiency over the years, many member states do not necessarily want the UN to have an effective Secretariat and secretary-general, since that could diminish their own ability to control what the UN does. We discuss issues of Secretariat reform later in the chapter.

The International Court of Justice. Although its predecessor, the Permanent Court of International Justice, enjoyed only a loose association with the League of Nations, the International Court of Justice (ICJ), the judicial arm of the UN, headquartered in The Hague, shares responsibility with the other major organs for ensuring that the principles of the Charter are followed. Its special role is providing states with an impartial body for settling legal disputes in accordance with international law and giving **advisory opinions** on legal questions referred to it by international agencies. All members of the UN are ipso facto parties to the ICJ Statute.

The General Assembly and Security Council play a joint role in electing the fifteen judges, who serve nine-year terms (five are elected every three years). Judges must have qualifications befitting appointment to the highest judicial body in their home country and recognized competence in international law. Together they represent the major legal systems of the world, but they act independently of their national affiliations, utilizing different sources of law set forth in Article 38 of the ICJ Statute as the basis for judgments. Their deliberations take place in private, their decisions are decided by majority vote, and decisions, including dissents, include the reasons on which they are based.

The ICJ has **noncompulsory jurisdiction**, meaning that parties to a dispute (only states) must all agree to submit a case to the court; it has no executive to enforce its decisions and no police to bring a party to justice. Enforcement therefore depends on the perceived legitimacy of the court's decisions, the voluntary compliance of states, and the "power of shame" if states fail to comply.

The ICJ has had 161 contentious cases brought before it between 1946 and 2015. It has never been heavily burdened, but its caseload has increased significantly in recent years as a result of the Cold War's end and greater trust in the court by developing countries. Also, many newer international legal conventions require the use of the ICJ to resolve disputes. Twelve cases were pending in late 2015, for example. To speed up what is often a lengthy process, the court instituted the option of using a chamber of five justices to handle cases by summary procedure.

ICJ cases have only rarely reflected the major political issues of the day because few states want to trust a legal judgment for the settlement of a largely political issue. The court has helped states resolve numerous territorial disputes (for example, the *Case Concerning the Land and Maritime Boundary Between Cameroon and Nigeria*), disputes over delimitation of the continental shelf (in the North Sea, for example), and fisheries jurisdiction (such as in the Gulf of Maine case). The ICJ has also ruled on the legality of nuclear tests, hostage taking, the right of asylum, use of force, environmental protection, application of the Genocide Convention in Bosnia, expropriation of foreign property, and Japan's whaling in the Antarctic.

On twenty-six occasions, the ICJ has issued advisory opinions on legal issues at the request of UN organs. Among the more prominent are the *Reparation for Injuries Suffered in the Service of the United Nations* opinion (1949), in which the UN's international legal personality was clarified, the *Certain Expenses of the United Nations* opinion (1962), which declared peacekeeping expenses part of the fiscal obligations of member states, and the *Difference Relating to Immunity from Legal Process of a Special Rapporteur of the Commission on Human Rights* opinion (1999). In the first, for example, the UN was accorded the right to seek payment from a state held responsible for the injury or death of a UN employee. With this case, the ICJ also established that it had the power to interpret the Charter, although no such power was expressly conferred upon it either by the Charter or by the court's own statute or rules. Two recent advisory opinions, *Legal Consequences Arising from the Construction of a Wall in the Occupied Palestinian Territories* (2004) and *Accordance with International Law of the Unilateral Declaration of Independence in Respect of Kosovo* (2010), represent more political issues, having been requested by the General Assembly.

Because only states can bring cases before the ICJ, the court cannot deal with disputes involving states and nonstate actors such as terrorist and paramilitary groups and private corporations. Furthermore, while judicial decisions are sources of international law under the court's statute, Article 38.1(d) also provides that the "decision of the Court has no binding force except as between the parties and in respect of that particular case." In other words, state sovereignty was intended to limit the applicability of ICJ judgments, unlike national courts that use precedents from prior cases to shape future judgments and, hence, the substance and interpretation of law. In reality, however, the ICJ has used many principles from earlier cases to decide later ones, which has contributed to greater consistency in its decisions and more respect for the court's ability to aid the progressive development of international law.

Some assessments of the ICJ focus on its relatively light caseload and slow processes, but other opinions stress its contributions to "the process of systematizing, consolidating, codifying and progressively developing international law."[29] Furthermore, with the creation of other judicial bodies, the ICJ is no longer the only site for adjudicating disputes, and there are many other ways to settle disputes besides resorting to adjudication. For example, there are a number of other international tribunals within the UN system. Some are tied to specialized agencies, such as the International Labour Organization's Administrative Tribunal and the International Centre for the Settlement of Investment Disputes within the World Bank. Others have been established to adjudicate specific issues such as the Law of the Sea Tribunal and the International Criminal Court (ICC). Still others are temporary bodies designed to deal with a particular problem, such as the UN Compensation Commission, which dealt with claims against Iraq following its invasion of Kuwait, and the ad hoc war crimes tribunals created to adjudicate crimes against humanity and war crimes in the former Yugoslavia, Rwanda, and Sierra Leone. The ICC, while not technically a part of the UN system, is discussed in Chapter 6.

The Trusteeship Council. This council was originally established to oversee the administration of the non-self-governing trust territories that carried over from the mandate system of the League of Nations. These territories were former German colonies, mostly in Africa, that were placed under the League-supervised control of other powers (Great Britain, France, Belgium, and Japan) because they were deemed unprepared for self-determination or independence. The eleven UN trust territories also included Pacific islands that the United States liberated from Japan during World War II. The council's supervisory activities included reporting on the status of the people in the territories, making annual reports, and conducting periodic visits to the territories. The council terminated the last trusteeship agreement when the people of the Trust Territory of the Pacific Islands voted in November 1993 for free association with the United States. The Trusteeship Council and its system of supervision provided a model for the peaceful transition to independence for colonial and dependent peoples, playing a role in the remarkable process of decolonization during the 1950s and 1960s. Thus, its very success spelled its demise.

To avoid amending the UN Charter, the council continues to exist, but it no longer meets in annual sessions. There has been periodic discussion about new functions for the Trusteeship Council. One proposal called for giving the council responsibility for monitoring conditions that affect the global commons (seas, seabed, and outer space). Another called for using it to assist "failed states."

The Specialized Agencies. A number of specialized agencies, including the ILO and Universal Postal Union, predate the UN itself and were brought into relationship with the UN under Article 57. The founders of the UN envisaged that functional agencies would play key roles, particularly in activities aimed at economic and social advancement. Thus, Articles 57 and 63 of the Charter called for the affiliation with the UN of various organizations established by separate international agreements to deal with issues such as health (WHO); food (Food and Agriculture Organization, or FAO); science, education, and culture (UNESCO); and economics (the IMF and World Bank). Today, nineteen specialized agencies are formally affiliated with the UN through agreements with ECOSOC and the General Assembly (see Figure 2.1). Like the UN itself, they have global responsibilities, but separate charters, memberships, budgets, and secretariats, as well as their own interests and constituencies.

Several factors complicate the relationship between ECOSOC and the specialized agencies. One factor is geographical dispersal. Several are headquartered in Geneva; others are in Rome, Paris, Montreal, Washington, London, Vienna, and Berne (Switzerland). In the field, each agency has often had its own separate building and staff. This dispersal affects efficiency, budgets, and coordination. Contemporary communications technologies such as video conferencing, however, lessen some of the effects of dispersal.

Another complicating factor is that historically the specialized agencies have operated quite independently, with ECOSOC having no control over their budgets or secretariats and no means other than persuasion to achieve integration and coordination. For example, the ILO's activities include employment promotion, vocational guidance, social security, safety and health, labor laws and relations, and rural institutions. These overlap with FAO's concern with land reform, UNESCO's mandate in education, WHO's focus on health standards, and the UN Industrial Development Organization's (UNIDO) concern with manpower in small industries. The result is constant coordination problems. The Bretton Woods institutions—the World Bank, IMF, and former General Agreement on Tariffs and Trade (GATT), now the World Trade Organization—have generally operated quite independently of ECOSOC and the rest of the UN system. The

WTO, created in 1995, is not even part of the UN system. The Chief Executives Board, chaired by the secretary-general, brings together all the executive heads of UN specialized agencies and programs twice a year to facilitate coordination.

The major economic institutions are discussed further in Chapter 5. We provide a brief overview here of the ILO, and in Chapter 7 we examine the WHO and its work on Ebola.

The origins of the ILO can be traced to the nineteenth century, when two industrialists, Welshman Robert Owen and Frenchman Daniel Legrand, advocated an organization to protect workers from abuses of industrialization and to support the growing labor movement in Europe and the United States. Labor's growing political importance and Owen and Legrand's ideas led to the adoption of the Constitution of the International Labour Organization in 1919 by the Paris Peace Conference. The constitution was based on the belief that world peace could be accomplished only by attention to social justice. Thus, the ILO became an autonomous organization within the structure of the League of Nations, an institutional model adopted by the United Nations.

The ILO's major activity is setting standards for treatment of workers. As of 2014, the ILO had concluded more than 190 conventions and supplementary protocols, of which 155 had received sufficient ratifications to come into force. In many countries, the international labor codes on such issues as the right to organize and bargain, the ban on slavery and forced labor, the regulation of hours of work, agreements about wages, and workers' compensation and safety are translated directly into domestic law. Among the eight conventions designated "fundamental" by the ILO are the conventions on forced labor, freedom of association, discrimination, and child labor. More than 138 states have ratified all these conventions; the United States has ratified but two, the forced labor and child labor conventions.

Under Article 33, the ILO can take action against states to secure compliance, but in practice, the ILO generally promotes compliance through the less coercive means of gathering member-state reports and hearing complaints of noncompliance. Using peer pressure and persuasion rather than hard sanctions, it makes recommendations to states on how their records can be improved and offers technical assistance programs to facilitate state compliance. Among functional organizations, the ILO is regarded as having the most effective system of monitoring. Rather than resorting to enforcement measures, however, it tends to work with the country in question and use technical assistance programs to facilitate compliance with labor norms.

The ILO, headquartered in Geneva, Switzerland, accomplishes its work through three major bodies, each of which includes a unique tripartite representation structure involving government officials, employers, and workers. This integration of governmental and nongovernmental representatives is a unique approach not duplicated in any other IGO. Nonetheless, the arrangement has been uniquely suited to represent both governmental and societal interests. Much like the General Assembly, the International Labour Conference meets annually; the Governing Body—the executive arm of the ILO, composed of fifty-six members representing twenty-eight governments, fourteen employers, and fourteen worker groups—establishes programs, and a Committee of Experts examines governments' reports on compliance with ILO conventions. The International Labour Office forms the permanent secretariat under the leadership of the director-general.

Global Conferences and Summits. Multilateral global conferences date back to the period after World War I when the League of Nations convened conferences on economic affairs and disarmament. Since the late 1960s, the UN has sponsored global conferences and summit meetings of heads of state and government on topics ranging from the environment, food supply, population, and women's rights to water supplies, children, and desertification, as shown in Box 2.2. These conferences and summits are ad hoc events, convened at the request of one or more countries, and authorized by the General Assembly or ECOSOC, with all member states eligible to attend. Names can be deceiving, particularly for those events since 1990 termed "summits," where the sessions for heads of state and government last one or two days and may or may not be accompanied by a conference running from two to six weeks. There was a large cluster of global conferences in the 1970s and another in the 1990s, with a lull in the 1980s and a deliberate effort to scale back since 2000.

UN-sponsored global conferences and summits serve a variety of purposes. They "seek to raise global consciousness about a particular problem, hoping to change the dominant attitudes surrounding the definition of the issue"; to educate publics and government officials; to generate new information; to provide opportunities to develop soft law, new norms, principles, and international standards; to highlight gaps in international institutions by providing new forums for debate and consensus-building; and to "set in motion a process whereby governments make commitments and can be held accountable."[30] The environmental conferences and the women's conferences, in particular, led governments to create appropriate national bodies to address the issues.

Global conferences and summits also provide opportunities for developing transnational issue networks by inviting participation and input from scientific and other expert groups, NGOs, and private corporations. Many have involved two conferences in the same location—the official conference with member states and a parallel NGO-organized conference. Participation has varied widely, from the UN Conference on the Human Environment (UNCHE) in Stockholm in 1972, which included 114 UN member states and more than 200 NGOs in the parallel Environment Forum, to the 2002 Johannesburg Summit on Sustainable Development, attended by approximately 21,000 people, including representatives of 191 states and some 8,000 representatives of NGOs and other organizations. These conferences contributed to the growth of NGOs and civil society; they helped to increase understanding of the links among issues as seemingly disparate as environmental protection, human rights (especially for women), poverty alleviation, and development and trade.

Global conferences typically have involved extensive preparatory processes, including in-depth studies by experts and preparatory meetings convened by committees known as "prepcoms" and involving both NGOs and states. This is where decisions are made on many key agenda items, experts brought in, and NGO roles at the conference itself determined. There may also be regional meetings to help build consensus on proposed conference outcomes. By one estimate, at least 60 percent of the final conference outcomes are negotiated during the preparatory process.[31] The background studies can also serve as wake-up calls to the international community, as, for example, when studies prior to the 1982 World Assembly on Aging showed that developing countries would face challenges of aging populations in fewer than fifty years.

The outcomes of UN-sponsored global conferences and summits include declarations and action plans. Several conferences in the 1970s also led to new institutions to meet conference goals, including the United Nations Environment Programme (UNEP) and the UN Development Fund for Women (UNIFEM). The 1992 Rio conference on the Environment and Development charged NGOs with key roles in implementing goals. The Platform of Action approved at the 1995 Fourth World Conference on Women in Beijing called for "empowering women" through access to all types of economic resources.

By the late 1990s, the difficulties of monitoring what was actually being done and integrating implementation of conference outcomes with the main UN organs, especially ECOSOC, had become increasingly problematic. The US Congress had joined sides with the critics to impose a moratorium on US participation in UN global conferences except for the Durban antiracism conference scheduled for 2001. In 2003, the General Assembly voted to end the practice of convening follow-up conferences. As a result, subsequent major UN-sponsored gatherings have been "summits" rather than global conferences. For example, the Millennium Summit in 2000 focused on mobilizing agreement on the eight Millennium Development Goals, thus deliberately addressing the need to integrate the development-related goals of various separate conferences. The 2005 World Summit focused on various UN reform proposals, with Secretary-General Kofi Annan putting forth his own program of action, "In Larger Freedom: Towards Development, Security, and Human Rights for All." Although leaders failed to act on Security Council reform, they did approve the creation

BOX 2.2. UN-Sponsored Global Conferences and Summits

Topic	Global Conference	Summit
Aging	1982, 2002	
Agrarian Reform and Rural Development	1989, 2006	
Children		1990
Climate	1979, 1990, 2007, 2010	2009
Desertification	1977	
Education	1990	
Education for Sustainable Development	2009	
Environment	1972, 2013	
Environment and Development	1992, 2012	
Financing for Development		2002, 2008
Food	1974, 2002	1996, 2009
Habitat (Human Settlement)	1976, 1996	
Human Rights	1968, 1993	
Illicit Trade in Small Arms	2001	
Information Society		2003, 2005
Law of the Sea	1958, 1973–1982	
Least-Developed Countries	1981, 1990, 2001, 2011	
Millennium Development Goals	2010	
New and Renewable Sources of Energy	1981	
Population	1974, 1984	
Population and Development	1994, 2014	
Racism	1987, 2001, 2009	
Science and Technology for Development	1979	
Social Development		1995
Sustainable Development		2002, 2015
Sustainable Development of Small Island States	1994, 2014	
UN Reform, New Millennium Challenges		2000, 2005
Water	1977	
Women	1975, 1980, 1985, 1995	2015

of a new Peacebuilding Commission, established a Human Rights Council to replace the Commission on Human Rights, strengthened UN oversight capacity, agreed on language endorsing the "responsibility to protect," condemned terrorism "in all its forms and manifestations," and recognized the serious challenge posed by climate change.[32] A 2009 summit dealt with the global financial and economic crisis, and Secretary-General Ban Ki-moon organized a summit on climate in 2014. In 2015, two successive summits dealt with the integration of development and climate change: the Sustainable Development Summit and the twenty-year follow-up to the 1995 Beijing conference on women.

UN-sponsored conferences and summits are an integral part of global governance, not just stand-alone events tied to the United Nations. As part of broader political processes, the conferences have mobilized energies and attention in a way that established institutions could not. They have pushed different parts of the UN system, although the record of implementation is uneven and much depends on NGOs' ability to pressure governments to live up to commitments they have made and to assist the UN in meeting the demands placed on it. Where summits can boost implementation is through peer pressure on leaders to pledge their countries' cooperation. There are, however, mixed opinions on the value of global conferences and summits. In one view, "conferences are one of the main devices . . . that are used to spawn, nurture, and massage new ideas as well as to nudge governments, international secretariats, and international civil service to alter their conceptions and policies."[33] In another view, the large conferences are too unwieldy, duplicate work of other bodies, and are an inefficient way to identify problems and solutions. Critics question whether the global conferences are just expensive media events whose declarations and programs of action have little value.[34]

The UN Conference on the Law of the Sea (UNCLOS) (1973–1982) illustrates a different type of UN-sponsored global conference, namely, one used to negotiate a major law-creating treaty for states to subsequently ratify. UNCLOS entailed a nine-year political process involving more than 160 governments in complex negotiations to update the law of the sea. This followed the independence of many new states in the 1960s and the endorsement by the UN General Assembly in 1967 of the principle that the high seas and deep seabed are part of the "common heritage of mankind." The Law of the Sea Convention, concluded in 1982, came into effect in 1994 and had been ratified by 167 states as of early 2015. Participants in the negotiations were official representatives of states; there was no formal participation by NGOs. Items were negotiated in committees of the whole, and the outcome was a legal document, not statements of goals and aspirations. A similar treaty-negotiating process began in 2009 for a successor agreement to the 1992 UN Framework Convention on Climate Change and 1997 Kyoto Protocol on climate change with the goal of adopting a comprehensive agreement to address climate change. As with UNCLOS, these negotiations, which concluded at the Paris Conference in 2015, were long and difficult, as discussed in Chapter 7.

PERSISTENT ORGANIZATIONAL PROBLEMS AND THE CHALLENGES OF REFORM

Like any long-standing organization, the UN has long been in need of reform. Indeed, one commentator called this "a constant refrain" at the UN—"never finished, never perfected."[35] Over the UN's history, there have been persistent calls for reform, including Charter revision. In the 1970s, the primary focus was on improving coordination of economic and social programs; in the 1980s, calls for financial reforms dominated the agenda; since the early 1990s, managerial reforms, improvement of the UN's ability to support peace operations, and Security Council reform have been among the major issues. All link directly to the first dilemma discussed in Chapter 1—the demands for governance and the UN's capacity to meet those demands.

To be sure, the UN has made many changes over the years, but rarely have these been enough to solve its institutional weaknesses. The UN is still hamstrung by pre–Cold War structures, redundant agencies, inadequate personnel policies, a lack of accountability, and inadequate resources. The membership of the Security Council is particularly problematic since its permanent members reflect the world of 1945, not the world of the twenty-first century.

How can UN reform occur? First, changes in the major organs of the UN require amending the UN Charter. This has happened twice thus far. In 1963, the Security Council membership was increased from eleven to fifteen, its voting majority was changed from seven to nine, and ECOSOC was enlarged from eighteen to twenty-seven members. In 1971, ECOSOC was expanded to fifty-four members. Like many constitutions, the UN Charter is designed to be difficult to amend. Under Articles 108 and 109, amendments must be approved and ratified by two-thirds of the UN member states, including all five permanent members of the Security Council. The principal reform that would require Charter amendment is the size and composition of the Security Council. It is also the most controversial.

Many changes, however, can and have been accomplished without amending the UN Charter. This includes the creation of new bodies such as the Peacebuilding Commission (2006), UN Women (2010), and the UNEP Assembly (2013) to meet new demands; addressing coordination, management, transparency, and accountability issues; and the termination of bodies that have outlived their usefulness, such as the Commission on Sustainable Development (2012). In 1997, for example, Secretary-General Kofi Annan merged three departments into one Department of Economic and Social Affairs, and all the Geneva-based human rights programs into the Office of the High Commissioner for Human Rights. He reduced the size of the Secretariat by almost 4,000, created the post of deputy secretary-general, grouped the central offices into five executive groups (their heads forming a cabinet), and promoted the idea of UN "houses" in developing countries to bring UN development agencies and programs together. Secretary-General Ban Ki-moon reorganized the departments of Peacekeeping Operations and Political Affairs, among other changes. In short, incremental changes are easier to effect than revolutionary changes.

The primary obstacles to UN reform, however, are not procedural but political. There are deep disagreements among the UN's members and between strong and weak states. All want to steer the organization in directions congruent with their objectives or try to prevent it from infringing on their interests. Everyone agrees that the UN needs reforming, but they disagree about the kind of reform needed and the purpose. Developed countries want more productivity and efficiency from the UN Secretariat, reductions in programs and activities, elimination of overlap, improved management, and better coordination. Developing countries are interested in greater economic and political equity through redistribution of resources and enhanced participation in key decisionmaking. They want more power within the system and more programs oriented toward development. They fear management reforms that would cost them their share of plum secretariat jobs and the loss of favored programs. NGOs want a UN more open and accountable to civil society, allowing them greater input and participation. In short, most reform proposals have hidden political agendas and policy goals. We focus here on four specific sets of issues: Security Council reform, financing, management, and integrating nonstate actors. Chapter 8 delves further into the politics and feasibility of future reform.

Security Council Membership and Voting

No UN reform issue is as controversial as the question of changing the Security Council's membership and voting rules. With the P-5 still limited to the five major victor nations of World War II, the Security Council has been viewed for many years as something of an anachronism. The P-5 underrepresent the majority of the world's population and the principal financial contributors to the UN (Germany and Japan contribute more financially than Russia, China, Great Britain, and France); Europe is overrepresented at the expense of Latin America, Africa, and Asia; China is the only Asian and developing country.

Should Security Council membership be expanded and diversified to accord more with representative principles? What arrangements can satisfy the criteria of representation and efficiency? Should voting be modified to alter the antidemocratic bias of the veto power? Would the legitimacy of Security Council actions be enhanced by diversifying the geographic representation and altering the voting structure? With the council's greater activity since the Cold War's end, these issues have gained increasing urgency, as the Asian, African, and Latin American states have challenged their exclusion from permanent seats and the disproportionate representation of developed countries, and as some developed countries have challenged their exclusion as well.

Virtually everyone agrees that more states should be added to the Security Council to alleviate the inequities in representation. The trick is to increase the number of members for geographic representation and enhanced legitimacy while maintaining a small enough size to ensure efficiency.[36] A second issue concerns whether the distinction between permanent and nonpermanent members should be kept and whether new permanent members would have veto power. Some proposals would give no veto power to the new permanent members, others would limit veto power to Chapter VII questions, still others would grant veto power comparable to what the P-5 currently enjoy, and some would eliminate the veto entirely on the grounds that it is undemocratic. The latter is a nonstarter for all permanent members, and Britain and France are hardly eager to give up their seats. In reality, as one observer noted, "new veto-wielding permanent members would only increase the likelihood of blockage and still further paralyze the organization."[37] Another noted that "without first tackling working methods [of the council], no real reform is proposed at all."[38] Box 2.3 summarizes the debate over Security Council reform.

Resolving these issues has proved impossible thus far. There is no agreement on what process or formula should be used to determine who would get new permanent seats. There are three likely African candidates for permanent membership (Nigeria, Egypt, and South Africa), but the African Union consensus position is to rotate Africa's representation on the council. Countries that know a rival is more likely to be a candidate tend to oppose adding any permanent seats. Thus, Italy opposes a seat for Germany, Pakistan opposes a seat for India, and Argentina challenges Brazil's candidacy. China has opposed seats for both India and Japan but champions Latin American and African participation to show its support for developing countries. China prefers to keep the size of the council small, to maintain its veto for "historic reasons," and to be the sole representative of a major continent.[39]

In advance of the World Summit in 2005, Secretary-General Kofi Annan and a number of member states pressed hard to get a resolution. Four countries that have quietly and sometimes not so quietly campaigned for permanent seats—Japan, Germany, India, and Brazil—went public on the issue in an effort to line up votes. This Group of Four (G-4) suggested a twenty-five-member council,

BOX 2.3. The Debate over Security Council Reform

Issue

Representation

Council needs greater representation of Africa, Asia, and Latin America

Permanent members should better reflect geopolitics and economics

Proposed additions: Germany and Japan

One member each from Asia and Latin America, two from Africa, but whom and how to select?

No permanent members

No new permanent members

Veto power

Require two vetoes to block a resolution

Eliminate entirely

Reduce scope for its use to Chapter VII decisions

Keep current P-5, but not give new permanent members veto power

Give all permanent members veto power

Efficiency

Size should be large enough to allow greater representation, but small enough to preserve the ability to act

Proposed size: 22–26 members

Who Decides

Reform of council membership requires Charter amendment, which takes a vote of two-thirds of the General Assembly members and must be ratified in accordance with their respective constitutional processes by two-thirds of the members of the UN, including all permanent members of the Security Council (Chapter XVIII, Article 108).

Reforms in methods of work may be made by the Security Council itself.

including six additional permanent seats, four of which would be reserved for themselves. The African Union supported a different plan, and a group of middle powers, including Italy and Pakistan, proposed still another.

In short, there is no agreement, but the G-4, along with many others, continues to push for change. As Edward Luck pointed out, the issue involves "profound and persistent divisions about which and how many countries should sit around the table; whether permanent status should be extended; what the balance among regions and groups should be; whether the veto should be retained, modified, or eliminated; how decisions should be made; and whether its working methods should be further refined. . . . The very fact that none of this has been resolved . . . testifies . . . to the divergent perspectives and interests among member states, and to the value capitals place on the work of the council."[40] More recently, Luck has proposed not tackling the permanent seat and veto issues, but rather expanding the council to twenty members, of whom fifteen would be nonpermanent members who would serve three-year terms and be eligible for reelection. Council decisions on nonprocedural matters would require the affirmative votes of twelve members, including the concurring votes of the P-5.[41]

Despite the frustration and disappointment in many quarters, the issue persists. The lesson, however, is that formal reforms such as this are difficult to achieve and likely to come only at glacial speed.

Yet despite these deep divisions and widely expressed concerns about the council's loss of legitimacy, new peacekeeping missions with enforcement powers have been authorized, such as in Mali in 2013 and the Central African Republic in 2014, and others have been expanded, as in the Democratic Republic of the Congo, as discussed in Chapter 4. The Security Council also played a role in the P-5+1 negotiations on Iran's nuclear program (with Germany as the +1), when council members unanimously adopted a resolution to monitor Iran's nuclear activities, in line with the agreement reached in July 2015, and to create a path for the incremental removal of the economic sanctions against the country. When crises break out, the international community still turns to the Security Council. States still want to become nonpermanent members, as participation is seen as a mark of status and prestige for a state and its diplomats (although Saudi Arabia took the unprecedented step of declining a seat in 2013 to protest the Council's failure to resolve the Syrian crisis and Iranian nuclear situation). States attach symbolic importance to Security Council endorsement of regional peacekeeping operations, such as the African Union's in Somalia. Thus, the council continues to be seen as the most authoritative body in the international community for dealing with threats to peace, and it retains considerable legitimacy despite its unrepresentative composition.

Financing

The UN has had long-standing financial problems because it has no independent source of money and depends almost entirely on its member states for assessed and voluntary contributions. In recent years, partnerships with major philanthropists such as Bill Gates and Ted Turner and some corporations have led to contributions to specific areas such as health, but these are relatively small relative to the UN's total budget and needs. As with Security Council reform, there has been no shortage of proposals for changing structures and methods of financing as well as for enhancing oversight and efficient use of resources. Although reform in UN financing does not require Charter amendment, it does require the support of a majority of members and, most important, support of the UN's major contributing states. If the UN's largest contributor, the United States, opposes adoption of the UN's budget unless changes are made, as happened in the 1980s, in the 1990s, and again in 2005, it can provoke a financing crisis for the organization unless a compromise is found.

Like the UN system itself, the UN's budget is complex; in fact, it comprises several budgets. The UN's regular budget covers its administrative machinery, major organs, and their auxiliary agencies and programs. It grew from less than $20 million in 1946 to more than $2.8 billion in 2015. Peacekeeping expenses constitute a separate budget (more than $8.4 billion in 2015), and each specialized agency also has a separate budget. These two types of budget expenditures are funded by member-state assessments according to a formula based on ability to pay. In addition, however, many economic and social programs, including UNICEF, UNDP, WFP, and the UN High Commissioner for Refugees (UNHCR), are funded by states' voluntary contributions, which frequently exceed the amounts of their assessments. Table 2.2 illustrates the relative size of each of these categories of budget expenditure based on assessed and voluntary contributions and changes between 1986 and 2015. The escalation of peacekeeping costs in the early post–Cold War years (1992–1995) and since 2005 is particularly notable.

The formulas for member states' assessed contributions for the regular budget and for peacekeeping operations are reevaluated every three years. The General Assembly's Committee on Contributions considers national income, per capita income, economic dislocations (such as from war), and members' ability to obtain foreign currencies. Initially, the highest rate (for the United States) was set at 40 percent of the assessed budget and the minimum rate at 0.04 percent for states with the most limited means. Over time, these rates have been adjusted: the US share was reduced to 22 percent, and the minimum dropped to 0.0001 percent. Between 1985 and 2002, for example, Japan's share increased from 11.82 percent to 18.9 percent, but the Soviet/Russian figure declined from 11.98 percent to 1.15 percent, a reflection of Japan's economic strength and Russia's decline. Between 1995 and 2005, China saw its assessment triple, from 0.72 to 2.05 percent; in 2014, it rose to 5.1 percent. Figure 2.2 shows the scale of assessments for major contributors and the majority of UN members for 2015. Three things are particularly striking: first, Russia's assessment, at 2 percent, is smaller than Brazil's and even Italy's; second, ten states contribute 68 percent of the UN's regular budget; and third, the other 183 UN members together contribute 32 percent.[42]

TABLE 2.2. UN System Expenditures (in $US millions)

Year	Assessed Contributions				Voluntary Contributions		
	Regular	Peacekeeping	Agencies	Total Assessed	Organs	Agencies	Total Voluntary
1986	725	242	1,142	2,109	3,075	951	4,026
1990	838	379	1,495	2,712	4,436	1,346	5,782
1995	1,181	3,281	1,847	6,309	5,778	1,159	6,937
2000	1,090	2,139	1,766	4,955	4,023	955	4,978
2004	1,389	3,645	2,000	7,034	9,529	2,165	11,694
2007	2,054	5,148	2,198	9,400	12,289	3,281	15,570
2013	2,606	7,258	3,390	13,254	1,440	27,296	28,736
2015	2,823*	8,466**	2,830	14,126	1,440	27,296	28,736

SOURCES: For figures prior to 2013: www.globalpolicy.org/finance/tables/finvol.htm; www.globalpolicy.org/finance/tables/tabsyst.htm; www.un.org/ga/search/view_doc.asp?symbol=A/69/305. For 2015 figures: *www.un.org/ga/search/view_doc.asp?symbol=ST/ADM/SER.B/889; figures: www.un.org/ga/search/view_doc.asp?symbol=A/C.5/69/17. For summary 2014–2015: www.un.org/en/ga/search/view_doc.asp?symbol=A/68/6/Add.1. **www.un.org/ga/search/view_doc.asp?symbol=A/70/6%20%28Introduction%29; www.un.org/press/en/2015/gaab4160.doc.htm. For projection 2016–2017: www.un.org/ga/search/view_doc.asp?symbol=A/70/6%20%28Introduction%29; www.un.org/press/en/2015/gaab4160.doc.htm.

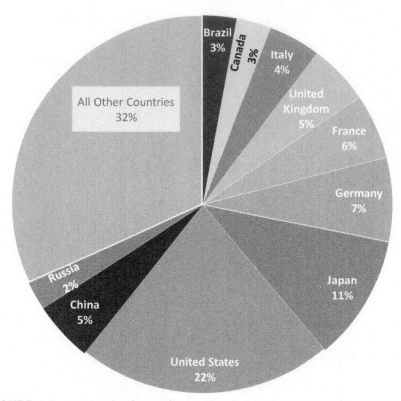

FIGURE 2.2. UN Members' Contributions Based on Scale of Assessments, 2014–2015
SOURCE: General Assembly Resolution 68/250, www.un.org/ga/search/view_doc.asp?symbol=ST/ADM /SER.B/889.

Not surprisingly, the UN has frequently experienced difficulties in getting states to pay their assessments. States fail to fulfill their legal obligations to pay for reasons ranging from technicalities in timing to poverty to politics to unhappiness with the UN in general or with specific programs and activities. The result has been periodic financial crises. The only sanction provided by the Charter in Article 19 is the denial of voting privileges in the General Assembly if a member falls more than two years in arrears, although that has never occurred. In the early 1960s, the Soviet Union, other Communist countries, and France refused to pay their peacekeeping assessments for operations in the Congo and Middle East. An ICJ advisory opinion confirmed their obligation to pay. During the 1980s and 1990s, the United States withheld part of its dues because members of Congress were unhappy with specific UN policies, the **politicization** of many agencies, and procedures that gave the United States, the largest contributor, little weight in budget decisions. In the late 1990s, the UN faced its most serious financial crisis, with member states owing more than $2.5 billion for current and past assessments. Only 100 of 185 members had paid in full. The United States, by far the biggest debtor, owed $1.6 billion, or two-thirds of the total due. The financial crisis prompted by these **arrearages** (unpaid assessments or debts) threatened the organization's ability to fulfill the various mandates given it by member states and illustrated the second dilemma mentioned in Chapter 1: the tension between demands for governance and institutional weakness arising from states' unwillingness (the United States being one example) or inability (the situation of many states in economic difficulties) to pay their assessed contributions. The crisis was partially resolved by an agreement struck in the US Congress and with the UN General Assembly to reduce the US assessments for the regular budget and peacekeeping and for payment of all arrears by 2003, subject to certain conditions.[43] Nonetheless, the financing problem persists, with the United States still owing a significant portion of the arrearages, which totaled $3.5 billion as of 2014.

Beyond states' assessed and voluntary contributions, the UN is limited in finding ways to finance its activities and programs. It has neither the authority to borrow money nor a history of private fund-raising. Although the short-term financial pressure would be significantly reduced if the United States and other member states paid their debts, the long-term problem will persist: namely, how to fund adequately the many economic, social, and security activities that member states have approved. Secretary-General Kofi Annan's millennial report, *We the Peoples*, noted, "When the scope of our responsibilities and the hopes invested in us are measured against our resources, we confront a sobering truth. The budget for our core functions . . . is about 4 percent of New York City's annual budget and nearly a billion dollars less than the annual cost of running Tokyo's fire department. Our resources are simply not commensurate with our global tasks."[44]

A variety of proposals have been made for dealing with the UN's persistent financing problems. All seek to provide a steady and predictable flow of resources—revenues that would be independent of states in particular. As Thomas Weiss notes, "Allowing the UN to manage such independent revenues would alleviate the world organization's reliance on member-states' largess and permit a more rational and less agency-driven agenda regarding priorities and resources availabilities."[45] Among the ideas are international taxes on arms sales, international air travel, petroleum trade (carbon tax), and current transactions (what is called the "Tobin tax"). Corporations such as Winterthur and Pfizer and private philanthropists such as Bill Gates and Ted Turner have provided resources for specific programs on children's health and the Global Fund to Fight AIDS, Tuberculosis, and Malaria, but such funds cannot be used to meet regular budget obligations. States are fundamentally reluctant, however, to see the UN's dependence on them for its financing reduced too much, as that would reduce their ability to control what the UN does.

Administration, Management, and Coordination

UN effectiveness has also been plagued by administrative problems. The UN Secretariat grew almost constantly until the 1990s, from 300 people in 1946 to 3,237 in 1964, 11,303 in 1974, and 14,691 in 1994. Staffing rose to 30,548 in 2006 (this figure included those on contracts of less than one year, who made up roughly one-sixth of the total). It has leveled off at around 41,400 in 2014 (or roughly 35,000 by an older method). This growth stemmed from both the expansion of the UN's membership and the proliferation of programs and activities, ranging from peacekeeping missions to technical assistance. As the UN bureaucracy expanded, charges of political bias and administrative inefficiency surfaced. The United States was particularly vocal in this regard. Studies conducted both by the UN itself and by some member states came to similar conclusions about the lack of coordination, the expansion of programs with little consideration of financial commitments, and weak to nonexistent program evaluation. And periodically charges of political bias, mismanagement, and inefficiency surfaced.

The first five secretaries-general paid little attention to internal management of the Secretariat and also had little incentive for change. Thus, it took the UN more than fifty years to adopt management systems such as program reviews, internal audits, performance evaluations for staff members, and effective recruitment and promotion practices. Even then, developed countries were more concerned about effective management, financial control, and clear objectives than were many developing countries.

When Kofi Annan became secretary-general in 1997, he was pressured by the United States in particular to reduce the size of the Secretariat by 25 percent and implement other reforms, as described earlier. In his "quiet revolution," departments were merged, administrative costs cut, and a code of staff conduct developed. In 2001 and 2002, more reforms were undertaken. In the area of peacekeeping, the Brahimi Report called for strengthening the secretariat's ability to support operations, and the General Assembly approved a 50 percent increase in staff for the Department of Peacekeeping Operations and more flexibility in administration.[46] A new system went into effect in 2001 for recruiting, placing, and promoting staff that gave more emphasis to merit, competence, and accountability for results than to tenure and precedent. These changes did not require Charter amendments.

The latter part of Kofi Annan's tenure as secretary-general was marred by the highly publicized Oil-for-Food Programme scandal, described earlier. In response to that scandal, the US government conducted six investigations of the UN and that program. Former US Federal Reserve chairman Paul Volcker chaired the UN investigation. As Annan admitted, "The inquiry committee has ripped away the curtain, and shone a harsh light into the most unsightly corners of our organization. . . . Who among us can now claim that U.N. management is not a problem, or is not in need of reform?"[47] Following the investigations, the Secretariat introduced measures to improve the performance of senior management, including monitoring of individual performance and a new Office of Internal Oversight Services with operational independence. Policies dealing with fraud, corruption, whistle-blower protection, financial disclosure, conflict of interest, and procurement contracts were adopted to prevent the type of personnel abuses found in the oil-for-food scandal.

Secretary-General Ban Ki-moon's follow-through with these reforms has met with criticism. As explained in Chapter 3, in 2010 the administrator of the Office of Internal Oversight Services, responsible for investigating fraud, abuse, and waste within the organization, publicly questioned that body's ability to act independently. There has been a growing number of problems within UN peacekeeping operations, including sexual misconduct, as discussed in Chapter 4. The number of women in leadership positions has also decreased under Ban. Clearly, Secretariat reform must be an ongoing process if the UN's bureaucracy is to grow in capacity, strengthen its management and working procedures, address internal divisions, and maintain its effectiveness and legitimacy.

The problem of multiple agencies engaged in similar tasks has plagued the UN system from the beginning. The founders designed the organization to be decentralized because this would increase the capacity of different groups to participate while minimizing the potential for politicization, but the lack of coordination in the area of economic and social development and in humanitarian crises has been particularly criticized. Numerous reports and recommendations have sought to improve ECOSOC's effectiveness as the main coordinating agency for economic and social programs, but that requires dialogues with the World Bank and IMF; more effective relationships with the specialized agencies, funds, and programs; and the greater involvement of NGOs in policymaking processes.

The problems of coordination and management are also evident in humanitarian crises produced by wars and natural disasters—whether they be crises that unfold over time, such as civil war, genocide, and state collapse in South Sudan; natural disasters, such as the 2010 Haitian earthquake and 2014 Philippine typhoon; or pandemics, such as Ebola in West Africa in 2014–2015. Historically, there has been a functional division of responsibilities among UN agencies: UNHCR manages refugee camps, UNICEF handles water and sanitation, WFP is responsible for food supplies and logistics, and WHO handles the health sector. In some situations, peacekeeping forces have safeguarded relief workers and supplies. Yet, as one observer described, "the United Nations did not respond as a system but rather as a series of separate and largely autonomous agencies. Each had its own institutional dynamics, formulated its own priorities, and moved according to a timetable of its own devising."[48]

The problem of coordination in emergencies, however, is compounded by the presence of hundreds of NGOs that vary in size and resources, have different cultures and philosophies, and resist efforts to harmonize activities. The UN Office for the Coordination of Humanitarian Affairs (OCHA) created in 1998 is headed by an undersecretary-general who is responsible for coordinating all emergency relief within and outside the UN system. Still, UN specialized agencies, private relief contractors, and NGOs frequently resist giving up their independence and compete for a share of the action. Just creating a UN office for coordination does not ensure meaningful coordination. Any proposal for change advantages some agencies, states, and NGOs while disadvantaging others.

Integrating Nonstate Actors

The increasing involvement of NGOs, other civil society organizations (CSOs), and private businesses with UN programs and activities demonstrates another area of needed reform: how to better integrate nonstate actors into the UN system. Prior to the Millennium Summit of 2000, the People's Millennium Forum brought together representatives of more than a thousand NGOs based in more than a hundred countries. Its participants resolved to create a global civil society forum to deal with UN institutions, member states, and other institutions.[49] As of 2014, more than 22,000 NGOs were registered with the UN and 4,189 organizations held consultative status. NGOs form key partnerships with the UN in areas of humanitarian aid, disaster relief, human rights and environmental monitoring, and development assistance. Other nonstate actors such as private foundations and corporations now play a substantial role in supplementing the limited financial resources of the UN system. The roles played by scientists, aid workers, medical personnel, and local farmers are just some of the examples of civil society engagement with the UN. NGOs are sometimes viewed as vehicles for democratizing the political processes at the UN, although many are not always inclusive or democratic themselves and often lack accountability. Coordinating and integrating these partnerships between the UN and nonstate actors is a continuing challenge. One scholar has described the task as "herding cats."[50] Thus, NGO access to various parts and activities of the UN system is an ongoing issue, as is the question of how well partnerships such as the UN Global Compact or funding from private corporations and foundations serve the UN's mission.

Still, the UN was created to promote and protect the interests of states as well as to preserve peace and security in the world and to promote economic and social development and human rights. It is far easier to understand the UN by looking at what it has and has not been able to do in relationship to these different issue areas than simply by knowing how it is structured and operates. In subsequent chapters, we shall do just that. First, however, it is important to understand the roles of states and coalitions of states, secretaries-general, civil society, NGOs, and other nonstate actors within the UN. We explore these various actors in the UN system further in Chapter 3.

NOTES

1. On the League, see F. S. Northledge, *The League of Nations: Its Life and Times, 1920–1946* (New York: Holmes and Meier, 1986); and F. P. Walters, *A History of the League of Nations* (New York: Oxford University Press, 1952).

2. Norman J. Padelford (executive officer for Commission IV of the UN Conference Secretariat), letter to family and friends, June 26, 1945.

3. Paul Taylor and A. J. R. Groom, eds., *The United Nations at the Millennium: The Principal Organs* (New York: Continuum, 2000). Works on the specific organs include Sydney D. Bailey, *The Procedure of the UN Security Council,* 3rd ed. (New York: Oxford University Press, 1999); David M. Malone, ed., *The UN Security Council: From the Cold War to the 21st Century* (Boulder, CO: Lynne Rienner, 2004); M. J. Peterson, *The UN General Assembly* (London: Routledge, 2006); and Simon Chesterman, *Secretary or General? The UN Secretary-General in World Politics* (Cambridge: Cambridge University Press, 2007).

4. The difference is exemplified in the two UN Web sites: one for the central organs, www.un.org, and one for the system as a whole, www.unsystem.org.

5. Harold K. Jacobson, *Networks of Interdependence: International Organizations and the Global Political System,* 2nd ed. (New York: Random House, 1984), 39.

6. M. J. Peterson, "General Assembly," in *The Oxford Handbook on the United Nations,* ed. Thomas G. Weiss and Sam Daws (Oxford: Oxford University Press, 2007), 98.

7. Erik Voeten, "Data and Analyses of Voting in the UN General Assembly," SSRN, July 17, 2012, http://ssrn.com/abstract=2111149.

8. Courtney B. Smith, *Politics and Process at the United Nations: The Global Dance* (Boulder, CO: Lynne Rienner, 2006), 218.

9. On the subject of consensus decisions and voting, see Simon Hug, "What's in a Vote?" paper prepared for presentation at the annual meeting of the American Political Science Association, New Orleans, August 30–September 2, 2012, http://papers.ssrn.com/sol3/papers.cfm?abstract_id=2106672.

10. Ian Johnstone, "The Security Council as Legislature," in *The UN Security Council and the Politics of International Authority,* ed. Bruce Cronin and Ian Hurd (New York: Routledge, 2008), 88–89.

11. John Langmore and Jeremy Farrall, "Can Elected Members Make a Difference in the UN Security Council? Australia's Experience in 2013-2014," *Global Governance* 22, no. 1 (Jan.–Mar. 2016): 59–78.

12. Sebastian von Einsiedel, David M. Malone, and Bruno Stagno Ugarte, "Conclusion," in *The UN Security Council in the 21st Century,* ed. Sebastian von Einsiedel, David M. Malone, and Bruno Stagno Ugarte (Boulder, CO: Lynne Rienner, 2016), 836.

13. Edward C. Luck, "The Security Council at Seventy," in *The UN Security Council in the 21st Century*, ed. Sebastian von Einsiedel, David M. Malone, and Bruno Stagno Ugarte (Boulder, CO: Lynne Rienner, 2016), 202.

14. Peter Wallensteen and Patrik Johansson, "The UN Security Council: Decisions and Actions," in *The UN Security Council in the 21st Century*, ed. Sebastian von Einsiedel, David M. Malone, and Bruno Stagno Ugarte (Boulder, CO: Lynne Rienner, 2016), 48.

15. David M. Malone, *The International Struggle over Iraq: Politics in the UN Security Council, 1980–2005* (New York: Oxford University Press, 2006), 173.

16. Ibid., 31.

17. On the debate on Security Council authority and legitimacy, see Ian Hurd, *After Anarchy: Legitimacy and Power in the United Nations Security Council* (Princeton: Princeton University Press, 2007) and "Theories and Tests of International Authority," in *The UN Security Council and the Politics of International Authority*, ed. Bruce Cronin and Ian Hurd (New York: Routledge, 2008), 23–39.

18. Michael J. Glennon, "Why the Security Council Failed," *Foreign Affairs* 82, no. 2 (2003): 16–35.

19. Bruce Cronin and Ian Hurd, "Conclusion: Assessing the Council's Authority," in *The UN Security Council and the Politics of International Authority*, ed. Bruce Cronin and Ian Hurd (New York: Routledge, 2008), 201.

20. Jeremy Greenstock, "The Security Council in a Fragmenting World," in *The UN Security Council in the 21st Century*, ed. Sebastian von Einsiedel, David M. Malone, and Bruno Stagno Ugarte (Boulder, CO: Lynne Rienner, 2016), 824.

21. Quoted in Somini Sengupta, "'Sclerotic' U.N. Security Council is Under Fire for Failing to Maintain Peace," *New York Times*, October 24, 2015.

22. Paul Taylor, "Managing the Economic and Social Activities of the United Nations System: Developing the Role of ECOSOC," in *United Nations at the Millennium*, ed. Paul Taylor and A. J. R. Groom (New York: Continuum, 2000), 108.

23. Brian Hall, "Blue Helmets," *New York Times Magazine*, January 2, 1994, 22.

24. Simon Chesterman, "The Secretary-General We Deserve?" *Global Governance* 21, no. 4 (2015): 507, 508.

25. Michael Barnett and Martha Finnemore, *Rules for the World: International Organizations in Global Politics* (Ithaca, NY: Cornell University Press, 2004).

26. Thomas G. Weiss, "The John W. Holmes Lecture: Reinvigorating the International Civil Service," *Global Governance* 16, no. 1 (2010): 41.

27. See UN Women, "Representation of Women in the United Nations System with Appointments of One Year or More," February 2015, www.unwomen.org/~/media/head quarters/attachments/sections/how%20we%20work/unsystemcoordination/data /secretariat/2013-projections/unsecretariat.pdf.

28. Kirsten Haack, "Breaking Barriers? Women's Representation and Leadership at the United Nations," *Global Governance* 20, no. 1 (2014): 38.

29. B. G. Ramcharan, "The International Court of Justice," in *United Nations at the Millennium*, ed. Paul Taylor and A. J. R. Groom (New York: Continuum, 2000), 177.

30. Michael Schechter, *United Nations Global Conferences* (New York: Routledge, 2005), 9.

31. Michael Schechter, "Making Meaningful UN-Sponsored World Conferences of the 1990s: NGOs to the Rescue?" in *United Nations–Sponsored World Conferences: Focus on*

Impact and Follow-Up, ed. Michael G. Schechter (Tokyo: United Nations University Press, 2001), 189.

32. United Nations, *World Summit Outcome,* A/60/L.1, sec. 81 (2005), www.un-ngls.org /un-summit-final-doc.pdf.

33. Louis Emmerij, Richard Jolly, and Thomas G. Weiss, *Ahead of the Curve: UN Ideas and Global Challenges* (Bloomington: Indiana University Press, 2001), 89.

34. Jacques Fomerand, "UN Conferences: Media Events or Genuine Diplomacy?" *Global Governance* 2, no. 3 (1996): 361–375.

35. Edward Luck, "Principal Organs," in *Oxford Handbook on the United Nations,* ed. Thomas G. Weiss and Sam Daws (Oxford: Oxford University Press, 2007), 653.

36. Peter Wallensteen, "Representing the World: A Security Council for the Twenty-First Century," *Security Dialogue* 25, no. 1 (1994): 67.

37. James A. Paul, "Security Council Reform: Arguments About the Future of the United Nations System" (1995), www.globalpolicy.org/security/pubs/secref.htm.

38. Edward C. Luck, "The UN Security Council," in *Irrelevant or Indispensable? The United Nations in the 21st Century,* ed. Paul Heinbecker and Patricia Goff (Waterloo, Canada: Wilfred Laurier Press, 2005), 148.

39. J. Mohan Malik, "Security Council Reform: China Signals Its Veto," *World Policy Journal* 22, no. 1 (Spring 2005): 19–29.

40. Edward C. Luck, "How Not to Reform the United Nations," *Global Governance* 11, no. 4 (2005): 410.

41. Luck, "The Security Council at Seventy," 206–207.

42. See General Assembly Resolution 68/250, www.un.org/ga/search/view_doc.asp ?symbol=ST/ADM/SER.B/889. Older data can be found on the Global Policy Web site, www.globalpolicy.org.

43. See Margaret P. Karns and Karen A. Mingst, "The United States as 'Deadbeat'? U.S. Policy and the UN Financial Crisis," in *Multilateralism and U.S. Foreign Policy: Ambivalent Engagement,* ed. Stewart Patrick and Shepard Forman (Boulder, CO: Lynne Rienner, 2002), 267–294.

44. Kofi Annan, *We the Peoples: The Role of the United Nations in the 21st Century* (2000), www.un.org/millennium/sg/report/full.htm.

45. Thomas G. Weiss, *What's Wrong with the United Nations and How to Fix It,* 2nd ed. (Cambridge: Polity, 2012), 196.

46. United Nations, *Report of the Panel on United Nations Peace Operations* (Brahimi Report), A/55/305-S/2000/809 (August 21, 2000).

47. Malone, *International Struggle over Iraq,* 133.

48. Larry Minear, "Humanitarian Action in the Former Yugoslavia: The UN's Role, 1991–1993," Occasional Paper no. 18 (Providence, RI: Thomas J. Watson Institute for International Studies, 1994), 28.

49. Chadwick F. Alger, "Widening Participation," in *The Oxford Handbook on the United Nations,* ed. Thomas G. Weiss and Sam Daws (Oxford: Oxford University Press, 2007), 701–715.

50. Michael Edwards, "Herding Cats?" *New Economy* 9, no. 2 (2002): 71–76.

3

〜

Actors in the
United Nations System

If the UN is the world's stage, then who are its key actors? The organization was formed by states, it depends on states for its sustenance, and it is directed by states on the supposition that it may be useful to them. Still, the UN has always drawn the interest of a variety of nonstate actors seeking to influence what happens there. It has always depended on outside experts to supplement the work of the Secretariat, members of the Secretariat are themselves important actors, and the UN increasingly works in partnerships with states and nonstate actors to accomplish its work.

The Charter accords special status to five states, giving them permanent membership on the Security Council and veto power. As discussed in Chapter 2, the makeup of the P-5 has been a subject of discussion and reform efforts for some time. Shifts in the relative influence and assertiveness of the P-5 members have been reflected in the activities of the Security Council as well as elsewhere within the UN system. Middle powers, emerging powers, and small states all have historically played important roles in the UN, particularly when acting through blocs and coalitions, as we examine below.

If the UN is but a venue for states, or just another diplomatic instrument for states to utilize, that is compatible with a realist view. But if it has become an actor in its own right, and if nonstate actors play influential roles within the UN system, the liberal perspective is more appropriate. In fact, the Secretariat, particularly the secretary-general and other senior officials, have acquired authority, influence, and legitimacy that enable them to act at times without the explicit direction of the governing bodies. Consistent with constructivist views, the UN's professional staff may influence the actions of member states and others because of their expertise and role as important sources of ideas. Feminist perspectives focus on the importance of bringing women into the policy process and leadership positions at the UN, as discussed in Chapter 1. This discussion of actors in the UN system must consider not only various member states but also coalitions and blocs, the secretary-general, the Secretariat, outside experts, and partnerships.

Increasingly, "the peoples" in whose name the UN Charter was drafted have exerted their voices through NGOs and other civil society groups. External experts, scholars, consultants, committed citizens, and certain NGOs have long worked with UN bodies and the Secretariat, but their roles as actors in the UN system have grown in recent years, as have partnerships with corporations, foundations, and other nonstate actors. This has led to the concept of the **third UN** to complement Inis Claude's distinction between the first UN, consisting of the arenas where member states debate issues and make recommendations and decisions, and the second UN, consisting of the UN and specialized agency secretariats. The third UN's roles include advocacy, research, policy analysis, the promotion of ideas, and mobilizing public support for UN activities.[1]

In examining the roles of various actors in the UN, we employ this concept of three UNs, particularly for analyzing the Secretariat and NGOs as well as other nonstate actors—the second and third UNs.

THE ROLE OF STATES

From a realist perspective, the UN is primarily an instrument of its dominant member states, one among many diplomatic tools used to serve their national interests. States may use the UN to gain a collective stamp of approval on specific actions, points of view, principles, and norms; they may seek to create new rules, enforce existing ones, and settle disputes. The UN and its agencies serve useful functions for states, including gathering and analyzing information, thereby improving the quality of information available to governments; providing forums for exchanging views and airing concerns; and offering opportunities to gather information about other governments' attitudes and policies, to the benefit of their own decisionmaking. This continuing interaction also enhances the value for states of maintaining a good reputation. The UN's decisionmaking processes encourage states to form coalitions and to link specific issues so as to enhance their bargaining power on those issues. Over time, states have used the UN system to create a variety of valuable programs and activities for addressing global problems, ranging from development assistance, disease eradication, and aid to refugees to peacekeeping, election monitoring, human rights promotion, and curbing ozone depletion.

The UN, however, is more than just an instrument of its member states. It exercises influence and imposes constraints on its members' policies and the processes by which those policies are formed. Year in and year out, the meetings of the General Assembly and other bodies set international, and hence national, agendas and force governments to take positions on issues such as terrorism, environmental degradation, states' human rights records, and the status of women. These meetings and ongoing data gathering on each state's economy, trade, balance of payments, population, and compliance with treaties also subject states' behavior to international surveillance. UN-approved rules, norms, and principles, whether on human rights, the law of the sea, ozone depletion, or the financing of terrorism, force states to realign their policies if they wish to maintain a reputation for law-abiding behavior and to enjoy the benefits of reciprocity from other states. Many of the ideas that have come out of the UN system over more than seventy years have led governments to change their own thinking about policy approaches to various issues. Particularly in democratic, pluralist societies, norms and rules created by the UN may be used by domestic interest groups to press for changes in national policies.[2] This reflects the liberal institutionalist view that the UN operates through the interaction between state members, coalitions, and groups with a two-way flow of influence between the organization and its member states. And like other IGOs, the UN thereby reduces cheating, increases transparency, and maximizes gains for all parties. In short, the UN may influence state preferences.

Intergovernmental organizations such as the UN depend on their member states. To be effective and hence relevant, the UN must be able in some ways and to some extent to influence even the largest, most powerful states in the system. It must be valued by them as a means of inducing other states to change their behavior, to redefine their interests, and to accept certain constraints. From the very inception of the UN in the 1940s, no state has been more critical than the United States. Yet the United States has a long history of conveying "mixed messages" concerning its support for international organizations, particularly the UN.[3] Over time, notes one scholar, "relations between the United States and the UN have oscillated between periods of friendship and friction."[4]

The Key Role of the United States

As the dominant power after World War II, the United States played an important role in shaping the international system's structure, including the establishment of many IGOs, from the UN to the Bretton Woods institutions, the International Atomic Energy Agency, and the United Nations Environment Programme. The provisions of the UN Charter, for example, were consistent with US interests, and until the 1960s the United States could often count on the support of a majority on most major issues. This enabled the United States to use the UN and its specialized agencies as instruments of its national policies and to create institutions and rules compatible with US interests.

Over time, the United States has used the UN for collective legitimation of its own actions, examples being Korea in 1950, the Cuban missile crisis in 1963, the Iran hostage crisis in 1979, the Gulf War in 1991, and the terrorist attacks on the World Trade Center and the Pentagon on September 11, 2001.

From the late 1960s to mid-1980s, however, the United States was much more ambivalent about international institutions in general and about parts of the UN system in particular. It withdrew from the ILO in 1978 (rejoining it more than two years later) and from UNESCO in 1984 (rejoining it in 2003), because of politicization and bureaucratic inefficiency. Developing countries' demands in the 1970s for a New International Economic Order (NIEO), their repeated res-olutions linking Zionism with racism, and their criticisms of American policies led Washington to oppose many UN-sponsored development programs and to view the UN as a hostile place. US alienation from the UN was borne out in the steep drop in US voting with majorities in the General Assembly. In the Security Council, the United States used its veto thirty-four times between 1976 and 1985 (see Table 2.1). In 1985, when Congress imposed conditions on contributions and withheld full payment as a strategy to force change, congressional support for paying UN dues started to decline.[5]

US antipathy to the UN moderated somewhat in the late 1980s. Changes in Soviet policy under Mikhail Gorbachev created opportunities for UN efforts to settle a number of regional conflicts. The UN's success in handling new peace-keeping challenges and the war against Iraq in 1991 generated widespread opti-mism about an expanding UN role in the post–Cold War era.

In 1993, the Clinton administration articulated a policy of assertive multi-lateralism designed to share responsibilities for global peace with other coun-tries by working through an invigorated UN, but the stance was short-lived. By the mid-1990s, problems with UN missions in Somalia, Rwanda, and Bosnia overshadowed successes elsewhere. The US experience in Somalia, in particu-lar, had a devastating effect on its relationship with the UN. The United States became unwilling to commit its own military personnel in UN peacekeeping operations and withdrew its support for new types of peacekeeping in general. It lost confidence in then secretary-general Boutros Boutros-Ghali and undertook a unilateral campaign to deny him a second term in 1996. Other unilateralist actions followed, including opposition to the convention banning antipersonnel land mines (1997), the Kyoto Protocol (1997), the International Criminal Court (1998), and the rejection of the Comprehensive Test Ban Treaty (1999). In addi-tion, Congress contributed to the UN's financial crisis by continuing to withhold US dues for the regular budget and for peacekeeping, as discussed in Chapter 2.

Given President George W. Bush's past statements and the records of his close associates, no one expected him to be a strong supporter of multilateralism or of the UN. His unprecedented decision in 2001 to renounce US signature of the Rome Statute creating the International Criminal Court (ICC) and active campaign against the court provoked widespread condemnation. Still, immediately following the terror attacks of September 11, 2001, the United States turned to the UN and received Security Council support for action in Afghanistan. Various measures were passed to restrict the ability of Al Qaeda to raise money and to support counterterrorism initiatives (discussed in Chapter 4). A year later, the United States undertook protracted negotiations through the UN to address the problem of Iraq and its presumed weapons of mass destruction. Yet when the United States chose to go to war against Iraq in 2003 without authorization from the Security Council, the international community viewed it as evidence that the United States did not consider itself bound by the obligations of the UN Charter. Nevertheless, the United States did return to the Security Council to secure UN help with the challenges of postwar Iraq and Afghanistan.

The United States under the administration of President Barack Obama projected a more positive yet still mixed message regarding US support for the UN. The appointment of Susan Rice as UN ambassador and the restoration of her position to cabinet status suggested a willingness to take the UN seriously. In 2009, the United States signed the Convention on the Rights of Persons with Disabilities—the first action on an international human rights treaty since 2002—although the US Senate failed to ratify the convention in 2013. In the Security Council, the United States supported stronger sanctions on Iran and North Korea for their nuclear programs as well as authorizing the use of armed force to protect civilians in both Libya and Côte d'Ivoire. It led the way on a Chapter VII resolution on the Ebola outbreak in 2014. Likewise, the negotiations by the P-5+1 with Iran over curbing its nuclear program were effectively led by the United States, as were the efforts to get the Security Council to tighten sanctions on Iran. The Obama administration also played a more active role in UN-sponsored efforts to address climate change, particularly in demonstrating leadership for the 2015 Paris agreement, as discussed in Chapter 7. In short, US interests can be and are still advanced through the UN, whether for national security, environmental protection, or poverty alleviation.

Several factors have shaped US ambivalence. More than in many other states, US policy is shaped by domestic politics, including presidential leadership (or lack thereof), relations between the executive and legislative branches of government, lobbying by domestic groups, public opinion, and the deep partisan divide between Democrats and Republicans.[6] The role of Congress is critical for the US relationship with the UN, as Congress controls the budget, an important source of US power in the UN. Although the Obama administration paid all US arrears in 2010, the congressional elections that year returned a Republican majority to the House of Representatives and renewed calls for cutting US contributions to the UN. In December 2015, Congress passed a spending bill that fully funded US assessed dues and provided $2.62 billion in support for UN peacekeeping operations. At the same time, the bill cut funds for renovations of the UN head-quarters in New York and prohibited all financial support for the Human Rights Council, the United Nations Population Fund, and the Arms Trade Treaty. The Obama administration also led the way to a deal in 2010 to increase the votes of China and other emerging powers in the IMF to give them a greater say, but only in that late 2015 spending bill did Congress finally approve the change.

What is widely seen as dysfunction in the US government, therefore, is af-fecting the ability of the United States to act within the institutions of the UN system. Divisions are also increasingly evident within the American public. Public opinion polls have long shown that the majority of Americans want the United States to cooperate fully with the UN and want to see the UN strength-ened to investigate human rights violations, arrest genocidal leaders, organize a permanent peacekeeping force, and address other global issues. However, polls in 2015 showed a deep partisan divide, with 60 percent of Democrats rating the UN as doing a good job, in contrast to 35 percent of Republicans.[7] Opposition to the UN and to US participation in the body has long been a core point for some American conservatives. A 2013 poll found that for the first time since 1964, more than 50 percent of respondents believed that "the US should mind its own business internationally and let other countries get along the best they can on their own"—a result that raised serious questions about future directions of American foreign policy.[8] US policy is also shaped by more general attitudes of American political culture, notably a belief in US **exceptionalism** that was rein-forced in the early years of the twenty-first century by its sole superpower status.

Despite mixed messages from the United States, historically "American pref-erences on many issues, embodied in US policies and backed by US power, have explained a great many . . . public policies emanating from the United Nations, its associated specialized agencies, and the managing institutions of the global economy."[9] Yet the UN has "always been and continues to be a West-ern organization," Donald Puchala argues, because "the 'West' . . . never was, nor is it now, solely the United States."[10] Whether the UN remains a Western organization remains to be seen, as China and other emerging powers exercise increasing influence. As one journalist noted, "The United States still has formi-dable strengths. . . . Its military has a global presence and a technological edge that no other country can yet match. But America will never again experience the global dominance it enjoyed in the 17 years between the Soviet Union's collapse in 1991 and the financial crisis of 2008. Those days are over."[11] Today, "there is much less deference to US preferences and privileges and much less sense that there are no alternatives," according to Bruce Jentleson.[12] There is also a vigorous debate about the degree to which American power and influence are declining as China and other emerging powers' influence and presence increases within and without the UN system, and governmental dysfunction and perceived American withdrawal from a leadership role in the world fuel concerns within and without the United States. Still, three long-time observers of the Security Council note, "even today, with US initiatives increasingly challenged by others, Washington's instincts and impulses continue to drive the Council more than any other single factor."[13]

Other Major Powers

Among the major powers in the UN system are the other four permanent members of the Security Council—anachronistic as the perpetuation of their status and the exclusion of emerging powers may be. The Soviet Union (now Russia), France, Great Britain, and China have had significant roles in shaping the organization's development and, like the United States, have not always been ready to commit themselves to using the UN as the major arena for their foreign policy. Japan and Germany have also been major players in the UN since the 1970s by providing funding.

The Soviet Union/Russia. The Soviet Union played a key (though largely negative) role in the UN during the Cold War period, clashing frequently with the United States and its allies. Between 1945 and 1975, the Soviet Union used its veto 113 times; more than half of the vetoes were on membership applications in the early 1950s, and the impasse over the membership of the divided states of Korea, Vietnam, and Germany continued until the 1970s. In the 1960s and 1970s, the Soviet Union often sided with the newly independent states in the General Assembly, supporting self-determination for colonial peoples and the New International Economic Order agenda. This strategy permitted it to vote with the majority in the General Assembly a high percentage of the time. For ideological reasons, the Soviet Union and other bloc members were not part of the Bretton Woods institutions, but they did participate in many other specialized agencies.

Significant changes in the actions and attitudes of the Soviet Union became evident in 1987, even before the Cold War's end. After years of opposition to UN peacekeeping, the Soviet Union agreed to having UN peacekeepers monitor and legitimize its troop withdrawal from Afghanistan and end the Iran-Iraq War. In the 1991 Gulf War, the Soviet Union abandoned its former ally Iraq and supported US-UN actions, albeit with reservations about the use of force. The Soviets wished not only to prevent bloodshed but also to assert what little influence they had left and to limit damage to their future interests in the region.[14] The Soviet Union's need for US economic and emergency aid to deal with its own internal problems and its desire for support in dealing with its crumbling empire overrode other considerations.

The speed and thoroughness of the Soviet Union's dismemberment in 1991 brought a number of changes. There was a period during the early 1990s when US-Russian cooperation reached a peak, with the countries voting together 89 percent of the time in the General Assembly. That dropped dramatically by the end of the decade, when agreement between the two fell to 40 percent and Russia opposed US and NATO intervention in Kosovo, for example, and endeavored to put together enough votes in the Security Council to condemn the action. Russia was then a much-diminished power with meager economic means and was moving in a different direction than the United States and its allies.[15]

Today, Russia is again a central player, and President Putin has taken a number of steps to ensure that it is recognized as such. Since 2005, Russia has been active in efforts to deal with Iran's nuclear program, including the P-5+1 negotiations that concluded in 2015. In 2013, Russia put forward the plan to dismantle Syria's chemical weapons capability that forestalled U.S. military intervention in Syria. However, Russia also cast its veto (with China) four times between 2011 and 2015 to block other action in the Syrian crisis, thus protecting its close ties with the Assad government and frustrating all diplomatic efforts. Russia did not veto the resolution that led to US and NATO military intervention in Libya in 2011, but quickly came to regret that when humanitarian intervention turned into regime change. That "shadow of Libya" has had a major influence on Russia's behavior since 2011.

Since 2014, Russia has demonstrated renewed assertiveness, particularly with its takeover of Crimea and actions in eastern Ukraine. This reflects President Putin's perception that Russian interests diverge from those of the West, which he sees as deliberately seeking to obstruct Russia's status as a great power. After almost thirty meetings on the Ukraine situation, Russia vetoed a Security Council draft resolution that proclaimed the referendum on Crimean secession from Ukraine illegal. In response, the General Assembly by a vote of 100 to 11 with 58 abstentions affirmed its commitment to Ukrainian sovereignty, political independence, unity, and territorial integrity and called on states, international organizations, and specialized agencies not to recognize the change in Crimea's status (GA Resolution 68/262). Still, in a move that signaled the UN's continued relevance for Russia, in February 2015 Russia proposed a Security Council resolution creating a cease-fire in eastern Ukraine that passed unanimously. Nonetheless, Russia has continued its pattern of using its veto more extensively than at any time since the early Cold War. Russia vetoed two Security Council resolutions in July 2015, one proposing the creation of an international tribunal on the downing of flight MH17 (the Malaysian airliner that crashed in eastern Ukraine in 2014) and one that would have marked the twentieth anniversary of the Srebrenica massacre in Bosnia and recognized it as an act of genocide. Furthermore, by sending Russian troops, planes, and advanced weaponry to Syria in late 2015, Russia ensured that it would be a central player in any resolution of the Syrian crisis.

In short, Russia is clearly a significant actor within the UN, particularly on peace and security issues, but not always in ways that many other states consider constructive. Indicative of its reduced economic status and limited influence over many other areas of UN activities, however, is its relatively low assessment, 2.0 percent for 2013–2015—the lowest of all major powers. By comparison, its assessment in 1991 was 8.7 percent.

France and Great Britain. France and Great Britain continue to be major actors in the UN and world politics despite their diminished status. As members of the P-5, they hold veto power; both continue to be significant donors, their 2013–2015 assessments being between 5 and 6 percent; and both have played active roles in post–Cold War UN peacekeeping and enforcement operations in the 1991 Gulf War, Bosnia, Afghanistan, and Libya. Since 1990, each has also assumed responsibility for subcontracted enforcement operations—Great Britain in Sierra Leone and France in Rwanda, Côte d'Ivoire, Democratic Republic of Congo, Mali, and the Central African Republic. As prominent players in the World Bank and IMF, both contribute senior personnel and financial resources and vote consistently with other large developed countries. Both have supported such initiatives as the International Criminal Court, the Kyoto Protocol, the land mines treaty, and the Comprehensive Test Ban Treaty, all of which were rejected by the United States. Continuing ties with their former colonies helps both Britain and France retain substantial influence and interests in Africa and in the developing world more generally. Yet both are part of the North, and that limits the extent of their influence.

Despite these commonalities, Great Britain and France have nevertheless carved different niches in UN politics. During the 1970s and 1980s, France tried to be a mediator between the South's NIEO agenda and the North's opposition to change. More than other developed countries, it was ready to accept state intervention in regulating commodity markets and financial compensation to developing countries for market failure. It has always been a strong supporter of UNESCO, which is based in Paris. On other issues, France's positions have paralleled those of other developed countries—for example, it voted with the United States and Great Britain in opposition to mandatory economic sanctions against South Africa in the 1970s and 1980s. France has long shown greater interest than Great Britain in developing and enforcing a common European position—that is, a common position on major issues among members of the European Union. France and Great Britain parted ways over US military action in Iraq in 2003, with France in opposition and Great Britain supporting the United States in the UN Security Council.

Great Britain has always had a prominent position in the UN, not only as a permanent member of the Security Council but also as a member of other restricted-member committees, notably the Geneva Group for review of budgets and programs. By tradition, the director of the UN Department of Political Affairs has always come from Britain. The country is always elected to membership in ECOSOC, and a British jurist has always held a seat on the ICJ. This privileged position also carries over to the specialized agencies: Britain has occupied leadership positions in the ILO and the WHO.[16]

Britain has had this leadership role for several reasons. British delegates and Secretariat members are frequently called on to exercise their skill in drafting, and continued ties to Africa and Asia through the Commonwealth give the British established contacts with many of the UN's members. Britain has been a leader, along with the United States, in promoting UN financial reform and accountability. And, through special voluntary contributions, it pays a larger share of UN expenses than its assessment. Both France and Britain want to keep their privileged positions and have opposed efforts to restructure the Security Council.

China. The fifth permanent member of the Security Council, China, historically was far less active or interested in international institutions generally and the UN in particular. The Republic of China originally held China's seat in the UN, which it continued to occupy long after the Chinese revolution brought the People's Republic of China to power in 1949 and sent the ROC government to Taiwan. (Neither government would accept the other's legitimacy.) In 1971, Third World votes granted the PRC the Chinese seat over US-led opposition, and Taiwan walked out of the body. Up to that time, the PRC had been a member of only one IGO. China is the only developing and non-Western country among the P-5, and its influence in the world and in the UN has been growing steadily in recent years.

During its first decade of UN membership, however, the PRC kept a low profile. Although it supported the G-77 and nonaligned group positions on decolonization and economic development issues and joined a number of UN specialized agencies, it remained uninvolved in security issues and "showed little interest in, or respect for, the norms, principles, and even rules of the international organizations it joined."[17] Only in 1981, when threatened with the loss of voting rights under UN's Article 19, did China begin to pay its share of peacekeeping assessments. In the late 1980s, China's move to a market economy, its subsequent rapid economic growth, and its increasing share of world trade made admission to the IMF, World Bank, and WTO essential. The PRC assumed

China's seats in the IMF and World Bank in 1980 and eventually gained its own seat on the Executive Board. In 2001, after fifteen years of negotiations, China was accepted into the WTO.

Over time, China's participation in various UN bodies has led it to redefine its interests and policies. For example, despite its resistance to international human rights norms, it fought hard to host the 1995 Fourth World Conference on Women because it believed that a successful conference would bring prestige to China. In the same year, China also agreed to accept selected ILO labor standards, and in doing so, it initiated a process to modify appropriate domestic laws. In 1992, it reversed its previous support for nuclear proliferation and signed the Nuclear Nonproliferation Treaty. Still, adjusting domestic practices to international norms in human rights and the environment has been a slow and incomplete process.

Historically, China has shown strong adherence to the principles of sovereignty and noninterference in the domestic affairs of states. Increasingly, these have created conflicts with its desire to be accepted as part of the international community. The 1989 Tiananmen Square massacre led to wide condemnation in the UN and in human rights circles. In 1990, China was confronted with a test of its commitment to the principle of collective security. Although it opposed using force to remove Iraq from Kuwait, it did not want to be the odd country out. This led it to abstain on key votes in the Security Council, a strategy that allowed it to register its objections but not bear responsibility for blocking international action. These same dilemmas came up repeatedly during the 1990s with the advent of more assertive peacekeeping operations under Chapter VII; China abstained on forty-one votes. By threatening to use the veto then agreeing not to block action, China could exercise influence consistent with its great-power status.

China's dramatic economic growth has now greatly bolstered its status as a rising major power with the world's second-largest economy. In 2000, its UN assessment was still only 0.9 percent of the UN budget. In 2013–15, that had risen to 5.1 percent, only slightly below that of France and Great Britain. In 2016, it became the second-largest contributor to peacekeeping operations. With a growing sense of national pride and increasing assertiveness, China's views have to be taken into account on both security and economic issues. Since 2000, China has contributed to UN peacekeeping operations in Liberia, Haiti, DRC, and South Sudan, among others, and provided a total of 3,079 personnel for ten missions in 2015. It contributed naval vessels to Security Council–authorized antipiracy efforts in the Indian Ocean. Its veto power and relationships have given it leverage with respect to efforts to deal with the crises in Darfur (Sudan), North Korea, Iran, and Syria. Regarding Darfur, China's rapidly rising need for oil along with its antipathy to sanctions and humanitarian interventions led it to oppose Security Council actions under Chapter VII. It also demonstrated its continuing adherence to the norm of noninterference in vetoing a 2007 draft resolution condemning the Myanmar military government's repressive policies as a threat to international peace and security. Only reluctantly has it acquiesced on UN-AU forces in Darfur, further sanctions against Iran in 2010, and UN-sanctioned intervention in Libya in 2011. China joined with Russia on four occasions between 2011 and 2015 to use its veto to block Security Council action in the Syrian crisis, suggesting some reluctance to use its veto in isolation. It abstained on the 2015 draft resolution marking the twentieth anniversary of the Srebrenica massacre that Russia vetoed because of the reference to genocide.

With respect to economic issues, China has historically supported the G-77 and the nonaligned group positions, pleading for special treatment as a developing nation. Yet as its economy has boomed, China has increasingly had to balance its own interests and those of other developing states.[18] China's interests are now more similar to those of other powerful states. Within the Bretton Woods institutions, China's influence is growing. The World Bank was one of the biggest funders of external aid to China in the 1990s; now China is a lender and the third-largest shareholder behind the United States and Japan. In the IMF its quota has been increased from 3.66 to 6.0 percent, and in 2015, its currency, the renminbi, became part of the IMF's basket of currencies along with the dollar, euro, pound, and yen. With the 2007–2008 global financial crisis, China's power in the G-20 expanded, buttressed by its huge foreign currency reserves. Its call for a new international currency to replace the dollar was but one indication of its growing assertiveness.

How China's economic power will be used within the UN remains unclear, but its president, Xi Jinping, pledged $2 billion toward implementation of the post-2015 development agenda at the 2015 Sustainable Development Summit along with $12 billion in investment in least-developed countries by 2030, $1 billion for the UN peace and development fund, $100 million for an AU emergency response unit, and 8,000 Chinese troops for a permanent UN peacekeeping force.[19] As one scholar notes, China wants "not only to assume a greater stake in international organizations but also to remake the rules of the game."[20] In 2015, China inaugurated the Asian Infrastructure Investment Bank (AIIB), capitalized with $50 billion from China, and with more than fifty charter members, including many US allies. It is widely seen as a rival to the World Bank and Asian Development Bank, and it is emblematic of China's increasing willingness to assert itself as a great power and to take what it regards as its rightful place in the world. At the Ten-Year Review of the World Summit on the Information Society in late 2015, China pushed for recognition of state sovereignty over the Internet and a greater say in how the Internet and cybersecurity are regulated worldwide.[21]

China's emergence as a major world power with considerable economic prowess guarantees that it will have growing influence on the UN stage. The nature of that role remains to be seen. As the most populous state in the world, the only non-Western member of the P-5, a nuclear weapons state with growing nonnuclear military capabilities, the second-largest economy behind the United States as of 2010, the largest donor of aid to African countries, and the world's largest emitter of carbon dioxide, China is unquestionably a key actor. As one US observer noted in 2015, "The UN offers a platform to showcase China's aspirations and growing capacity for constructive global leadership. . . . To be sure, China's embrace of UN norms remains uneven, particularly when it comes to human rights. Beijing is also skeptical of Western-led armed humanitarian intervention. . . . Still, it frames this resistance as fealty to the core UN Charter principles of territorial integrity, sovereign equality, and nonintervention." He added that China views the UN as a valuable instrument and has been more active in peacekeeping than any other P-5 member; it abandoned its stance that, as a developing country, it would not reduce its carbon emissions; and it has actively contributed to and supported the sustainable development goals.[22]

Germany and Japan. The ranks of the world's major powers include Germany and Japan, yet neither is a permanent member of the Security Council; indeed, their historical experiences as the defeated World War II powers have had a major impact on their individual willingness and capacity to make certain international commitments. Because of Germany's pivotal geographic position in Cold War Europe, there was a concerted effort to bring it into organizations such as NATO and the European Economic Community (precursor of the EU). Yet it was not until 1973 that the two German states—the Federal Republic of, or West, Germany and the German Democratic Republic, or East Germany—were admitted into the UN.

Japan joined the UN almost twenty years earlier, in 1956. During those early years, Japan kept a low profile; it concentrated on a few selective issues, such as keeping the People's Republic of China out of the UN and supporting the UN as a guarantor of the peace. In the 1970s, Japan's role in UN politics shifted markedly. Japan joined with the less developed countries to uphold the right of self-determination for the Palestinian people, accept the role of the Palestine Liberation Organization in the UN, and support other Arab causes. These positions reflected Japan's national interest given its dependency on Middle East oil producers.[23]

The decade of the 1990s was pivotal for Germany and Japan in the UN. In both countries, the 1991 Gulf War stimulated debates over their international roles. Both were asked to make significant monetary contributions to the war, yet neither was a member of the Security Council, nor had they been consulted. Both had constitutional impediments to participation in any collective enforcement or peacekeeping operation. In 1992, the Japanese Diet (Parliament) approved legislation permitting up to 2,000 Japanese troops to be deployed in UN peacekeeping missions under limited conditions. Japan's participation in the UN operation in Cambodia, known as the United Nations Transitional Authority in Cambodia (UNTAC), set a precedent for participation in other UN operations in Mozambique, East Timor, Haiti, South Sudan, and elsewhere. Still, while it is the third-largest contributor to the peacekeeping budget at 10.8 percent between 1994 and 2014, Japan has contributed just 9,300 troops and other personnel for UN missions.

In 1994, the German Constitutional Court ruled that German military forces could participate in UN peacekeeping operations. Germany has now sent more than 7,000 soldiers to UN and UN-mandated operations in Kosovo, Ethiopia, Georgia, Liberia, Lebanon, Sudan, and Afghanistan. It played a particularly vital role in the UN-authorized NATO operation in Afghanistan, supporting the reconstruction program, providing security assistance forces, funding humanitarian programs in education and culture, and training police.[24] Like Japan, while Germany's peacekeeping assessment is relatively high (7 percent), its personnel contributions have been comparatively small and totaled only 200 scattered across five missions in 2015. Generally, Germany prefers NATO and EU military missions, where there is greater control over the military personnel and greater credit to be gained.[25]

Both Germany and Japan are major UN financial supporters. Japan is the second-largest contributor to the UN: its assessed contribution was set at 10.8 percent for 2013–2015, which is equivalent to the combined share of France and Great Britain. Both Japan and Germany are major contributors to the IMF, World Bank, and WTO. Both seek permanent seats on the UN Security Council and both, along with Brazil and India (and other countries), have become increasingly insistent that the council must be reformed to more accurately reflect the distribution of power in the twenty-first century.

Middle Powers: The Traditional and Emerging Powers

The P-5 and other major powers are not the only states that matter in the UN. In fact, multilateral diplomacy in the UN system opens many opportunities for a group of states known as middle powers, as well as small states, to exercise influence. And a number of middle powers are among those countries categorized as rising or emerging powers. Categorizations such as these are always subject to dispute, but they provide a way of identifying and analyzing the roles of different states.

The so-called middle powers have played an important role in UN politics. This group of states can be characterized according to the kinds of policies they pursue, including multilateralism, compromise positions in disputes, and coalition-building to secure reform in the international system. Canada, Australia, Norway, and Sweden as well as Argentina, Brazil, India, South Africa, and Nigeria have been considered the traditional middle powers, which during the Cold War era were seen as uniquely able to facilitate UN activity when disputing parties were wary of great-power involvement but less so of middle-power mediation. During the 1944 Dumbarton Oaks conference, Canadian prime minister Mackenzie King called for a special position in the UN for Canada and others. His argument was that states ought to have a role commensurate with their contribution and that a division between the great powers and the rest was unworkable. Although a provision for special status for middle powers failed to become part of the UN Charter, the notion persisted.

When UN peacekeeping was developed in the 1950s, middle powers became frequent contributors of peacekeeping troops. Canada has played a particularly vital role, providing leadership, helping to train peacekeepers, setting up command structures, and providing communication and linguistic facilities and medical expertise. Its political culture has influenced preferences in the UN "for pragmatic non-ideological compromise, a belief in pluralism and tolerance, and a commitment to the orderly mediation and resolution of conflicts."[26] During the Cold War, Canada tried to maintain a line between taking independent action through the UN and supporting its neighbor to the south. During the Gulf War, Canada was reluctant to support military action, preferring to give sanctions more time. That was true in 2003 as well, when Canada offered no support to the US position on Iraq, preferring instead to continue inspections of Iraq's nuclear facilities.

Since the 1990s, Canada's role in the UN has come under greater domestic scrutiny. How could the country support more than one-quarter of its troops in UN peacekeeping when other domestic policy commitments were pressing? Widely publicized misconduct by Canadian troops in Somalia and the former Yugoslavia, and the subsequent government cover-up, stimulated a public debate over training and racism in the Canadian military and its continued ability and willingness to serve in more expensive and dangerous operations. The result was a decrease in the number of troops in UN peacekeeping operations. Although the country has sent more than 120,000 peacekeepers worldwide over the last sixty years and was the leader in troop contributions in the early 1990s, it now ranks only sixty-eighth out of 124 countries participating, with just 118 military and civilian personnel in 2015. For a number of years, Canada turned its energy to issues of human security. It managed the negotiations for the convention banning antipersonnel land mines, helped to draft guidelines for humanitarian intervention, and hosted the first **conference of parties** to the Kyoto Protocol on Climate Change in 2005. Nevertheless, in 2010 Canada failed to win a seat on the UN Security Council, the first time its bid had failed. With the election of a new Canadian government headed by Justin Trudeau in 2015, there was renewed optimism that Canada would revive its traditional support for multilateralism and cooperation with the UN.

Australia is also a strong supporter of the UN, although the extent of its participation has varied according to the exigencies of domestic politics. Its commitment to peacekeeping has tended to be concentrated on conflicts in Southeast Asia. It played a key diplomatic role in the Cambodian peace process and provided the force commander for UNTAC. Australia was also involved in Papua New Guinea and East Timor, providing military forces, police, and civilian personnel, totaling about one-half of the 11,000-person force in the UN Transitional Administration in East Timor (UNTAET).[27]

Beyond peacekeeping, Australia has been a crucial player in leading and supporting coalitions. It helped establish the Cairns Group of Fair Trading Nations—a coalition that crossed both the East-West and North-South divides—to push reform in international agricultural trade during the GATT trade negotiations in the early 1990s, for example. It also provided the intellectual and diplomatic leadership for the difficult negotiations in support of a freer, more open, and nondiscriminatory international trade regime in agriculture.[28]

India occupies a unique position as a traditional middle power and now as an emerging power. As a traditional middle power, for example, India had long participated in peacekeeping operations in the Middle East and Africa, a role that served its aspiration for international recognition and for a permanent seat on the Security Council. Indian generals commanded operations in Korea, Congo, Sierra Leone, Bosnia, and the Middle East. Participation in peacekeeping also helped India project its image as a nonaligned state and its claim to leadership in the **Nonaligned Movement (NAM)**. India helped create the movement in the 1950s and then used it to reinforce its activist multilateral agenda. In the first UN General Assembly session in 1946 and later in the nonaligned summits, India spoke out about racism in South Africa and led the push to end apartheid and colonialism. However, through its refusal to sign the Treaty on the Non-Proliferation of Nuclear Weapons (NPT, 1970) and the Comprehensive Nuclear Test Ban Treaty (1996), and by testing a nuclear device in 1998, India has also been a spoiler in UN efforts to curb nuclear proliferation. It argues vociferously that the NPT is discriminatory since there is no provision for adding new nuclear weapon states, such as India itself. Because of its huge population and rapidly growing economy, India is important to climate change negotiations, but it has been slow to accept the need to commit itself to reducing carbon dioxide emissions. India continues to aspire to a permanent seat on the Security Council, and to be a major contributor of troops and other personnel for peace-keeping, ranking third in 2015. India's UN assessment, however, remained well below 1 percent due to the extreme poverty of a significant portion of its large population.

Since the 1990s, India and other emerging economic powers have played an increasing role in UN politics on both security and economic issues. In the 1990s, Brazil became a significant contributor to peacekeeping operations, concentrating first on the former Portuguese colonies (Angola and Mozambique), where common language provided a link. Since 2004, Brazil has commanded the UN force in Haiti and provided almost a fifth of its personnel. The Brazilian military's extensive experience in infrastructure-building, development, and managing political unrest has made it a valuable partner in Chapter VI operations. Like India, Brazil seeks a permanent seat on the Security Council. Unlike India, it has been readier to commit to a target for reducing carbon dioxide emissions, it dismantled its nuclear program in the 1990s, and it has worked to reduce the destruction of the Amazon rain forest. Brazil's economy is also large enough that its UN 2013–2015 assessment was 2.9 percent, ranking ahead of Russia's. However, Brazil was experiencing significant economic and political problems beginning in 2015 that tarnished its image as a rising power.

Nigeria has often been seen as a middle power with immense potential. In the 1990s, it orchestrated the Economic Community of West African States' (ECOWAS) interventions in Liberia and Sierra Leone, providing both financing and manpower for the operations. In 2005, it provided much of the manpower for the UN-authorized African Union peacekeeping force in Darfur (Sudan) and hosted negotiations between the Sudanese government and the rebels. The Boko Haram terrorist group's raids and killings in recent years, however, have turned the tables, with Nigeria's smaller neighbors (Niger, Chad, Cameroon, and Benin) joining it to create a regional joint military force in 2015.

On economic issues, Brazil, India, Nigeria, Turkey, South Africa, and China have found their voices inside and outside the United Nations. For example, they have played a leading role in the Group of 20 advanced developing countries that have pushed hard for greater concessions on agricultural and other trade in WTO negotiations. India, China, Brazil, and others have pushed for a greater say in the World Bank and IMF, where they have been underrepresented. As discussed further in Chapter 5, most of these initiatives are occurring outside of the UN itself, underscoring the limited role the UN plays in global economic issues.

The essence of the middle powers' and emerging powers' role lies in the importance of secondary players in international politics: there must be followers as well as leaders. These countries can be both. They can also be challengers to entrenched institutions. Unquestionably, in a period when power and influence in the world are shifting, coalitions and roles within the UN system will also shift. Fostering cooperation in the future is likely to require leadership based not only on military capability and economic strength but also on diplomatic skill and policy initiatives—strengths that middle and emerging powers as well as small and developing states can contribute.

Small and Developing States

For small states everywhere, and for the majority of less developed countries, the UN has facilitated a number of foreign policy objectives. First, membership in the UN is a symbol of statehood and sovereignty. Second, small states in particular use the UN and the specialized agencies as arenas for bilateral and multilateral discussions, even if they concern non-UN matters. With limited diplomatic and economic resources, less developed countries find in the UN a cost-efficient forum where they can forge multilateral ties and conduct bilateral talks on a range of issues. The fall General Assembly sessions are vehicles for conducting other business among representatives and visiting ministers. Third, small states, especially the small European and Latin American states, have used the UN to promote the expansion of international law in an effort to constrain the major powers and protect small-power interests. Fourth, the UN enlarges the "voice" of small states and offers opportunities to set the global agenda. For example, because Kuwait was a UN member, Iraq's invasion and occupation in 1990 immediately gained attention, and there was strong support for sanctions and even the use of force. Yet Georgia was not successful in doing likewise in the face of Russia's intervention in 2008; Ukraine was somewhat more successful in that it secured a General Assembly resolution in 2014 criticizing Russia's takeover of Crimea and activities in eastern Ukraine. Costa Rica was influential in the formation of the Commission on Human Rights in the 1940s and the new post of UN High Commissioner for Human Rights in the 1990s, viewing each as essential to the pursuance of its human rights agenda.[29] When it assumed leadership of the Nonaligned Movement and the Organization of the Islamic Conference (now the Organisation of Islamic Cooperation or OIC) in 2003, Malaysia assumed a proactive role on a number of issues within the UN. One scholar noted, "Malaysia's influence in world politics has been far greater than its national power potential, almost approximating to that of a middle power, and in the main this was due to its imaginative foreign policy and high profile diplomacy."[30]

Because small and less powerful states do not have the diplomatic resources to deal with all issues in depth, participation in the UN tends to force them either to specialize in particular issues or to follow the lead of larger states within the Group of 77 or other coalitions. Participation in the UN not only aids in achieving foreign policy objectives directly but also provides small states with more avenues, including opportunities for interest aggregation through the formation of coalitions to enhance weak states' influence. With the proliferation of UN-related bodies, small states may also seek the body most favorable to their interests—a phenomenon known as "forum shopping."

Small and weak states have been able to bargain with major powers in the UN for their support on certain important issues in return for economic concessions. In the 1991 Gulf War, for example, some small states that were nonpermanent members of the Security Council at the time agreed to support US-UN action in return for favors. Ethiopia extracted a promise from the United States to broker a peace between the government and Eritrean rebels. Egypt and Malaysia received financial "rewards." For Yemen, however, the consequence of opposition to the Gulf War was the withdrawal of US aid and commitments. In 2003, the smaller nonpermanent members of the Security Council such as Guinea, Angola, and Cameroon were courted extensively by both sides in the divisive debate over Iraq, but in this instance were not receptive to financial inducements.

Developing countries are the major beneficiaries of most UN economic and development programs. They may apply to the World Bank and UN development agencies for projects, technical assistance, and structural adjustment funds to augment their economic development plans. They are also the beneficiaries of funds from various UN agencies and programs, including WHO, the World Food Programme, the International Fund for Agricultural Development, UNHCR's refugee programs, and the UN Disaster Relief Organization's emergency disaster funds.

Since 1990, it is also developing countries that have been the primary contributors of troops and other personnel for UN peacekeeping operations. The top seven contributors in 2015 were Bangladesh, Pakistan, India, Nepal, Ethiopia, Senegal, and Rwanda. It is financially remunerative for countries to make their personnel available, but the current situation has led to charges that the rich countries pay in money while the poor countries pay in blood. Chapter 4 will examine some of the other problems that this pattern raises.

Although there have long been weak and quasi states in the international system, one of the major developments since the Cold War's end has been the phenomenon of fragile and failing states. Somalia has been a prime example of a failed state since its central government collapsed in 1991; other examples of failing or failed states, some of which have now partially recovered, include the Democratic Republic of the Congo, Sierra Leone, Afghanistan, Haiti, and East Timor. The most recent UN member, South Sudan (a member since 2011), also falls in this category. Problems emanating from weak, failing, and failed states include spillover in the form of refugees from civil wars; groups such as the Taliban and Al Shabab that use neighboring states as sanctuaries; terrorist groups such as Al Qaeda in the Islamic Maghreb that exploit the weakness of states surrounding the Sahara; violence bordering on genocide in countries such as the Central African Republic, Burundi, and South Sudan that puts civilians at high risk in an era when the responsibility to protect civilians is an emerging norm; and an inability to control piracy emanating from the territory of countries such as Somalia. These problems have led to two dilemmas. Do such states merit continuing representation in international bodies, including the UN? And what actions should be taken to rebuild them, and by whom? International law assumes that states not only have control of their territory but also have the capacity to govern and to comply with international obligations. As discussed further in Chapter 4, the UN has taken on the tasks of **statebuilding** in a number of instances, including Kosovo and East Timor (which became a new state in 2002). The dilemmas of what to do about failed and failing states persist.

Although small and developing countries gain voice and influence through coalitions and blocs, all member states participate in one or more such groupings. As in any parliamentary or legislative body, coalition-building is a primary strategy for garnering a majority of votes in favor of or in opposition to proposals for action.

COALITIONS, BLOCS, AND THE IMPORTANCE OF CONSENSUS

Early in the UN's history, states in the same geographic region, or those sharing economic or political interests, formed coalitions to shape common positions on issues and to control a bloc of votes.[31] The UN Charter itself specified that the General Assembly should give consideration to "equitable geographic distribution" in electing the nonpermanent members of the Security Council and members of ECOSOC, though it offered no guidance about how to do so. By informal agreement, these five groups came to correspond roughly to the major regions of the world: Western European and Others (includes the United States, Israel, and Canada), Eastern Europe, Africa, Latin America and the Caribbean, and Asia. (See Box 3.1.) Each regional group determines the rules and procedures for selecting candidates. For the Security Council, the Latin American group tends to give preference to the larger states (Argentina, Brazil, and Colombia), but the African group rotates candidates among all of its member states.

The European Union (EU) has developed the most formalized process for continual consultation among its member states and for delegating responsibility to articulate common policies. It constitutes a sizable voting bloc, with twenty-eight members, and is collectively the largest donor, contributing 35 percent of the UN regular budget and 36.8 percent of the UN peacekeeping budget. Members generally act as a single unit in the UN, voting as a bloc on social and economic issues. On issues of security, however, the EU members have found

---

BOX 3.1. **Caucusing Groups in the United Nations (Number of Member States)**

Regional Groups

African Group (54)
Asia-Pacific Group (55)
Latin American and Caribbean Group (33)
Western European and Others Group (29)
Eastern European Group (23)

Other Multilateral Groups

Group of 77 (ca. 132)
Association of Southeast Asian Nations (ASEAN) (10)
Nonaligned Movement (ca. 120)
Organisation of Islamic Cooperation (57)
Nordic Group (5)
European Union (28)

Sources: www.un.org/depts/DGACM/RegionalGroups.shtml, www.nti.org/treaties-and-regimes/non-aligned-movement-nam.

---

it more difficult to take common positions, as illustrated in the divisions over the Middle East, the 2003 Iraq War, and the 2011 Libya intervention. In 2011, the EU's participation status was upgraded, allowing EU representatives to present common bloc positions in General Assembly debates, circulate documents, present proposals and amendments, and exercise the right of reply with regard to EU positions. EU representatives are still seated among the observers, however, and have no right to vote or put forward candidates.

Subregional groups often show remarkable unity in the General Assembly as well as in other bodies. For example, high cohesion can be found among the five Nordic states and the members of the Caribbean Community.

Coalitions are important because the General Assembly body functions like a national parliament, each state having one vote and decisions being made by a majority (either simple or two-thirds under specified circumstances). Just as a majority political party (or a coalition) can control most decisions, so can a stable coalition comprising a majority of UN member states. These coalitions within the UN have tended to persist for long periods; their presence led to the practice of consensus decisionmaking in the General Assembly, as described in Chapter 2.

During the Cold War, two competing coalitions were composed of states aligned with either the United States or the Soviet Union. The Eastern European states could be counted on to vote consistently with the Soviet Union, thus forming a true bloc. Many nonaligned states also voted regularly with the Soviet bloc. Throughout the mid-1950s, the Western European, Latin American, and British Commonwealth states voted closely with the United States on issues that involved Cold War competition and also often on human rights, social concerns, and UN administration. Despite some internal tensions, that US-dominated coalition held a controlling position in UN General Assembly voting until 1955.

Beginning in 1960 with the influx of new African and Asian states, a new coalition emerged, the Group of 77, whose members constituted more than two-thirds of the UN's membership. By 1971, the G-77 had become the dominant coalition, based upon its high level of cohesion on development-related issues. As such, it was able to set agendas in the General Assembly, ECOSOC, and many specialized agencies. The G-77 was often supported by the Eastern European bloc when the Soviet Union took advantage of opportunities to escape its minority position and accuse the West of being responsible for the problems of developing countries. Once the PRC held the Chinese seat, it also supported G-77 demands for economic change. The cohesion among the G-77 reached its peak in the mid-1970s. Thereafter, differences in social and economic conditions among Asian, African, and Latin American countries made common policy positions more difficult to forge, and the G-77's influence declined. Instead, the G-20 emerged first in the WTO as a voice of developing countries. In many UN bodies, including the General Assembly, the divide between developed and developing countries (North versus South) still shapes coalitions on issues of economic inequality and development. But on many specific policies, cohesion has weakened and differences among coalition members have become more pronounced.

Other interests can also serve as the basis for coalitions in the UN. For example, the thirty landlocked countries that first coalesced during the law of the sea negotiations in the 1970s and early 1980s have tended to vote together on specific issues of trade and transportation; they have also convened UN-sponsored meetings to address their particular needs. So, too, have the forty-four members of the Alliance of Small Island States, who are among the strongest advocates for action on climate change. The member states of the Organization of Petroleum Exporting Countries (OPEC) once provided leadership for the G-77 and the proposed New International Economic Order in the 1970s, but are far less cohesive and influential in the current era of low oil prices. Another group, the UN Democracy Caucus, came together in 2004 to push for good-governance norms in UN development programs and international financial institutions' aid programs as well as for a human rights agenda. The group has since become largely inactive.

States sharing particular political interests have used their contacts with each other to influence politics within the UN. For example, the Commonwealth—fifty-three states, most of which were formerly part of the British Empire—operates as a coalition at the UN as well as at the intergovernmental and societal levels. The Nonaligned Movement, previously a strong bloc of like-minded states opposing colonialism, racism, and Cold War alignments, has refocused its energies since the Cold War's end on representing small non-Western states. NAM tries to promote common positions within the Security Council and elsewhere and works closely with the G-77.

In addition to coalitions and blocs, UN members also have often formed ad hoc informal groups of three to six states, referred to as "friends" or "contact" groups, to support UN peace-related actions. In the late 1970s, the Contact Group on Namibia worked alongside the Security Council in the search for a peaceful solution to the problem of South West Africa, or Namibia, which had been under South African control as a League of Nations mandate since the end of World War I. That group involved high-ranking members of five UN missions (Canada, France, Germany, Great Britain, and the United States) in a decade-long series of negotiations that eventually led to independence for a democratic Namibia. Subsequently, contact groups were formed as part of efforts to settle conflicts in Central America, the former Yugoslavia, and, more recently, Ukraine. The UN, the United States, Russia, and the EU make up the so-called Middle East Quartet, formed in 2004 to seek a peaceful settlement of the Israeli-Palestinian conflict, though the group is now generally regarded as useless.

Friends of the Secretary-General have generally included at least one interested member of the P-5. The "friends" keep in close contact with the secretary-general and support efforts to keep a peace process on track and coordinate the work of mediators, either before reaching a formal agreement or in implementing an agreement. The groups are kept small so that meetings can be quickly convened. More than one country is used to exert pressure on parties and present a common view to the international community. Friends groups have been formed, for example, for Haiti (Canada, France, United States, Venezuela), Georgia (France, Germany, Russia, Great Britain), and Tajikistan (Afghanistan, Iran, Turkey, United States, Uzbekistan).[32]

Groups and coalitions, then, provide order and some coherence in a UN of 193 member states and a crowded agenda. Some serve primarily parliamentary-style functions of putting issues on the table, establishing negotiating positions, garnering votes, and engaging in bargaining. Still others have complemented the UN secretary-general's role as a mediator by bringing the assets of several countries to bear on efforts to find a peaceful settlement to a difficult conflict.

THE SECRETARY-GENERAL
AND THE UN SECRETARIAT AS KEY ACTORS

The international prominence of the UN's secretary-general (UNSG) has contributed to the emergence of the UN itself as an autonomous actor in world
politics. Both the secretary-general and other senior UN Secretariat officials,
however, wield significant influence within the UN itself and occasionally over
member states. They form the so-called second UN. Both command authority
to shape agendas and frame issues. Both are often asked to recommend "what
is the right thing to do." Both tend to emphasize their "neutrality, impartiality,
and objectivity in ways that make essentially moral claims against particularistic
self-serving states."[33] Some constructivists have made the argument that international organizations such as the UN have autonomy because they are bureaucracies and their authority is based on impersonal rules. As two scholars described
the process, "IOs, through their rules, create new categories of actors, form new
interests for actors, define new shared international tasks, and disseminate new
models of social organization around the globe."[34] Acting autonomously may
mean that the bureaucracy develops its own views and manipulates material and
information resources. These characteristics may lead to undesirable outcomes
such as tunnel vision, bias, and reluctance to embrace reform.

The Secretary-General

For more than seventy years, secretaries-general have exercised their leadership
by taking advantage of opportunities for initiatives, applying flexible interpretations of Charter provisions, seeking mandates from UN policy organs as necessary, and developing their own political roles and that of the institution (see
Box 2.1). Their personalities and interpretations of the UN Charter, as well as of
world events, have combined to increase the power, resources, and importance
of the position. More than just a senior civil servant, the UN secretary-general
is an international political figure "subject to the problems and possibilities of
political leadership."[35] There has long been a debate, however, as to whether the
role calls for someone who is more a "general" or a "secretary." To what extent
is the UNSG free to give orders versus taking them from the member states and
serving as chief administrative officer?[36]

The UN secretary-general is well placed to serve as a neutral communications
channel and intermediary for the global community. Although she or he represents the institution, she or he can act independently of the policy organs even
when resolutions have condemned a party to a dispute, maintaining lines of communication and representing the institution's commitment to peaceful settlement
and alleviation of human suffering. Although these tasks call for diplomatic skills,

it has become essential for the UNSG also to have strong managerial and budgetary skills.

The most important resource for UNSGs is the power of persuasion. The "force" of majorities behind resolutions may lend greater legitimacy to initiatives, though it may not ensure any greater degree of success. Autonomy can also be a source of the secretary-general's influence. For example, during the Security Council's 2002–2003 debate over Iraq's failure to disarm and cooperate with UN inspections and whether to authorize a US-led war, Kofi Annan steered an independent course by pushing for Iraqi compliance, council unity, and peace. This type of approach facilitates a UNSG's ability to serve as a neutral intermediary. U Thant stated, "The Secretary-General must always be prepared to take an initiative, no matter what the consequences to him or his office may be, if he sincerely believes that it might make the difference between peace and war."[37] Annan put it more bluntly: "I know some people have accused me of using diplomacy. That's my job."[38]

Dag Hammarskjöld, the second secretary-general, played a key part in shaping the role and the UN during the critical period of 1953–1961. Hammarskjöld articulated principles for UN involvement in peacekeeping. He demonstrated the UNSG's efficacy as an agent for peaceful settlement of disputes, mediating the release of eleven US airmen under the UN command in Korea who had been imprisoned by the Communist Chinese, and seeking a solution to the secession of the Congo province of Katanga just before his death in 1961. Hammarskjöld also oversaw the initiation of UN peacekeeping operations with the creation of the United Nations Emergency Force (UNEF) at the time of the 1956 Suez crisis. He is generally credited with inventing the idea of preventive diplomacy.

Javier Pérez de Cuéllar, the fifth secretary-general, presided over the UN's transformation from the brink of irrelevance in the 1980s to an active instrument for resolving conflicts and promoting international peace at the end of the Cold War. In his persistent, patient, low-key approach to Israel's 1982 invasion of Lebanon, the Falklands/Malvinas War, the Iran-Iraq War, and the ongoing problems in Cyprus, Namibia, and Afghanistan, he epitomized the ideal intermediary.

Secretary-General Boutros Boutros-Ghali pushed the boundaries of the office further with the benefit of independent UN information-gathering and analytical capability. He prodded states, including the United States, to take action in Somalia. He engaged the UN in civil conflicts in Cambodia, Bosnia, and Haiti. This activism and his antagonistic relationship with the United States led to his defeat for a second term in 1996.

Kofi Annan, a Ghanaian national, became the seventh secretary-general and the first from within the UN bureaucracy. A much quieter individual than his predecessor, Annan nevertheless pledged change, and proved to be even more of an activist. He carried out extensive administrative and budgetary reforms within the UN, including structural changes within the Secretariat, discussed in Chapter 2. He strengthened liaisons between various departments and NGOs and initiated dialogue with business leaders. He built a better relationship with the US Congress, an important step given Congress's failure to fully fund US dues to the UN for much of the 1990s. Having won the Nobel Peace Prize for himself and the organization, a widely respected Annan won reelection in 2001. He used his bully pulpit as UN head, including his annual reports to the General Assembly, to speak out on controversial issues such as HIV/AIDS, changing interpretations of state sovereignty, and the emerging norm of humanitarian intervention, and to initiate programs such as the Global Compact on Corporate Responsibility with private corporations. He took the unprecedented step of publishing reports on the UN's failures in the disastrous massacre in the UN-declared safe area of Srebrenica, in the Rwandan genocide, and in security for UN personnel in Iraq. His prestige and authority were damaged, however, by the oil-for-food scandal discussed in Chapter 2. As one close observer of the UN noted, both Boutros-Ghali and Annan "shared a reputation as proponents of big ideas, bold doctrines, and a generous interpretation of the scope and authority of the office."[39]

Still, even activist secretaries-general can find their influence limited. Mark Malloch Brown, former administrator of UNDP, left that post to serve as deputy secretary-general and *chef de cabinet* to Kofi Annan. He later remarked, "I found when it came to management and budgetary matters that the secretary-general was less influential than I had been as administrator of UNDP. Whereas I had had a cooperative board that was not infected by bitter political confrontation, he was hostage to intergovernmental warfare."[40] This suggests that individual personality is not the only variable affecting the secretary-general's ability to act independently.

Ban Ki-moon, the eighth secretary-general, had a very different approach to the role than his two immediate predecessors. While he proclaimed climate change to be a high priority early on, he had difficulties translating that general commitment into action, as discussed in Chapter 7. His low-profile approach did work in Myanmar, where he got the government to accept international assistance after the devastation caused by Cyclone Nargis in 2008. Ban's reluctance to speak out when his words would antagonize the United States, Russia, or China, however, met with sustained criticism, as did his handling of the Sri Lankan war when he selected an inappropriate negotiator with ties to India. In 2010, the outgoing undersecretary-general of the Office of Internal Oversight Services, Inga-Britt Ahlenius, wrote a scathing critique of Ban's management practices, particularly his efforts to undercut the independence of the internal

PHOTOGRAPH 3.1. Secretary-General Ban Ki-moon meets with Pope Francis at the Vatican, April 28, 2015

Source: UN Photo 629741/Mark Garten.

investigations division. She called Ban secretive, his actions "reprehensible," and his leadership "deplorable," concluding that "the secretariat now is in a process of decay."[41] That and other criticisms did not affect the campaign for his reelection at the end of 2011, as he also had his supporters. As one journalist has remarked, "While Ban has been a letdown on many fronts, it's worth asking whether anyone else could have done better—at least on Syria. . . . The fact is that when the great powers squabble, there's little that anyone in the organization can accomplish, be they competent or not. . . . The big powers, tired of locking horns with Annan, wanted someone bland and pliable to replace him, and the colorless South Korean fit the bill."[42] Nonetheless, evaluation of Ban highlights tensions among those such as the United States who prefer the secretary-general to be an efficient manager and an instrument of members, those who are content with a weak individual who does not exercise leadership, and those who prefer a more independent figure willing to take initiative and direct a powerful bureaucracy.

In addition to the UNSG, **special representatives of the secretary-general** (SRSGs) who are now appointed in conjunction with all UN peacekeeping missions and often serve as mediators, can exercise significant independent influence.

Among the most notable special representatives have been Sergio Vieira de Mello, the SRSG successively in Lebanon, Kosovo, East Timor, and Iraq;[43] Martti Ahtisaari, winner of the 2008 Nobel Peace Prize, who served as SRSG in Namibia and Kosovo; and Lakhdar Brahimi, who, among his many important UN posts, served as SRSG in Haiti, South Africa, Afghanistan, Iraq, and Syria.

Between 1997 and 2013, thematic SRSGs dealt with thirty-two different topics, ranging from the impact of armed conflict on children and HIV/AIDS in Africa to the MDGs, the Global Compact on Corporate Responsibility, migration, and sexual violence in conflict. These individuals represent the secretary-general by "becoming a presence themselves—not necessarily with office space in New York, but certainly as a distinct voice and promoters of ideas in direct consultation with diplomats and the media as well as with governments, relevant agencies, and NGOs worldwide."[44]

The directors-general of the specialized agencies also wield considerable power. Diplomatically, they carry the same rank as the UNSG, historically a factor complicating efforts of the latter to coordinate initiatives across different parts of the UN system. But the role of the second UN extends beyond these high-level officials, and it is to that we turn.

The UN Secretariat as Bureaucracy and Actor

The UN's Secretariat and the secretariats of the specialized agencies share some of the characteristics of bureaucracies more generally. They derive authority in performing "duties of office" from their rational-legal character and from their expertise; they derive legitimacy from the moral purposes of the organization and from their claims to neutrality, impartiality, and objectivity; and they derive power from their missions of serving others. The different agencies within the UN system tend to be staffed by technocrats—individuals with specialized training and knowledge who shape policy options consistent with that expertise. "In fact," Michael Barnett and Martha Finnemore note, "the organization will not readily entertain policy options not supported by its expertise. Professional training, norms, and occupational cultures strongly shape the way experts view the world. They influence what problems are visible to staff and what range of solutions are entertained."[45]

The Secretariat includes the under- and assistant secretaries-general, the heads of departments such as peacekeeping and electoral assistance, the high commissioners for refugees and for human rights, the heads of programs such as UNDP and UNICEF, and the head of UN Women—the new UN organization that became operational on January 1, 2011. These senior-level officials can be influential in building awareness of issues and calling attention to specific problems such as child soldiers, violence against women, refugee crises, or torture in China. Staff in the field with development or peace operations can significantly shape the success or failure of those operations by their actions. As an example, Chapter 6 examines the leadership role that high commissioners for human rights have played.

The UN's bureaucrats play a significant role in shaping the agendas of various meetings. The ways in which they understand particular conflict situations can also influence how member states view them. For example, Barnett and Finnemore show how the UN staff defined the situation in Rwanda in 1994 as a civil war and failed to see that the unfolding genocide was quite different from violence against civilians in other ethnic conflicts. "Because Rwanda was a civil war there was no basis for intervention," they note. "The rules of peacekeeping . . . [at that time] prohibited peacekeeping in a civil war and in the absence of a stable cease-fire . . . but also shaped its [the Secretariat's] position on how peacekeepers might be used in this volatile situation."[46] Furthermore, Secretary-General Boutros-Ghali did not make the argument for intervention. Thus, the UN's failure to stop the genocide in Rwanda was "the predictable result of an organizational culture that shaped how the UN evaluated and responded to violent crises."[47]

Examples of such Secretariat influence in defining issues can be drawn from other UN agencies. In the mid-1980s, for example, HIV/AIDS was viewed as solely a health problem and, hence, the province of the medical professionals in WHO. Only gradually did other UN agencies demonstrate the scope of the epidemic's effects and the necessity for interagency collaboration in dealing with the problem. The influence of liberal economists in the IMF and World Bank has long been noted as a major factor shaping the way those institutions' bureaucracies think about and address development issues and financial crises. For example, Tamar Gutner has examined the poor fit of the IMF with the Millennium Development Goals, describing it as "the major IO least capable of embracing any bold new initiatives for poverty reduction in general, and the MDGs in particular." There was a fundamental difference between the IMF's primary mission and the poverty reduction strategies of the MDGs that made the IMF ill equipped to engage in activities and processes that involvement with the MDGs called for.[48]

Yet influence in the UN is not limited to states, secretaries-general, directors-general, or bureaucrats. Increasingly, nonstate actors have come to play leading roles as part of the third UN.

NONSTATE ACTORS: THE THIRD UN

Four types of nonstate actors make up the third UN. These include nongovernmental organizations; academics and experts who serve as consultants; prominent individuals and independent commissions; and more recently, corporations and foundations. Their interactions with the first and second UNs influence thinking and policies; they may provide services and other resources, including funding in the case of corporations and foundations. They are characterized by their independence from governments and from the UN Secretariat. None are monolithic. And "deciding who is in or out of the third UN depends on the issue and the period in question."[49]

NGOs as Actors in the UN System

The rapid growth in numbers, roles, and influence of NGOs in global politics generally and within the UN system is one of the striking developments since the Cold War's end. The members of these organizations are private individuals or associations that come together around some common purpose. To some, these groups together form the basis of a global civil society. Some NGOs are formed to advocate a particular cause such as human rights, peace, or environmental protection. Others are established to provide services such as disaster relief, humanitarian aid, or development assistance. Some are in reality government-organized nongovernmental organizations (dubbed GONGOs). Scholars and analysts distinguish between not-for-profit groups (the vast majority) and for-profit corporations; it is also common to treat terrorist, criminal, and drug trafficking groups separately.

The estimates of numbers of NGOs vary enormously. The 2014–2015 *Yearbook of International Organizations* identified more than 8,000 nongovernmental organizations that have an international dimension in terms of either membership or commitment to conduct activities in several states. Exclusively national NGOs number in the millions. Many large international NGOs (INGOs) are transnational federations linking a number of national groups. Examples include the International Federation of Red Cross and Red Crescent Societies, Oxfam, Médecins Sans Frontières (Doctors Without Borders), World Wildlife Fund, Human Rights Watch, Amnesty International, and Save the Children.

Article 71 of the UN Charter authorized ECOSOC (but not the General Assembly) to grant consultative status to NGOs. Resolution 1296, adopted in 1968, formalized the arrangements for accrediting NGOs whose influence occurred primarily within ECOSOC's subsidiary bodies, and particularly within the Commissions on Human Rights, Status of Women, and Population. The UN-sponsored global conferences beginning in the 1970s greatly increased the visibility and power of NGOs. In the conferences focusing on women, the environment, human rights, population, and sustainable development, NGOs found valuable new outlets for their activities. In many cases, groups participated in preconference meetings with delegates, organized their own parallel meetings on topics of interest, published materials to increase public awareness of the issues, provided input to official conference documents, and developed networks with other NGOs to enhance their influence. At the conferences themselves, the rules for NGO participation have varied. While some conferences permitted NGO lobbying and NGO roles in implementation, others limited participation to informal activities. Those experiences strengthened the NGOs' resolve to gain greater formal access and clearer rules for participation.

ECOSOC Resolution 31, in 1996, granted access to national-level NGOs, enlarging the number of NGOs with consultative status to about 3,000. Those NGOs have broad access to UN bodies: they may consult with officers from the Secretariat; place items on agendas in ECOSOC, the functional commissions, and other subsidiary bodies; attend meetings; submit statements; and make oral presentations with permission. Still, NGOs have lobbied for greater participation rights through the Conference of Non-Governmental Organisations in Consultative Status with the United Nations Economic and Social Council (CoNGO). The 2004 Cardoso Report called for enhanced relationships between the UN and all relevant civil society partners but failed to acknowledge the multiple ways NGOs already took part in UN activities.

In the General Assembly, four NGOs—the International Federation of the Red Cross and Red Crescent Societies, the International Committee of the Red Cross, the Inter-Parliamentary Union, and the Sovereign Military Order of Malta— have special privileges to participate as observers in all assembly sessions. Since the late 1980s, NGOs have had access as petitioners to some assembly committees, notably the Third Committee (Social, Humanitarian, and Cultural) and the Second Committee (Economic and Financial).

In 1997, NGOs first gained limited access to Security Council meetings. Through the NGO Working Group on the Security Council (organized by Amnesty International, the Global Policy Forum, EarthAction, and the World Council of Churches, among others), NGOs that provide relief aid in humanitarian emergencies have gained a voice in council deliberations. For example, Oxfam, CARE, and Doctors Without Borders have spoken on the Great Lakes crisis in Africa, and discussions on AIDS have included NGO representatives. Informal consultations between NGOs, the Security Council president, and council members are now a common practice.

Whether NGOs are recognized through ECOSOC accreditation is now largely an academic question since they have found various other ways for influencing UN policymaking and implementation. Women's NGOs, which have a long history of networking with women in governments and various UN bodies, have effectively used these informal links and during the four world conferences on women pressed for mainstreaming women's and gender issues. A coalition of NGOs, the Global Call to Action Against Poverty, promoted the Millennium Development Goals by mobilizing local community leaders and groups.

By contrast, however, the UN Development Programme does not engage systematically with any NGOs, and its advisory committee actually shields UNDP from such interactions. This is particularly troubling since UNDP resident co-ordinators have been designated by Secretary-General Ban to lead UN country teams, overseeing multisector and multiagency UN programs that frequently involve NGO participation. Several UN specialized agencies and programs have long welcomed the involvement of NGOs. Only the ILO, however, has formalized their participation in the unique tripartite system of representation. UNESCO, for example, has an extensive network of national commissions, scientific councils, and more than six hundred NGOs in consultation. UNICEF and the United Nations Development Fund for Women also have long histories of recognizing the importance of NGOs. In a number of specialized agencies, though, it has been a long struggle to incorporate NGOs in a meaningful way. In many cases, NGOs are contractors providing services under the aegis of the specialized agencies rather than stakeholders in programs.

The barriers to NGO participation do not lie just within the UN. A 2004–2005 survey of UN system agencies conducted by the UN Non-Governmental Liaison Services (UN-NGLS) found that NGOs' lack of funding to participate in meetings and follow-up was a significant constraint. NGOs themselves acknowledge the difficulty in balancing the interests and desires of groups from the developed world with those from the developing world, for example. Even when NGOs participate, they may only have an impact on low-level policy issues rather than on core economic questions. As one NGO questioned, "We are being listened to but are we being heard?"[50]

NGO participation in the loosely UN-related international financial organizations has been quite uneven. Beginning in the late 1970s, women's and environmental NGOs pressured the World Bank, for example, to adopt a women-in-development and environmentally friendly agenda, often targeting specific bank projects such as big dams. In 1994, the bank turned to a more participatory development approach, increasingly using NGOs to collaborate on and administer projects. The bank admitted, however, that "CSOs [civil society organizations] invited to consultation meetings were those who were easily accessible and approving of the government and the Bank's preferred strategies. Moreover, CSOs who were invited often did not get enough timely and appropriate information about the issues at stake, the options being considered, and how the PRSP [Poverty Reduction Strategy Papers] process works, thus limiting their ability to effectively participate in the process."[51] The IMF has, likewise, been slow to develop formal contacts with NGOs because its specialized focus on monetary policy has not lent itself easily to NGO input. Yet even the IMF felt NGO influence during the Jubilee 2000 campaign for debt reduction orchestrated by a wide range of NGOs, religious groups, trade unions, and business associations.

NGOs at the UN are most influential in the areas of human rights, environmental protection, development, and humanitarian aid. They are given the

greatest access and hold the most influence when they are contributing specialized information.[52] Service providers have the most influence on what happens
in the field with UN programs, especially when program delivery is subcontracted to them. But NGOs vary enormously in their capacity, resources, and
willingness to collaborate with others. There is competition among those seeking subcontracts for humanitarian and development projects and competition
generally for funding. And NGO field personnel have been accused of egregious
misconduct. For example, more than sixty-seven individuals from forty aid
agencies were cited for distributing food in return for sexual favors in refugee
camps during the civil war in Sierra Leone. UNHCR and Save the Children,
in turn, were accused of hiding the scope of the scandal.[53] For better or worse,
NGOs are an integral and important part of the third UN.

For several decades, there have been proposals to give civil society actors a
forum of their own. The People's Millennium Forum, held in 2000, was an ad
hoc version of such a forum that brought together representatives of more than
one hundred NGOs. Although the names have varied—a UN Parliamentary Assembly, a Forum of Civil Society, a Second Assembly—the ideas are basically
the same. To proponents, nonstate actors—including NGOs—should have a
venue for consultations among themselves and should be given standing within
the UN system. Such an assembly would give voice to heretofore unrepresented
groups, add transparency to the international political process, and potentially
add accountability. It would also require UN Charter revision.

Yet there are deep divisions among member states, the UN Secretariat, and
NGOs and other nonstate actors themselves over greater nonstate participation.
Many governments have mixed or even negative feelings about NGOs. For example, repressive governments often feel threatened by the pressures of human
rights NGOs and in many parts of the world have cracked down on domestic NGOs and ties to international NGOs; developed countries have not always
welcomed NGO pressure for economic justice; the Nonaligned Movement and
small countries have opposed expanding NGO access to the General Assembly; and the UN Secretariat has feared that greater NGO involvement would
be costly both in stretching material resources and in complicating procedures
already deemed cumbersome.

NGOs do not speak with one voice on the issue of participation within the
UN system or on any other issue. There are differences in interest and perspective, often leading to conflict among NGOs, the not-for-profit business associations, and private companies. The not-for-profit business associations have
been included within the NGO sector by the UN, even though their individual members are businesses. NGOs have been especially upset by the ease with
which businesses and MNCs have acquired status and participatory rights by
their presence on national delegations and through the Global Compact, while

NGOs are typically not represented on national delegations and have to undergo strenuous examination to gain consultative status. Even among the NGOs themselves, there are significant divisions between the traditional NGOs (which they say represent "the people") and social movements like indigenous people, and between the larger more established NGOs and smaller local ones.

Academic and Expert Consultants

Almost from its inception, the UN has drawn on the knowledge of outside experts to study specific issues and prepare reports. These have in a number of cases included individuals who later were awarded Nobel Prizes for their work in economics, such as Jan Tinbergen, W. Arthur Lewis, Gunnar Myrdal, and Amartya Sen. Much of this work took place in the 1950s and 1960s and contributed to early understandings of economic development. The UN System of National Accounts was the product of a committee of experts convened by the UN Statistical Office. Similarly, measures for full employment, economic development, and international economic stability were developed by outside experts. Sen, for example, wrote both for the ILO World Employment Programme in the 1970s and for UNDP's *Human Development Report* in the 1990s.

Independent Commissions

The third UN also includes independent commissions composed of prominent individuals such as former foreign ministers, heads of government, and ambassadors. The commission may be established by the UN, a government, or others; often, there is a team of academic researchers who provide study papers for the commission, which typically presents its report to the UNSG. Since the late 1960s, when a commission led by former Canadian prime minister Lester Pearson produced the report *Partners in Development* (1969), there have been a large number of other commissions, several of which are discussed in later chapters. These include the Commission on Environment and Development, chaired by Norwegian prime minister Gro Harlem Brundtland in the 1980s; the Commission on Global Governance, whose 1995 report *Our Global Neighborhood* helped to make the concept of global governance more widely known; and the Commission on Civil Society, led by former Brazilian president Fernando Henrique Cardoso, whose 2004 report was mentioned above. In 2004, Secretary-General Kofi Annan convened the High-Level Panel on Threats, Challenges, and Change as part of the preparation for the World Summit planned in conjunction with the UN's sixtieth anniversary in 2005. Two more recent independent commissions were created in 2011 and 2014 by the Human Rights Council to investigate violations of international human rights law in Syria and of international humanitarian law in Gaza.

What differentiates the independent commissions from the academic and expert consultants is the collective weight they bring to their recommendations. With high-level individuals from different parts of the world participating in deliberations, lending their names to its report, and, in many cases, advocating adoption of a commission's recommendations, they combine "knowledge with political punch and access to decisionmakers." Thus, independent commissions have been a major factor in "nourishing ideas"—a major contribution of the UN overall. They have also been important vehicles for the prominent participants to "voice criticisms at higher decibel levels and make more controversial recommendations than when they occupied official positions."[54]

Public-Private Partnerships

Since the late 1980s, the variety of public-private partnerships involving private corporations and most UN specialized agencies, funds, and programs, including UNDP, World Bank, WHO, UNICEF, and UNEP, has mushroomed with the recognition that such partnerships can contribute to achieving internationally agreed-upon goals. UNSG Kofi Annan's Global Compact initiative was an important milestone, as was the 2002 Johannesburg World Summit on Sustainable Development, which called for the creation of Partnerships for Sustainable Development, several hundred of which have now been created. Partnerships have become a major source of funding for the UN and have influenced ideas of how development should be achieved and who should deliver it, as well as the architecture of the UN itself. Some are large, institutionalized multi-stakeholder arrangements; others are more temporary with fewer actors. Not all are about raising money, as they may also involve mobilizing corporate knowledge, personnel, and expertise to achieve policy objectives. Catia Gregoratti notes, for example, how UN-business partnerships have "refashioned not only ideas of how development should be achieved and who should deliver it but also the institutional architecture of the UN itself."[55] Such partnerships have become widespread throughout the UN system, particularly in areas of development, health, women, and children. Their functions range from advocacy, developing standards of conduct, and business development in LDCs to providing funding, goods, and services.

The UN has also entered into partnerships with foundations such as the Bill and Melinda Gates Foundation, the Howard G. Buffett Foundation, and the UN Foundation, created by Ted Turner. The Gates and Buffett foundations, for example, are funding the World Food Programme to buy surplus crops from poor farmers in Africa and Central America in order to feed WFP recipients facing hunger and starvation—a project that is intended to help developing-country farmers produce more food and sell it in some of the poorest regions of the world. The Gates Foundation has been particularly active in the health area, working with WHO, UNICEF, the Global Alliance for Vaccines and Immunization, and the Global Fund, among others, to eradicate polio, tuberculosis, and malaria, support immunization programs, fund AIDS research, fight Ebola during the 2014 epidemic, and strengthen health care delivery systems.

Partnerships with corporations and foundations enable the UN to tap financial and other resources beyond those of its member governments and form a growing aspect of the UN's role in global governance.

CONCLUSION

States remain major actors in the UN system, although their sovereignty may be eroding and their centrality may be diminished by the activism of the UN bureaucracy, NGOs, and other nonstate actors. Across the years, they have used the United Nations for foreign policy purposes and have been affected in turn by the organization's actions. With proliferating demands for UN action on security, economics, human rights, and other issues, the political will, or commitment, of member states remains a critical factor in determining whether sufficient action is taken and sufficient resources are made available. Yet ideas for what to do and resources in the field for addressing economic and social problems have increasingly come from NGOs and other nonstate actors such as public-private partnerships with corporations and foundations.

The third dilemma—the dilemma of who provides leadership—is not necessarily resolved by the wealthiest and most powerful states. As we have discussed, the United States has continued to send mixed messages about its willingness and ability to provide leadership and funding, and many view its role as waning. The willingness of China, a rising power, to exercise more leadership and responsibility for global public goods will be a major issue in coming years. The willingness of other powerful states to share financial burdens, to participate in UN peace operations, and to provide other kinds of leadership, and of middle and emerging powers to be leaders or followers is essential. Likewise, the ability and willingness of small states to support global initiatives and to fulfill their own commitments are part of the picture.

The fourth dilemma , the need for inclusiveness, is also present in the tensions surrounding the increasing role of nonstate actors. On the one hand, NGOs provide more access for civil society and potentially for members of marginalized groups. On the other hand, NGOs are not necessarily or inherently democratic and representative entities, and they lack accountability other than to their members and funders. Increased inclusion of NGOs is opposed by some states, so while they are not necessarily relegated to the backstage area of the UN, neither are they likely to displace states in the spotlight. Nevertheless, the proliferation of NGOs and other nonstate actors, the emergence of global civil society and of public-private partnerships, and the roles of the secretary-general and UN bureaucracy as actors are developments that complicate and enrich the cast of characters on the UN's stage.

NOTES

1. Thomas G. Weiss, Tatiana Carayannis, and Richard Jolly, "The 'Third' United Nations," *Global Governance* 15, no. 1 (2009): 123.

2. Margaret P. Karns and Karen A. Mingst, eds., *The United States and Multilateral Institutions: Patterns of Changing Instrumentality and Influence* (Boston: Unwin Hyman, 1990).

3. Edward C. Luck, *Mixed Messages: American Politics and International Organization, 1919–1999* (Washington, DC: Brookings Institution Press, 1999).

4. Lise Morjé Howard, "Sources of Change in United States–United Nations Relations," *Global Governance* 16, no. 4 (2010): 485.

5. Margaret P. Karns and Karen A. Mingst, "The United States as 'Deadbeat'? U.S. Policy and the UN Financial Crisis," in *Multilateralism and U.S. Foreign Policy: Ambivalent Engagement,* ed. Stewart Patrick and Shepard Forman (Boulder: Lynne Rienner, 2002), 267–294.

6. Alynna J. Lyon, *US Politics and the United Nations: A Tale of Dysfunctional Dynamics* (Boulder, CO: Lynne Rienner, 2016).

7. Frank Newport, "Americans Continue to See UN as a Poor Problem-Solver," Gallup Poll, February 2015, www.gallup.com/poll/181721/americans-continue-poor-problem-solver .aspx.

8. Andrew Kohut, "Americans: Disengaged, Feeling Less Respected, but Still See U.S. as World's Military Superpower," Pew Research Center, April 1, 2014, available at www .pewresearch.org/fact-tank/2014/04/01/americans-disengaged-feeling-less-respected-but -still-see-u-s-as-worlds-military-superpower.

9. Donald J. Puchala, "World Hegemony and the United Nations," *International Studies Review* 7, no. 4 (2005): 575.

10. Ibid., 576.

11. Gideon Rachman, "Think Again: American Decline," *Foreign Policy,* January–February 2011, 63.

12. Bruce W. Jentleson, "The John Holmes Memorial Lecture: Global Governance in a Copernican World," *Global Governance* 18, no. 2 (2012): 141.

13. Sebastian von Einsiedel, David M. Malone, and Bruno Stagno Ugarte, "Conclusion," in *The UN Security Council in the 21st Century,* ed. Sebastian von Einsiedel, David M. Malone, and Bruno Stagno Ugarte (Boulder, CO: Lynne Rienner, 2016), 831.

14. See Ken Matthews, *The Gulf Conflict and International Relations* (London: Routledge, 1993), 81.

15. Michael Grossman, "Role Theory and Foreign Policy Change: The Transformation of Russian Foreign Policy in the 1990s," *International Politics* 42, no. 3 (2005): 334–351.

16. For extensive treatment of the British position, see A. J. R. Groom and Paul Taylor, "The United Kingdom and the United Nations," in *The United Nations System and the*

Politics of Member States, ed. Chadwick F. Alger, Gene M. Lyons, and John E. Trent (Tokyo: United Nations University Press, 1995), 376–409.

17. Ann Kent, *Beyond Compliance: China, International Organizations, and Global Security* (Stanford, CA: Stanford University Press, 2007), 63.

18. Ann Kent, "China's International Socialization: The Role of International Organizations," *Global Governance* 8, no. 3 (2002): 349.

19. Jane Perlez, "Xi Jinping's U.S. Visit," *New York Times*, September 28, 2015; Michelle Nichols, "China Pledges $2 Billion to Help Poor States Meet U.N. Goals," Reuters, September 26, 2015.

20. Elizabeth C. Economy, "The Game Changer: Coping with China's Foreign Policy Revolution," *Foreign Affairs* 89, no. 6 (2010): 143.

21. Dan Levin, "China Asserts Itself in U.N. Internet Policy," *New York Times*, December 17, 2015.

22. Stewart M. Patrick, "Xi Said Yes: How China Got Engaged at the UN," *The Internationalist*, September 22, 2015, available at http://blogs.cfr.org/patrick/2015/09/22/xi-said-yes-how-china-got-engaged-at-the-un.

23. See Sadako Ogata, "Japan's Policy Towards the United Nations," in *United Nations System and the Politics of Member States*, ed. Chadwick F. Alger, Gene M. Lyons, and John E. Trent (Tokyo: United Nations University Press, 1995), 231–270. See also Reinhard Drifte, *Japan's Quest for a Permanent Security Council Seat: A Matter of Pride or Justice?* (New York: St. Martin's Press, 2000).

24. Mary N. Hampton, "Germany," in *Politics of Peacekeeping in the Post–Cold War Era*, ed. David S. Sorenson and Pia Christina Wood (London: Frank Cass, 2005), 43–44.

25. Jennifer Fraczek, "Germany's Minimalistic Role in UN Missions," Deutsche Welle, June 26, 2014.

26. Keith Krause, David Dewitt, and W. Andy Knight, "Canada, the United Nations, and the Reform of International Institutions," in *The United Nations System and the Politics of Member States*, ed. Chadwick F. Alger, Gene M. Lyons, and John E. Trent (Tokyo: United Nations University Press, 1995), 171.

27. Hugh Smith, "Australia," in *Politics of Peacekeeping in the Post–Cold War Era*, ed. David S. Sorenson and Pia Christina Wood (London: Frank Cass, 2005), 9–13.

28. Andrew F. Cooper, Richard A. Higgott, and Kim Richard Nossal, *Relocating Middle Powers: Australia and Canada in a Changing World Order* (Vancouver: University of British Columbia Press, 1993).

29. Alison Brysk, "Global Good Samaritans? Human Rights Foreign Policy in Costa Rica," *Global Governance* 11, no. 4 (2005): 445–466.

30. Quoted in Sally Morphet, "Multilateralism and the Non-Aligned Movement: What Is the Global South Doing and Where Is It Going?" *Global Governance* 10, no. 4 (2004): 533.

31. Courtney B. Smith, *Politics and Process at the United Nations: The Global Dance* (Boulder, CO: Lynne Rienner, 2006), esp. chap. 3.

32. See Teresa Whitfield, *Friends Indeed? The United Nations, Groups of Friends, and Resolution of Conflict* (Washington, DC: United States Institute of Peace Press, 2007).

33. Michael Barnett and Martha Finnemore, "The Power of Liberal International Organizations," in *Power in Global Governance*, ed. Michael Barnett and Raymond Duvall (New York: Cambridge University Press, 2005), 170, 173.

34. Michael Barnett and Martha Finnemore, *Rules for the World: International Organizations in Global Politics* (Ithaca, NY: Cornell University Press, 2004), 3.

35. Oran R. Young, *The Intermediaries: Third Parties in International Crises* (Princeton: Princeton University Press, 1967), 283.

36. Simon Chesterman, ed., *Secretary or General? The UN Secretary-General in World Politics* (Cambridge: Cambridge University Press, 2007).

37. Ibid., 284.

38. Barbara Crossette, "Kofi Annan Unsettles People, as He Believes U.N. Should Do," *New York Times,* December 31, 1999.

39. Edward C. Luck, "The Secretary-General in a Unipolar World," in *Secretary or General? The UN Secretary-General in World Politics,* ed. Simon Chesterman (Cambridge: Cambridge University Press, 2007), 202.

40. Mark Malloch Brown, "The John W. Holmes Lecture: Can the UN Be Reformed?" *Global Governance* 14, no. 1 (2008): 10.

41. Quoted in Colum Lynch, "Departing U.N. Official Calls Ban's Leadership 'Deplorable' in 50-Page Memo," *Washington Post,* July 20, 2010, A14.

42. Jonathan Tepperman, "Where Are You, Ban Ki-moon?" *New York Times,* September 24, 2013.

43. Samantha Power, *Chasing the Flame: One Man's Fight to Save the World* (New York: Penguin, 2008).

44. Manuel Frölich, "The Special Representatives of the UN Secretary-General," in *Routledge Handbook of International Organizations,* ed. Bob Reinalda (New York: Routledge, 2013), 186.

45. Barnett and Finnemore, "The Power of Liberal International Organizations," 174. The ideas in this section draw heavily from pages 171–178.

46. Barnett and Finnemore, *Rules for the World,* 151–152.

47. Ibid., 155.

48. Tamar Gutner, "When 'Doing Good' Does Not: The IMF and the Millennium Development Goals," in *Who Governs the Globe?* ed. Deborah D. Avant, Martha Finnemore, and Susan K. Sell (New York: Cambridge University Press, 2010), 266–291.

49. Weiss, Carayannis, and Jolly, "The 'Third' United Nations," 127.

50. Quoted in ibid., 132.

51. World Bank, *World Bank–Civil Society Global Policy Dialogue Forum,* Washington, DC, April 20–22, 2005, Summary Report.

52. Jonas Tallberg, Lisa Maria Dellmuth, Hans Agné, and Andreas K Duit, "NGO Influence in International Organizations: Information, Access, and Exchange," *British Journal of Political Science,* published online September 2015 and available at http://dx.doi .org/10.1017/5000712341500037x.

53. Ian Smillie and Larry Minear, *The Charity of Nations: Humanitarian Action in a Calculating World* (Bloomfield, CT: Kumarian, 2004), 38–41.

54. Weiss, Carayannis, and Jolly, "The 'Third' United Nations," 133.

55. Catia Gregoratti, "UN-Business Partnerships," in *Routledge Handbook of International Organizations,* ed. Bob Reinalda (New York: Routledge, 2013), 311.

4

꠱

Maintaining International Peace and Security

Many of today's armed conflicts are more intractable and less conducive to political resolution. Many of them result from entrenched
long-term conflict punctuated by episodic relapse into large-scale
violence. . . . A growing number of violent extremist and terrorist
groups represent a particularly malignant threat to international peace
and security. . . . [T]he Panel believes that by "uniting our strengths"
to maintain international peace and security, the United Nations can
better respond to the volatile scenarios that lie ahead.

—2015 Report of the High-Level Independent Panel on Peace Operations

War, *the* fundamental problem in international politics, has been the primary
factor motivating the creation of IGOs, from the Concert of Europe in the nineteenth century to the League of Nations and the United Nations in the twentieth
century. Despite being the most destructive century in human history, the twentieth century was also the century of creating ways to prevent wars.

The nature of wars and conflicts has changed in significant ways in the past
seventy years, and concepts of security have also evolved. Studies of war have
shown a sharp decline in interstate wars (wars between two or more states), and
none between major powers or advanced industrial countries since 1945. This
trend provoked one scholar to write, "War has almost ceased to exist."[1] Yet in
2014–2015, China's provocative actions in the South China Sea as well as Russia's
interventions in Ukraine and Syria renewed concerns about the potential for
major-power interstate conflicts.

While the number of wars between countries declined, intrastate (internal) armed conflicts rose dramatically from the mid-1950s to the mid-1990s, declined until 2005, then reversed again thereafter. This trend resulted from struggles for self-determination, such as those of the Tamils in Sri Lanka; the collapse of weak states, as in Somalia; ethnic conflicts, as in the former Yugoslavia and Rwanda; and civil wars between governments and opposition groups, such as the North-South civil war in Sudan (1983–2005) and more recently in South Sudan. Some civil wars have been internationalized, with intervention by other states in support of either the government or opposition groups, such as in the Democratic Republic of Congo (1996–2001) and Nigeria (2015–). The cross-border diffusion of armed conflict and regional actor involvement is found in a number of contemporary conflicts, including those in Syria, Libya, Yemen, and Nigeria. There is also troublesome evidence that recurrences—where conflicts terminated or became inactive for a period of time only to reignite—prevent a sustained downward trend. From a regional perspective, the Middle East and portions of Africa have seen increases in violence. Yet research also shows a decline in the onset of new conflicts, which is encouraging, and a dramatic decline in deaths from war.

Still more troubling, however, is the rapid spread of violent extremist and transnational terrorist groups using deliberately shocking violence such as beheadings; exploitation of often distorted religious symbols; skillful employment of social media and global connections for moving information, money, and weapons; and rigid demands that pose a major threat to peace and, in some cases, even the existence of states. A 2014 RAND Corporation report noted, "Since 2010, there has been a 58 percent increase in the number of jihadist groups, a doubling of jihadist fighters and a tripling of attacks by Al Qaeda affiliates."[2] These developments have introduced new and dangerous dimensions to the ways in which terrorism undermines international peace and security and, hence, to the role the UN can play. Further complicating this growing threat is the nexus of terrorism, internal conflicts, and transnational criminal activities that fuel the violence, such as in the looting of valuable resources in Eastern Congo, drug trafficking in Colombia and Afghanistan, and sale of antiquities by ISIS. As a 2011 World Bank report noted, these forms of conflict and violence do not "fit neatly either into 'war' or 'peace,' or into 'criminal violence' or 'political violence.'"[3] They have also increasingly included attacks by governments and armed groups against civilians, including appalling sexual violence against women and the forcible recruitment of children to fight.

Many post–Cold War conflicts have been accompanied by humanitarian crises, including ethnic cleansing or genocide, famine, and the deliberate targeting of civilians and humanitarian workers. The numbers of refugees and internally displaced persons have risen dramatically—and often in very short periods of time—reaching 60 million in 2015 (as discussed in Chapter 7) and overwhelming the capacity of the UN High Commissioner for Refugees. These humanitarian crises have provoked intense debates about the idea of state sovereignty as responsibility and the legitimacy of international armed intervention under UN auspices to protect human beings. The primary threats to peace and security that the UN's Charter was designed to deal with were interstate wars. Even though the majority of all conflicts since 1945 have been within states, until the Cold War's end the Security Council rarely determined that civil wars were threats to international peace and security. Since 1990, however, conflicts within states have been the council's primary focus. The UN's member states have empowered it to play a much more active role in dealing with these conflicts and with postconflict peacebuilding and statebuilding efforts, though not without many heated debates and much inconsistency in responses. Traditionally, security meant *state* security—the security of borders, control over population, and freedom from interference in the government's sovereignty over its internal affairs. With the body of internationally recognized human rights norms steadily expanding in the second half of the twentieth century, the balance between the rights of sovereign states and the rights of people began to shift. Increasingly, it was argued that *human* security should take precedence over security of governments or states. This shift has provided support for the new norm of a responsibility to protect populations at risk that encompasses both R2P and its twin, protection of civilians (POC). These emerging norms have been used to justify armed intervention to protect human beings against the violence of governments, paramilitary forces, militias, and police. Yet as Rwanda, Darfur, Libya, and Syria illustrate, the Security Council has been inconsistent in applying R2P, as further discussed below.

The changing nature of conflicts, complex humanitarian crises, and transnational terrorism are the main challenges to peace and security in the twenty-first century. Added to them is the threat of the spread of weapons of mass destruction, particularly nuclear and chemical weapons. These threats are not new, but the linkages between them are, and they present major challenges to the UN and international efforts to maintain peace and security.

LINKING INTERNATIONAL RELATIONS THEORIES

International relations theorists differ sharply in their views of the causes of war and whether and how international institutions can respond to the use of armed force and conflicts. Realists come in "hard" and "soft" varieties when dealing with threats of force, breaches of the peace, and conflict resolution. The "hard" variety hold firm to traditional realist views about states' likely use of force and the role of power struggles among states in prompting conflict. They don't see many differences between the dynamics that give rise to interstate and intrastate conflicts. Security dilemmas affect parties to both. In realists' eyes, balance-of-power politics, alliances, and force itself are key means to resolve conflicts since IGOs do not provide effective mechanisms. Should any consideration be given to intervention by a third party, only major powers have the resources to influence the parties or intervene effectively, but their incentives to do so are often limited.

The "soft" variety of realists comes closer to liberals in some respects, as they envisage a broader range of options and actors. Diplomacy and mediation are among the options "soft" realists consider valuable for dealing with conflicts and use of force, in order to change parties' cost-benefit analyses in favor of peaceful settlement versus war. They also recognize the role of IGOs as interveners.

Liberals have traditionally supported international law and organization as approaches to peace; hence, the concepts embodied in the UN Charter reflect liberal theory. They also believe that economic interdependence and the spread of democracy will reduce the incidence of armed conflicts. This so-called liberal democratic peace is a basis for contemporary postconflict peacebuilding activities. Liberals also see NGOs and IGOs, as well as individuals, states, and ad hoc groups, as among the actors that may play roles as third parties in peaceful efforts to settle disputes, stop fighting once it has started, secure a settlement, and build conditions for peace. Thus, while liberals don't oppose the use of force when necessary, they prefer to use nonmilitary means, including sanctions and diplomacy, to avert or end armed conflicts.

Since the mid-1990s, constructivism has contributed substantially to understanding the evolution and role of norms as well as to reconceptualizing security itself. Constructivists have examined how norms on the use of force and which groups should be protected have changed.[4] They have shown how norms against specific weapons, such as the taboos on the use of chemical and nuclear weapons, have evolved over time. They have traced the emergence of the R2P norm and the role of NGOs in the conventions banning land mines and cluster munitions.

Feminism also lends a distinct perspective to understanding peace and conflict. This view highlights the role of gender in violent conflict, as women and girls are often targeted victims. Feminist scholars also highlight connections between women's security, human security, and international peace and stability. This view calls for increased female recruitment in peacekeeping and peacebuilding operations and for women in leadership positions. Some feminists provide a gendered lens to creating more inclusive societies that may prevent wars and conflict in general and reject an approach to politics that reflects **militarized masculinity**.

Much of the rich recent literature on interstate and civil wars as well as on conflict resolution draws on multiple schools of thought, with no definitive theory setting forth clear conditions under which wars will occur or peace will be secured—and by whom. The contextual factors shaping human choices—the choice for war and the choice to settle a dispute peacefully—defy tidy theorizing. In short, we know a lot about both choices, but not enough to lay out a single theory to guide the maintenance of international peace and security.

MAINTAINING PEACE AND SECURITY: THE UN CHARTER AND ITS EVOLUTION

Maintaining peace and security has always been the primary purpose of the UN, but how the UN undertakes this task has changed over time in ways never envisaged by the founders. Many provisions of the Charter that lay largely unused during the forty years of the Cold War have seen far more use since 1989. Over time, the UN has also created new ways of addressing security threats and seeking to secure peace—demonstrating the flexibility of the UN Charter.

The United Nations Charter in Article 2 (sections 3, 4, and 5) obligates all members to settle disputes by peaceful means, to refrain from the threat or use of force, and to cooperate with UN-sponsored actions. This normative prohibition was a direct outgrowth of the Kellogg-Briand Pact, concluded in 1928. The use of force for territorial annexation is now widely accepted as illegitimate—witness the broad condemnation of Iraq's invasion of Kuwait in 1990 and the large number of states that contributed to the US-led multilateral effort to reverse that occupation, as well as the General Assembly's condemnation of Russia's annexation of Crimea in 2014. The use of force in self-defense against armed attack is accepted and was the basis for the Security Council's authorization of US military action after the September 2001 terrorist attacks. International norms prescribe, however, that the response must be proportional to the provocation—the basis for widespread condemnation of Israel's large-scale military responses in 2006, 2009, and 2014 to rockets fired by Hezbollah and Hamas from Lebanon and Gaza, respectively. A large majority of states accept the legitimacy of using force to promote self-determination, replace illegitimate regimes, and correct past injustices. The UN Security Council refused in 2003, however, to authorize use of force against Iraq, leading the United States to form an ad hoc coalition to remove Saddam Hussein from power. In 2011, the council did authorize "all necessary means" to stop the Libyan government from using force against its citizens. When the US and NATO military operation turned from humanitarian intervention to regime change, however, Russia, China, and a number of other countries drew lessons that have since blocked efforts to gain council approval of intervention in Syria and even efforts by the EU to use naval forces to stop trafficking of migrants in the Mediterranean. As discussed in Chapter 2, the Security Council has primary responsibility for maintenance of international peace and security (Article 24), and there continues to be a strong consensus on its authority to (de)legitimize the use of force.

Chapter VI specifies the ways in which the Security Council can promote **peaceful settlement** of disputes. For example, under Article 34, the Security Council may investigate disputes that threaten international peace and security. Throughout the Cold War years, the Security Council relied on the Charter's peaceful settlement mechanisms in responding to the many situations placed on its agenda. And, as discussed later in this chapter, when peacekeeping—peace operations with lightly armed troops to maintain a truce or cease-fire agreement—was first undertaken in the late 1940s and 1950s, it was under Chapter VI, since there is no specific provision in the Charter for this.

Chapter VII—what some would call the "teeth" of the Charter—specifies actions the UN can take with respect to threats to the peace, breaches of the peace, and acts of aggression. The Security Council can identify aggressors (Articles 39 and 40), decide what enforcement measures should be taken (Articles 41, 42, 48, and 49), and call on members to make military forces available, subject to special agreements (Articles 43–45). Because the Cold War made concurrence among the Security Council's permanent members almost impossible to achieve, Chapter VII was invoked on only two occasions during this period. Since 1989, however, the situation has changed dramatically, and Chapter VII has been invoked on many occasions to authorize the use of force and various types of sanctions by the UN alone, by a regional organization, or by a **coalition of the willing** led by a particular country such as the United States (Haiti), Australia (East Timor), and Great Britain (Sierra Leone). Today, it is common for most UN peace operations to have a mandate under Chapter VII.

Chapter VIII recognizes the rights and responsibilities of regional organizations to "make every effort to achieve peaceful settlement of local disputes" before referring them to the Security Council. When a regional organization seeks to use force, however, Security Council authorization is required to maintain the UN's primacy with respect to international enforcement. In some cases, a regional IGO has acted first and sought Security Council authority retroactively. Since 2003, NATO, the EU, and the African Union have emerged as the primary regional organizations involved in peace operations, often in partnership with the UN (and each other)—as exemplified by the AU–UN Mission in Darfur.

Because the UN's founders did not envision a major role for the UN with respect to arms control and disarmament, the UN Charter contains only two short references to this aspect of maintaining international peace and security. In Article 11, the General Assembly is authorized to consider principles governing disarmament and the regulation of armaments and may make recommendations to the Security Council or member states. In Article 26, the Security Council, with the assistance of the Military Staff Committee, which has been moribund from the beginning, is charged with formulating plans for "the establishment of a system for the regulation of armaments." Nonetheless, the advent of nuclear weapons in 1945 put disarmament and arms control on the UN's agenda, with the General Assembly's very first resolution calling for the creation of the Atomic Energy Commission to propose ways of ensuring that atomic energy was used only for peaceful purposes. Over time, the UN General Assembly has played a key role in developing arms control and disarmament norms and international law, although the most fruitful negotiations have often taken place outside the UN. Since the early 1990s, the Security Council has played an active role in efforts to deal with Iraq, Iran, and North Korea's nuclear programs, utilizing sanctions and monitoring that complement the work of the International Atomic Energy Agency, as discussed later in this chapter.

Over its history, the UN has addressed security threats in a variety of ways, utilizing the provisions of Chapters VI, VII, and VIII of the Charter, and also creating new approaches such as **preventive diplomacy** and deployment, mediation by the secretary-general, both traditional and complex peace operations, targeted sanctions, and enhanced monitoring procedures. Despite continuing concerns about its makeup, the Security Council remains the central organ dealing with threats to peace and the changing nature of those threats. Indeed, it has become much more active within the UN system since 1990. It has created ad hoc criminal tribunals to prosecute war crimes and crimes against humanity, established reporting and monitoring mechanisms to prevent the proliferation of nuclear weapons along with a variety of counterterrorism measures, condemned sexual violence and rape as tools of war, mandated gender-sensitive elements of UN activities relating to peace and security, increased attention to protection of civilians, and refined the use of various types of sanctions as tools for enforcement. These initiatives illustrate how the UN has evolved as an institution. Yet the 2015 Report of the High-Level Independent Panel on Peace Operations called attention to the need for far closer cooperation between the Security Council, UN Secretariat, and various UN agencies as well as cooperation with member states, regional organizations, civil society, and think tanks to meet the security challenges of the future.[5]

MECHANISMS FOR PEACEFUL SETTLEMENT
AND PREVENTIVE DIPLOMACY

From ancient times, there has been agreement about the desirability of settling disputes peacefully. The 1899 and 1908 Hague Conferences laid the foundations for mechanisms still in use today with the Convention for the Pacific Settlement of International Disputes. The assumption is that war is a deliberate choice for settling a dispute and that it is possible to create mechanisms that will influence actors' choices. They call for third-party roles variously labeled "good offices," "inquiry," "mediation," "conciliation," "adjudication," and "arbitration." The mechanisms were incorporated into both the League of Nations Covenant and Chapter VI of the UN Charter.

Among the peaceful settlement approaches, the UN has employed good offices and mediation led by the secretary-general, a special representative of the secretary-general, contact groups, or friends of the Secretary-General, as discussed in Chapter 3. For example, Secretary-General Javier Pérez de Cuéllar secured agreement on the Soviet Union's withdrawal from Afghanistan, and Alvaro de Soto, his special representative, mediated an end to the conflicts in Central America in the late 1980s. With the advent of more complex peace operations since 1990, SRSGs not only have been responsible for securing an end to armed conflict (a peacemaking role) but also often head peacekeeping and peacebuilding operations (coordination and managerial roles). They must engage in ongoing mediation among the parties to the conflict, troop contributors, UN agencies, regional organizations, key regional states, and NGOs involved in the postconflict environment. Most SRSGs are career UN diplomats who have both close personal relationships with the secretary-general and other high-level UN officials as well as the ability to be effective diplomats outside the UN.[6]

Adjudication and arbitration of conflicts relating to peace and security may take place in the International Court of Justice, ad hoc war crimes tribunals, the International Criminal Court, and arbitration panels. The Permanent Court of Arbitration (PCA), for example, has ruled on a number of border disputes, such as between Ethiopia and Eritrea (2002) and between northern and southern Sudan (2009). In 2015, it took on the South China Sea case brought by the Philippines against China. Several contentious ICJ cases have involved peace and security issues, among them the case concerning US intervention in Nicaragua in the 1980s and cases involving French nuclear testing in the South Pacific. The former, however, demonstrated the limitations of adjudication for dealing with peace and security issues. Despite the fact that the court found that US mining of Nicaragua's harbors, attacks on port installations, and support for the contras infringed upon the prohibition against the use of force, the United States rejected the ICJ's jurisdiction in the case, and it had little impact on the conflicts in Central America.

Preventive diplomacy, an innovative approach to peaceful settlement introduced by Secretary-General Dag Hammarskjöld in the late 1950s, is "action to prevent disputes from arising between parties, to prevent existing disputes from escalating into conflicts and to limit the spread of the latter when they occur."[7] Most often, it takes the form of diplomatic efforts, sometimes coupled with economic sanctions or arms embargoes. Preventive deployment is intended to change the calculus of parties regarding the purposes to be served by political violence and to deter them from choosing to escalate the level of conflict. The UN's deployment of 1,000 peacekeeping troops to Macedonia between late 1992 and 2001 cost $300 million, as opposed to an estimated $15 billion had the violence in other regions of the former Yugoslavia spread to Macedonia.[8] Successful preventive diplomacy depends on timeliness, which has provoked debate within the UN about early warning systems; indeed, the costs of waiting tend to be much higher than those of preventive action. Preventing conflicts is rarely easy, and opportunities are frequently missed. Since the 1990s, the International Crisis Group has emerged as an important actor providing early crisis warnings and actively helping policymakers in the UN, regional IGOs, donor countries, and countries at risk to better prevent and manage conflicts.

Political missions are at the heart of the UN's preventive activities. Composed of largely civilian international officials and experts, headed by a UN SRSG, they are charged with "fostering sustainable political settlements." Some staff may focus on human rights or legal issues; others may be constitutional experts, while still others provide technical support for managing elections. There were twenty-three such missions in the field in late 2015, ranging from a large one in Afghanistan to small ones in Nepal and Burundi. They have "a track record in helping fragile states avoid full-scale conflict—but they are typically support actors rather than the stars of conflict prevention."[9] They are also chronically underresourced.

Preventive diplomacy is widely recognized today as an area in need of greater attention. The UN *2005 World Summit Outcome* stressed the importance of preventing armed conflict, promoting a "culture of prevention," and developing "a coherent and integrated approach."[10] In Resolution 1325 (2000), the Security Council made an appeal for the greater participation of women in the prevention of conflicts and highlighted the important role of local conflict resolution approaches. In 2008, the UN created the Mediation Standby Team—something like a mobile SWAT team for preventive diplomacy, consisting of eight individuals from around the world with expertise on key issues such as cease-fires, transitional justice, constitution writing, security arrangements, and power sharing—which can deploy

within seventy-two hours to help address crises. The UN also created three regional offices for preventive diplomacy in Central Asia, West Africa, and Central
Africa, and has endeavored to strengthen the intelligence-gathering capabilities
of the Department of Peacekeeping Operations. Yet Secretary-General Ban Ki-
moon noted in 2011 that "no matter how accurate the early warning, the real test
is whether it leads to early action . . . the challenge the international community
can find hardest to meet."[11]

COLLECTIVE SECURITY, ENFORCEMENT, AND SANCTIONS

The concept of collective security was at the heart of President Woodrow Wilson's proposal for the League of Nations as an alternative to the traditional
balance-of-power politics that had frequently led to wars. Collective security is
based on the conviction that peace is indivisible and that all states share an interest in countering aggression whenever and wherever it may occur. It assumes
that potential aggressors will be deterred by the united threat of counterforce
mobilized through an international organization such as the League or the UN.
If enforcement is required, then a wide range of economic and diplomatic sanctions as well as armed force may be utilized.

Chapter VII of the UN Charter provides the legal basis for the UN's collective
security role and for enforcement decisions that bind all UN members, speci-
fying actions the UN can take with respect to threats to the peace, breaches of
the peace, and acts of aggression. Because of the P-5's veto power in the Security
Council, the UN is a limited collective security organization. Korea in 1950 and
the 1991 Gulf War in response to Iraq's invasion of Kuwait came the closest to
being collective security actions. Bosnia and Kosovo, Afghanistan, the 2003 Iraq
War, and Libya are cases that illustrate the controversies surrounding collective
security. They each involved application of Chapter VII authority, involving both
armed forces and sanctions.

Collective Security Efforts Involving Armed Force

The UN has never had the capability to undertake enforcement itself. Instead,
it authorizes member states generally, specific states, a regional organization, or
UN or non-UN peacekeeping forces to employ coercive armed force—in effect,
subcontracting to others what it cannot do itself. All but one of the actions below
have occurred since 1990. The authorization of peacekeepers to use force under
Chapter VII is discussed below in the section on complex, multidimensional
peace operations. The issues surrounding intervention in situations of humanitarian crisis—an increasingly controversial subject since the late 1990s—are discussed in the section "Humanitarian Intervention (R2P and POC): Providing

Human Security" later in this chapter. Here we look at several situations when the Security Council authorized the use of coercive armed force and two situations where authorization was sought but denied.

Korea: Authorization Given. The sanctioning of UN forces to counter the North Korean invasion of South Korea in 1950 was made possible by the temporary absence of the Soviet Union from the Security Council in protest against the UN's refusal to seat the newly established Communist government of the People's Republic of China. Thus, the UN provided the framework for legitimizing US efforts to defend the Republic of Korea and mobilizing other states' assistance. An American general was designated the UN commander, but he took orders directly from Washington. Some fifteen states contributed troops during the three-year war.

The 1991 Gulf War: Authorization Given. The end of the Cold War led many to speculate that the UN Security Council could finally function as a collective security body. The first test of that belief came with Iraq's invasion and annexation of Kuwait (a UN member state) in the summer of 1990. That triggered a period of unprecedented activity by the council. Unity among the P-5, including the Soviet Union (despite its long-standing relationship with Iraq), facilitated the passage of twelve successive resolutions during a four-month period, activating Chapter VII of the Charter. The most important of these was Resolution 678, passed in November 1990, which authorized member states "to use all necessary means" to reverse the occupation of Kuwait.

The military operation launched under the umbrella of Resolution 678 was a US-led multinational effort resembling a subcontract on behalf of the organization. US commanders did not regularly report to the secretary-general, nor did senior UN personnel participate in military decisionmaking. Coalition forces did not use the UN flag or insignia. After the fighting ceased in late February 1991, a traditional lightly armed peacekeeping force known as the United Nations Iraq-Kuwait Observer Mission (UNIKOM) was organized to monitor the demilitarized zone between Iraq and Kuwait.

The US-led military action in the Gulf coming right at the end of the Cold War was widely regarded as exemplifying a new and stronger post–Cold War UN. Yet it also came under critical scrutiny.[12] Many developing countries supported the action but were troubled by the autonomy of the US-led operation. The Gulf War marked only the beginning, however, of efforts to deal with Iraq's threats to regional peace.

Bosnia and Kosovo: Authorization Given, Authorization Denied. In 1992, the UN Security Council again invoked Chapter VII, calling on member states to "take all necessary measures" nationally or through regional organizations to facilitate delivery of humanitarian aid in war-torn Yugoslavia. Various peacemaking efforts and the UN peacekeeping force (UN Protection Force for Yugoslavia or UNPROFOR) had failed to stop the escalating fighting in Bosnia-Herzegovina, one breakaway province. The resolution authorized the creation of UN "safe areas" in six Bosnian cities and enforcement of a no-fly zone over Bosnia, removal of heavy weapons from urban centers, economic sanctions on Serbia and Montenegro, and air strikes against Bosnian Serb forces attacking the safe areas. US and European forces under NATO auspices implemented the no-fly zone over Bosnia and eventually, in 1995, conducted air strikes against Bosnian Serb positions that helped create conditions for negotiating a peace agreement. Not only was this the first time the UN had ever cooperated with a regional alliance, but it was also NATO's first-ever enforcement action.

NATO's second enforcement action occurred in the former Yugoslav province of Kosovo, where the ethnic Albanian majority sought independence. It was extremely controversial because it was not authorized by the UN Security Council. In March 1999, NATO began more than two months of aerial bombing in Kosovo and parts of former Yugoslavia itself after Yugoslav (Serbian) rejection of a negotiated settlement for Kosovo and growing evidence of ethnic cleansing. Secretary-General Kofi Annan captured the dilemma Kosovo posed when he stated, "It is indeed tragic that diplomacy has failed, but there are times when the use of force may be legitimate in the pursuit of peace. . . . [But] the Council should be involved in any decision to resort to the use of force."[13] Russia, China, and other countries loudly protested the illegality of NATO intervention, but Great Britain maintained that a Security Council resolution was not necessary when there was "overwhelming humanitarian necessity."[14] Others noted that NATO's military action worsened the humanitarian crisis by prompting a huge refugee outflow, civilian casualties of bombing, and destruction of infrastructure such as power plants and bridges on the Danube River.[15]

The NATO-led action in Kosovo brought to the fore a major issue relating to the UN's collective security and enforcement role, namely, whether and when a regional organization or individual member state, including major powers such as the United States, must obtain authorization from the Security Council to use force.

Afghanistan: Authorization Given. Within twenty-four hours of the September 11, 2001, terrorist attacks on the US, the UN Security Council approved Resolution 1368, which, among other things, recognized the US right to self-defense under Article 51. The United States interpreted the resolution as providing an international legal basis for its military action against the Taliban regime and Al Qaeda camps in Afghanistan one month later. Following the Bonn Conference establishing the Afghan Interim Authority in December 2001, Security Council Resolution 1386 authorized a British-led International Security Assistance Force (ISAF) with enforcement power under Chapter VII to help the Afghan transitional authority maintain security.

In 2003, NATO took control of ISAF, with the US continuing combat operations against Al Qaeda and the Taliban under Operation Enduring Freedom. Under UN Security Council Resolution 1776 (2007), ISAF was mandated to disarm militias, reform the justice system, train a national police force and army, provide security for elections, and combat the narcotics industry. The growth of Taliban attacks from 2006 on blurred the distinction between US-led combat operations and NATO-ISAF actions, as the latter took on more offensive operations. At its height, in early 2011, ISAF had more than 130,000 troops from forty-eight countries, with the United States, United Kingdom, Germany, and Italy contributing the bulk of the force. At the end of 2014, Afghan forces took over full responsibility for security and the ISAF mission was completed, although some US and NATO forces remained thereafter in training and support roles. Beyond its authorizing role, the UN has been involved in humanitarian assistance, human rights monitoring, organizing elections, and peacebuilding tasks in Afghanistan.

2003 Iraq War: Authorization Denied. The greatest problems regarding the legitimacy of the use of force arise when it is neither a clear case of self-defense (individual or collective) in response to an armed attack nor authorized by the Security Council. Hence, the story of US efforts to secure Security Council authorization for enforcement actions against Iraq in late 2002 and 2003 is a very different and controversial one. During that period, the United States expended a great deal of diplomatic effort in trying to muster Security Council support for a Chapter VII operation against Iraq. President George W. Bush warned Iraq that force would be used to uphold the objectives set by the Security Council unless it agreed to be peacefully disarmed of all weapons of mass destruction and accept the return of UN weapons inspectors. In November, the Security Council unanimously passed a new resolution (1441) reinforcing the inspections regime imposed after the Gulf War and giving Iraq a last opportunity to provide full information on its WMD and missile programs. Although unwilling to authorize states in advance to use force against Iraq, the council did state that lack of cooperation, lies, and omissions would constitute a material breach that could lead to action. Despite UN and IAEA reports showing that Iraq was cooperating with the inspections regime, the United States and Great Britain sought Security Council authorization in early 2003 for military action to disarm Iraq. They withdrew their draft resolution in the face of opposition from the three other P-5 members (France, Russia, and China), as well as most nonpermanent members, including Germany. As one analyst has noted, their skepticism or opposition was "not surprising, given their different interests, their different views of war, their different assessments of any threat posed by Iraq, and their stated concerns about U.S. dominance."[16]

By deciding to go to war in Iraq in March 2003 in defiance of the majority of the Security Council, however, the United States, Great Britain, and their coalition allies posed a serious challenge to the authority of the council to authorize the use of force. And because a major argument for military action involved what has been called "anticipatory self-defense"—or preventive action—the question was whether military action can be taken unilaterally in response to nonimminent threats. In short, the war in Iraq raised a host of questions of principle and practice concerning the UN's role in enforcement, including the fundamental question of the UN's relevance. Did the Security Council's failure to support the US action in Iraq illustrate the UN's ineffectiveness and confirm its waning legitimacy, especially in the face of a superpower with overwhelming military power and a willingness to pursue its own agenda without Security Council authority, as some have argued? Or did the Security Council work as its founders envisioned, not supporting UN involvement unless all the P-5 members and a majority of nonpermanent council members concurred? The debate was an intense one, with the supporters of the US position deriding the UN for its lack of follow-up to the sanctions, and opponents of the US-led war applauding the UN's stance and appreciative of the UN role in postconflict peacebuilding.[17] Yet as the debate over UN relevance raged, "the occupying powers soon realized . . . that *some* form of UN involvement was essential to help overcome the difficulties created by the occupation's lack of legitimacy and public support."[18] Hence, as in Afghanistan, the UN became involved in peacebuilding activities.

Libya: Humanitarian Intervention Authorized. The story of Security Council authorization for the use of "all necessary measures" in Libya in 2011 illustrates how attitudes can change when the consequences of enforcement action become evident. The mass demonstrations that marked the 2011 Arab Spring turned into civil war in Libya, as the eastern half of the state declared autonomy and factions in the military and government defected from the government ruled by Col. Muammar el-Qaddafi for more than forty years. Qaddafi publicly predicted "rivers of blood" and "hundreds of thousands of dead"; he threatened to use all weapons available, and he referred to the protestors as "cockroaches," the same term used by Hutus to dehumanize the Tutsi during the 1994 Rwandan genocide. Libyan delegates at the UN claimed that Qaddafi threatened, "Either I rule you or I kill you."[19] The international community feared a humanitarian crisis and the threat this posed both to Libya's people and to the large number of foreign nationals in Libya.

The UN Security Council initially imposed targeted sanctions on Libya, freezing assets, imposing an arms embargo, and referring the matter to the ICC (Resolution 1970). Citing "widespread and systematic attacks," the council stated that government actions "may amount to crimes against humanity" and that Libyan authorities had a responsibility to protect the population. Libya's own ambassador to the UN resigned. With violence mounting, the Security Council passed Resolution 1973, authorizing UN members to "to take all necessary measures" to protect civilians, establish a no-fly zone, enforce the arms embargo, and undertake air strikes and military action, short of landing troops. It was the council's first approval of enforcement of R2P. The resolution received ten affirmative votes and five abstentions (Russia, China, India, Germany, and Brazil), thanks in no small part to the support of the Organisation of Islamic Cooperation, the Gulf Cooperation Council, and the Arab League, and the fact that Qaddafi had few friends.

Like other UN-authorized operations requiring strong military assets, enforcement began with air strikes by the United States, France, Italy, Canada, and Britain designed to protect civilian supporters of the secessionists and establish a no-fly zone. NATO subsequently took over the bulk of military operations, aided by Qatar, Jordan, the United Arab Emirates, and Sweden. Yet, as the intervention dragged on in 2011, concerns even among R2P's advocates grew that it had become a justification for war. The legacy of these concerns cast a shadow on the Security Council's ability to act in the civil war and subsequent humanitarian crisis in Syria, as discussed further below.

Anti-Piracy Enforcement: Authorization Given. In a further illustration of the changing nature of security threats, piracy—an ancient problem—has become a contemporary problem. Although piracy had been a problem in Southeast Asia, particularly in waters of the Indonesian archipelago, it was brought under reasonable control through regional efforts after 2000. More than one hundred pirate attacks were launched on ships in the Gulf of Aden and off the coast of Somalia in 2008, however, significantly disrupting major shipping routes. For the first time, in December 2008, the Security Council unanimously authorized the use under Chapter VII of "all necessary means" against piracy and armed robbery at sea by states and regional and international organizations (Resolutions 1846 and 1851). NATO and EU member countries sent ships for a multinational naval task force, as did other countries, including India, Russia, Japan, South Korea, and China. The council was careful to make clear, however, that its authorization applied only to the situation in Somalia and "shall not affect the rights or obligations or responsibilities of

Member States under international law . . . [nor] be considered as establishing customary international law" (Resolution 1851). Between 2008 and early 2011, more than four hundred ships were hijacked, boarded, or fired upon by pirates operating from Somalia. As a result of both the naval enforcement and efforts to address Somalia's own problems, piracy off the Somali coast diminished by 2012, although it increased off the West African coast and elsewhere.

As the above cases illustrate, the authorization of armed force under Chapter VII has become more frequent since 1990 in a variety of circumstances and with varied purposes. The result has been a system of what one scholar describes as "selective" rather than "collective" security and a record that is "distinctly patchy." He notes that the reasons have to do with whether the council discussed a situation at all, failed to act, or could not agree on a course of action, as well as with the actual employment of forces undermined by inadequate resources, various difficulties, failures, and controversies.[20] Various types of sanctions have also become integral to the UN's enforcement efforts.

Enforcement Through Sanctions

Sanctions have long been a favorite tool in states' efforts to get others to do what they wanted them to do. Unilateral sanctions, however, have always been problematic because they do not close off alternative markets and sources of supply for the target state(s). Organizing multilateral sanctions without a multilateral forum or organization through which to reduce the diplomatic transaction costs of securing other states' cooperation is a difficult undertaking. Hence, beginning with establishment of the League of Nations, multilateral organizations significantly enhanced the potential for using sanctions as an instrument of security governance.

Until 1990, the UN had imposed mandatory sanctions under Chapter VII only twice: economic sanctions against the white minority regime in Southern Rhodesia after it unilaterally declared its independence from Great Britain in 1965, and an arms embargo on South Africa in 1977. Since 1990, sanctions have become a key enforcement instrument. Beginning with the sanctions imposed on Iraq in 1990, the UN Security Council utilized different forms of sanctions in fourteen situations over the next eleven years, leading one study to dub the 1990s "the sanctions decade."[21] Over the twenty-year period from 1992 to 2012, the council imposed sanctions in twenty-two situations. Fourteen of the cases involved peace enforcement, all but one in intrastate conflicts; four related to terrorism (Libya, Sudan, the Taliban/Al Qaeda); three related to proliferation of WMD, specifically nuclear weapons (Iraq, Iran, North Korea); four related to nonconstitutional changes in governments (Haiti, Guinea-Bissau, Côte d'Ivoire); and one related to protecting civilians under R2P (Libya). As the authors of one major project on sanctions note, "Because the affirmation of an international norm is embedded in the *signaling* aspect of every episode, sanctions function as a central mechanism for the strengthening and/or negotiation of international norms."[22]

We look first at the experience with comprehensive sanctions imposed on Iraq beginning in 1990 and then at lessons learned from that and sanctions on Angola, and at the effectiveness of targeted sanctions.

Iraq and the Problems with Comprehensive Sanctions. When Iraq invaded Kuwait in August 1990, the Security Council immediately invoked Chapter VII to condemn the invasion and demand withdrawal. Subsequent resolutions imposed economic and transport sanctions against Iraq and established a sanctions committee to monitor implementation. Following the Gulf War, on April 3, 1991, the council passed Resolution 687, enumerating terms of the cease-fire agreement and a far-reaching plan for dismantling Iraq's weapons of mass destruction. The earlier comprehensive sanctions were to continue until all the provisions were carried out to the Security Council's satisfaction. The only exception was oil sales authorized under the 1995 Oil-for-Food Programme to pay for food and medical supplies.

The Iraq sanctions became highly controversial as they produced a mounting humanitarian crisis among ordinary Iraqis (aggravated by the government's diversion of funds from the Oil-for-Food Programme). Evidence of malnutrition, contaminated water supplies, infectious disease, and high infant and child mortality rates generated widespread sympathy and calls for ending sanctions. The Iraqi government also exacerbated the crisis for political purposes and rejected international proposals to alleviate it. Over time, sanction fatigue grew among neighboring and other nations that had traditionally relied on trade with Iraq, and compliance eroded as unauthorized trade and transport links multiplied. The United States and Great Britain, however, insisted on complete compliance before the sanctions could be lifted and rejected proposals by Russia, France, and other countries to reward Iraq's cooperation and encourage further progress by partially lifting sanctions. The result was a stalemate, and Saddam Hussein had no incentive to cooperate.[23]

The sanctions were finally lifted in May 2003 following the US invasion of Iraq. In retrospect, former Canadian UN ambassador David Malone concludes, "On many levels, the Program worked: it saved many lives, it drove the disarmament process, and it prevented rearmament by keeping the lion's share of Iraq's oil wealth and imports—which could be used to produce WMD—out of the hands of Saddam Hussein. . . . [T]he Iraqi military and weapon programs had, in fact, steadily eroded under the weight of sanctions."[24] Still, the sanctions created broad resentment of the United States and its allies and may have had the unintended consequence of fueling militant Islam and anti-Western sentiments in Iraq and elsewhere.

Applying Lessons About Sanctions. Sanctions were among several approaches used by the UN in the 1990s to end a bitter civil war in Angola that began in 1974. Next to the Iraq sanctions, by 2002 the Angolan sanctions were the longest in effect. They had little impact until 1999, however, because there had been almost no monitoring to ensure compliance. That changed when an independent panel of experts was created by the Security Council to investigate sanctions violations and recommend ways to enhance compliance. By mid-2001, the monitoring group reported that arms deliveries were greatly reduced, countries were no longer providing safe havens to officials of the rebel National Union for the Total Independence of Angola (UNITA), and diamond export revenues (targeted by the sanctions) had dropped. Long considered a failure, Angola became "one of the most important developments in sanctions policy in recent years."[25]

The Security Council drew three important lessons from the experience with comprehensive sanctions on Iraq and the experience with sanctions on Angola. The first involved the large-scale negative humanitarian effects of sanctions, especially general trade sanctions. This changed many people's perception of the pain/gain trade-offs of sanctions. The second problem was that strangling a target state's economy did not necessarily impose any economic pain on government leaders or their personal wealth and resources, and prospects for compliance were low unless sanctions affected them specifically. Third, in intrastate conflicts and failed states, generalized sanctions were largely ineffective in an environment without normal governmental controls over taxation, documentation of imports and exports, or borders.

In short, a major lesson was that sanctions must be tailored to the specific situation if they are to be effective. Since 1994, no new comprehensive sanctions have been initiated by the Security Council. Instead, targeted sanctions have been used, including arms embargoes (the most common), diplomatic sanctions (suspensions from IGO membership, limiting diplomats' travel), financial sanctions (freezing assets of governments and individuals, investment bans, limits on banking services), travel bans and aviation sanctions (prohibiting international transit by air and naval carriers), and commodity sanctions (e.g., oil, timber, and diamonds) (see Table 4.1). Targeting has involved not just "what" but also "who." Targets have included entire governments, government leaders, rebel factions, terrorist groups, leaders' family members, and other select individuals. Humanitarian impact assessments are standard practice now, though they are often difficult to conduct.

The UN's extensive use of sanctions since 1990 has highlighted the challenges of making them work. Since 2000, independent expert panels have gathered data on violators, supply routes, networks, and transactions in conjunction with all UN-imposed sanctions; the Security Council has named and shamed violators by publicly identifying them. Still, as one group of scholars concludes, "smart

TABLE 4.1. Selected Types of UN Sanctions, 1990–2015

Type of Sanction	Target Country or Entity	Years
Comprehensive Sanctions	Iraq	1990–2003
	Yugoslavia	1992–1995
	Haiti	1993–1994
Arms Embargo	Iraq	1990
	Yugoslavia	1991–1996, 1998–2001
Note: "Targeted" in each of these categories indicates that the relevant UN sanctions committee maintains a list of specific individuals and entities that are targeted by the sanction.	Angola and UNITA	1993–2002
	Libya	1992–2003
	Somalia	1992–
	Afghanistan	1990–2000
	Sierra Leone (rebels only)	1998–
	Al Qaeda and Taliban	1999
	Liberia (militias)	2003–
	DRC	2003–2008
	DRC (militias)	2008–
	Côte d'Ivoire	2004–
	Sudan (militias)	2004–
	Iran	2006–
	North Korea	2006–
	Libya	2011–
	Taliban (targeted)	2011–
	ISIS & Al Nusra Front	2014–
Export or Import Limits (ban exports of selected technologies, diamonds, timber, etc., or place embargo on imports of oil, etc.)	Cambodia (timber, oil)	1992–1994
	Angola (diamonds)	1993, 1998–2002
	Sierra Leone (oil, diamonds)	1997–1998, 2000–2003
	Liberia (diamonds)	2001–2007
	Liberia (timber)	2003–2006
	Côte d'Ivoire (diamonds)	2004–
	Somalia (charcoal)	2012–
	North Korea (luxury goods)	2016–
Asset Freeze	Libya	1993–1999
	Yugoslavia	1992–1995, 1998–2000
	Angola (UNITA only)	1998–2002
	Al Qaeda/Taliban (targeted)	2000–
	DRC (militias)	2003–
	DRC (targeted)	2008–
	Côte d'Ivoire (targeted)	2004–
	Sudan (targeted)	2004–
	Lebanon (targeted)	2005–
	Iran (targeted)	2006–
	North Korea (targeted)	2006
	ISIS & Al Nusra Front	2014–
	Central African Republic	2015–
	South Sudan	2015

(continues)

TABLE 4.1.   Selected Types of UN Sanctions, 1990–2015   *(continued)*

Type of Sanction	Target Country or Entity	Years
Denial of Visas (travel bans)	Libya	1992–1999
	Angola (UNITA only)	1997–2002
	Sudan	1998–
	Al Qaeda and Taliban	1999–2001
	Al Qaeda (targeted)	2002–
	Afghanistan	2001–2003
	Liberia (targeted)	2003–
	DRC (militias)	2004–
	DRC (targeted)	2008–
	Côte d'Ivoire (targeted)	2004–
	Sudan (targeted)	2004–
	Iran (targeted)	2006–
	North Korea (targeted)	2006–
	Taliban (targeted)	2011–
	ISIS & Al Nusra Front	2014–
	South Sudan	2015–
Cancellation of Air Links	Libya	1992–1999
	Afghanistan	1999–2001

sanctions may satisfy the need . . . to 'do something,' . . . and they may serve to unify fraying coalitions and isolate a rogue regime. But they are not a magic bullet for achieving foreign policy goals."[26] Operational effectiveness is impeded by legal loopholes and lack of trained staff and adequate budgets in both the UN Secretariat and member governments, a problem exacerbated by weak border controls and corruption in many countries. Compliance by all UN members cannot be taken for granted.

One difficulty in establishing the effectiveness of targeted sanctions is determining that it was sanctions and not something else that induced compliance. Another is that each sanctions case is unique and past successes cannot predict future outcomes. Studies have shown that the success rate is higher for modest policy changes than for regime change or efforts to compel a target country to take actions it resists. Arms embargoes are among the least effective sanctions, while commodity sanctions, particularly those targeting the diamond trade, are "highly effective." Efforts to coerce a target were least successful, while those seeking to constrain or signal were much more successful.[27]

Sanctions can also have unintended consequences. They create incentives for evasion (e.g., black markets), contribute to corruption and criminality, place burdens on neighboring states, strengthen authoritarian rule, and divert resources.

Ineffective sanctions have also been shown to harm the legitimacy and authority of the Security Council itself.[28]

Nevertheless, sanctions continue to be a major tool in UN enforcement efforts. They have even been imposed on parties to the civil war in the UN's newest and arguably weakest member, South Sudan, in an effort to force compliance with a cease-fire. We examine their use in connection with efforts to address terrorism and nuclear proliferation later in the chapter.

PEACE OPERATIONS: PEACEKEEPING AND PEACEBUILDING

Although the UN has used the enforcement powers embodied in Chapter VII extensively since 1990, its conflict management role before and after 1990 has been most notable in the evolution of peacekeeping and the complex activities related to peacebuilding. Despite the debate over the UN's continuing relevance and effectiveness following the US intervention in Iraq and deep Security Council divisions, there has been a dramatic increase in UN peace operations of various types since 2003. This illustrates the continuing vitality of these approaches to conflict management.

Peacekeeping, first developed to provide observer groups for cease-fires in Kashmir and Palestine in the late 1940s, was formally proposed by Lester B. Pearson, the Canadian secretary of state for external affairs, at the height of the Suez crisis in 1956 as a means for securing the withdrawal of British, French, and Israeli forces from Egypt, pending a political settlement. Its development enabled the UN to play a positive role in dealing with regional conflicts at a time when hostility between East and West prevented the use of the Chapter VII provisions for sanctions and collective security. Since the Cold War's end, peace-keeping's use has broadened to include a variety of tasks, sometimes blurring the line with enforcement. The UN and some regional IGOs have deployed various types of peace operations to help maintain cease-fire agreements, stabilize conflict situations to create an environment conducive to peaceful settlement, help implement peace agreements, protect civilian populations at risk in humanitarian crises, and/or to assist in laying the foundations for durable peace. With more than sixty operations since 1948, the majority of them initiated since 1990, peacekeeping in various forms has become "one of the most visible symbols of the UN role in international peace and security."[29]

Distinguishing Between Enforcement and Peacekeeping

The UN traditionally defined peacekeeping as "an operation involving military personnel, but without enforcement powers, undertaken by the United Nations to help maintain or restore international peace and security in areas of conflict."[30] Since there is no Charter provision for peacekeeping, it lies in a gray zone between the peaceful settlement provisions of Chapter VI and the military enforcement provisions of Chapter VII and is sometimes referred to as "Chapter VI and a half." Some operations in the 1990s crossed that gray zone and more closely resembled enforcement, creating controversy and operational problems that we address below. Since the Cold War's end, the UN has noted, "peacekeeping has evolved from a primarily military model of observing cease-fires and the separation of forces after inter-state wars, to incorporate a complex model of many elements—military, police and civilian—working together to help lay the foundations for sustainable peace."[31] It has become common, therefore, to distinguish between traditional peacekeeping and complex, multidimensional peacekeeping and peacebuilding operations. Thus, peacekeepers' tasks have varied significantly with the Security Council mandates for different types of operations, as outlined in Box 4.1.

The key distinction between enforcement and peacekeeping lies in three principles that guide UN peacekeepers: consent of the parties to the conflict, impartiality, and use of military force only as a last resort and in self-defense or in defense of the mandate. All three have become more problematic with the development of different types of peace operations, particularly those in intrastate conflicts. In more muscular operations—that is, operations with more troops, more heavily equipped than traditional peacekeepers, and with a mandate that permits the use of force other than in self-defense—the line between peacekeeping and enforcement is clearly blurred, for in many situations there has been no peace to keep, no cease-fire to monitor, and no consent for the mission from local parties that are not states or include a failed state, such as in Somalia and the Democratic Republic of the Congo. Therefore, the resolutions for most UN peace operations now invoke Chapter VII, not only to provide the legal basis for a range of actions but also to show the council's political resolve and remind member states of their obligations under Article 25 to give effect to council decisions.

In principle, peacekeeping has numerous advantages over enforcement. First, no aggressor need be identified, so no one party to the conflict is singled out for blame—making it easier to get approval for an operation. This is also why it is important for UN peacekeepers to maintain credibility as an impartial force; otherwise, they can be perceived as favoring one or more parties and become a target themselves, as has happened in several situations since 1990, including Somalia, Bosnia, Mali, and Côte d'Ivoire.

Second, in peacekeeping, there is at least nominal consent to cooperate with peacekeepers. Yet consent is problematic with armed rebel and militia groups that operate independently, as they do in the DRC. Even having given consent, states may prohibit certain actions and impede the operation, as Eritrea did by denying UN peacekeepers permission to use helicopters and land patrols to

BOX 4.1. Types of Peace Operations Tasks

Traditional Operations

These include the following:

Observation, Monitoring, and Reporting
- cease-fires and withdrawal of forces
- investigating complaints of violations

Separation of Combatant Forces
- establish buffer zones
- use of force only for self-defense

Complex, Multidimensional Operations

The above tasks, plus many of the following:

Observation and Monitoring
- democratic elections
- human rights
- arms control

Limited Use of Force
- maintain or restore civil law and order
- disarm combatants
- demining

Humanitarian Assistance and Intervention
- open food and medical supply lines; guard supplies
- protect aid workers
- protect refugees
- create safe havens

Peacebuilding
- rebuild and train police and judiciary
- organize elections and promote civil society
- repatriate refugees

Statebuilding
- security sector reform (military and police)
- strengthen rule of law, rebuild judiciary
- reform bureaucracy, reduce corruption
- promote market-led development
- provide interim civil administration

monitor the cease-fire line with Ethiopia. Governments may call for premature withdrawal of a mission (that is, before the mandate has been fulfilled), as Egypt did in 1967. Peacekeepers may be taken hostage, as has happened in Bosnia, Sierra Leone, and the Syrian Golan Heights. In short, as one scholar has commented, "peacekeeping operations are increasingly being tested by deteriorating consent. . . . [Yet] consent should not be understood to require absolute deference to the wishes of the host government, or scaling back the more intrusive aspects of the peacebuilding agenda at the first sign of resistance."[32]

A third advantage of peacekeeping over enforcement is that most operations have required relatively small numbers of troops from contributing states, a critical factor since peacekeeping operations rely on ad hoc military units, or subcontracting to a coalition of states or regional IGOs. The size of peacekeeping forces has varied from small monitoring missions numbering fewer than 100 troops to major operations requiring 20,000 or more, such as in Cambodia, Somalia, and Bosnia in the early 1990s and the DRC and Darfur since 2004.

Who Are the UN's Peacekeepers?

Since the permanent UN military forces envisioned by the Charter (Articles 43–45) were never created, the UN has relied on ad hoc military, civilian, or police units volunteered by member states for its peacekeeping operations. During the Cold War, peacekeepers were drawn almost exclusively from the armed forces of nonpermanent members of the Security Council, often nonaligned members, small states, or middle powers such as Canada, India, Sweden, Ghana, and Nepal. With post–Cold War multidimensional operations, the majority of contingents continue to come from countries other than the P-5, and most come from countries in the global South, with the top six contributors in 2016 being Bangladesh, Pakistan, India, Rwanda, Nepal, and China. Sweden and Canada now contribute only a handful of personnel for peacekeeping. Major powers including the United States, Great Britain, France, and Russia have also contributed forces since 1990, especially to much larger peace operations. China first made personnel (civilian police) available for the stabilization mission deployed in Haiti in 2004; it ranked sixth in contributions in 2016 (more than any other P-5 member) and made a major pledge for a future standby force of 8,000, plus creating two training centers. Overall, in mid-2016, the UN had more than 104,000 troops, police, and military observers deployed in sixteen missions, with 123 member states making contributions ranging from 1 to 8,496 persons.

An important innovation in personnel followed Security Council Resolution 1325 (2000), which called for greater participation of women in peacekeeping and protection activities. As of late 2015, there were more than 4,000 women in UN peace operations overall. This represented a quadrupling of female military and police personnel since the first statistics were published in 2005, but women

PHOTOGRAPH 4.1.   Tara Yonjan, vehicle mechanic, with two of her colleagues from the Nepalese Contingent at UN Post 8-31's workshop, near Shaqra, South Lebanon, October 10, 2012

SOURCE: UN Photo 542740/Pasqual Gorriz.

still made up barely 3 percent of personnel. The impetus for adding women came both from women's NGOs' advocacy prompted by sexual violence in conflicts and from gender-based violence committed by peacekeepers themselves. Female peacekeepers serve as role models to local women, address needs of female ex-combatants, and help make the peacekeeping force more approachable to local women.[33]

It has become increasingly difficult to get states to contribute military forces (or other types of personnel) for peace operations. As a result, it is not uncommon for the number of troops and police to be significantly lower than the numbers authorized by the Security Council. For example, the joint UN-AU mission in Darfur, authorized in 2007, was still at barely 85 percent of authorized troop strength at the end of 2010. Under complex peacekeeping with the higher likelihood of casualties, many member states have been less willing to allow their troops to participate. Furthermore, some countries' units have proven more effective than others, making them more desirable. Civilian police units have proven even harder than military units to recruit for peace operations, as few states have police officers readily available or trained for international duties and situations that are likely to be very different from what they are accustomed to. And few states have women military or police to offer.

Sexual misconduct by some peacekeepers has created thorny issues for the UN Departments of Peacekeeping Operations (DPKO) and Field Support that oversee operations and for contributing states. The problem has existed at least since the 1990s, but become significantly worse with operations in the Democratic Republic of Congo and, most recently, Central African Republic. The UN declared a zero-tolerance policy in 2003 and endeavored to improve training and enforcement, but it has been hampered by the difficulties in recruiting enough troops for peacekeeping and the fact that only troop-contributing member states can discipline personnel. A panel report on the problem in late 2015 led Secretary-General Ban Ki-moon to appoint a special coordinator to improve the handling of the sexual abuse issue in early 2016, even as further reports of abuse tarnished the UN's reputation.[34] In March 2016, the Security Council passed a resolution on the subject (Resolution 2272), authorizing the UNSG to repatriate military or police units where there is credible evidence of widespread or systematic sexual exploitation; to replace all units from contributing countries that fail to take appropriate steps to address allegations; to ensure that replacement units come from countries that uphold the highest standards; and to take immediate steps to prevent future incidents, strengthen complaint procedures, and assist victims. For many countries, there are important goals to be served by peacekeeping participation. The difference between poorer countries' military salary levels and those paid by the UN makes troop contributions economically attractive. Small states such as Fiji and Nepal gain prestige, valuable training, and field experience by participating in UN peacekeeping. Canada and the Nordic countries long saw peacekeeping contributions as a way to underscore their commitment to multilateralism, as noted in Chapter 3. Brazil, Japan, and Germany's contributions, by contrast, reflect their desire to secure permanent seats on the Security Council. China's participation reflects its shifting interests and growing role as a major power in global governance. However, with the decline in peacekeepers from Western developed countries and the heavy UN reliance on personnel from African and South Asian countries, there are fears that future UN peacekeeping could be undermined if developing countries perceive that they bear an unfair burden with their personnel serving (and sometimes dying) and rich countries paying.

Regional and subregional organizations have also become involved with UN peacekeeping operations, sometimes as partners, sometimes being delegated responsibility or authorization by the Security Council, and sometimes transitioning to a UN operation. The sheer number of new operations (fifteen) that the UN undertook between 1989 and 1993 taxed its capacity. Between 1990 and

2003, two African subregional organizations, ECOWAS and the Southern African Development Community (SADC), undertook peace operations in Liberia, Sierra Leone, Guinea-Bissau, Côte d'Ivoire, Mali, the DRC, and Lesotho. The Organization of American States (OAS) was part of a joint UN operation in Haiti in 1993; NATO sent peacekeepers to Bosnia, Kosovo, and Afghanistan; and Russia and the Commonwealth of Independent States took on peacekeeping roles under UN supervision in Moldova, Georgia, and Tajikistan. By the late 1990s, there were more regional IGO peace operations than UN operations, a trend that shifted again after 2003. As discussed below, what was initially an African Union operation in Darfur became a joint UN-AU hybrid mission in 2007; the AU has also been responsible since 2007 for an operation in Somalia authorized by the Security Council.

The difficulty of recruiting adequate forces for peacekeeping has led to periodic proposals for a permanent or standby peacekeeping force and/or pledged national contingents. Few countries have stepped up. Efforts were again made at the seventieth General Assembly in 2015 with some significant commitments, including one from China, mentioned above. International peacekeeping centers have also been established in many countries and on all continents to train military, police, and civilians for these operations, which continue to range from traditional missions to complex, multidimensional ones.

Traditional Peacekeeping

All of the conflicts where traditional peacekeeping has been employed have been between states. Peacekeepers' purpose was to contain fighting and monitor a cease-fire agreement until negotiations could produce a lasting peace agreement. The peacekeepers were either unarmed or lightly armed and often stationed between hostile forces to monitor truces and troop withdrawals, provide a buffer zone, and report violations, and they were authorized to use force only in self-defense. Their size and limited capacity meant that they could not stop a party determined to mount an offensive, as Israel has repeatedly shown in attacking Lebanon despite the presence of the United Nations Interim Force in Lebanon (UNIFIL).

Kashmir and Cyprus are the sites of two long-standing traditional peacekeeping missions. In Kashmir, UN observers have monitored a cease-fire line between Indian and Pakistani forces in the disputed area of Kashmir since 1948 with little movement toward a settlement. The United Nations Force in Cyprus (UNFICYP) was established in 1964 to monitor a cease-fire between local Greek and Turkish Cypriot forces and continues to patrol a buffer zone between the two communities today. The presence of UN peacekeepers and a variety of diplomatic initiatives have failed to produce a settlement of the Cyprus conflict.

In the late 1980s, traditional peacekeepers facilitated the withdrawal of Soviet troops from Afghanistan, supervised the cease-fire in the eight-year war between Iran and Iraq, and monitored the cease-fire along the Iraq-Kuwait border after the 1991 Gulf War. The Nobel Peace Prize for 1988 was awarded to UN peacekeeping forces in recognition of their "decisive contribution toward the initiation of actual peace negotiations."

Traditional peacekeeping is still important in the Middle East, where UN forces remain in place in Lebanon and on the Syrian-Israeli border. Peacekeeping continues despite the war in Syria, though some contingents were withdrawn after suffering casualties and kidnapping. It was also used to monitor the cease-fire between Ethiopia and Eritrea (2000–2008).

Traditional peacekeeping is useful primarily where there is a cease-fire or peace agreement and a limited mandate. Most operations since 1990, however, have been complex ones with broader mandates, often with Chapter VII authorization to use "all necessary means," and a variety of tasks intended to lay the foundations for long-term stability in internal or civil conflicts. The guiding principles of peacekeeping—consent, impartiality, and limited use of force—still hold, although some situations have challenged their viability. Monitoring remains a core task for most operations.

Complex, Multidimensional Peacekeeping

The Cold War's end, the UN's successful experience with peacekeeping in the late 1980s, and its active role in responding to Iraq's invasion of Kuwait increased world leaders' enthusiasm for employing UN peacekeepers in still more missions. Peace agreements ending conflicts in Central America, southern Africa, and Southeast Asia called for new types of missions. Weak state institutions, the rise in civil wars, and complex humanitarian emergencies in the former Yugoslavia, Angola, Mozambique, Somalia, Rwanda, Congo, and Sierra Leone demanded larger, more muscular, and more complex operations. While troop contingents in such operations have engaged in observer activities characteristic of traditional operations, they have also been called on to monitor the cantonment, disarmament, and demobilization of military forces and clear land mines. Other military personnel, civilians, and police along with NGOs and UN agencies such as UNHCR, UNICEF, UNDP, and the Electoral Assistance Division (established in 1992) have been involved in restoring law and order, repatriating and resettling refugees, organizing and supervising democratic elections, monitoring and promoting human rights, and rebuilding the police and judiciary. In four cases—Namibia, Cambodia, Kosovo, and East Timor—the UN has also provided interim or transitional civil administration (see Table 4.2).

Many of these tasks are associated with the concept of postconflict **peacebuilding**—which can be defined as "external interventions that are intended to

TABLE 4.2. Complex UN Peacekeeping Operations (Representative Cases)

Country	Somalia	Cambodia	E. Timor	E. Timor	Bosnia/Croatia	DR Congo	Sudan–Darfur	DR Congo	Mali
Mission	UNOSOM II	UNTAC	UNTAET	UNMIT	UNPROFOR	MONUC	UNAMID	MONUSCO	MINUSMA
Dates	5/93–5/95	7/91–4/95	10/99–5/02	8/06–12/12	2/92–12/95	11/99–7/10	7/07–	5/10–	4/13–
Maximum Strength									
Troops	28,000	15,900	6,281		38,599	19,815	17,711	19,815	9,149
Police		3,600	1,288	1,608	803	1,229	5,109	1,270	1,058
Observers			118	19	684	760	235	760	40
Civilians	2,800	2,400	2,482	1,266	4,632	3,756	3,876	3,769	1,260
Military Liaisons				34					
Chapter VII Authority	✓		✓		✓	✓	✓	✓	✓
Military Tasks									
Monitor Cease-fire	✓	✓	✓		✓	✓	✓		✓
Peace Enforcement	✓	✓	✓		✓	✓	✓		
Disarmament	✓	✓				✓			✓
Demining	✓	✓				✓			
Refugee & Humanitarian Aid									
Refugee Return	✓	✓	✓		✓	✓			✓
Assist Civilians	✓	✓	✓		✓	✓	✓		✓
Protect Int'l Workers						✓	✓		✓
Civil Policing									
Police Retraining			✓	✓		✓		✓	
Electoral Assistance									
Monitor Elections		✓	✓	✓		✓			
Legal Affairs									
Constitution/Judicial Reform	✓		✓			✓		✓	
Human Rights Oversight		✓	✓	✓		✓	✓	✓	✓
Administrative Authority		✓	✓						

reduce the risk that a state will erupt into or return to war."[35] Of the fifty-six peacekeeping operations the UN undertook between 1988 and 2015, the majority have involved peacebuilding tasks, some of which the UN and other actors have initiated even before a conflict is fully ended. The specific contours of a peace operation whose mandate includes peacebuilding depend on the nature of the conflict situation as well as the consensus and political will among the Security Council members. Regional organizations, including ECOWAS, EU, AU, and NATO, have all been involved in these operations, often in partnership with the UN (and each other), as discussed above. The task of coordinating all the actors and activities can be a significant challenge. Typically, this falls to the special representative of the secretary-general overseeing the mission.

Short case studies of nine UN missions since 1990 show various aspects of complexity, including elements of enforcement, peacebuilding, and statebuilding. Somalia, the former Yugoslavia, the DRC, and Mali illustrate dilemmas in peacekeeping operations where there is no peace to be kept and assorted non-state parties to the conflict; Namibia and Cambodia illustrate peacebuilding missions; and Kosovo, East Timor, and South Sudan exemplify statebuilding exercises. The AU–UN Mission in Darfur (UNAMID), discussed later in the section "Humanitarian Intervention (R2P and POC): Providing Human Security," illustrates the effort to combine a regional organization's capabilities with those of the UN.

No Peace to Keep: Somalia, Former Yugoslavia, Democratic Republic of the Congo, and Mali.   *Somalia.* More than twenty years after conflicts first erupted in Somalia and the former Yugoslavia, the problems these two situations posed for UN peacekeepers still exemplify some of the major dilemmas the UN faces. In 1992, civil order had totally collapsed, and warring clans had seized control of Somalia. Widespread famine and chaos accompanied the fighting. The control of food was a vital political resource for the Somali warlords and supplies of food a currency with which to pay the mercenary militias. The Security Council was slow to react, making the assumption—consistent with the norms of traditional peacekeeping—that it needed the consent of the Somali warlords to provide humanitarian assistance. A small contingent of five hundred lightly armed Pakistani troops (the UN Operation in Somalia, or UNOSOM I) was finally deployed in August 1992 with a mandate to protect relief workers, but it was inadequate for the task at hand.

In December 1992, faced with a mounting humanitarian crisis, the Security Council authorized a large US-led military-humanitarian intervention (Unified Task Force, or UNITAF, known to the American public as Operation Restore Hope) to secure ports and airfields and to assist humanitarian relief efforts. Neither the outgoing Bush administration nor the incoming Clinton administration would agree to enlarge the mission's objectives to impose a cease-fire and disarm the factions, leading to prolonged disagreement with the UNSG about the mission.

Despite these problems, UNITAF was largely successful in achieving its humanitarian objectives, supplying food to those in need and imposing a de facto cease-fire in specific areas. In 1993, the Security Council created UNOSOM II—a larger and more heavily armed force than a traditional peacekeeping contingent but smaller than UNITAF and lacking much of the heavy equipment and airpower the United States had brought to Somalia. It was authorized to use force when disarming the factions, but the killing of first Pakistani and then American soldiers in 1993 made the UN one of the players in the Somali conflict and led to the withdrawal of the US contingent in March 1994. The UN itself withdrew in March 1995 without having helped the Somalis to establish an effective government or end their internal strife.

UNOSOM remains a controversial undertaking.[36] Its difficulties led to reluctance, especially on the part of the United States, to undertake such activities in the future. It had major implications for the UN's handling of the conflict that broke out almost simultaneously in the former Yugoslavia and of the 1994 genocide in Rwanda. The UN largely ignored the continuing problems in Somalia until 2007, when the Security Council authorized an African Union peace operation (AMISOM) to protect Somalia's transitional government and lay the foundation for transitioning to a future UN role. Instead, the Security Council enlarged AMISOM's mandate and authorized a UN support role that continues in 2016.

Former Yugoslavia/Bosnia and Herzegovina. After Yugoslavia's disintegration into five separate states in the early 1990s, the fiercest fighting was in Bosnia-Herzegovina, where Muslim Bosnians, Croats, and Serbs were heavily intermingled. Nationalist leaders of each group fueled ancient suspicions and hostilities; each group's military and paramilitary forces attempted to enlarge and ethnically cleanse its territorial holdings. The resulting war killed more than 200,000 people, produced millions of refugees, and subjected thousands to concentration camps, rape, torture, and genocide.

Between 1991 and 1996, the Security Council devoted a record number of meetings to debates over whether to intervene in the former Yugoslavia, to what end, and with what means. Initially the UN deferred to European Union diplomatic efforts to find a peaceful settlement and negotiate a cease-fire agreement. The mandate of the UNPROFOR peacekeeping mission, organized in 1992, was gradually broadened from maintaining a cease-fire in Croatia, disbanding and demilitarizing regular and paramilitary forces, and delivering humanitarian assistance to creating safe areas for refugees in Bosnia, relieving the besieged city of

Sarajevo, protecting basic human rights, and using NATO to enforce sanctions, a no-fly zone, and safe areas, as well as conducting air strikes. In short, what began as a traditional peacekeeping mission was transformed into a much more complex one involving use of force bordering on enforcement, as explained earlier. The lightly armed UN peacekeepers encountered massive and systematic violations of human rights, a situation demanding more vigorous military action, and very little interest by the parties in making peace.

By late 1992, the Security Council had invoked Chapter VII, calling on member states to "take all necessary measures," and repeatedly invoked it to expand UNPROFOR's mandate. Yet Security Council resolutions did not produce the manpower or logistical, financial, or military resources needed to fulfill the mandates. All sides interfered with relief efforts and targeted UN peacekeepers and international aid personnel. UN personnel were reluctant to use the authority given them to call for NATO air strikes. The UN "safe areas" were anything but safe for the civilians who had taken refuge in them. Srebrenica, in particular, became a humiliating defeat when UN peacekeepers failed to prevent the massacre of more than 7,000 Bosnian Muslim men and boys by Bosnian Serbs in July 1995.[37]

The UN's peacekeeping role in Bosnia and Croatia ended with the US-brokered Dayton Peace Accords of November 1995, and UN blue helmets were replaced by the NATO Implementation Force (IFOR) of 60,000 combat troops. Alongside NATO, many IGOs and NGOs have been involved since 1995 in implementing different parts of the Dayton Accords and dealing with Bosnia's extensive needs. The UN itself was charged with monitoring and reforming Bosnia's police forces— a difficult task because of the shortage of international police personnel and high levels of distrust among the three Bosnian groups.[38]

The Bosnian experience demonstrates the dangers of complex operations that require greater use of force without the political will to turn them into full-blown enforcement operations. Since the late 1990s, the UN has confronted similar challenges in a number of conflict situations, including Liberia, Sierra Leone, Côte d'Ivoire, Haiti, and the Democratic Republic of the Congo. None has been as complex or as deadly as the DRC.

Democratic Republic of the Congo: The "Infinite Crisis." The UN's involvement in the DRC exemplifies most clearly a multidimensional mission operating in a situation of internationalized civil war with multiple belligerents, continuing violence, large-scale humanitarian crisis, lootable resources to fuel the fire, and a weak, failing state. The DRC has ten times more people and fifty times more territory than Bosnia; the conflict there has been hugely violent and complex at times. The death toll since 1998 is more than 5.4 million people, making this the world's deadliest conflict since World War II. Only after more than five years

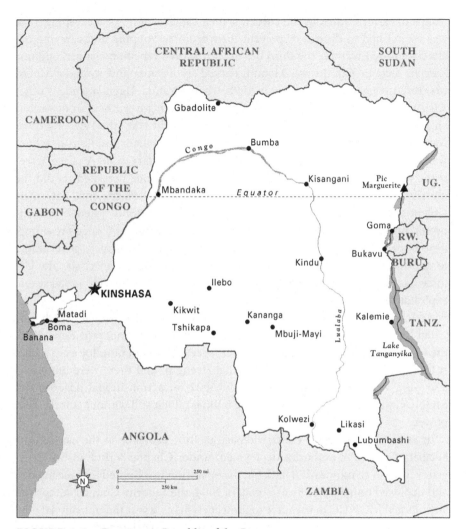

FIGURE 4.1. Democratic Republic of the Congo

of fighting (and a peace agreement) did the UN peacekeeping force there reach one-sixth the size of IFOR and receive Chapter VII authority. It has been the UN's largest operation in recent years.

Crises in the Congo have threatened international peace and security in several different periods. The first occurred when the Congo gained independence from Belgium in 1960 and civil order collapsed, leading to a four-year UN peace operation that presaged many post–Cold War complex operations and failed to create much stability. The second followed the genocide in Rwanda in 1994, when Hutu extremists responsible for the genocide fled to UN-run refugee camps in eastern Zaire, as the DRC was then called, but no peacekeeping force was established to disarm or prevent them from regrouping and carrying out attacks inside Rwanda. The third began with a 1996 rebellion against longtime Zairian dictator Col. Joseph Mobutu backed by Uganda and Rwanda. Mobutu's ouster triggered a wider war in 1998, when Rwanda, Uganda, and six other African countries intervened in support either of the government or of various antigovernment militias. Dubbed "Africa's First World War," the 1998–2002 war was incredibly complex. It was also disastrous for civilians, millions of whom were displaced and died of war-related diseases and starvation. A peace agreement was signed in late 2002, but smaller-scale violence persisted, as did the massive humanitarian crisis, with large population displacements, extremely violent systematic rapes, and collapse of the health and food systems. The economic interests of neighboring states and various militias in Congo's resources have impeded peacemaking efforts. The inability of the Congolese government to control its own troops has contributed to the humanitarian crisis. The UN force has been tarnished by failure to protect civilians and by widespread sexual exploitation and abuse by its own peacekeepers.

African countries in the SADC mediated the Lusaka Agreement, which provided the basis for the UN Organization Mission in the Democratic Republic of the Congo (MONUC) as a small observer force of 4,900 to monitor a cease-fire. It took three years, however, to reach that strength, and there were numerous cease-fire violations. With agreement in 2002 on a transitional government, MONUC was tasked to help disarm the militias, albeit still without enforcement power.

In 2003, an upsurge of ethnic violence in Ituri province in the east led the Security Council to authorize deployment under Chapter VII of an EU emergency force to reinforce MONUC, but the operation was limited to three months and deployed only in the city of Bunia. In 2004, the Security Council authorized an enlarged MONUC to use force to protect civilians, assist the transitional government, fill the security vacuum, and disarm and repatriate former armed militias, including the Rwandan Hutu *genocidaires*. In short, it took four years for MONUC's mandate to evolve from traditional peacekeeping as an observer force to a complex, multidimensional operation involving peace enforcement and protection of civilians. Still, the force was understaffed for its mission and the UN peacekeepers became targets themselves—just as in Somalia.

In 2006, with the added support of a second EU rapid-reaction force, EU funding, and MONUC's presence, the Congo held its first multiparty presidential and parliamentary elections in forty years. Remarkably, the elections were considered reasonably free and fair. To many, this appeared to signal the success of UN-led peacebuilding efforts. MONUC had also succeeded in ending the fighting between regional and national groups. Living conditions for the majority of Congolese improved, international donors increased funding for the DRC, violence against civilians disappeared, displaced persons returned to their villages, trade resumed within the country, and humanitarian organizations gained access to much of the country.[39]

Despite these signs of progress, violence persisted and, in 2008, worsened in Congo's eastern provinces, particularly North and South Kivu. The Hutu militias, various Congolese militias, the Rwandan and Ugandan governments, and the Uganda-based Lord's Resistance Army were all still active in the region. Looting of the DRC's rich natural resources continued to support the armed groups, and the humanitarian crises continued, with the worst instances of sexual violence in the world committed by militias and Congolese government troops alike.

The Security Council successively increased MONUC's size and mandate in an effort to address the persistent violence in the east and continue peacebuilding activities. In 2009, tensions with the government led to a request that the UN withdraw all peacekeeping forces by mid-2011. Under diplomatic pressure, the DRC and UN reached agreement on a smaller stabilization mission (UN Organization Stabilization Mission in the Democratic Republic of the Congo, or MONUSCO after its French name).

Still, violence and political instability persisted in the Congo. In 2012, a new rebel group, M23, backed by Rwanda and Uganda, emerged to pose serious security problems. During the fall of the city of Goma to M23, Congolese troops fled and MONUSCO forces provided little resistance (or protection for civilians). This galvanized the Security Council to impose targeted sanctions on M23; negotiate a Framework Agreement signed by the UN, AU, SADC, International Conference on the Great Lakes Region, and eleven neighboring countries; and authorize an intervention force and use of surveillance drones to monitor DRC's borders. Of these steps, the last two proved to be the most significant in the short run at least, but raised serious questions about the nature of UN peacekeeping in the longer run.

The Force Intervention Brigade, composed of 3,000 South African, Tanzanian, and Malawian crack troops with tanks and helicopter gunships, was initially deployed in mid-2013 under MONUSCO and alongside the Congolese army to demobilize and disarm the militant groups. The use of the intervention brigade has raised concerns from aid organizations about the risks to their personnel on the ground, as well as for future peacekeeping operations and the willingness of troop-contributing countries to put their soldiers at greater risk. While the Security Council was careful to make clear that the force set no precedents for "the agreed principles of peacekeeping," others see it as a "stronger approach that can give peacekeeping operations more strength in the future and help resolve knotty problems."[40] A 2014 assessment of the legal issues raised by the brigade's mandate notes that because it makes MONUSCO a party to the armed conflict, in this and other "high-threat environments" UN peacekeepers may be seen as "taking sides."[41]

This conflict is far more complex than either Somalia or Bosnia. The DRC is a weak state that continues to teeter on the brink of failure. Because it is in the heart of Africa, the conflict has implications for much of the continent but limited importance to the major powers. In addition to national and regional causes of the violence, there are long-standing local conflicts over land, the DRC's rich resources, and political power that need to be addressed. The DRC's huge size and its virtually unusable roads and railroads have presented enormous logistical and operational difficulties and required the use of more expensive air transport. The peacekeepers themselves have exacerbated the problems, failing to protect civilians from rape and abuse and engaging in corrupt practices and sexual exploits themselves (with more than 200 recorded cases since the 2000s). A culture of impunity has pervaded MONUSCO.

The Congo case underscores the Security Council's difficulty in crafting an overall strategy for dealing with complex conflicts. It also raises the difficult question of whether it is better to undertake a weak operation or none at all when there isn't the will for a robust one. A weak operation raises expectations that civilians will be protected and peace kept, but hundreds of thousands have died and thousands more have suffered rape and other major human rights abuses, despite and even because of the presence of UN peacekeepers.

Mali: When Peacekeepers Meet Terrorists. Mali exemplifies a complex operational environment where UN peacekeepers are called upon to engage in activities that come close to enforcement operations and face problems of coordination with regional organizations. Since the former French colony gained independence in 1960, the country has witnessed repeated conflicts as the Tuaregs, an ethnic group from the northern region, have campaigned for self-determination. In early 2012 this group joined forces with Al Qaeda in the Islamic Mahgreb (AQIM) and seized control of northern Mali. The group had links to transnational organized crime, and kidnappings for ransom were a major problem. In December 2012, the Security Council finally authorized an ECOWAS/AU plan for an African-led International Support Mission to Mali (AFISMA); shortly thereafter, France intervened to prevent the rebels from seizing parts of southern Mali, including the capital. In April 2013, the Security Council took the further step of authorizing the UN Multidimensional Integrated Stabilization Mission in Mali (MINUSMA) in response to growing attacks on civilians, use of child soldiers, disappearances, rape, forced marriages, and displacement of half a million people forced to flee their homes.

With the lessons of past peacekeeping failures in mind and deep concerns about involving the UN in offensive operations against the rebels or Islamist

PHOTOGRAPH 4.2. The UN Multidimensional Integrated Stabilization Mission in Mali (MINUSMA) honors peacekeepers killed during an ambush in the Timbuktu region on July 2, 2015

Source: UN Photo 637628/Marco Dormino.

groups, the council gave MINUSMA a robust Chapter VII mandate to support the establishment of government authority throughout the country, protect civilians as well as UN personnel, and pave the way for humanitarian aid. Resolution 2100 did not explicitly authorize offensive operations against the Islamic extremists, but it did authorize French troops to "use all necessary means" to support MINUSMA as it took over from the AU/ECOWAS operation.

Coordinating these different elements has been a major challenge. In 2014, the African countries formed a rapid intervention force to fight armed terrorists and criminal groups and to strengthen MINUSMA's ability to stabilize Mali. The operation has also included a multinational intelligence unit made up of Swedish and Dutch personnel. And, with the signing of a peace agreement in late 2014, Security Council Resolution 2227 added the traditional peacekeeping task of cease-fire monitoring to MINUSMA's mandate.

One analyst described MINUSMA as "a potentially flawed peace operation" and accused the Security Council of creating a peacekeeping operation with no peace to keep.[42] Others also acknowledge that this model is not ideal for addressing the threats posed by asymmetrical conflict consistent with terrorism. Indeed, the operation came at a high cost to the UN. Between April 2013 and December 2015, 56 peacekeepers were killed and 166 wounded. Targeted attacks

on UN personnel raised concerns that troop-contributing countries would reduce the number of peacekeepers they contribute and prompted discussions
about whether employing private security contractors or creating a UN guard
force was feasible and/or desirable. As in the DRC, the conflict has evolved into
a regional problem, with many groups streaming into Mali with different agendas and tactics. The UN has found regional rivalries, the lack of national and
regional consensus, and the lack of resources particularly challenging. The situation was further complicated by a hostage-taking terrorist incident in late 2015
that dramatized the limited security even in Mali's capital.

Complex Peacekeeping: "The UN at War?" The DRC and Mali raise questions
about the nature of such UN peacekeeping operations and the line between
peacekeeping and enforcement. They led one researcher to describe "the UN
at war."[43] The mandate for MINUSMA and for the combined AU, ECOWAS,
Malian, and French special forces effectively conducting war against AQIM, for
the use of drones for reconnaissance in the DRC, and for a multinational intelligence unit in Mali all amount to something much closer to enforcement
than to traditional peacekeeping. The authorization to use force also jeopardizes
the safety of peacekeepers themselves as well as UN civilian and humanitarian workers. There are, indeed, concerns within the UN Secretariat and in the
field about the implications of these developments, and there exists no consensus among member states about their desirability, and wariness among troop-
contributing countries about the risks to troops themselves.

Experiments in Peacebuilding: Namibia and Cambodia. Postconflict peacebuilding activities have been part of most complex, multidimensional UN peace
operations since the Cold War's end, typically involving a variety of UN agencies
and other IGOs as well as NGOs. Secretary-General Boutros Boutros-Ghali put
forward the concept in *An Agenda for Peace* (1992), but the roots lie in the UN's
role in the process of decolonization in the 1950s and 1960s. The core ideas involve preventing renewed hostilities and aiding countries in building the foundations for long-term stability, including democratic polities. When the UN first
undertook some of these tasks, however, there were serious questions regarding
its authority for doing so, given Article 2(7) of the UN Charter—the demarca-
tion between states' sovereignty and UN authority. In a short period at the beginning of the 1990s, however, the Security Council authorized several missions
that crossed the line, and the Security Council's endorsement of *An Agenda for
Peace* marked their acceptance. There are often long lists of military and civilian
tasks associated with peacebuilding operations, as both Box 4.1 and Table 4.2
illustrate, underscoring the complexity and multidimensionality of many missions. In some situations, the UN has gone beyond peacebuilding to activities

PHOTOGRAPH 4.3. Senegalese police officers serving with the UN Multidimensional Integrated Stabilization Mission in Mali (MINUSMA), patrolling the streets of the city of Gao, Mali, November 28, 2015
SOURCE: UN Photo 559898/Marco Dormino.

associated with actual statebuilding—that is, working with local actors to create the foundations and institutions of a government. We look briefly at five missions the UN has undertaken—in Namibia, Cambodia, Kosovo, East Timor, and South Sudan—to illustrate the peacebuilding and statebuilding aspects of contemporary peacekeeping.

Namibia. A former German colony (South West Africa) that was administered by South Africa as a League of Nations mandate after World War I, Namibia became the object of intense international efforts through the UN to secure its independence. In the late 1970s, the Security Council approved a plan setting the terms for this with the approval of South Africa and the main Namibian liberation group. Implementation stalled, however, for a decade until there was agreement on the withdrawal of both Cuban and South African troops from neighboring Angola. The UN Transition Assistance Group (UNTAG) in Namibia, deployed in April 1989, had the most ambitious and diverse mandate of any UN mission to that time. It included the supervision of the cease-fire between South African and rebel forces (known as the South West Africa People's Organization, or SWAPO), monitoring the withdrawal of South African forces from Namibia and the confinement of SWAPO forces to a series of bases, supervising the civil police force, securing the repeal of discriminatory and restrictive legislation, arranging for the release of political prisoners and the return of exiles, and creating conditions for free and fair elections, which were subsequently conducted by South Africa under UN supervision. With military and civilian personnel provided by 109 countries, UNTAG played a vital role in managing the process by which Namibia moved step by step from war to a cease-fire, full independence, and political stability. This success led the UN to undertake other multidimensional peacebuilding missions, not all of which enjoyed the same success. Among them was the Cambodian peace operation.

Cambodia. In 1991, following the twenty-year civil war in Cambodia, the Agreements on a Comprehensive Political Settlement of the Cambodia Conflict were signed in Paris with US, Soviet, Chinese, and Vietnamese support. In essence, the agreements "charged the UN—for the first time in its history—with the political and economic restructuring of a member state as part of the building of peace under which the parties were to institutionalize their reconciliation."[44]

The UN Transition Authority in Cambodia (UNTAC) deployed in 1992 with a mandate calling for up to 22,000 military and civilian personnel. Its military component was charged with supervising the cease-fire and disarming and demobilizing forces. Civilian personnel had responsibility for Cambodia's foreign affairs, defense, finance, and public security over an eighteen-month transition period. UN personnel also monitored the police, promoted respect for human rights, assisted in the return of 370,000 Cambodian refugees from camps in Thailand, organized the 1993 elections that returned civil authority to Cambodians, and rehabilitated basic infrastructure and public utilities. According to then Secretary-General Boutros-Ghali, "Nothing the UN has ever done can match this operation."[45]

UNTAC helped end the civil war and bring a peace of sorts to most of the country, although it was unable to achieve a complete cease-fire, demobilize all forces, or complete its civil mission. Cambodia, therefore, illustrates the difficulty of carrying out all aspects of a complex peacekeeping and peacebuilding mission. The UN conducted a successful election in 1993, but Cambodia was not a stable state, as UNTAC's mandate had not included building an effective legal system and constitutional process or promoting economic development.

The UN and Statebuilding. The UN undertook still more extensive statebuilding responsibilities in Kosovo, East Timor, and South Sudan. In neither Kosovo nor East Timor, however, was there a prior peace agreement or an existing state; both were provinces of other countries (Yugoslavia and Indonesia); both involved the use of force by a coalition of the willing—the United States and NATO for Kosovo and a UN-authorized Australian-led force for East Timor. In the case of Kosovo, its international legal status was among the questions to be determined. In South Sudan, a new state quickly collapsed in violence despite the UN presence.

Kosovo. Following NATO bombing of Serbia and intervention to protect Albanian Kosovars in 1999 from ethnic cleansing by Serbian-Yugoslav military forces, the Security Council authorized the UN Mission in Kosovo (UNMIK) to undertake wide-ranging civilian administrative functions in conjunction with a NATO peacekeeping force (known as KFOR). These duties included maintaining civil law and order, aiding the return of refugees, coordinating humanitarian relief, supporting the reconstruction of key infrastructure, promoting Kosovo's autonomy and self-government, and helping determine Kosovo's future legal status. The UN SRSG coordinated the work of several non-UN organizations, among which various functions were divided. The UN itself had chief responsibility for police, justice, and civil administration.

Among the problems the Kosovo mission faced was the Albanian Kosovars' desire for independent statehood, since the mandate called for the respect of Yugoslavia's (now Serbia's) sovereignty and the protection of Serbs living in Kosovo. When and how could the UN's interim administration end, since Serbia, supported by Russia and others, vigorously opposed independence? A second problem was the difficulty of recruiting adequate numbers of police for UNMIK. Third, the partner organizations had different objectives and cultures, and the UN had no authority to impose coordination. Fourth, the economy became extensively criminalized, with little done by UNMIK to curb transnational drug, organ, and human trafficking. Over time, Kosovars also complained that "the quality of the UN international staff has declined and is constituted primarily of nationals from countries less democratic than Kosovo."[46] All these difficulties contributed to skepticism about the outcome of this effort at statebuilding.

In February 2008, the Kosovo Provisional Self-Government declared the country's independence. Despite recognition from 108 UN members, including the United States and many EU members, and an ICJ advisory opinion in 2010 declaring that Kosovo's independence was not a violation of international law, Kosovo remains in limbo. NATO still maintains troops there, and UNMIK, along with the UN SRSG, still holds executive authority. It is unclear when and how the situation will be resolved and the UN's statebuilding role will be terminated.

East Timor. The UN statebuilding effort in East Timor (now Timor-Leste) also began in 1999. Unlike Kosovo, the UN's charge was unequivocal in East Timor: to lead the territory to statehood. The UN peace operation followed almost fifteen years of diplomatic efforts to resolve the status of East Timor—a former Portuguese colony seized by Indonesia in the mid-1970s. Violence had broken out, Indonesian troops failed to restore order, and almost a half million East Timorese were displaced. The Security Council initially authorized Australia to lead a multilateral force to restore order, then created the UN Transitional Administration in East Timor (UNTAET) with a mandate to exercise all judicial, legislative, and executive powers to assist in the development of civil and social services, provide security, ensure the delivery of humanitarian aid, promote sustainable development, and build the foundation for stable liberal democracy. As in Kosovo, the UN's role involved collaboration with other IGOs as well as with NGOs. There was no road map to follow. Indonesian-backed militias had wrought total destruction, and all civilian administrators had left. Sergio Vieira de Mello, the SRSG who went to East Timor from Kosovo, noted, "We had to feel our way, somewhat blindly, towards [the two-phased strategy of devolving executive power] wasting several months in doing."[47]

Despite Timorese complaints of delay and insufficient empowerment, elections were held in 2002 and an independent Timor-Leste recognized. A small UN operation continued to provide support for stability, democracy, justice, law enforcement, and external security until 2005, when it was terminated despite Timor's lack of economic development and still shaky political institutions. With riots and renewed political instability in 2006, it was a "failed state in the making."[48] The Security Council authorized the new UN Integrated Mission in Timor (UNMIT) to support the state and relevant institutions to ensure stability and security. In 2012, following a two-year transition process that included national elections, the formation of a new government, and work with the parliament, civil society, and the media to create a resilient state, UNMIT terminated its mission. As this case shows, if a statebuilding process is flawed, ends too quickly, or lacks sufficient resources, further international involvement may well be required.

South Sudan. The challenges of statebuilding are even more evident in the Republic of South Sudan, which gained independence following the 2005 Comprehensive Peace Agreement ending the Sudan's long-running civil war and the resulting 2011 referendum in the south. It came into existence, however, with unresolved disputes with Sudan over borders and division of oil revenues, little infrastructure, and few government institutions. The UN Mission in South Sudan (UNMISS) authorized by the Security Council in July 2011 (Resolution 1996) is tasked with supporting the development of state institutions and has a Chapter VII mandate to use force to protect civilians. The DPKO, however, had great difficulty securing commitments for troops and equipment, especially much needed helicopters, for UNMISS. A separate UN Interim Security Force was authorized for Abyei—a territory claimed by both Sudan and South Sudan.

Little more than two years after independence, the new country descended into civil war as a result of splits between the president, Salva Kiir, and his vice president, Riek Machar. By early 2014, more than 1 million people had been displaced and more than 10,000 killed; ethnic cleansing bordering on genocide between Dinka and Nuer elements accompanied great brutality in killing; tens of thousands of people took refuge within UN bases, yet the bases and UN peacekeepers were also attacked by heavily armed militias. The enormous humanitarian crisis includes the threat of widespread famine. In 2015, the Security Council withheld targeted sanctions to encourage the parties to honor the cease-fire agreement reached in late August. Still, by late 2015, it remained to be seen whether the civil war was truly ended and, if so, what role the UN would undertake going forward.

In many respects, the situation in South Sudan resembles that in the DRC far more than the cases of Namibia, Cambodia, Kosovo, or East Timor. It is perhaps instructive that there was no desire to create a transitional administration or international authority in South Sudan. As the International Crisis Group report of April 2014 noted, "The country needs fundamental reworking of the governance agreement between and within elites and communities if a negotiated settlement is to lead to a sustainable peace."[49]

Evaluating Success and Failure in Peacekeeping and Peacebuilding

What defines success in peacekeeping and peacebuilding? An end to fighting? A political solution in the form of a peace agreement? A period of years (two, five, ten?) without renewed violence? The establishment of a functioning government? The successful holding of free elections? A democratic state? The completion of a mandate? Because the mandates of missions differ significantly, the answer must be linked to the mandates. Yet, the various stakeholders in peace operations may well have different standards for judging success.[50] The local population may define success in terms of returning to their homes; troop-contributing states may see success in terms of mission termination; the Secretariat may link it to mandate completion (e.g., elections held); the Security Council may define it in terms of long-term stability. And in complex missions, there may be elements of both success and failure.

With respect to interstate wars, there is strong evidence that traditional peacekeeping missions reduce the risk of another war.[51] The first UN Emergency Force averted war between the Arab states and Israel for eleven years, and the UN Force in Cyprus has averted overt hostilities between the Greek and Turkish communities on Cyprus, although it could not prevent the 1974 invasion by Turkish forces. There has been no renewal of hostilities either between Iraq and Iran or between Iraq and Kuwait, and for years UN monitors' presence has helped India and Pakistan to avoid war and contain intermittent hostilities along the line of control in disputed Kashmir. These experiences demonstrate, however, that having international monitors for a truce does not necessarily resolve the underlying conflict. Fighting may resume, even with UN monitors in place, especially as the UN has historically been reluctant to condemn states for violations for fear of jeopardizing its impartiality. "This unfortunately undermined the organization's ability to use the spotlight of international attention to help maintain peace," noted one scholar.[52]

The majority of UN peace operations since 1990 have been multidimensional missions. Research shows that such operations have reduced the risk of war by half, whereas enforcement missions have been more associated with unstable peace.[53] Yet there is a disturbing rate of conflict recurrence within five years, despite negotiated agreements and the presence of peacekeepers.[54]

Precisely because complex peacekeeping missions combine different types of tasks, the assessment of these operations may be mixed. In Somalia, UN and US forces were successful in achieving the humanitarian tasks but failed in the pacification and nation-building tasks. Cambodia is regarded as a short-run success with longer-term mixed reviews. Likewise, Timor-Leste achieved independence, but the UN left too soon, had to return, and the long-term prognosis is uncertain. The long-term outcome also remains in doubt in the DRC, Mali, Central African Republic, Darfur, and South Sudan. Some tasks such as arms control verification, human rights monitoring, and election supervision tend to be successful because they resemble traditional peacekeeping, are generally linked to a peace agreement and, hence, involve consent of the parties. Alex Bellamy and Paul Williams, for example, found that the UN operation in Côte d'Ivoire had qualified success in limiting and containing violence and some success with regard to democratization, but failed to promote disarmament, demobilization, and reintegration.[55]

Studies of various types of peace operations have yielded many insights into the situational difficulties that can affect success and failure, particularly in civil wars. These include factors relating to the conflict itself and factors relating to the mission. Clearly, the desire of combatants for peace makes a huge difference, along with their consent and cooperation with the mission. The number and coherence of belligerents, the deadliness of the conflict, the roles of neighboring states, the presence of spoilers, a coerced peace, and the availability of lootable natural resources such as diamonds, timber, and oil can affect the outcome of peace operations. As one scholar has observed, "If peacekeepers tend to deploy only to relatively easy cases . . . [s]uch a policy would help the UN and the international community to avoid embarrassing failures, but . . . it will also ensure the irrelevance of peacekeeping." In fact, peacekeepers are more likely to be deployed after wars that end in a stalemate, especially long wars, and where there are three or more parties; they are less likely to be where access to primary commodities is at stake.[56] It is noteworthy that more than half of all UN peace operations have been in Africa, including nine of the sixteen missions in 2015.

With regard to the mission, the political will of UN member states to make necessary resources available (including sufficient forces and authority to use them) is key. The difficulty of a peace operation's mission as well as the clarity and feasibility of the mandate set forth in one or more Security Council resolutions are important variables. So are the leadership, command structure, and quality of personnel, including the energy, skill, and improvisational ability of the SRSG heading the mission. Studies have also shown that learning and adaptation by UN personnel both in the field and at UN headquarters in New York make a critical difference.[57] The timing of both deployment and withdrawal is critical. Many critiques of the Cambodian mission note the long delay in deployment, for example, reflecting the UN's average deployment timetable of four to six months during the 1990s. The Brahimi Report on UN peace operations in 2000 concluded that the first twelve weeks after a cease-fire or agreement were key.[58] After that, peace may begin to unravel and the parties may lose confidence in the process. With improved military planning following that report, the UN succeeded in deploying approximately 6,000 troops to each of four operations in Burundi, Haiti, Eastern Congo, and Côte d'Ivoire within a few weeks in 2004. But in 2011, it took months to assemble the personnel for UNMISS.

In multidimensional operations, other factors in success include the demobilization and demilitarization of soldiers; the wide deployment of police monitors along with police and judicial reform; the extensive training of election monitors; gender training for peacekeeping troops, appointment of women protection advisers in missions where sexual violence has been a feature of the conflict, and the deployment of women peacekeepers; and, most critically, continuous political support.

Research on peace operations in difficult civil wars and peacemaking efforts has shown that peacekeeping has little or no significant effect on mediation or negotiation success, while failed peacekeeping efforts have a negative effect on diplomatic initiatives in both interstate and civil wars.[59] For example, in the DRC case, the Security Council delayed establishment of MONUC until after the Lusaka Agreement was in place, with consequent large loss of civilian lives in the interim. Yet MONUC did not facilitate conclusion of a comprehensive agreement that would hold, nor was it able to stop the fighting entirely and the horrific violence against civilians. Therefore, as a recent study concludes, "It might be too much to expect those [missions in the most difficult conflicts] to make a significant difference in the behavior of implacable enemies."[60]

Success in one dimension is not necessarily followed by success in another. The results of various studies can, in fact, be confusing since they often draw on different data sources. One study found that peacebuilding efforts in more than half of the civil wars ending between 1945 and 1999 failed by either the standard of merely keeping the peace or that of no renewed fighting and improved governance when assessed two or five years afterward. They further found, however, that UN multidimensional missions significantly increased the chances for success, especially in civil wars. Another study found that 60 percent of UN peacebuilding missions between 1987 and 2007 experienced no renewed conflict within five years.[61]

Peacebuilding and statebuilding missions clearly are expensive and take time to achieve results. With regard to statebuilding, the dominant assumption has been that nation-states can be rebuilt in a relatively short time span despite the fact that nation-building historically has been a bloody and rarely, if ever, democratic process. "Fixed timelines, often designed to reassure skeptical domestic audiences in troop-contributing countries," one analyst concludes, "work only if all local parties are committed to peace and will therefore do worse if the operation leaves than if it stays."[62] Various international agencies involved in supporting statebuilding efforts all have different approaches, assumptions, and mandates. A recent study notes that "the weight of the evidence is increasingly pointing to the conclusion that, if democracy is the measure of a successful outcome, peacebuilding has a poor track record." Local conditions may be favorable or unfavorable, and the outcomes may be a mixture of liberal and illiberal outcomes.[63]

In short, there is no formula for peacebuilding and statebuilding. Each situation is unique and requires getting the implementation environment right. The UN and other international actors involved in such efforts have often paid insufficient attention to local dynamics and whether local actors are truly interested in the liberal democratic type of state that peacebuilders typically seek to create.[64] Drawing on extensive interviews in the DRC and Timor-Leste, one scholar has shown how divergent understandings can be. In her view, a peacebuilding mission is effective only "when a large majority of the people involved in it view it as such"—an approach that takes into account both external and local stakeholders' assessments.[65] Another scholar, too, has found that local aid recipients want more ownership of the peacebuilding process. "We do not wish to be measured and held accountable to externally developed criteria," she quotes some as saying. "We need tools we can understand and use in our own contexts . . . we want a bottom-up process; we are our own experts."[66] She concludes that the UN has been slow to learn lessons from more than sixty years of experience and that the challenge of moving away from templates and getting agreement on basic measures for peacebuilding and statebuilding is both technical and political—further testimony to the difficulty of evaluating success and failure in these peace operations.

Improving the UN's Operational Capability

Clearly, the UN itself cannot ensure that all the factors making for a successful operation are met; that depends also on the commitments of states and nonstate actors, the major powers, and participating regional organizations. Nevertheless, in response to the increased demand for peacekeeping the UN has taken a number of steps to bolster its capacity to manage a large number of complex operations and to address the difficulties and failures it has encountered. We look here briefly at two particular areas: the Departments of Peacekeeping Operations and Field Support, and the Peacebuilding Commission, created in 2006.

Improving Capacity: Departments of Peacekeeping Operations and Field Support. Major reforms of the Department of Peacekeeping Operations (DPKO) were undertaken during the 1990s, notably a 50 percent increase in staff, the addition of military staff from member states, and the addition of experts in demining, training, and civilian police. A further set of reforms followed the Report of the Panel on United Nations Peace Operations, known as the Brahimi Report for its chair, Algerian diplomat Lakhdar Brahimi. That 2000 report called for strengthening the planning and management of complex peace operations, improving the Secretariat's information-gathering and analysis capacity for conflict prevention, and increasing staff levels. Those changes were essential to prepare for more robust peacekeeping.[67] Some of its recommendations have been implemented, including the creation of strategic deployment stocks and the use of rapid-deployment teams.

Secretary-General Ban Ki-moon restructured DPKO again in 2007, creating a separate Department of Field Support; the two departments then embarked on an ongoing reform process to improve the planning, management, and conduct of UN peacekeeping operations. A 2015 report, however, noted that "Secretariat departments and United Nations agencies, funds and programs struggle to integrate their efforts in the face of competing pressures, at times contradictory messages and different funding sources. United Nations bureaucratic systems configured for a headquarters environment limit the speed, mobility, and agility of response in the field." It called for "an awakening" at UN headquarters to the "distinct and important needs of field missions," including a restructuring of the Secretariat peace and security architecture, creation of a new deputy secretary-general position, and establishment of analysis and planning capacity to support peace operations.[68]

In 2014 Ban Ki-moon commissioned a High-Level Independent Panel on Peace Operations. It highlighted the successes of close to forty missions and noted the adaptability of the peacekeeping approach over several decades. It found several areas in need of reform. One persistent issue is force capacity and the ability to respond quickly. Beyond this, the report called for "four essential shifts." First, it recommended that the DPKO make political solutions the center-piece of engagement. Second, it identified a need for a more integrated approach, with "sequenced and prioritized mandates" and an incremental approach to mission development. Third, the report highlighted the need for a "more inclusive peace and security partnership" through strengthened global and regional partnerships as well as integration with local governments and communities. Fourth, it called for more overall accountability, inclusiveness, and oversight. The panel strongly warned about the UN's venture into fighting terrorism and moving away from strict neutrality, stating, "The Panel believes that United Nations troops should not undertake military counter-terrorism operations. Extreme caution should guide the mandating of enforcement tasks to degrade, neutralize or defeat a designated enemy. Such operations should be exceptional, time-limited and undertaken with full awareness of the risks and responsibilities for the United Nations mission as a whole."[69] Finally, the report acknowledged a "credibility gap" as increasing expectation of UN abilities meets increased challenges on the ground and issues with capacities. In September 2015, the secretary-general initiated more reform efforts, including the development of "light teams" consisting of several experts that could mobilize quickly and integrate security, development, and human rights components in a conflict-specific approach.

Improving Support for Peacebuilding: The Peacebuilding Commission (PBC). The PBC is composed of thirty-one UN member states, including the P-5, top providers of financial aid, military personnel, civilian police, relevant regional organizations, the World Bank, IMF, regional banks, and relevant UN staff. It serves as an intergovernmental advisory body to marshal resources and advise on strategies for reconstruction, institution-building, and sustainable development. It was established following the World Summit in 2005 to provide sustained oversight and coordination of peacebuilding missions—more oversight than the Security Council was able to provide, given the extended time frames, complex mandates, and variety of actors involved in such missions. It forms what are known as "country-specific configurations" for each of the countries in which it is involved and is complemented by the Peacebuilding Fund, financed by voluntary contributions and a small Peacebuilding Support Office (PBSO) within the UN Secretariat.

The first two countries referred to the PBC by the Security Council were Burundi and Sierra Leone; subsequently, the Central African Republic, Liberia, and Guinea-Bissau were added. In each of the countries, consultations between the PBC and government identify critical areas for consolidating peace, such as strengthening the rule of law, security sector reform, promoting good governance and youth employment, and specific projects for funding by the Peacebuilding Fund and international and national donors. The fund also supports projects in non-PBC countries to avert the risk of relapse into conflict, help implement peace agreements, or strengthen peacebuilding efforts.

In 2015, the PBC underwent the first part of an extensive review, which found that peacebuilding is often an afterthought and continues to be conceived as a postconflict activity rather than as a set of activities that can take place during any phase of the conflict cycle. The relapse of conflict is a by-product of this neglect and has great human and financial cost. The report introduced the idea of "sustaining peace" and identified several pillars of peace, which include not only quieting the guns but also integrating human rights and development. It found that states were both the cause of some UN failures and the source of certain solutions. It also highlighted the need for better financing and longer-term commitments to conflict situations and called for a more integrated approach within the UN itself with public and private actors, as well as domestic, regional, and international actors sharing responsibility.[70]

Whether the PBC truly improves the UN's ability to build on the lessons of the complex operations to create and sustain more integrated missions remains to be seen. Of the first countries on the PBC's agenda, only Liberia has remained free of political violence since its civil war ended in 2003, and it had a UN peacekeeping mission deployed across the country at the time it was placed on the PBC's agenda. There has been considerable disappointment on the resource-mobilization side, as increased fund-raising capacity has been a major reason for countries to seek to be on the PBC's agenda. Sierra Leone has benefited from major World Bank and EU investments in youth unemployment and energy in addition to African Development Bank (AfDB), UN, and UK funding. PBC work in Guinea-Bissau was halted after the 2012 coup, and fund-raising for the Central African Republic failed to obtain pledges in 2009 and was halted in 2012.[71] Burundi experienced a failed coup in 2015 and considerable violence.

Many complex peacekeeping operations since 1990 have also involved major humanitarian emergencies. Calls for international responses to human suffering, despite the long-standing norm of noninterference in states' domestic affairs, triggered debate about an emerging norm of humanitarian intervention based on the evolution of humanitarian and human rights norms, the new concept of a "responsibility to protect," and the emerging concept of "human security."

HUMANITARIAN INTERVENTION (R2P AND POC): PROVIDING HUMAN SECURITY

Horrific as some earlier twentieth-century conflicts had been, many post–Cold War conflicts were marked by large-scale humanitarian disasters: displaced populations, refugees, mass starvation, deliberate targeting of civilians, rape as a tool of ethnic cleansing, widespread abuses of human rights, and even genocide. An estimated 35 million people faced humanitarian crises during the 1990s alone. UN peace operations and agencies such as the UNHCR and OCHA have been challenged as never before. The very fact that the Security Council repeatedly referred to humanitarian crises as threats to international peace and security under Chapter VII marked a sea change: during the Cold War, not one council resolution had mentioned humanitarian intervention.

While the UN Charter precludes the United Nations from intervening in matters within states' domestic jurisdiction (Article 2, section 7), the once-rigid distinction between domestic and international issues has weakened and humanitarian crises resulting from both interstate and civil wars have come to be viewed as justifications for UN action. The UN's responses, however, have been inconsistent and selective. In April 1991, after the Gulf War's end, Western powers created safe havens and no-fly zones to protect Iraqi Kurds in northern Iraq and Shiites in the south, but did not seek UN authorization for those actions. The UN's intervention in Somalia was initiated for humanitarian reasons, as was NATO's in Kosovo. Other interventions motivated in part by humanitarian crises included Haiti, Bosnia, Sierra Leone, East Timor, and DRC. Varying great-power interests and political will in the Security Council, as well as selective media and NGO attention, all play a role in determining which situations get attention. Rwanda still offers the most striking example of UN failure.

Rwanda: A Failure of Political Will

The UN was still engaged in Somalia when humanitarian disaster on a massive scale erupted in Rwanda. In April 1994, following the death of President Juvenal Habyarimana (a Hutu) in a mysterious plane crash, Hutu extremists in the Rwandan military and police began slaughtering the minority Tutsi as well as moderate Hutus. In a ten-week period, more than 800,000 men, women, and children were killed out of a total Rwandan population of 7 million. When the Tutsi-dominated Rwandan Patriotic Front (RPF) seized the capital, Kigali, approximately 2 million Rwandans fled their homes in the largest and most rapid migration of the twentieth century. Media reports led to a public outcry to "do something." Yet the UN's experience in Somalia produced a pattern of paralysis, halfhearted action, and then belated intervention, spearheaded by France.

The roots of the Rwandan conflict between the Hutu and the Tutsi go back to colonial times, when first German and then Belgian rulers favored the minority Tutsi over the majority Hutu. Periodic outbreaks of devastating ethnic violence gave way to open fighting in 1990 between the Hutu-dominated government and the RPF, based in neighboring Uganda. A 1993 peace agreement led to establishment of the UN Assistance Mission in Rwanda (UNAMIR) to monitor the cease-fire and investigate allegations of noncompliance. Initially, the UN Secretariat saw the violence in April 1994 as a renewal of civil war.[72] Despite the reports of massacres and pleas from the UN commander for reinforcements, in a bizarre move the Security Council voted to reduce UNAMIR's strength from 2,539 troops to 270. Four weeks later, responding to public pressure for action and finally acknowledging the genocide taking place, the council voted to deploy 5,500 troops to protect civilians and to deliver humanitarian aid. Few countries were willing to volunteer troops, however, and the human tragedy mounted, as is graphically shown in the film *Hotel Rwanda*.

Ten weeks after the massacres began, the Security Council finally invoked Chapter VII to authorize member states (led by France) to mount a temporary operation in Rwanda and pave the way for a reconstituted UNAMIR. Only then, under an onslaught of media coverage, did the United States finally send in personnel, supplies, and equipment to aid the refugees (but not the victims of genocide within Rwanda). UNAMIR belatedly established a humanitarian protection zone in southeastern Rwanda in an attempt to ensure the safety of threatened civilians. It provided security for relief supply depots and escorts for aid convoys. Its personnel restored roads, bridges, power supplies, and other infrastructure destroyed by the civil war. The mission ended in April 1996, not because peace had been restored or humanitarian needs fulfilled but because the new (Tutsi-led) government requested the departure of UN troops.

Earlier action by the Security Council almost certainly would have reduced the scale of genocide in Rwanda. The Independent Inquiry on Rwanda reported that "the responsibility for the failings of the United Nations to prevent and stop the genocide in Rwanda lies with a number of different actors, in particular the Secretary-General [then Boutros Boutros-Ghali], the Secretariat [in which Annan was head of the Department of Peacekeeping Operations at the time], the Security Council, UNAMIR and the broader membership of the United Nations."[73] All agreed that "never again" would they fail to respond to genocide.

The Origins of R2P

As Rwanda illustrated, force may be the only way to halt genocide, ethnic cleansing, and other crimes against humanity. Given their colonial experiences, however, many Asian and African countries are skeptical about altruistic claims by Western countries. Along with Russia and China, they have insisted on Security Council authorization as a prerequisite for intervention. The controversy over NATO's intervention in Kosovo in 1999 without Security Council authorization led Secretary-General Kofi Annan to call for a new international consensus on how to approach the issues of humanitarian intervention. In response, the government of Canada along with major foundations created the International Commission on Intervention and State Sovereignty to examine the legal, moral, operational, and political questions relating to humanitarian intervention. Its 2001 report endorsed the "responsibility to protect" and set forth criteria for military intervention dealing with right authority, just cause, right intention, last resort, proportionate means, and reasonable prospects.[74] Annan himself vowed in accepting the report, "Of all my aims as Secretary-General, there is none to which I feel more deeply committed than that of enabling the United Nations never again to fail in protecting a civilian population from genocide or mass slaughter."[75]

A key part of R2P that is often overlooked is that it does not just or primarily concern military intervention. As one member of the International Commission has commented more recently, "R2P is about a whole continuum of reaction from diplomatic persuasion, to pressure, to non-military measures like sanctions and International Criminal Court process, and only in extreme, exceptional and last resort cases military action."[76] States have primary responsibility to protect their own people; only if they fail to do so does the UN have responsibility for acting under the Charter. The World Summit in 2005 endorsed R2P, and in 2006, the Security Council approved Resolution 1674, which called for the protection of civilians in armed conflict. Altogether, between 2006 and late 2015, the Security Council approved thirty-nine resolutions referring to R2P and/or POC.

Darfur: Testing "Never Again" and R2P

The collective political will of UN members to intervene for humanitarian purposes was tested again beginning in 2003 when the western region of Darfur in Sudan presented yet another horrific humanitarian disaster. Fighting between government forces and rebels from the Sudanese Liberation Army and the Justice and Equality Movement forced thousands to flee their homes after attacks from government-backed Arab militias (known as Janjaweed), many seeking shelter in neighboring Chad. During the next year, the humanitarian disaster grew to 100,000 refugees, more than 1 million internally displaced persons, and an estimated 10,000 killed. Aid efforts by UN agencies and NGOs were frequently blocked by the Sudanese government. It was May 2004, however, before the Security Council addressed the issue, merely calling for the Sudan to disarm the Janjaweed and cease fighting. That toothless action was followed by promises to aid an African Union monitoring force. Secretary-General Annan pushed for more concerted action, supported by US secretary of state Colin Powell, who in mid-2004 labeled Darfur a clear case of genocide.[77] With both China and Russia opposing coercive measures, the Security Council in 2005, acting under Chapter VII, referred the Darfur crisis to the new International Criminal Court for action against those responsible for the genocide. By that time, between 180,000 and 300,000 people had died and 2.4 million individuals had been displaced. The Sudanese government announced it would not cooperate with the ICC, however. The "never again" promise following Rwanda's genocide looked hollow.

The AU monitoring force deployed in 2005 was insufficient for the task, even with NATO and EU assistance. Only in spring 2007 did Sudan accept the proposed UN-AU force of some 21,000 troops, having refused to accept UN peacekeepers. Negotiations still dragged on for months, with the Sudanese government even refusing to grant visas to the UN team tasked with assessing the possible mission. It proved difficult to secure sufficient commitments of troops, helicopters, and ground support. When initially deployed in January 2008, UNAMID was composed largely of AU personnel rehatted, still undermanned and poorly equipped. In 2015, UNAMID had more than 17,000 troops, more than 3,000 police, and an international civilian staff that exceeded 800, in addition to local civilians and UN volunteers. It has faced major logistical challenges, given the remoteness of the Darfur region and lack of roads and other infrastructure.

UNAMID also demonstrates the problems a humanitarian intervention inadequately equipped even for peacekeeping can encounter when it does not have sufficient support from major powers, is faced with opposition from both government and rebel forces, and lacks good leadership. A scathing report published in 2014 recounts the failure of the peacekeepers to prevent the abduction of civilians and to confront the Sudanese government over its deliberate targeting of civilians and peacekeepers alike.[78] It also notes the failure of DPKO, the AU, and the Security Council to respond effectively to recommendations to terminate the mission.[79] Efforts to deal with the conflict in Darfur continue also to be complicated by the ICC's indictment of Sudan's president, Omar al-Bashir, for war crimes committed in Darfur, and by the independence of South Sudan in 2011, where yet another conflict and major humanitarian crisis bordering on genocide has unfolded since 2014.

Why Libya and Not Syria?

R2P and POC have been particularly affected by the inconsistency between the UN's response to the crisis in Libya in 2011 and its failure to respond to the civil war in Syria. After the wave of anti-government protests throughout the Middle East and North Africa in 2011, known as the Arab Spring, spread to Syria, the Syrian government responded with armed force against growing protests. In June 2013, as the death toll passed 100,000, the UN Security Council attempted to pass a resolution condemning Syria's actions. Russia and China both vetoed the resolution, as discussed in Chapter 2. Russia, an ally of Syria, and China viewed the 2011 intervention in Libya as overstepping the original Security Council mandate and opposed a replay in Syria. Despite efforts by two SRSGs, former UN secretary-general Kofi Annan and Algerian diplomat Lakhdar Brahimi, the Syrian crisis proved beyond diplomatic resolution. It worsened in 2013 when allegations surfaced that the Syrian government had used chemical weapons against its civilians. UN reports also accused both government troops and rebel forces of committing war crimes and crimes against humanity.

There is little doubt that the inability of the Security Council to act—even to condemn the use of force against civilians by the Syrian government and the humanitarian crisis—has been shameful. In fact, in August 2012, the General Assembly, by a vote of 133 in favor with 12 opposed and 31 abstentions, deplored the council's failure to respond to the crisis and condemned the "widespread and systematic gross violations of human rights" by the Syrian government and pro-government militias (Resolution 66/253B). Secretary-General Ban Ki-moon himself criticized the council's failure in 2015, as discussed in Chapter 2. Yet international military intervention has not generally been considered the appropriate response, as some point out that "it was very difficult to see how an external military intervention in Syria could do more good than harm."[80] Clearly, many states remain wary of approving an outside intervention in an intrastate conflict without that state's consent and when the interests of several great powers oppose intervention.

Since the 2011 intervention in Libya, there has been vigorous debate about "why Libya and not Syria" and whether the UN's failure to intervene in Syria marks the death of R2P. This would not be the first prediction of the "sunset of humanitarian intervention" and R2P.[81] Yet there is consensus that the situations were not directly comparable. The UN-sanctioned intervention in Libya had strong endorsements from four regional organizations—the Arab League, Gulf Cooperation Council (GCC), Organisation of Islamic Cooperation, and African Union—and Qaddafi had few friends. Plus the United States, Britain, and France were willing to act and believed that they could foil Qaddafi's threat of mass atrocities relatively quickly and easily. Because NATO's intervention turned into regime change, however, the doubts that Russia, China, Brazil, India, and others had quickly turned to opposition, creating a "shadow of Libya" effect over Security Council discussions of possible action in Syria.

To be sure, the humanitarian crisis in Syria has been far greater than any imagined in Libya. As of late 2015, the war's toll included more than 50 percent of the country's population displaced (about 12 million), more than 4 million Syrian refugees outside the country (with most in Turkey, Lebanon, and Jordan), and an estimated 250,000 deaths. The emergence of ISIS in 2014 and 2015 greatly complicated the conflict and humanitarian crisis. There has been no call from other international organizations for intervention, the Arab states are divided, Iran is a major backer of President Assad, and the United States has been unwilling to intervene. Perhaps most important, Assad has two P-5 friends—Russia and China—exercising their veto power in the Security Council. Only with the emergence of ISIS has the United States become involved militarily, as discussed later in this chapter. Peace initiatives have largely been fruitless, although a further diplomatic push following Russia's military intervention on behalf of the Syrian government in late 2015 opened new possibilities. In December 2015 the council unanimously passed Resolution 2254, calling for a "credible, inclusive and nonsectarian governance" within six months and "free and fair elections, pursuant to the new constitution." The resolution also called for UN-sponsored talks between the Syrian government and opposition forces and acknowledged that a cease-fire must be accompanied by a parallel political process.

The debate about the future of R2P is likely to persist. Almost simultaneously with the intervention in Libya and the beginning of Syria's civil war, the Security Council authorized the UN Operation in Côte d'Ivoire (UNOCI) to use "all necessary means" to protect civilians (Resolution 1975) and, in effect, help oust Laurent Gbagbo, who had refused to leave office after losing the presidential election in 2010. The bigger debate concerns whether R2P has a future and to what degree it has been internalized. As one of R2P's ardent proponents suggests, "Syria demonstrates, if there was any doubt, that a robust R2P response is never automatic. . . . [A]nd [Syria] was distinctly more complicated, chancy, and confused than Libya."[82]

The Dilemmas of R2P and POC

These cases highlight four essential problems that the UN and international community face with humanitarian intervention. The first is selectivity. Why did the UN authorize a humanitarian mission in Somalia but ignore the long-running civil war in Sudan in the early 1990s when there was large-scale loss of life as a result of deliberate starvation, forced migrations, and massive human rights abuses? Why Libya and not Syria? As one author wrote, "Aren't the two regimes equally murderous?"[83] Why have humanitarian crises bordering on genocide in South Sudan and Central African Republic failed to attract major attention?

Second is the problem of timely action. International action was too little and too late to save thousands of human lives in Somalia, Rwanda, the DRC, and Darfur. Mobilizing a force takes time—unless one or more major powers (or alliance such as NATO) deem it in their national interest to act. That is one of the reasons there have been repeated recommendations for a small rapid-reaction force available to the UNSG to protect civilians caught in humanitarian disasters. Still, learning from peacekeepers' experience, the best such a force might do is to draw international attention to a crisis and hope that a larger response will be forthcoming.

Third, application of R2P requires political will. When the major powers have no strategic interests, they are apt not to respond, as Rwanda illustrates. When P-5 states have conflicting interests, as in Syria, the Security Council is stymied and it is impossible for the UN to implement R2P. Both Russia and China have traditionally opposed using enforcement measures for internal disputes, upholding the norm of noninterference. Both had economic interests in the Sudan and preferred not to jeopardize their ties with Sudan's government to support Darfur. Likewise, the European Union and the United States put priority on the 2005 peace accord ending the long civil war in southern Sudan and on cooperation with the Sudanese government in the war against terrorism, resulting in a very delayed response. Islamic countries are divided on Syria. "Major and minor powers alike are committed only to stopping killing that harms their national interests," a *Washington Post* article concluded. "Why take political, financial and potential military risks when there is no strategic or domestic cost to remaining on the sidelines?"[84]

Finally, R2P brings up the tension between legality and legitimacy. The UN Charter (Article 2, section 7) precludes UN intervention "in matters which are essentially within the domestic jurisdiction of any state." NATO's intervention in Kosovo to protect civilians from ethnic cleansing was not authorized by the UN Security Council. Thus, it was illegal under the UN Charter, though it was deemed ethically justifiable and legitimate even by Secretary-General Annan. The Libyan intervention was authorized by the Security Council, hence legal. But was it legitimate? Was it really to protect civilians?

Regardless of selectivity, egregious errors, and continuing controversy, the very fact that debate has been taking place over the legitimacy of humanitarian intervention for almost two decades and that the Security Council has repeatedly referred to humanitarian crises as threats to international peace and security under Chapter VII is a huge change. The fact that protection of civilians is incorporated into the mandates of virtually all UN peace operations since 2006 testifies to the acceptance of human security as an important goal.

Still, the problem of sexual abuse by UN peacekeepers clearly indicates that the UN is failing some of those whom it is supposed to protect, especially women and children. The allegations discredit the UN and what it stands for; they raise serious questions about the UN's need to better track abuse cases, to remove offending units, to monitor whether offenders are prosecuted by troop- and police-contributing countries, and to hold governments accountable when they fail to discipline their troops. Since the presence of women in peace operations has been shown to mitigate instances of sexual abuse, the UN is making more efforts to recruit female military, police, and civilian personnel.

Humanitarian concerns have long motivated advocates of arms control and disarmament, who see particular weapons as inhumane or who want to eliminate wars entirely by eliminating the weapons of war. The history of disarmament and arms control efforts is a mixed one, however. Advocates have been highly successful in getting the subject established permanently on the UN's agenda. But Inis Claude notes that "it is important to avoid confusing long hours of international debate, vast piles of printed documents, and elaborate charts of institutional structure with meaningful accomplishment."[85] Still, there have been some notable achievements, particularly with regard to controlling chemical, biological, and nuclear weapons of mass destruction.

ARMS CONTROL AND DISARMAMENT

The UN Charter did not envision a major role for the UN with respect to arms control and disarmament, although Article 26 did empower the Security Council to formulate plans for regulation of armaments. Disarmament had been discredited during the interwar era because it had failed to avert the outbreak of World War II. The Charter had just been signed, however, when the use of two atomic bombs on Japan on August 6 and 9, 1945, signaled the advent of nuclear weapons. This immediately put disarmament and arms control on the UN's agenda, with the General Assembly's very first resolution calling for the creation of the Atomic Energy Commission to study how to ensure that atomic energy was used for only peaceful purposes. Hence, the nuclear threat not only transformed world politics but also made the UN a key place for pursuing disarmament and arms control agreements. As with all international treaties, the UN is the depository for such agreements.

Although nuclear weapons are the highest-profile issue, arms control and disarmament efforts have also been directed at chemical and biological weapons, conventional weapons, missile technology, small arms, antipersonnel land mines, cluster munitions, and the arms trade. The primary goal has been to conclude international conventions limiting or banning various categories of weapons; reducing arms expenditures, transfers, and sales; and establishing mechanisms for monitoring and enforcing states' compliance. Since the 1990s, an added challenge has been limiting nonstate actors' access to arms and, in particular, preventing terrorist and other groups from gaining access to WMD.

The UN General Assembly has played a key role in developing arms control and disarmament norms and international law, including the Treaty on Nuclear Non-Proliferation (1967), the Comprehensive Test Ban Treaty (1996), and the Arms Trade Treaty (2014). It has created various bodies to deal with these issues, including the Disarmament Commission in 1952 and the Conference on Disarmament in 1979 to serve as the primary multilateral disarmament negotiating forum. There have been several reorganizations with accompanying name changes, reflecting a debate about which countries should participate in disarmament negotiations. In reality, the most fruitful negotiations on most issues have often taken place outside the UN among the relevant major powers. The recent cases of land mines and cluster munitions have demonstrated the ability of middle powers and coalitions of NGOs to provide leadership for diverse groups of states to pursue arms control initiatives without major-power participation in view of "a widespread sense that the UN [particularly the Conference on Disarmament] has become dysfunctional and moribund as a forum for negotiating arms control and disarmament treaties."[86]

The Challenges of Limiting Proliferation of Nuclear Weapon Capability

Even at the height of the Cold War, following U.S. president Dwight D. Eisenhower's Atoms for Peace proposal in 1954, the United States and the Soviet Union collaborated in creating an international agency to help spread information about the peaceful uses of atomic energy and to provide a system of safeguards designed to prevent the diversion of fissionable material. The International Atomic Energy Agency was established in 1957 as a specialized agency of the UN. The Cuban missile crisis in 1963 provided impetus for the two superpowers to sign the Partial Test Ban Treaty. They then participated in UN-organized negotiations for a treaty banning the spread of nuclear weapons. The Treaty on the Non-Proliferation of Nuclear Weapons (NPT) was signed by the two superpowers in 1967 and then opened to other nations to sign. It entered into force in 1970. Currently, 191 states are parties to the NPT.

The essence of the NPT is a bargain that in return for the pledge of non-nuclear-weapon states (NNWS) not to develop weapons, they will be aided in gaining access to peaceful nuclear technologies. In addition, the declared nuclear-weapon states (NWS) promised to give up their weapons at some future time. In essence, the NPT created a two-class system of five declared nuclear-weapon states (the United States, the Soviet Union/Russia, Britain, France, and China) and everyone else as non-nuclear-weapon states. Although accepted by most states, this two-class system has always been offensive to some, most notably India, which conducted a peaceful nuclear test in 1974 and five weapons tests in 1998. All but five states (North Korea, which withdrew in 2003, India, Pakistan, Cuba, and Israel) are now parties to the NPT. Three states that previously had nuclear weapons programs (South Africa, Brazil, and Argentina) became parties in the 1990s along with three states (Belarus, Kazakhstan, and Ukraine) that gave up nuclear weapons left on their territory after the dissolution of the Soviet Union. In 1995, the UN NPT Review Conference approved an indefinite extension of the treaty, conditioned on renewed efforts toward disarmament and a pledge by the nuclear-weapon states to conclude a Comprehensive Test Ban Treaty. The latter was drafted under UN auspices in 1996, but ratification stalled in 1998 when the US Senate rejected the treaty and India and Pakistan conducted weapons tests.

The IAEA is a critical part of the nuclear nonproliferation regime, especially its safeguard system of inspections that provides transparency about the security of non-nuclear-weapon states' nuclear power plants—that is, that nuclear fuel is not being diverted from peaceful to weapons purposes. The IAEA system is supplemented by the export control agreements of the forty-four-member Nuclear Suppliers Group.

Although the IAEA system appeared operational and reliable for many years, the discovery of a secret Iraqi nuclear weapons program in 1991—in direct violation of Iraq's IAEA safeguard agreements and its obligations under the NPT—brought the entire system under scrutiny. That drew the UN Security Council into discussion of arms control issues for the first time. The Gulf War cease-fire resolution (Security Council Resolution 687) created the Iraq disarmament regime, with the most intrusive international inspections ever established. To oversee the destruction of Iraq's chemical and biological weapons and missiles as well as production and storage facilities, and to monitor its long-term compliance, the Security Council created the UN Special Commission for the Disarmament of Iraq (UNSCOM). The IAEA was responsible for inspecting and destroying Iraq's nuclear weapon program. The comprehensive sanctions imposed on Iraq following its invasion of Kuwait remained in place to enforce compliance with the disarmament regime as well as other provisions of the cease-fire.

Between 1991 and 1998, inspectors moved all over Iraq, carrying out surprise inspections of suspected storage and production facilities, destroying stocks of materials, and checking documents. Iraq continually thwarted UNSCOM and IAEA inspectors, removing equipment, claiming to have destroyed material without adequate verification, arguing that some sites were off-limits, and complaining about the makeup of the commission. It severed all cooperation in November 1998, and inspectors were withdrawn. The successor to UNSCOM, the UN Monitoring, Verification, and Inspection Commission (UNMOVIC), was allowed to begin inspections anew in November 2002. Along with the IAEA, it was able "to verify the non-existence of a reconstituted Iraqi programme and rebuff various misleading allegations," only to have its work cut short by US military action against Iraq in March 2003.[87]

The problems that the IAEA and UNSCOM encountered in Iraq mirror the broader problems with international enforcement and with two other states that have nuclear programs—North Korea and Iran. As a consequence of the revelations about Iraq's nuclear program in 1991, the IAEA Board of Governors strengthened nuclear safeguards. The Security Council has also been actively involved in efforts to enforce North Korea's and Iran's compliance with the NPT, while ad hoc groups of states have managed diplomatic initiatives. The two cases have followed different paths.

In 1993, North Korea refused to admit inspectors to suspected sites and threatened to withdraw from the NPT. In 2002, it expelled the IAEA's inspectors and abrogated a 1994 agreement that renewed inspections. Then it withdrew from the NPT, produced additional plutonium for bombs, tested its first device (2006), declared itself an NWS, and refined its missile technology. In response, the Security Council approved targeted sanctions on North Korea, but they have not curbed its nuclear program (see Table 4.1). In early 2016, North Korea conducted a fourth test, provoking strong international protests and additional sanctions. China and Russia have condemned its bluster about nuclear strikes, but their influence has not proven decisive. North Korea's isolation from the world gives it little incentive to reach an agreement like that reached with Iran in 2015. The Six Party Talks were suspended in 2009. This makes it likely that North Korea will continue to develop its stockpile and delivery systems, increasing the threat it poses to the region and the world.

The extent of Iran's nuclear program eluded IAEA inspectors until 2003. Indeed, many of Iran's activities were permissible under the NPT, but because they were carried out surreptitiously, the United States and Europeans in particular worried that it sought to develop the capacity to build and deliver nuclear weapons despite its repeated denials.

With respect to Iran (or any other country that is party to the NPT), when the IAEA determines that it is not in compliance with its treaty obligations with respect to full inspections, uranium enrichment, or potential weapon development, the issue may be referred to the Security Council for enforcement action. The EU initially led negotiations with Iran to try to secure an agreement that would bring it into compliance. China and Russia, as well as some nonpermanent council members, opposed the use of sanctions. Then in September 2005, the IAEA's board voted twenty-two to one, with twelve abstentions, to report Iran's "many failures and breaches of its [NPT] obligations" to the Security Council.[88] When the Security Council took up the issue in 2006, Iran threatened to withdraw from the NPT and to retaliate if sanctions were imposed. Nonetheless, the council approved and repeatedly extended sanctions on Iran under Chapter VII (see Table 4.1). The 2008 resolution (1747), for example, authorized inspections of sea and air cargo to and from Iran, tightened monitoring of Iranian financial institutions, extended travel bans and asset freezes, and enlarged the list of targeted individuals and companies. Mindful of the lessons from the 1990s sanctions on Iraq, the Security Council created a monitoring committee and clearly spelled out humanitarian exemptions as well as the actions Iran needed to take for the sanctions to be suspended or terminated.

Iran continued to deny it was seeking to develop nuclear weapons, but the evidence of its increasing number of centrifuges and other activities led to mounting concern and speculation about US and/or Israeli military strikes. In search of a peaceful resolution, the P-5 plus Germany (P-5+1) proposed to offer economic incentives and civilian technology transfer if Iran permanently gave up its nuclear program. Active negotiations began in 2012. Over the subsequent three years, Iran remained a party to the NPT and permitted IAEA inspections, albeit keeping some sites "off-limits." It also signaled its interest in a deal that would secure the ending of sanctions. Intense negotiations in 2014 and 2015 sought to resolve what capabilities Iran would be allowed to keep, the length of time an agreement would be in effect, and the speed and conditions for lifting UN sanctions. In July 2015, agreement was reached between the P-5+1 and Iran and endorsed unanimously by the Security Council. The resolution set provisions for terminating all UN sanctions following a verification process whereby the IAEA establishes that "all nuclear material in Iran remains in peaceful activities." By early 2016, the IAEA had certified Iran's compliance with the agreement, which triggered the lifting of many but not all of the UN sanctions.

The danger of failing to halt North Korea's and Iran's nuclear programs is threefold: first, the greater risk of weapons being used; second, the risk that other countries in both regions will feel pressured to reconsider their non-nuclear status; and third, that one or both will supply nuclear weapons to Al Qaeda, ISIS, or some other nonstate group. These risks clearly threaten the entire NPT regime. Following the discovery in early 2004 that Pakistan's chief nuclear scientist, Dr. A. Q. Khan, ran a secret global network of nuclear suppliers, it became clear that new strategies were needed to prevent proliferation. As a result, the Security Council approved Resolution 1540 (April 2004), which affirms WMD proliferation as a threat to international peace and directs states to enact and enforce domestic legislation to protect materials and block illicit trafficking in WMD material. Some member states and NGOs thought this was an "unprecedented intrusion into national law-making authority" because of its legislative character.[89] The Security Council's 1540 Committee reviews member states' reports on their compliance. That 129 states submitted reports by April 2006 was seen by experts as a measure of initial success.[90] The reporting requirement can be a burden on many countries, especially smaller developing ones, but overall the resolution is considered a "partial success" even if reporting is uneven.[91]

The key difference between the conventions dealing with chemical and biological weapons and the NPT is the acceptance by all parties of a total ban on the possession, development, and use of chemical and biological weapons of mass destruction. In other words, there is no two-class system. Yet the failure of the NWS under the NPT's two-class system to move in the direction of disarmament continues to rankle. The US invasion of Iraq in 2003 on the grounds that its supposed WMD programs threatened regional and global security appears to have led North Korea and Iran, for example, to conclude that their only defense or leverage against the world's sole superpower would come through the acquisition of nuclear weapons. Thus, the challenge of preventing nuclear proliferation has become more serious, not less so, since the Cold War's end. The fear that nuclear as well as chemical and biological weapons could be acquired and used by terrorist groups is likewise very real.

The Syrian Conflict and the Organization for the Prohibition of Chemical Weapons

A taboo on the use of chemical weapons has existed for more than a century. The issue is especially troublesome, however, because many of the ingredients in chemical weapons, unlike nuclear weapons, are used in ordinary industrial and agricultural production. Because it is therefore impractical to eliminate their manufacture, the focus of arms control and disarmament efforts is on their use. A declaration of the Hague Conference of 1899 first articulated the norm banning asphyxiating shells; the 1925 Geneva Protocol reaffirmed it based on reactions to the use of chemical weapons in World War I; and a follow-up campaign successfully defined their use as "a practice beyond the pale of civilized nations" and "an especially inhumane method of warfare."[92] Thus, there is a rather remarkable history of nonuse of chemical weapons since the 1920s. The Chemical Weapons Convention (CWC) itself was signed in 1993, having been blocked by Cold War politics, and called for the complete destruction of all weapons and production facilities in a phased process. The Organisation for the Prohibition of Chemical Weapons (OPCW) began operations in early 1997 and has since conducted hundreds of inspections at military and industrial facilities. As of 2015, global stockpiles of chemical weapons had verifiably been reduced by more than 90 percent since 1997, but among the largest stockpiles were those in Syria.

The civil war that began after the Syrian government violently put down demonstrations during the 2011 Arab Spring has threatened international peace and security in a number of ways since then. One of those challenges has been the use of chemical weapons. In the summer of 2013, there were numerous reports that the Syrian government had used chemical weapons against its own citizens in Damascus. A French government report confirmed the use of sarin gas, a clear violation of the 1925 Geneva Protocol (Syria was not a signatory of the CWC). Following the US threat of military intervention, a remarkable diplomatic initiative led to an agreement between the United States and Russia outside the Security Council by which Syria would declare all of its chemical weapons stockpiles and sites within a week and join the CWC. There would be OPCW inspectors on the ground within two months with access to all sites, and the country's chemical weapons would be eliminated by June 2014. The agreement was unanimously endorsed by the Security Council, with the OPCW establishing the necessary procedures to carry out the disarmament process. Denmark, Norway, the United Kingdom, and the United States were all part of the operation that removed 1,300 metric tons of weapons from Syria in a short period of time, despite the country being torn apart in a brutal civil war.[93] In January 2014, the first shipment of weapons was loaded on a Danish ship, and six months later the last 8 percent were shipped out. Destruction of the weapons themselves was carried out at sites in several countries, including on a special US Navy vessel, and Syria's facilities were destroyed or permanently sealed. For its work, the OPCW received the 2013 Nobel Peace Prize. Concerns persist about whether Syria declared its entire stockpile, and there were reports of the use of chlorine and mustard gas in 2015 by the Syrian government and ISIS, respectively. Still, the OPCW reported that 98 percent of chemical weapons within Syria had been destroyed—a remarkable achievement.[94]

COPING WITH TERRORISM

Terrorism is an old threat to individual, state, and regional security that is now universally recognized as a threat also to international peace and security. Since the 1967 Arab-Israeli War and Israeli occupation of the West Bank and Gaza, much terrorist activity has originated in the Middle East, rooted in the Palestinians' quest for self-determination, rivalries among various Islamic groups, and the rise of Islamic fundamentalism. Since 1980, religious-based groups (Islamic and others such as Hindu nationalists) as a proportion of active terrorist groups have increased significantly. Of particular importance was the development of Al Qaeda—the shadowy network of Islamic fundamentalist groups in many countries—led by Osama bin Laden, which was linked to the 1993 New York World Trade Center bombing, the 1998 attack on US embassies in Africa, the 1999 attack on the USS *Cole*, and the 9/11 attacks as well as bombings in Madrid, London, and other cities. The increased ease of international travel and telecommunications have made **transnational terrorism** less confined to a particular geographic place and enabled terrorist groups not only to form global networks but also to move money, weapons, and people easily from one area to another—thus creating a global problem. Weak, failed, or conflict-ridden states such as Somalia, Afghanistan, Iraq, Libya, and Syria are important because they create gaps in international efforts to control borders and the flow of people, money, and arms as well as to deny terrorists sanctuaries for training camps and operations.

From the late 1960s through the 1970s, airline hijackings were a popular terrorist method for projecting a message. Hostage taking has been another tactic. The most common terrorist incidents involve the use of bombs on airplanes, trucks, cars, and ships or the use of suicide bombers. Prominent examples include Pan American Flight 103, which blew up over Lockerbie, Scotland, in 1988, and the 1998 attacks on the US embassies in Kenya and Tanzania. In addition, although the four planes involved in the 9/11 attacks were initially hijacked, they were turned into lethal weapons of mass destruction in a new twist on the old car-bomb strategy. Suicide bombings were pioneered by young members of the Tamil Tigers in Sri Lanka and then adopted by young

Palestinians during the Second Intifada and the 9/11 hijackers, as well as groups in Iraq, Afghanistan, Pakistan, and elsewhere. Concerns about terrorist groups gaining control of WMD or the materials to produce them magnify the importance of controlling these weapons, particularly nuclear materials, as discussed earlier in this chapter.

The rapid emergence of ISIS in 2014 introduced a new and dangerous dimension to terrorism, although experts were divided on whether it should be viewed as a terrorist organization or a quasi state given its seizure of territory and declaration of a caliphate (a single, transnational Islamic state based on sharia law). Its brutal treatment of non-Muslim and non-Arab minorities, Shiites, and all who opposed it included beheadings, mass slaughter, and slavery (particularly of women and children). With its control and administration of territory and cities in Iraq and Syria, including tax collection and public services, ISIS clearly was different. It also attracted thousands of "foreign fighters" to Syria (and subsequently to Libya) and drew declarations of allegiance from other jihadist groups in Afghanistan, Egypt, Libya, Nigeria, Yemen, and elsewhere. The destruction of a Russian civilian airliner and the Paris and Brussels bombings in late 2015 and early 2016 rapidly changed perceptions of ISIS from quasi state to global terrorist network with a growing ability to orchestrate attacks in a variety of locations. At the same time, the taking of hostages and suicide bombings by Al Qaeda affiliates in various parts of West Africa suggested a competition between ISIS and Al Qaeda for dominance among Islamic extremists. The Security Council responded to these changed perceptions of ISIS by approving a new resolution cosponsored by Russia and the United States and largely drafted by members' finance ministers to improve implementation of existing sanctions and to block ISIS's and other groups' funding sources.

Speaking at a special Security Council session in 2014, Secretary-General Ban Ki-moon said that "the world is witnessing a dramatic evolution in the nature of the terrorist threat."[95] Indeed, that drama continues to unfold. Among the changes is the targeting of the UN itself, with attacks on UN personnel in Iraq, Nigeria, Somalia, and Mali. Al Qaeda and other extremist groups have attacked UN personnel in more than seventy cases since 2005. The Al Nusra Front took a number of UN peacekeepers hostage in the Syrian Golan Heights. Clearly, groups associated with transnational terrorism have goals that are "seemingly irreconcilable with the principles of the UN Charter," as they reject the Westphalian state system, international law, and human rights norms.[96] Links with organized crime pose added challenges, as profits from drug smuggling, weapons and antiquities trafficking, and kidnapping are funding various extremist groups and have destructive impacts on local economies and societies. By April 2016, the unfolding drama also included a significant shrinkage in the territory ISIS controlled in Iraq and Syria.

In short, as David Rothkopf has noted, "terrorism is spreading worldwide. . . . [And] global terror trends are heading in an ever more dangerous direction."[97] This poses major challenges for the UN. Compliance and enforcement are major issues, as is the need for capacity-building in various approaches to counterterrorism.

International efforts to address the problem have long been hobbled by the inability to agree on a definition of terrorism. The problem is "how to formulate the term without criminalizing all armed resistance to oppressive regimes[,] . . . how to distinguish legitimate armed struggle from terrorism and how much emphasis to place on identifying root causes of grievances that lead individuals and groups to adopt terrorist methods."[98] This is often cast as the problem of distinguishing "freedom fighters" from terrorists.

The UN system is the hub for many counterterrorism efforts because of its global reach, legitimacy, and legal authority, although limited resources and operational capacity mean that a number of counterterrorism activities take place elsewhere. Currently, thirty-five bodies within the UN system are engaged in counterterrorism efforts.

Since 1972, the UN General Assembly has played a major role in developing the normative framework defining terrorism as a shared problem (without agreeing on a definition of terrorism itself) and concluding a series of fourteen international law–creating treaties and four protocols. They create norms outlawing terrorist acts against civil aviation, airports, shipping, diplomats, and nuclear materials. The most recent conventions address the problems of terrorist bombings, financing, nuclear terrorism, and unlawful acts relating to civil aviation. Since the 9/11 attacks there has been a more concerted effort to secure universal ratification, with technical assistance provided to countries whose legal systems are weak. According to some experts, the dramatic increase in ratifications since 2001 shows that "the United Nations has been successful in creating a stronger legal foundation among states for institutionalizing the battle against terrorism," with more than one hundred states having acceded to or ratified at least ten of these conventions.[99] None of the UN conventions and protocols on terrorism has a treaty-monitoring mechanism, however.

In 1996, the UN General Assembly drafted the Comprehensive International Convention on Terrorism, but differences about how to define terrorism held up adoption. In 2004, the secretary-general's High-Level Panel on Threats, Challenges, and Change proposed a definition and called on the General Assembly to conclude the convention.[100] The *2005 World Summit Outcome* endorsed these recommendations, including language that condemned terrorism "in all its forms and manifestations, committed by whomever, wherever and for whatever purposes, as it constitutes one of the most serious threats to international peace and security."[101] This is seen as a major step toward a consensus definition, but still not sufficient to allow conclusion of the comprehensive convention.

In 2006, the General Assembly adopted the United Nations Global Counter-Terrorism Strategy (A/RES/60/288)—the first attempt to provide a comprehensive global framework for addressing the problem of terrorism. That strategy is built around four pillars: addressing conditions conducive to the spread of terrorism, preventing and combating terrorism, building state capacity, and defending human rights while combating terrorism. The strategy is subject to review every two years, with the tenth review scheduled in 2016. The Counter-Terrorism Implementation Task Force (CTITF), composed of representatives from thirty UN entities, including various specialized agencies, DPKO, the Counter-Terrorism Executive Directorate (CTED), the 1540 Committee, and Interpol, works to ensure overall coordination of activities throughout the UN system. Its mission is also to promote counterterrorism strategy, provide member states with policy support and technical assistance, and discuss strategies for future efforts.

The Security Council began to address the question of terrorism only in the 1990s, led by the US push for sanctions against Libya, the Sudan, Afghanistan, and Al Qaeda for their roles in supporting terrorism. In 1992, the Security Council invoked Chapter VII to condemn terrorist acts and Libya's role in them. To pressure Libya into giving up the two men indicted for the bombings of Pan American Flight 103, the Security Council imposed travel and diplomatic sanctions, flight bans, and an embargo on aircraft parts in 1992 and 1993. These were lifted in 2003 after Libya delivered the two suspects for trial and paid compensation to the families of those killed.

Sanctions were imposed on the Taliban regime in Afghanistan in 1999, including an arms embargo, aviation and financial sanctions, a ban on the sale of acetic anhydride (which is used in processing opium into heroin), diplomatic restrictions, and a travel ban. UN members had concluded that it was impossible for the UN to maintain neutrality in Afghanistan's civil war and that only the Taliban's removal would end Afghanistan's support for terrorism (including harboring the Al Qaeda leader Osama bin Laden), its role in the heroin trade, and its harsh treatment of women. The Security Council set up an office for sanctions-monitoring assistance for the six neighboring countries. Although diplomatic isolation was effective, other sanctions did not persuade the Taliban to end its support for terrorism until after the US intervention in October 2001 led to regime change. In 2011, the Security Council split the sanctions regime targeting Al Qaeda and the Taliban, creating a separate sanctions list of individuals, groups, and undertakings associated with Al Qaeda. This was further strengthened in 2014.

Sanctions, then, have been one major approach for the Security Council in responding to terrorism. The global regime to counter terrorism also includes several UN Security Council resolutions adopted under Chapter VII authority that impose other types of legal obligations on member states. The first and most important is Resolution 1373, adopted in 2001 following the 9/11 attacks. It was unprecedented in obliging all states to block the financing and weapons supply of terrorist groups, freeze their assets, prevent recruitment, deny them safe haven, and cooperate in information sharing and criminal prosecution. It also urged member states to sign and ratify the twelve antiterrorism conventions existing at the time. In addition, as discussed in Chapter 2, Resolution 1373 established the Counter-Terrorism Committee (CTC), a committee of the whole Security Council that monitors states' capabilities to deny funding or haven to terrorists. In 2004, the council established the CTED to provide it with more permanent and expert staff.

A key aspect of Resolution 1373 is its reporting requirements. The CTED assists CTC members in reviewing and analyzing reports from member states concerning their counterterrorism actions. In an extraordinary show of compliance, every UN member state submitted a report for the first round, leading one group of experts to state, "Member state compliance with CTC reporting requests has been greater than for any previous Security Council mandate."[102] The reports provide a large body of information on the counterterrorism capabilities of most UN members, but they pose a significant burden for processing, particularly on top of the Resolution 1540 reports, leading to "reporting fatigue." Between 2005 and 2015, the CTED also conducted sixty-six site visits. As these visits have expanded, the CTC seemed to be "maximizing the functionality and minimizing the politics, bringing enhanced legitimacy to the CTC's engagement with member states."[103]

The CTED is specifically designed to strengthen the counterterrorism capabilities of member states through technical assistance and training for bureaucrats. It has assisted states in drafting legislation, helped them adapt money-laundering laws and controls on informal banking systems, and provided training in counterterrorism standards. Half of CTED's forty staff members are legal experts specialized in legislative drafting, border and customs controls, and policy and law enforcement. In addition, the UN Office on Drugs and Crime's Terrorism Prevention Branch assists states in ratifying and implementing the conventions and strengthening national criminal justice systems.

Resolutions 1373 and 1540 (discussed above) along with their respective committees and professional staff not only expanded the UN's counterterrorism activities but also shifted primary responsibility for dealing with the issue from the General Assembly to the Security Council. With the General Assembly's adoption in 2006 of the Global Counter-Terrorism Strategy and the work of the

CTITF, the pendulum shifted back somewhat more to the assembly. However, the interrelated crises in Libya, Mali, and the Sahel after the ouster of Libyan leader Muammar Qaddafi in 2011, followed by rising concerns about ISIS and the flow of foreign fighters in 2014–2015, demonstrated that the Security Council is still central to UN counterterrorism efforts. It involved sanctions committees, the CTED, and other bodies in assessing the interrelated threats relating to the territorial gains by armed Islamist groups and by the proliferation of arms and materiel in the region (Resolution 2017) and to the Integrated Strategy for the Sahel—the UN's first such regional-level plan involving counterterrorism.[104]

In sum, while there are many things that the UN has done in dealing with the evolving threats that terrorism poses to international peace and security, there are also clear limits to what the UN can do. Its operational capacities in relevant areas are limited and its intelligence-gathering capacity essentially nonexistent. Still, it has played a key role in the establishment of international norms and law and in the use of sanctions to enforce those rules and impose costs on violators, albeit with more success against states than nonstate actors; it has also facilitated enhancement of the capacities of weaker states to counter the threat of terrorism.

FUTURE CHALLENGES FOR
THE UN'S ROLE IN PEACE AND SECURITY

The UN's experience in dealing with changing threats to international peace and security has highlighted a number of lessons that represent important issues for the future. These tie directly to the four dilemmas around which this book is organized.

Dilemma 1: Changing Threats Versus the Limits on the UN's Role

A major lesson from more than seventy years of UN efforts to provide collective security and enforcement, and especially from the peace operations since 1990, is that although international military action (in contrast to sanctions) should be authorized by the Security Council, the actual work of applying force has to be subcontracted to a coalition of the willing led by one or more major powers with sufficient military capabilities. States never have and never will empower the UN with the means to exercise coercion. "The U.N. itself can no more conduct military operations on a large scale on its own than a trade association of hospitals can conduct heart surgery," Michael Mandelbaum has noted.[105]

In peace operations where the line between peacekeeping and enforcement is blurred and the situation requires some use of military force, UN-appointed commanders need clear operational mandates from the Security Council and DPKO spelling out how they can use force to disarm local militias, deliver humanitarian

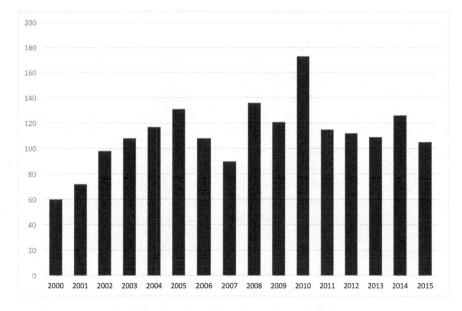

FIGURE 4.2. UN Peacekeeping Fatalities by Year, 2000–2015

SOURCE: Department of Peacekeeping Operations, www.un.org/en/peacekeeping/fatalities/documents /stats_1.pdf.

relief, and protect civilians. More than this, they require sufficient military strength and the continuing political support of member states to carry out their tasks under circumstances of adversity. When UN peacekeepers use force, they give up the UN's impartial position to confront one or more belligerent groups—a danger first evident in Somalia in 1994 and more recently in the DRC with the Force Intervention Brigade. When the UN is viewed as taking sides, it loses its essential credibility and commitment to rule of law and compromises its legitimacy and distinct capacity for impartiality. It also runs a greater risk that more peacekeepers will lose their lives. This is reflected in Figure 4.2, which illustrates the rising cost, with almost 1,700 peacekeepers killed between 2000 and 2015. Furthermore, as the seeming impotence of the UN force in South Sudan has revealed, ambitious objectives, robust mandates, and substantial support cannot guarantee desired outcomes.

What is often referred to as the problem of political will of member states has several dimensions. First, it is important to emphasize that as an IGO, the UN depends on its members' support to act. When the necessary political will is lacking, one or both of the following may occur: the Security Council may not address or act on a given issue, and member states may fail to provide the personnel, financial, or logistical support necessary to implement resolutions passed by the council. Although much has been made in recent years of the need to prevent outbreaks of violence and horrendous crimes against humanity, prevention is more easily talked about than done. And member states have been notably reluctant to provide the UN Secretariat with significant early-warning capability that would aid preventive efforts.

Funding for peacekeeping operations has long been a problem. Observer missions are generally funded from the UN's regular budget, whereas full-scale peace operations are funded through special peacekeeping assessments. Yet member states, large and small, are frequently in arrears, and with more and larger peace operations, the financial strains have increased. In 1987, the cost of peacekeeping was $240 million; in 1995, it reached $3.36 billion; after dropping for several years, it passed the $7 billion mark in 2010. The approved 2015–2016 peacekeeping budget was $8.2 billion; outstanding overall contributions to peacekeeping in June 2015, however, were $4.80 billion, with the US owing $363 million.[106]

The recruitment of forces for UN peacekeeping continues to be a significant problem. As peacekeeping demands have increased, military units have been drawn from many more countries. For poor developing countries, there are financial benefits because UN pay scales are far higher than their own (but arrearages of richer countries can make payments slow in coming). The greater risk of casualties, however, has made many developed countries more reluctant to participate—hence the ethical and operational questions discussed earlier. The possibility of "subcontracting" various peacekeeping tasks to a regional organization, such as the African Union, is consistent with Chapter VIII of the UN Charter, but there are significant limits on the capacity of most regional organizations other than NATO. Police units are particularly difficult to recruit in sufficient numbers. The same is true for female peacekeepers. The problem of sexual abuse by peacekeepers and governments' failure to address it may now force the UN to decline offers of troops from offending countries.

Finally, the UN's managerial capacity, especially with respect to peacekeeping operations, is an increasingly contentious issue as operations and bureaucracies have become larger, more complex, and more expensive, and have involved coordination among military and civilian components, various UN agencies, regional organizations, and NGOs. Flexibility and adaptability are casualties of size and complexity. Although reform initiatives since the mid-1990s have improved coordination and management of peace operations, much still needs to be done in this regard. For many, however, the most serious issue relating to the UN's ability to address changing threats to international peace is the very composition and operation of the Security Council, as discussed in Chapter 2. Although the legitimacy of Security Council authority is still high, there is widespread recognition of the need for change. The challenge is twofold: first, how to get agreement on reform among the P-5, and second, how to reach agreement among a majority of the rest of the UN's 193 members.

Dilemma 2: Changing Norms and Challenges to Sovereignty

Although consent of parties remains key to traditional and complex peacekeeping, the emergence of R2P reflects the recognition that sovereignty carries responsibilities, including the responsibility to protect individuals. "Surely," Secretary-General Annan concluded in 1999, "no legal principle—not even sovereignty—can ever shield crimes against humanity."[107] Indeed, the UN Charter itself makes clear that sovereignty cannot stand in the way of responses to aggression and threats to peace or states' obligations to meet their commitments under the Charter. International customary and treaty law also limits sovereignty. Thus, Iraq could not use sovereignty as a defense against the intrusive arms control inspections and sanctions after the Gulf War. Nor did states raise objections on the grounds of sovereignty to the extensive reporting requirements of Resolution 1373 and the CTC or the requirements of Resolution 1540 to prevent nuclear materials from falling into the wrong hands.

Changing norms, however, do not ensure that responses to all humanitarian crises and conflicts will be uniform. As the discussion on humanitarian intervention makes clear, selectivity, timing, political will, and legality have been and are likely to be ongoing problems. These issues touch directly on sovereignty, which may be used to justify a state's unwillingness to carry out Security Council decisions or to accept UN involvement in certain conflicts. And as China and Russia continue to be assertive, their strong affinity for upholding the norms of state sovereignty and noninterference (an affinity shared by many developing countries) makes future humanitarian interventions even more problematic.

Dilemma 3: The Need for Leadership
Versus the Decline of US Dominance

As Kosovo and the US invasion of Iraq in 2003 illustrated, a sole superpower determined to take action will not be deterred by the absence of Security Council authorization. The acrimonious, divisive debate in the UN about the war in Iraq was widely regarded as raising serious issues about the future effectiveness of the UN, and especially of the Security Council. It was "at least as much about American power and its role in the world as about the risks posed by Iraq's weapons."[108] And, as the 2011 action in Libya showed, the United States under President Obama has been more inclined to forge international consensus and limit its role in international interventions. Yet a major dilemma for the UN is that when security threats have required more complex and more coercive responses, historically only the United States, some of its NATO allies, and a few other developed states have had the capability to carry out Security Council mandates involving the use of force. China's rise and Russia's renewed assertiveness have not yet changed the equation of international power and willingness to take responsibility, leaving it unclear who will provide leadership and resources to address threats to international peace if the United States is unable or unwilling to do so.

As discussed in Chapter 3, the US record on multilateralism in general and the UN in particular has been one of mixed messages throughout the twentieth century and into the twenty-first. Historically, the United States was supportive of traditional UN peacekeeping and provided logistical support and equipment to most operations. But as UN involvement deepened with more complex and muscular operations, the US has continued to impose more restrictions on participating in operations outside of its direct national interest. President Obama supported humanitarian intervention in Libya only after a coalition had been forged and the Security Council authorized action, affirming that even for the United States, the UN has a unique capacity to confer legitimacy. The US military remains predominant, yet as China's military capability and international ambitions grow, it remains to be seen whether China will accept greater responsibility for supporting the UN in upholding international peace and security.

Dilemma 4: The Need for Inclusiveness

Since 2000, the UN Security Council has paid increased attention to inclusiveness in relation to conflict prevention, peacebuilding, and protection of civilians, as noted earlier. Resolution 1325 (2000), in particular, recognized that women and girls are often disproportionately harmed by armed conflict and called for special measures to protect women and girls from sexual violence in conflicts as well as increased presence and participation of women in peace and security initiatives. Still, significant gaps remain in the implementation of the women, peace, and security agenda, and especially in the mandate to improve protection. Some argue that the focus on an inclusive approach to peace and security has been more rhetorical than real. A 2014 report found that progress on inclusiveness has triggered pushback by members of the Security Council, who protest that the focus of the council should be specifically on situations of "sexual violence in armed conflict and post-conflict situations" and not more broadly on "conflict-related sexual violence."[109] In spite of several council resolutions to address the gaps in implementation of Resolution 1325, problems persist. And it remains to be seen how well Resolution 2272 (2016) authorizing the UNSG to take action against peacekeepers charged with sexual abuse is implemented.

The recruitment of women peacekeepers—albeit in relatively small numbers—is yet another step in response to the dilemma of inclusiveness and, most important, to meeting the very real needs for the special roles women can play in peace operations. It has been hoped that the presence of women in mixed-gender units would curb the problem of sexual abuse. Yet the numbers thus far make definitive conclusions difficult. Resolution 2122 (2013), for example, noted that the Secretariat had not met the council's call as of that point for more women protection advisers for deployments in CAR, Côte d'Ivoire, Darfur, DRC, Mali, Somalia, and South Sudan. Finally, as noted in Chapter 2, the Security Council has since the mid-1990s under the Arria formula invited NGOs and other nonstate actors to participate in informal council sessions. Beginning in 2012 and now written into Resolution 2242 (2015) is provision for gender advisers, women protection advisers, and representatives of concerned civil society groups to participate in such sessions. Thus, the council has tried to address the demand for inclusiveness and need for greater consultation with those who can provide a clearer sense of what is happening on the ground and in the field where UN operations are already under way or where conflict and violence may have erupted and been brought to the council's attention.

Traditionally, international peace and security have meant states' security and the defense of states' territorial integrity from external threats or attack. As suggested by our discussion of humanitarian intervention and the R2P norm, the concept of human security—the security of human beings in the face of many different kinds of threats—has begun to take hold. These concerns are reflected in the discussions in Chapters 5, 6, and 7 about the need to eradicate poverty and reduce the inequalities exacerbated by globalization, promote sustainable development and greater respect for human rights norms, and address the growing security threats posed by epidemics, displacement, and environmental degradation.

NOTES

1. John Mueller, "War Has Almost Ceased to Exist: An Assessment," *Political Science Quarterly* 124, no. 2 (2009): 297–321.

2. David Rothkopf, "We Are Losing the War on Terror," *Foreign Policy*, June 10, 2014.

3. World Bank, *World Development Report 2011: Conflict, Security, and Development* (Washington, DC: World Bank, 2011), 2.

4. Martha Finnemore, *The Purpose of Intervention: Changing Beliefs About the Use of Force* (Ithaca, NY: Cornell University Press, 2003).

5. *Report of the High-Level Independent Panel on Peace Operations*, S/2015/446 and A/7095, www.un.org/sg/pdf/HIPPO_Report_1_June_2015.pdf.

6. On the role of SRSGs, see Timothy D. Sisk, "Introduction: The SRSGs and the Management of Civil Wars," *Global Governance* 16, no. 2 (2010): 237–242, and other articles in the "Special Focus" section of this issue of the journal.

7. Boutros Boutros-Ghali, *An Agenda for Peace: Preventive Diplomacy, Peacemaking, and Peacekeeping* (New York: United Nations, 1992), 45.

8. Michael E. Brown and Richard N. Rosecrance, *The Costs of Conflict: Prevention and Cure in the Global Arena* (Lanham, MD: Rowman and Littlefield, 1999), 225.

9. Richard Gowan, "Multilateral Political Missions and Preventive Diplomacy," United States Institute of Peace Special Report 299, December 2011, 2, 10.

10. United Nations, *World Summit Outcome*, A/60/L.1, sec. 81, 22 (2005).

11. United Nations Secretary-General, *Preventive Diplomacy: Delivering Results*, S/2011/552, August 26, 2011, www.un.org/wcm/webdav/site/undpa/shared/undpa/pdf /SG%20Report%20on%20Preventive%20Diplomacy.pdf.

12. Two helpful sources are Abram Chayes, "The Use of Force in the Persian Gulf," in *Law and Force in the New International Order*, ed. Lori Fisler Damrosch and David J. Scheffer (Boulder, CO: Westview Press, 1991), 3–11; and Ken Matthews, *The Gulf Conflict in International Relations* (London: Routledge, 1993).

13. United Nations Press release, SG/SM/7263, AFR/196, December 16, 1999, www .un.org/docs/sg/sgsm.htm.

14. Adam Roberts, "NATO's 'Humanitarian War' over Kosovo," *Survival* 41, no. 2 (1999): 106.

15. Alynna J. Lyon, "Beyond Rwanda and Kosovo: The Interactive Dynamics of International Peacekeeping and Ethnic Mobilization," *Global Society* 19, no. 3 (2005): 267–288.

16. Adam Roberts, "The Use of Force," in *The UN Security Council: From the Cold War to the 21st Century*, ed. David M. Malone (Boulder, CO: Lynne Rienner, 2004), 141.

17. See Michael J. Glennon, "Why the Security Council Failed," *Foreign Affairs* 82, no. 3 (2003): 16–35; and responses, Edward C. Luck, "The End of an Illusion," Anne-Marie Slaughter, "Misreading the Record," and Ian Hurd, "Too Legit to Quit," all published in *Foreign Affairs* 82, no. 4 (2003): 201–205. See also the debate "The United Nations Has Become Irrelevant," *Foreign Policy* 138 (September–October 2003): 16–24.

18. Mats Berdal, "The UN After Iraq," *Survival* 46, no. 3 (2004): 82.

19. "'Fundamental Issues of Peace, Security at Stake, Secretary-General Warns," United Nations Security Council, Department of Public Information, February 25, 2001.

20. Adam Roberts, "The Use of Force: A System of Selective Security," in *The UN Security Council in the 21st Century*, ed. Sebastian von Einsiedel, David M. Malone, and Bruno Stagno Ugarte (Boulder, CO: Lynne Rienner, 2016), 349–350.

21. For a set of excellent studies of the "sanctions decade," see David Cortright and George A. Lopez, *The Sanctions Decade: Assessing UN Strategies in the 1990s* (Boulder, CO: Lynne Rienner, 2000).

22. Thomas Biersteker, Sue E. Eckert, Marcos Tourinho, and Zuzana Hudáková, *The Effectiveness of United Nations Targeted Sanctions: Findings from the Targeted Sanctions Consortium (TSC)*, November 2013, 15, http://graduateinstitute.ch/un-sanctions.

23. Ramesh Thakur, *The United Nations, Peace, and Security* (New York: Cambridge University Press, 2006), 145.

24. David M. Malone, *The International Struggle over Iraq: Politics in the UN Security Council, 1980–2005* (New York: Oxford University Press, 2006), 135.

25. David Cortright and George A. Lopez, *Sanctions and the Search for Security* (Boulder, CO: Lynne Rienner, 2002), 71.

26. Gary Clyde Hufbauer et al., *Economic Sanctions Reconsidered*, 3rd ed. (Washington, DC: Peterson Institute for International Economics, 2007), 141.

27. Biersteker et al., *The Effectiveness of United Nations Targeted Sanctions,* 1.

28. Ibid.

29. Thakur, *The United Nations, Peace, and Security,* 37.

30. United Nations, *The Blue Helmets: A Review of United Nations Peace-Keeping,* 3rd ed. (New York: UN Department of Public Information, 1996), 4. This is an excellent resource on peacekeeping operations up to the mid-1990s. The UN Web site is a valuable resource on all past and current UN operations: www.un.org/Depts/dpko/home.htm. See also the *Annual Review of Global Peace Operations,* a project of the Center on International Cooperation at New York University since 2006 and published by Lynne Rienner (online since 2015), as well as articles and data published in the journal *International Peacekeeping.*

31. United Nations, *Peacekeeping Operations: Principles and Guidelines* (New York: UN Department of Peacekeeping Operations, Department of Field Support, 2008), 18.

32. Ian Johnstone, "Managing Consent in Contemporary Peacekeeping Operations," *International Peacekeeping* 18, no. 2 (2011): 172.

33. Sahana Dharmapuri, "Not Just a Numbers Game: Increasing Women's Participation in UN Peacekeeping," Providing for Peacekeeping no. 4, International Peace Institute, July 2013, www.operationspaix.net/DATA/DOCUMENT/8074~v~Not_Just_A_Numbers_Game _Increasing_Womens_Participation_in_UN_Peacekeeping.pdf.

34. "Taking Action on Sexual Abuse and Exploitation by Peacekeepers," Report of an Independent Review on Sexual Exploitation and Abuse by International Peacekeeping Forces in the Central African Republic, December 17, 2015, www.un.org/News/dh /infocus/centafricrepub/Independent-Review-Report.pdf.

35. Michael Barnett et al., "Peacebuilding: What Is in a Name?" *Global Governance* 13, no. 1 (2007): 37. The authors' central point is that the different agencies involved in peacebuilding define and use this term in very different ways.

36. For further discussion, see Walter Clarke and Jeffrey Herbst, "Somalia and the Future of Humanitarian Intervention," *Foreign Affairs* 75, no. 2 (1996): 70–85; and Enrico Augelli and Craig N. Murphy, "Lessons of Somalia for Future Multilateral Humanitarian Assistance Operations," *Global Governance* 1, no. 3 (1995): 339–366.

37. United Nations, *Report of the Secretary-General Pursuant to General Assembly Resolution 53/35: The Fall of Srebrenica,* UN Doc. No. A/54/549, November 15, 1999, www.un.org /peace/srebrenica.pdf.

38. See Georgios Kostakos, "Division of Labor Among International Organizations: The Bosnian Experience," *Global Governance* 4, no. 4 (1998): 461–484.

39. Séverine Autesserre, *The Trouble with the Congo: Local Violence and the Failure of International Peacebuilding* (New York: Cambridge University Press, 2010).

40. Nicholas Kulish and Somini Sengupta, "New U.N. Brigade's Aggressive Stance in Africa Brings Success, and Risks," *New York Times,* November 13, 2013.

41. Scott Sheeran and Stephanie Case, "The Intervention Brigade: Legal Issues for the UN in the Democratic Republic of the Congo," International Peace Institute, 2014, 16, http:// reliefweb.int/sites/reliefweb.int/files/resources/ipi_e_pub_legal_issues_drc_brigade.pdf.

42. Richard Gowan, "Diplomatic Fallout: A Summer of Political Storms Looms for U.N.," *World Politics Review,* June 3, 2013.

43. John Karlsrud, "The UN at War: Examining the Consequences of Peace-Enforcement Mandates for the UN Peacekeeping Operations in the CAR, the DRC, and Mali," *Third World Quarterly* 36, no. 1 (2015): 40–54.

44. Michael W. Doyle, *UN Peacekeeping in Cambodia: UNTAC's Civil Mandate* (Boulder, CO: Lynne Rienner, 1995), 26.

45. "The 'Second Generation': Cambodia Elections 'Free and Fair,' but Challenges Remain," *United Nations Chronicle,* November–December 1993, 26.

46. Quoted in Andrea Kathryn Talentino, "Perceptions of Peacebuilding: The Dynamic of Imposer and Imposed Upon," *International Studies Perspectives* 3, no. 2 (2007): 163. For an earlier assessment of the UN mission in Kosovo, see Alexandras Yannis, "The UN as Government in Kosovo," *Global Governance* 10, no. 1 (2004): 67–81.

47. Sergio Vieira de Mello, "Message to the UNITAR-IPS-JIIA Conference." See also Sergio Vieira de Mello, "How Not to Run a Country: Lessons from Kosovo and East Timor," UNITAR-IPS-JIIA Conference to Assess the Report on UN Peace Operations, Singapore, February 2001.

48. International Crisis Group, "Timor-Leste: Security Sector Reform," *Asia Report* no. 143 (January 17, 2008): 1.

49. International Crisis Group, "South Sudan: A Civil War by Any Other Name," ICG Africa Report no. 217, April 2014, www.crisisgroup.org/en/regions/africa/horn-of-africa /south-sudan/217-south-sudan-a-civil-war-by-any-other-name.aspx.

50. Paul F. Diehl, *Peace Operations* (Malden, MA: Polity, 2008), 108. See also Séverine Autesserre, *Peaceland: Conflict Resolution and the Everyday Politics of International Intervention* (New York: Cambridge University Press, 2014), chap. 1.

51. Paul F. Diehl, "Forks in the Road: Theoretical and Policy Concerns for 21st Century Peacekeeping," *Global Society* 14, no. 3 (2001): 337–360.

52. Virginia Page Fortna, "Interstate Peacekeeping: Causal Mechanisms and Empirical Effects," *World Politics* 56 (July 2004): 510.

53. Virginia Page Fortna, *Peace Time: Cease-Fire Arrangements and the Durability of Peace* (Princeton: Princeton University Press, 2004), 283–285.

54. Paul Collier et al., *Breaking the Conflict Trap: Civil War and Development Policy* (Washington, DC: World Bank and Oxford University Press, 2003). For further research results along these lines, see Virginia Page Fortna, *Does Peacekeeping Work? Shaping Belligerents' Choices After Civil War* (Princeton: Princeton University Press, 2008); and Michael W. Doyle and Nicholas Sambanis, *Making War and Building Peace* (Princeton: Princeton University Press, 2006).

55. Alex J. Bellamy and Paul D. Williams, "The New Politics of Protection? Côte d'Ivoire, Libya, and the Responsibility to Protect," *International Affairs* 87, no. 4 (July 2011): 825–850.

56. Virginia Page Fortna, "Does Peacekeeping Keep Peace? International Intervention and the Duration of Peace After Civil War," *International Studies Quarterly* 48, no. 2 (2004): 283. For other studies, see Virginia Page Fortna, *Peace Time;* Virginia Page Fortna, *Does Peacekeeping Work?;* M. Gilligan and Stephen J. Stedman, "Where Do the Peacekeepers Go?" *International Studies Review* 5, no. 4 (2003): 37–54; Stephen J. Stedman, Donald Rothchild, and Elizabeth M. Cousens, *Ending Civil Wars: The Implementation of Peace Agreements* (Boulder, CO: Lynne Rienner, 2002); and James Cockayne, Christoph Mikulaschek,

and Chris Perry, *The United Nations Security Council and Civil War: First Insights from a New Dataset* (New York: International Peace Institute, 2010).

57. See Lise Morjé Howard, *UN Peacekeeping in Civil Wars* (New York: Cambridge University Press, 2008); James Dobbins et al., *The UN's Role in Nation-Building: From the Congo to Iraq* (Santa Monica, CA: RAND, 2005).

58. United Nations, *The Report of the Panel on United Nations Peace Operations* (Brahimi Report), A/55/305-S/2000/809, 2000.

59. J. Michael Greig and Paul F. Diehl, "The Peacekeeping-Peacemaking Dilemma," *International Studies Quarterly* 49, no. 4 (2005): 621–645.

60. Paul F. Diehl and Alexandru Balas, *Peace Operations*, 2nd ed. (Malden, MA: Polity, 2014), 154.

61. See Doyle and Sambanis, *Making War and Building Peace*; Charles T. Coll, "Knowing Peace When You See It: Setting Standards for Peacebuilding Success," *Civil Wars* 10, no. 2 (2008): 173–194.

62. William J. Durch, "Are We Learning Yet? The Long Road to Applying Best Practices," in *Twenty-First-Century Peace Operations*, ed. William J. Durch (Washington, DC: United States Institute of Peace Press, 2006), 594.

63. Michael Barnett, Songying Fang, and Christoph Zürcher, "Compromised Peacebuilding," *International Studies Quarterly* 58, no. 3 (2014): 608.

64. Stein Sundstøl Eriksen, "The Liberal Peace Is Neither: Peacebuilding, State Building, and the Reproduction of Conflict in the Democratic Republic of Congo," *International Peacekeeping* 16, no. 5 (2009): 652–666.

65. Autesserre, *Peaceland*, 23.

66. Erin McCandless, "Wicked Problems in Peacebuilding and Statebuilding: Making Progress in Measuring Progress Through the New Deal," *Global Governance* 19, no. 2 (2014): 240–241.

67. United Nations General Assembly and Security Council, *Report of the Panel on United Nations Peace Operations*, A/55/305-S/2000/809 (August 21, 2000), www.un.org/peace/reports/peace_operations/.

68. *Report of the High-Level Independent Panel on Peace Operations*, A/7095-S/2015/446 (2015), 9, 10, 15–16, www.un.org/sg/pdf/HIPPO_Report_1_June_2015.pdf.

69. General Assembly, "Comprehensive Review of the Whole Question of Peacekeeping Operations in All Their Aspects," A/70/95–S/2015/446, June 17, 2015, 12, www.un.org/sg/pdf/HIPPO_Report_1_June_2015.pdf.

70. See United Nations, "Letter Dated 29 June 2015 from the Chair of the Secretary-General's Advisory Group of Experts on the 2015 Review of the United Nations Peacebuilding Architecture Addressed to the Presidents of the Security Council and of the General Assembly," www.un.org/en/peacebuilding/pdf/150630%20Report%20of%20the%20AGE%20on%20the%202015%20Peacebuilding%20Review%20FINAL.pdf.

71. Security Council Report, "The Security Council and the UN Peacebuilding Commission," Special Research Report, April 18, 2013, www.securitycouncilreport.org/special-research-report/the-security-council-and-the-un-peacebuilding-commission.php.

72. Michael Barnett, *Eyewitness to a Genocide: The United Nations and Rwanda* (Ithaca, NY: Cornell University Press, 2002).

73. United Nations, *Report of the Independent Inquiry into the Actions of the United Nations During the 1994 Genocide in Rwanda,* S/1999/1257, December 15, 1999, www.un.org /news/ossg/rwanda_report.htm.

74. ICISS, *The Responsibility to Protect: Report of the International Commission on Intervention and State Sovereignty* (Ottawa: International Development Research Centre for ICISS, 2001), 32.

75. United Nations press release, SG/SM/7263, AFR/196, December 16, 1999, www.un.org /Docs/SG/sgsm.htm.

76. Gareth Evans, "The Responsibility to Protect After Libya and Syria," address to Castan Centre Human Rights Law Conference, Melbourne, July 20, 2012, www.gevans.org /speeches/speech475.html.

77. Secretary Powell's remarks were contained in testimony before the US Senate Foreign Relations Committee and reported in the news. See Glenn Kessler and Colum Lynch, "U.S. Calls Killings in Sudan Genocide," *Washington Post,* September 10, 2004.

78. Colum Lynch, "They Just Stood Watching," *Foreign Policy,* April 7, 2014.

79. Colum Lynch, "A Mission That Was Set Up to Fail," *Foreign Policy,* April 8, 2014.

80. Luke Glanville, "Syria Teaches Us Little About Questions of Military Intervention," in E-IR's edited collection *Into the Eleventh Hour: R2P, Syria and Humanitarianism in Crisis* (2014), www.e-ir.info/2014/2002/2007/syria-teaches-us-little-about-questions-of-military -intervention.

81. Thomas G. Weiss, "The Sunset of Humanitarian Intervention? The Responsibility to Protect in a Unipolar Era," *Security Dialogue* 35, no. 2 (2004): 135.

82. Thomas Weiss, "After Syria, Whither R2P?" in E-IR's edited collection *Into the Eleventh Hour: R2P, Syria and Humanitarianism in Crisis* (2014), www.e-ir.info/2014/2002/2002 /after-syria-whither-r2012p.

83. Fred Kaplan, "It's Not What We Ought to Do, but What We Can Do," *Slate,* August 19, 2011.

84. Morton Abramowitz and Samantha Power, "A Broken System," *Washington Post,* September 13, 2004.

85. Inis L. Claude Jr., *Swords into Plowshares: The Problems and Progress of International Organization,* 3rd ed. (New York: Random House, 1964), 267.

86. Thakur, *The United Nations, Peace, and Security,* 165.

87. Trevor Findlay, "Weapons of Mass Destruction," in *Multilateralism Under Challenge? Power, International Order, and Structural Change,* ed. Edward Newman, Ramesh Thakur, and John Tirman (New York: UN University Press, 2006), 228.

88. Mark Landler, "Nuclear Agency Votes to Report Iran to U.N. Security Council for Treaty Violations," *New York Times,* September 25, 2005.

89. Thakur, *The United Nations, Peace, and Security,* 169. On the legislative character, see also Ian Johnstone, "The Security Council as Legislature," in *The UN Security Council and the Politics of International Authority,* ed. Bruce Cronin and Ian Hurd (New York: Routledge, 2008), 80–104.

90. Olivia Bosch and Peter van Ham, "UNSCR 1540: Its Future and Contribution to Global Non-Proliferation and Counter-Terrorism," in *Global Non-Proliferation and Counter-*

Terrorism: The Impact of UNSCR 1540, ed. Olivia Bosch and Peter van Ham (London: Chatham, 2007), 212.

91. Waheguru Pal Singh Sidhu, "Weapons of Mass Destruction: Managing Proliferation," in *The UN Security Council in the 21st Century,* ed. Sebastian von Einsiedel, David M. Malone, and Bruno Stagno Ugarte (Boulder, CO: Lynne Rienner, 2016), 340.

92. Richard Price and Nina Tannenwald, "Norms and Deterrence: The Nuclear and Chemical Weapons Taboo," in *The Culture of National Security: Norms and Identity in World Politics,* ed. Peter J. Katzenstein (New York: Columbia University Press, 1996), 129.

93. Naftali Bendavid, "Removal of Chemical Weapons from Syria Is Completed," *Wall Street Journal,* June 23, 2014.

94. Charbel Raji, "100% of Declared Chemical Weapons Materials Destroyed or Removed from Syria," OPCW-UN Joint Mission in the Syrian Republic, June 23, 2014, http://opcw.unmissions.org/LinkClick.aspx?fileticket=pbq2OEoBdL8%3d&tabid=54.

95. United Nations, "Secretary-General's Remarks to Security Council High-Level Summit on Foreign Terrorist Fighters," September 24, 2014, www.un.org/sg/statements/index.asp?nid=8040.

96. Maurcio Artinano, Peter Blair, Nicolas Collin, Beatrice Godefroy, Conor Godfrey, Brieana Marticorena, Daphne McCurdy, Owen McDougall, and Steve Ross, *Adapting and Evolving: The Implications of Transnational Terrorism for United Nations Field Missions* (Princeton: Woodrow Wilson School for Public and International Affairs, Princeton University, 2014).

97. David Rothkopf, "We Are Losing the War on Terror."

98. M. J. Peterson, "Using the General Assembly," in *Terrorism and the UN: Before and After September 11,* ed. Jane Boulden and Thomas G. Weiss (Bloomington: Indiana University Press, 2004), 178.

99. David Cortright et al., "Global Cooperation Against Terrorism: Evaluating the United Nations Counter-Terrorism Committee," in *Uniting Against Terror: Cooperative Nonmilitary Responses to the Global Terrorist Threat,* ed. David Cortright and George Lopez (Cambridge, MA: MIT Press, 2007), 27.

100. See the High-Level Panel's report, *A More Secure World,* www.un.org/secureworld.

101. *2005 World Summit Outcome,* General Assembly A/60/L.1, section 81, www.un-ngls.org/un-summit-FINAL-DOC.pdf.

102. Cortright et al., "Global Cooperation Against Terrorism," 29.

103. J. Cockayne, A. Millar, and J. Ipe, "An Opportunity for Renewal: Revitalizing the United Nations Counterterrorism Program," Center for Global Counterterrorism Cooperation, September 2010, www.globalct.org/resources_publications.php.

104. Peter Romaniuk, "Responding to Terrorism," in *The UN Security Council in the 21st Century,* ed. Sebastian von Einsiedel, David M. Malone, and Bruno Stagno Ugarte (Boulder, CO: Lynne Rienner, 2016), 291.

105. Michael Mandelbaum, "The Reluctance to Intervene," *Foreign Policy,* no. 93 (Summer 1994): 11.

106. See "United Nations Peacekeeping Operations," fact sheet, March 31, 2015, www.un.org/en/peacekeeping/archive/2015/bnote0315.pdf.

107. Kofi Annan, *Annual Report of the Secretary-General to the General Assembly,* SG /SM7136 GA/9596, September 20, 1999.

108. Jane Boulden and Thomas G. Weiss, "Whither Terrorism and the United Nations?" in *Terrorism and the UN: Before and After September 11,* ed. Jane Boulden and Thomas G. Weiss (Bloomington: Indiana University Press, 2004), 17.

109. Security Council Report, "Women, Peace and Security," no. 2, 2014, www.security councilreport.org/atf/cf/%7B65BFCF69B-66D27–64E69C-68CD63-CF66E64FF96 FF69%67D/cross_cutting_report_62_women_peace_security_2014.pdf.

5

Economic Development and Sustainability

> We are at a historic crossroads, and the direction we take will deter-
> mine whether we will succeed or fail in fulfilling our promises. With
> our globalized economy and sophisticated technology, we can decide
> to end the age-old ills of extreme poverty and hunger. Or we can con-
> tinue to degrade our planet and allow intolerable inequalities to sow
> bitterness and despair.
>
> — Synthesis Report of the Secretary-General
> on the Post-2015 Sustainable Development Agenda

Since the UN's founding, fundamental changes have taken place in international economic relations and in understandings of development. The global economy has been reshaped by many dichotomies, including globalization tempered by state fragmentation, unprecedented wealth in some locations coupled with the deepening of poverty in others, and major advances in technology complicated by the unanticipated and sometimes unwanted consequences of technological advancement.

The paradigms used to explain these global economic trends are also chang-ing. Where once development was conceived largely in terms of national eco-nomic growth and measured by changes in aggregate and per capita income, a more holistic view has emerged in the broad concept of **human development**: the notion that the general improvement in human well-being and **poverty alleviation** is a primary development objective—an objective that cannot be reached by increasing gross national product (GNP) alone. The notion of human development itself was reframed in 2015 as the UN took a more integrated approach that views reducing poverty and inequality as part of a broader social and environmental context focused on sustainable development.

Historically, much of the activity related to managing international economic relations more generally has taken place outside the UN itself in what are called the Bretton Woods institutions (the World Bank, the International Monetary Fund, and the General Agreement on Tariffs and Trade, since succeeded by the World Trade Organization) and, since the mid-1970s, in the Group of 7 (G-7), which is composed of the major industrialized countries. Since the 2008–2009 global financial crisis, the Group of 20 (G-20) developed and emerging economies has also been involved in international economic governance. The World Bank and IMF are UN specialized agencies that technically report to ECOSOC; however, they have traditionally operated independently. Nonetheless, the UN and UN-sponsored global conferences have provided much of the intellectual leadership in developing key ideas and frameworks for thinking about development, and UN programs and specialized agencies have undertaken major development tasks, working with other actors in partnerships for development.

THE ORGANIZATION OF THE UN SYSTEM
FOR PROMOTING ECONOMIC DEVELOPMENT

The UN Charter

The UN Charter's provisions on economic and social development reflected a liberal vision of building institutions and programs to promote prosperity and peace through international cooperation and industrial change. These were also strongly influenced by European social democracy and the American New Deal of the 1930s, both of which envisioned expanding the role of government to deal with social and economic problems. Thus, achieving "international cooperation in solving international problems of an economic, social, cultural, or humanitarian character" is among the provisions of the Charter's Chapter I and is described in Article 55 as "necessary for peaceful and friendly relations among nations." Yet the specific provisions for carrying out this broad mandate are limited, particularly when contrasted with the extensive sections on managing threats to international peace and security.

In Article 13, the General Assembly is given responsibility for providing general direction, coordination, and supervision for economic and social activities through its Second Committee. Chapter X empowers ECOSOC specifically to undertake studies and prepare reports, make recommendations, prepare conventions, convene conferences, create specialized agencies, and make recommendations for their coordination. And, as discussed in Chapter 2, the founders of the UN envisaged that the specialized agencies affiliated with the UN would play key roles in carrying out operational activities aimed at economic and social advancement, coordinated through ECOSOC. One group of scholars describes ECOSOC as "something of a mailbox between the General Assembly and the rest of the socioeconomic agencies."[1]

Indeed, there was never the expectation that economic activities would be centralized in an "economic security council." Instead, authority on economic issues was dispersed all over the UN system. One could argue that the very characteristics of the issue area of economics—many subissues affecting everyone differently—mean that authority will always be divided, just as it is in most national governments.[2] Over time, the UN has established organizations to address various economic issues and developed several approaches to fulfilling the operational side of its mandate to promote economic and social advancement. These include the commitment to technical assistance; educational and training programs; the creation of regional commissions to decentralize planning and programs; information gathering, especially by the functional commissions; setting international goals for development; the work of the Bretton Woods institutions; seeking to redress the imbalance in less developed countries' international trade relationships; and the activities of various specialized agencies and programs as well as partnerships with other international organizations and NGOs in promotion of development.

UN Approaches to Development

Technical Assistance and the UN Development Program. In the late 1940s, experts realized that less developed countries lacked the necessary capital for infrastructure development. Discussion on how investment could be channeled grew out of a 1948 General Assembly mandate and US president Harry Truman's 1949 inaugural address. The World Bank, which had already been established, was concentrating on the rehabilitation of war-torn Europe; its strict terms made borrowing problematic for developing countries. Debate between the developed and developing countries was intense, with the latter arguing for a large fund to finance all types of investment, while the former envisaged a much smaller fund to establish research institutes, finance regional training centers, conduct natural resources surveys, and support other preinvestment projects.

The developed countries won the debate. What emerged in 1950 was the UN Expanded Programme of Technical Assistance (EPTA), which, by later in the same decade, had become the primary UN development agency.[3] Through that program, the UN awarded fellowships for advanced training, supplied equipment for training purposes, and provided project experts recruited from around the world. Many projects were jointly funded by the UN and specialized agencies such as WHO, FAO, UNESCO, or one of the regional economic commissions discussed below. EPTA pioneered the approach of asking governments to review their needs and develop plans and administrative machinery for country programs to establish the principle of country ownership and control. Today, regular UN budget funds for technical assistance are frequently augmented by voluntary contributions from member states. This development assistance consists of grant aid, not loans; hence, it does not create future burdens for recipient countries.

In 1965, the General Assembly created the United Nations Development Programme to enhance coordination of the various types of technical assistance programs within the UN system. As noted above, UNDP reports to the UN General Assembly, not ECOSOC—illustrating again the decentralized UN approach. And over the years, UNDP itself has become more decentralized. One scholar who has conducted extensive field observations of UNDP's work describes UNDP as a "decentralized complex of relatively autonomous (and creative) people and organizations involving independent experts, short-term alliances, and joint projects."[4]

Working in more than 170 countries, UNDP's contribution can be seen in three areas. First, UNDP focuses UN activities in recipient countries through a resident representative. These representatives are expected to assess local needs and priorities, coordinate technical assistance programs, serve as representatives for some of the specialized agencies, and generally link the United Nations with the recipient government. Although the resident representative positions have grown in significance, the resources at their disposal are still dwarfed by those of the World Bank and major bilateral aid donors, let alone private investors. This limits their power to coordinate country-based activities. The relative autonomy of the specialized agencies makes coordination even more difficult.

Second, UNDP has played an important role in developing and institutionalizing core development ideas. Among the most influential is the annual publication of the *Human Development Report*, beginning in 1990. The reports call attention to new development dimensions and new policies and provide annual updates of the Human Development Index (HDI) for all countries. Based on a composite of indicators for health, education, and income, the HDI helps decisionmakers set priorities for development assistance. The reports draw attention to core ideas reflecting UN system-wide priorities, such as "Making New Technologies Work for Human Development" (2001), "Human Mobility and Development" (2009), and "Sustaining Human Progress: Reducing Vulnerabilities and Building Resilience" (2014). In addition to the global reports, UNDP encourages and supports national and regional reports on human development, thus enabling specific countries and groups to choose additional culturally appropriate indicators for both economic development and political governance. The most well-known of these regional reports is the *Arab Human Development Report*, published annually since 2002. The 2004 edition was particularly noteworthy for singling out repressive Arab governments as responsible for the poor development record in the region.[5] Thus, over time UNDP has acquired a "special voice and pulpit and authority to develop alternative ideas."[6]

Third, UNDP's expanded mission calls for stimulating institutional capacities not just in states, its original focus, but also within civil society organizations, regional institutions, and other stakeholders. This broad-based institutional focus is consistent with the idea that institutions are critical for sustainability and that partnerships among institutions are necessary. Thus, UNDP provides technical assistance in collaboration with other donors and supports various state and civil society activities.

Regional Commissions. One key ECOSOC innovation was the establishment of regional economic commissions. In 1947, two of what became a network of five regional commissions were formed: the Economic Commission for Europe (ECE) and the Economic Commission for Asia and the Far East (renamed in the 1970s the Economic and Social Commission for Asia and the Pacific, or ESCAP, after the Commission for Western Asia was formed). Shortly thereafter, in 1948, the Economic Commission for Latin America (ECLA) came into being, and ten years later, the Economic Commission for Africa (ECA) was formed. These commissions are designed to stimulate independent regional approaches to development with studies and initiatives to promote regional projects. In both 1977 and 1979, the UN General Assembly expanded the tasks of the commissions to become coordinating agencies for intersectoral, subregional, regional, and interregional UN-related projects.[7]

The UN's regional approach has met with considerable success in articulating new approaches to economic development and in promoting regional and subregional institutions. The European commission under the leadership of the Swedish development economist Gunnar Myrdal provided an early impetus to European integration. The Latin American group played an important role during the 1950s in critiquing the liberal economic model's applicability to dependent states. Under the leadership of Raúl Prebisch, ECLA encouraged states to adopt import substitution policies to escape economic dependency. Many of its ideas formed the theoretical basis for the New International Economic Order proposals of the 1970s, especially in the area of commodity policy. The Economic Commission for Africa in the late 1960s helped draw attention to women's roles in development when it organized the first regional workshop on the topic. And the ECA through its role in the Lagos Plan of Action for Economic Development of Africa, 1980–2000, spearheaded an alternative economic view with its goals of self-reliance, sustainability, and democratizing the development process.

In terms of institution-building, the regional commissions have been responsible for laying the groundwork for a plethora of other regional arrangements, by either directly proposing a new institution, giving financial impetus to new organizations, or actively supporting their creation. ECLA contributed to the establishment of the Central American Common Market (CACM) and the Inter-American Development Bank (IDB), pushing regional industrialization projects. ECA was instrumental in support of the African Development Bank. Sometimes the success of those regional organizations, such as the Association of Southeast Asian Nations (ASEAN), has led to a weakening of the regional commission. ESCAP has become less powerful and more ceremonial, and it has turned its attention away from economic issues.

All the commissions produce high-quality economic surveys of their respective regions, as well as country plans used by national governments and other multilateral institutions. All address the diverse issues of trade, industry, energy, and transportation. Yet disputes among members, such as Arab versus non-Arab states in the Commission for Western Asia, and the lack of resources and expertise in Africa, have hampered the work of some commissions.

Information Gathering: The Functional Commissions. The functional commissions reporting to ECOSOC cover a wide range of responsibilities, but among their most important is gathering, analyzing, and disseminating different types of information. Several of these commissions have played instrumental roles in development. Here we focus on the Statistical Commission, while the Commission on the Status of Women is discussed later in this chapter. Two are discussed in later chapters—the now-defunct Commission on Human Rights (Chapter 6) and the Commission on Sustainable Development (Chapter 7). The work of the Commission on Transnational Corporations was incorporated into UNCTAD in 1994.

The UN's seminal role in the evolution of development thinking owed much to what in the late 1940s and 1950s was a very small community of development scholars as well as to the organization's growing research capacity. That included new ways of measuring and quantifying different types of indicators for development. Creating that statistical system was, in the words of one scholar, "one of the great and mostly unsung successes of the UN Organization."[8]

Beginning in 1945, the UN Statistical Commission worked to set international standards for gathering and reporting statistics. In the early years, this meant establishing standards for national accounts, for example. Then, as new ideas permeated the system, various UN agencies recognized the need to collect data that had not previously been collected by member states, let alone analyzed and disseminated worldwide. This included trends in world trade, population growth, food, and industrial production.

In the 1970s and 1980s, the UN emphasis turned to standardizing social statistics on such issues as fertility, hunger, and nutrition. As more attention was being paid to the roles of women in development and the status of women generally, there was a recognized need to collect data by gender. As a result, the UN Commission on the Status of Women compiled and published *The World's Women: Trends and Statistics, 1970–1990*, the first such compilation—an invaluable resource that is updated every five years.[9] In addition to the HDI, developed by UNDP in the early 1990s, several other indexes have since been introduced, including the Gender Development Index, the Gender Empowerment Measure, the Human Poverty Index, and the Worldwide Governance Indicators. The last of these is unique because it measures dimensions of governance, including accountability, political stability, effectiveness, rule of law, and control of corruption.

In short, the information gathering and analyses undertaken by various UN agencies, including the Statistical Commission, are critical for member states' development planning and for UN policy debates. They have also contributed to another major approach: setting goals.

Setting Goals. By the early 1960s, decolonization had produced the demographic shift in UN membership that dramatically changed the focus of the organization's agenda as discussed in Chapters 1 and 2. With a push from President John F. Kennedy's address to the General Assembly in 1961, that body proclaimed the 1960s as the "United Nations Development Decade." This marked a new role: setting internationally agreed upon goals and targets as a way of mobilizing support for the steps both developed and developing nations needed to take to accelerate progress. The first decade succeeded in spurring attention to development issues, adoption of national planning as a development tool, new studies of links between trade and development, and efforts to increase capacity to adapt science and technology to developing countries' needs. In addition, it saw the creation of new institutions, including UNDP, the World Food Programme, the United Nations Conference on Trade and Development, and the United Nations Industrial Development Organization.

The first development decade was followed by three subsequent development decades. In each, there were clearly articulated goals: targets for annual aid to developing states and targets for increases in the average annual growth rates of developing countries, as well as their exports, domestic savings, and agricultural production.

The development decades, however, are not the only examples of UN goal setting to provide guidelines for economic and social development. Other goals have included eradication of smallpox, expansion of education, reductions in child mortality, increases in life expectancy, and expansion of development. Significant progress has been achieved for many goals in many countries, and the goal of eradicating smallpox was completely achieved. Not surprisingly, the greatest shortfalls have been in sub-Saharan Africa and the least developed

countries. One group of analysts notes that "expectations about performance in
the 1960s raised the stakes in later decades, and economic performance increasingly fell below the more ambitious economic targets."[10]

The most recent UN goal-setting initiative involves the Sustainable Development Goals (SDGs), approved in 2015. They constitute a new approach—one
that endeavors to bring together much of what has been learned over the past
seventy years of development efforts and builds on the Millennium Development Goals that were approved in 2000, which brought together all parts of the
UN system for the first time ever. For that reason, these two successive goal-
setting initiatives are discussed separately below. Some of the most important
UN system economic activities, however, especially in terms of leadership and
funding, are found in the Bretton Woods institutions, which have long been
viewed as outside the UN system.

The Bretton Woods Institutions. The origins of the Bretton Woods institutions
can be found in the Great Depression of the 1930s, predating the founding of
the UN itself. Not only were millions of people impoverished, but the prices
of most raw materials also plummeted, causing the people in Europe's African
and Asian colonies and the independent countries of Latin America to suffer.
Countries adopted "beggar thy neighbor" policies, raising barriers to imports
and causing world trade to collapse. With that collapse, US and British economists realized that international institutions were needed to help countries with
balance-of-payments difficulties, provide stable exchange rates and economic
assistance, and promote nondiscrimination in and reciprocal lowering of barriers to trade. The lesson was confirmed by the realization in 1944–1945 that
recovery and rebuilding after World War II would require more capital than
war-ravaged countries alone could expect to provide. Hence, in 1944, a meeting at Bretton Woods established the International Bank for Reconstruction and
Development (IBRD, known as the World Bank), the International Monetary
Fund, and a nascent trade arrangement (which became the General Agreement
on Tariffs and Trade). When the UN was subsequently established, these institutions became specialized UN agencies reporting to ECOSOC. Yet, having
overwhelming economic resources and a high degree of legal autonomy, they
quickly became central parts of international economic relations.

The International Bank for Reconstruction and Development, or World Bank. The
World Bank's initial task was to facilitate reconstruction in post–World War II
Europe. In fact, because the task proved so great, the United States financed the
bulk of it bilaterally through the European Recovery Program (or Marshall Plan)
rather than multilaterally through the bank. During the 1950s, the bank shifted
focus from reconstruction to development. Unlike the UN, where member

assessments provide the financing, the bank generates capital funds largely from international financial markets and, to a lesser extent, from its member states. Unlike the UN, which offers grants, the bank lends money at market interest rates to states for major economic development projects. Its lending is not designed to replace private capital but to facilitate its operation by funding projects that private banks would not support, such as infrastructure (dams, bridges, highways), primary education, and health. Unlike private banks, the World Bank attaches conditions to its loans in the form of policy changes it would like to see states make to promote economic development and alleviate poverty.

To aid the World Bank in meeting the needs of developing countries, the International Finance Corporation (IFC) and the International Development Association (IDA) were created in 1956 and 1960, respectively. IDA provides capital to the poorest countries, usually in the form of no-interest ("soft" or concessional) loans with long repayment schedules (fifty years), to allow the least developed countries more time to reach "takeoff," sustain growth, and hence develop economically. Such funds have to be continually replenished or added to by major donor countries. The creation of IDA was a direct response to pressure from the developing countries for concessional loans. The IFC provides loans to promote the growth of private enterprises in developing countries. In 1988, the Multilateral Investment Guarantee Agency (MIGA) was added to the World Bank group. This agency's goal—to augment the flow of private equity capital to less developed countries—is met by insuring investments against losses. Such losses may include expropriation, government currency restrictions, and losses stemming from civil war or ethnic conflict. The World Bank family of institutions now also incorporates the International Centre for Settlement of Investment Disputes (ICSID). The World Bank, like the other development organizations, the UN itself, and major donor governments, provides funding for development projects, working with both governments and other donors to establish priorities. What the bank has funded, to whom those funds are given, and the conditions attached have changed over time, reflecting new thinking about development itself.

During the 1950s and early 1960s, the emphasis was on funding major infrastructure projects, with funds allocated only to governments; such projects (dams, hydroelectric plants, highways, airports) were viewed as vital to jump-start the development process. In the late 1960s and early 1970s, there was a move to fund projects meeting **basic human needs**, programs in education, the social sectors, and health. Beginning in the 1980s, the bank moved to support private-sector participation and greater NGO voice and participation in projects. With its sister institution, the IMF, the bank pushed a staunchly neoliberal economic agenda of **privatization**, opening markets for capital and trade flow, and **structural adjustment programs**, as explained below.

While the UN itself was increasingly marginalized in economic matters, it continued to serve as a forum for critics of the effects of these priorities, and offered new ideas and approaches. Most notable were the linkages between women and development and between the environment and development and poverty alleviation, as shown below. Thus, by the 1990s, when the bank added environmentally sustainable development, good governance, and poverty alleviation to its priorities, it was the result of influences from elsewhere within the UN system as well as from NGOs.[11] Currently, the World Bank's 188 members, together with its affiliates such as IDA, provide over $30 billion annually to 100 countries for more than 300 projects. Though their initial mandates differed, the bank now also works closely with the IMF.

The International Monetary Fund. The IMF's chief function at the outset was to stabilize currency exchange rates by providing short-term loans for member states with temporary **balance-of-payments** difficulties. Funds to meet such needs were contributed by members according to quotas negotiated every five years and payable both in gold and in local currency. Members could borrow up to the amount they had contributed. Stable currency values and currency convertibility facilitate trade, and trade was viewed as a critical engine for development. At the outset, it was thought that states' balance-of-payments shortfalls would be short-lived, and the IMF was to fill the gap.

Increasingly, developing states were experiencing long-term structural economic problems, plagued by persistent high debts and continual balance-of-payments disequilibrium. States could not develop under those conditions. Thus, beginning with the 1982 Mexican debt crisis, the IMF took on the role of intermediary in negotiations between creditors and debtor countries, and also became involved in dictating policy changes as conditions of lending. The IMF came to believe, as did the World Bank, that such changes were essential prerequisites to development. As a result, although the IMF was never intended to be a development institution, its responsibilities have increasingly overlapped with those of the bank and its activities extended into areas of economic activity that the UN has never touched.

Beginning in the 1980s, the IMF insisted on structural adjustment programs, requiring countries to institute economic policy reforms or achieve certain conditions, often referred to as conditionality, in return for economic assistance from both multilateral and bilateral lenders. Labeled the "Washington Consensus," the conditions included trade liberalization, economic reforms to eliminate subsidies and introduce user fees, and government reforms such as cutting waste and privatizing public enterprises, consistent with liberal economic theory. The IMF monitored the adjustment programs and determined whether performance criteria were met. During the 1997–1998 financial crisis in Asia, for example, the fund pushed Indonesia to change its entire economic system. In the 1990s, the IMF was also instrumental in the transitions of Russia and other former Communist countries to market economies. The very large size of IMF aid packages for several countries, including Mexico, Russia, and South Korea, effectively placed the IMF in the position of "bailing out" countries on the verge of economic collapse where there were concerns about contagion to other countries. The World Bank and the IMF were both involved in structural adjustment lending (the fund through short-term emergency loans and its negotiating and monitoring roles, the bank through aid for long-term structural reforms).

For almost three decades since the 1980s, vehement criticisms have focused on structural adjustment programs and the imposition of conditionality. Many believe these exact excessive social and economic costs and represent a cookie-cutter approach to complex problems without regard for particular local situations. In this view, bank and fund programs disproportionately affect the already disadvantaged sectors of the population: the unskilled, women, and the poor. Some have been especially outraged by intrusions of these institutions into areas of domestic policy traditionally protected by state sovereignty.[12] Criticism even emerged from within the institutions themselves, some noting that the bank and fund have not followed their own procedures, that bailouts have gone to countries making unwise economic decisions, and that states have been pushed too soon to open their economies to the risks in volatile international financial flows.[13]

Beginning in 2009, the IMF discontinued structural performance criteria for loans, even for loans to low-income countries, in response to both its critics and the 2008 global financial crisis. This represented a substantial overhaul of its lending framework. The amount of the loans can now be greater, and loans are to be tailored according to the respective state's needs, a direct response to the criticism of the cookie-cutter approach of structural adjustment lending. Monitoring of the loans will be done more quietly to reduce the stigma attached to conditionality. Also in response to previous criticism, the IMF has urged lending to programs that encourage social safety nets for the most vulnerable groups. Ideas that were previously unacceptable to the IMF—that capital flows may need regulation and that states might take a proactive role in coordinating economic development—became more acceptable in response to the market failures of the global financial crisis.[14] In all these new emphases, the fund is working closely with the World Bank and other donors.

The global financial crisis of 2008–2009 brought out both the strengths and the weaknesses of the fund. As the crisis manager, the IMF sharply increased its concessional lending and provided policy advice. Emergency loans were made to Pakistan, Guatemala, numerous African countries, Iceland (the first to a developed country), and Hungary. The fund established new credit lines with expanded flexibility for programs and attached fewer conditions. As a result, the fund was revitalized by the crisis, leading to a number of reforms. It played a major role in the euro zone crisis that followed, bailing out both Ireland and Greece. In 2014, the fund provided $17 billion to help the embattled pro-Western government in Ukraine, albeit imposing stringent austerity measures similar to those imposed in earlier crises.

Critics of IMF crisis responses have focused on the so-called moral hazard problem of IMF rescue packages that seemingly encouraged international investors and states to engage in still more reckless behavior because they could count on the fund's safety net. Whose interests was the fund serving? Others think that more money and fewer conditions would help pull countries out of crisis faster. Some critics have focused on the secrecy of negotiations between the fund and member countries. The IMF itself has retreated somewhat from its earlier commitment to fiscal discipline and free markets, encouraging governments to continue spending to stimulate growth. In 2014, IMF managing director Christine Lagarde endorsed internal studies that showed the need to reduce income inequality to achieve sustainable growth and social stability.

Governance within the bank and fund has also come under increasing scrutiny in recent years. By convention, the IMF managing director has always been a European and the World Bank president an American. Both positions carry wide-ranging power and authority. Everyday policies are made by limited-member executive boards operating under **weighted voting systems** that guarantee the voting power of the major donors commensurate with their contributions. Domination by the few opens both institutions to criticism from developing countries that have little power within the two institutions. In the IMF, for example, the United States commands 16.43 percent of shares (and votes), Japan 6.13 percent, Germany 5.30 percent, and France and the United Kingdom each 4.02 percent. With reforms approved in 2010, China saw its share increased to 6.06 percent (third-highest behind the United States and Japan) and it gained a separate executive director for that increased share, while India and Brazil also had increases in their quotas and votes. It took until late 2015, however, for the US Congress to ratify the changes.

Although changing economic power is reflected in bank and fund voting, key Western power is still reflected in the two bureaucracies, which employ economists trained largely in Western countries in the same liberal economic tradition as US decisionmakers. Both institutions are also criticized for being secretive and lacking transparency, even though the establishment of the Independent Evaluation Office and more extensive use of the Internet in the IMF have improved the situation. For these reasons, the least-developed countries have traditionally supported the UN's development-related institutions and ideas, where they enjoy a louder voice.

CARTOON 5.1. "New Economic Order," by Paresh Nath, *Khaleej Times*, July 28, 2015

Frustration with the delay in implementing IMF reforms, however, and the continuing dominance of Western developed countries in both the World Bank and IMF, led the BRICS countries to initiate the New Development Bank and China to create the Asian Infrastructure Investment Bank in 2015 as alternative sources of development funding. Both are based in Shanghai, with China providing significant portions of their funding.

Trade Issues and the GATT, UNCTAD, and WTO. Initially, the Bretton Woods institutions were to include a body called the International Trade Organization. That organization was expected to provide a general framework for trade rules and a forum for ongoing trade discussions. Lack of support in the US Senate, however, killed the proposed organization in 1948. In its place, the General Agreement on Tariffs and Trade was established "temporarily" to provide a framework for trade negotiations. GATT provided an approach to international trade based on principles of trade liberalization, nondiscrimination in trade, and reciprocity. With only a loose link to the UN, GATT and its small staff oversaw trade negotiations in eight successive multilateral rounds of negotiations.

During those rounds, most decisions were taken bilaterally, then multilateral-ized. Each successive round produced tariff cuts on an increasing volume of trade. Gradually, beginning in the late 1960s, treatment for the developing countries was improved, with preferential access to developed-country markets and the elimination of subsidies and rules governing nontariff trade barriers such as government procurement and technical barriers.

UNCTAD. Yet within GATT, the interests of the industrialized countries took precedence. Through the 1950s, many less developed countries grew increasingly dissatisfied with GATT's emphasis on trade in manufactured products and its lack of interest in the commodity problem and in trade as a way to transfer economic resources from rich countries to poor ones. Frustrated by the slow response of the Bretton Woods institutions generally to their development needs and by the developed countries' dominance of these institutions, developing countries proposed an international conference to establish principles and policies to govern international trade relations and to guide trade policies. Thus, in 1964, the UN Conference on Trade and Development became a permanent body reporting to the General Assembly, but with its own secretary-general. UNCTAD supporters resisted becoming a separate specialized UN agency, preferring to draw strength from the General Assembly, where developing countries commanded a majority of votes.

UNCTAD's founding conference in 1964 recommended a number of general principles to govern international trade relations as well as recognizing the need for a system of **trade preferences**. Reciprocity, a core GATT principle, was viewed as serving only to perpetuate dependency and underdevelopment. The inherently unequal international liberal trading system could not be made more equal without major changes. Thus, the developing countries argued that they needed special concessions—including preferential access to developed-country markets—to improve their trade. UNCTAD emphasized that the developed countries had a major role to play in addressing the problems of trade affecting developing countries. And it brought into the open the growing split—which persists today—between developed and developing countries over issues relating to trade and development.

UNCTAD continues to meet every four years, and the Trade and Development Board, its permanent governing organ, meets annually. The UNCTAD secretariat has been important in shaping its work because of its close ties with the G-77; it also provides research, analysis, and training for government officials to remedy the limited expertise of many developing countries' governments on complex international trade issues. UNCTAD's dynamics were long shaped by a pattern of group bargaining, prompted by the G-77's high degree of unity and the one-state/one-vote mode of majority decisionmaking. Despite efforts to develop operational responsibilities, it has functioned largely as a forum for debate, negotiation, and legitimation of new norms. It was the primary forum for articulating the major challenges to the predominant liberal thinking about economic development, including the New International Economic Order, discussed below.[15] It has failed to win support, however, from major donor countries and from many mainstream professional economists.[16]

Currently, UNCTAD meetings address such issues as commodity diversification, trade and commercial negotiations, transportation, macroeconomic policies, multinational corporations, and debt financing. Although it sponsors programs for the least-developed countries, including the landlocked and small-island developing countries, its activities have diminished. Even with the divergence in developing countries' interests and few substantial achievements over more than fifty years, many still view UNCTAD positively as a valuable forum.

The World Trade Organization. Although the interests of the industrialized countries took precedence in GATT, gradually, under pressure from the G-77 and UNCTAD, more favorable, preferential treatment for less developed countries was achieved. The eighth or Uruguay Round of GATT negotiations concluded in December 1993 with the establishment of a true global trade organization—the World Trade Organization. The agreement also addressed two topics previously excluded from the GATT rules but critical for developing countries: agriculture and textiles.

Although the WTO has no formal relationship with the UN, it does provide a unified organizational structure for managing the growing complexity of global trade issues. WTO membership stood at 162 in 2015, with members conducting 96.4 percent of the world's trade. Like GATT before it, it is based on a contractual framework. Previously negotiated trade agreements are still valid, and joining the WTO involves negotiating the terms of a country's accession to those agreements. For example, when China became a member in 2001 after fifteen years of negotiations, the document setting forth the terms of accession was nine hundred pages long, and China's government had to revise many laws that restricted foreign access to its economy. To assist states in becoming liberalized, the WTO and UNCTAD secretariats jointly operate the International Trade Centre in Geneva to provide technical cooperation to developing and transitional countries in trade promotion and export development.

The WTO has been subject to many of the same criticisms as the World Bank and the IMF, particularly from those who see the organization as still representing more the interests of the developed world. Yet it functions very differently. It is a one-state/one-vote organization, unlike the IMF and World Bank; decision-making is generally by consensus, and a state's market share is its primary source of influence. The most recent Doha Round of trade negotiations—labeled the "Development Round"—began in 2001 and reached an impasse in 2008, with the United States, Japan, and the European Union on one side and the G-20 emerging countries, led by India, Brazil, and China, on the other. The latter insisted on the opening up of developed-country agricultural markets, while the United States and EU resisted. An agreement in late 2014 between India and the United States on the issue of food subsidies and stockpiles broke some of the logjam, allowing implementation of the Trade Facilitation Agreement concluded in 2013 and the first trade reform steps since the creation of the WTO itself in 1995.

There are serious doubts among trade experts, however, about whether another comprehensive WTO agreement is possible. Reaching agreement among 162 countries is a major challenge. The complexities of new trade issues in a world of globalized production networks for automobiles and other products are huge. Because of these difficulties, bilateral and regional trade agreements have proliferated in recent years, leaving the future of WTO-based world trade governance uncertain. Still, among the WTO's important innovations are its trade dispute mechanisms. In particular, the Dispute Settlement Unit has become one of the busiest international adjudicatory bodies, with the EU, United States, and China as complainants or respondents in an overwhelming number of the cases.

Although the WTO and UNCTAD-operated International Trade Centre assists developing countries with the technicalities of trade liberalization and negotiation, less developed countries have generally turned to the UN specialized agencies and programs for development assistance. To illustrate the work of UN specialized agencies as well as UN programs and partnerships, we look at agricultural development and emergency food aid.

The Specialized Agencies, Programs, and Partnerships. The nineteen specialized agencies are an integral part of the UN's approaches to international development and trade (see Figure 2.1), since development involves a variety of activities. Trade, for example, requires the means to transport goods and facilitate communications, hence the need for ocean shipping and air transport, hence the International Maritime Organization (IMO), the International Civil Aviation Organization (ICAO), the International Association of Transport Airlines (IATA), and the International Telecommunication Union (ITU). Industrial development depends on specific skills, with the UN Industrial Development Organization (UNIDO) supplying the expertise. Agricultural development has been promoted through a group of UN-related organizations, the Food and Agriculture Organization and the International Fund for Agricultural Development (IFAD), both UN specialized agencies. They are complemented by the

World Food Programme, created in 1963, and the Consultative Group on International Agricultural Research (CGIAR), established in 1972, among others. We examine briefly the role of the food agencies in promoting development.

Agricultural Development. The core organization of the international food regime, the FAO, was established in 1945 with the objective of increasing agricultural productivity to eliminate hunger and improve nutrition. Its experts provide policy and technical assistance to improve agriculture generally consistent with free trade principles. Based in Rome, it serves as a knowledge and information center for agricultural activities, including fishing and forestry. During the 1960s, the FAO supported the development and dissemination of high-yield strains of grain and rice that produced the "green revolution" for developing countries. In the 1980s and 1990s, sustainable agriculture and rural development became the organization's primary focus, in keeping with the changing ideas about development.

The rural extreme poor are the target population for the International Fund for Agricultural Development, established in 1977 following the 1974 World Food Conference. IFAD finances and cofinances projects to improve agricultural methods in rural areas, including critical ancillary activities such as financial services and off-farm employment. Because East Asia's rural poverty rates have dropped dramatically since the 1980s, worldwide extreme poverty rates have been reduced from 47 percent to 14 percent, but the persistence of African rural poverty means that 50 percent of IFAD funding goes to that continent.

Emergency Food Aid. In the international headlines responding to food emergencies during natural disasters, war, or famine is the World Food Programme, with its operational capacities to deliver food aid to food-deficit countries. The WFP's mission also includes aid in more protracted situations and for development. In 2015, the WFP fed more than 80 million people in eighty-two countries. In late 2015, it found itself working in six emergencies—Syria, Iraq, Yemen, South Sudan, Nepal, and the Ebola-affected regions in Guinea, Liberia, and Sierra Leone. Its resources, which come entirely from voluntary contributions, were stretched beyond capacity. Of the total estimated need of $7.9 billion, it had received only $4.4 billion. As a result, it was forced to cut the daily food allotments for Syrian refugees, for example.

More than 11,500 employees direct WFP's various field activities, including delivering food supplies, running food-for-work programs where individuals build roads or irrigation systems in exchange for food, and providing school-based feeding programs so that children remain in school. The WFP partners with more than 3,000 local NGOs and community-based organizations to actually distribute the food. Food used for emergency aid is generally donated by developed countries, often from agricultural surpluses. A new approach with funding from private foundations is testing whether the WFP can buy surplus crops from poor farmers in Africa and Central America to feed WFP recipients facing hunger. That "purchase for progress" project is intended to both help food-deficit populations and stimulate production by developing-country farmers.

Partnerships. Increasingly, the WFP partners with private donors such as MNCs. MasterCard, for example, provides cash and in-kind services in advance of emergencies, Unilever is working to improve the nutrition content of the food delivered, and PepsiCo is a primary donor in the Syrian refugee emergency; all are indicative of emerging public-private partnerships. CGIAR, a consortium of fifteen research centers such as the International Rice Research Institute (Philippines) and the International Institute of Tropical Agriculture (Nigeria), conducts scientific research on crops in developing countries. It exemplifies partnerships among various donors that include the UN's FAO and IFAD, the World Bank, the European Commission, the Bill and Melinda Gates Foundation, and donor states.

Many of the relationships among the UN agencies, NGOs, and the private sector were established during the UN-sponsored world food conferences in 1974, 1996, and 2002, which brought together various constituencies and called attention to a variety of agricultural and food problems. At the 2002 World Food Summit, for example, many traditional issues filled the agenda: food aid to end hunger, emergencies, food safety and phytosanitary regulations, and securing food under conditions of limited water supplies. Among the new issues were the New Partnership for Africa's Development (NEPAD) and the International Treaty on Plant Genetic Resources for Food and Agriculture, which engaged the debate on genetic engineering of food crops. More than 650 labor, human rights, and farmer groups participated in the conference, along with 180 countries. This was a clear signal that collaboration with NGOs would increase along with partnerships with multinational corporations such as the Italian food giant Parmalat, which provided funding for the summit.

The specialized agencies illustrate the UN's tendency, in common with many governments, to create new agencies and programs. Some institutions have been established because thinking about development has changed and new institutions meet new needs more readily than old institutions can be reformed. Thus, the UN system has evolved over time in its efforts to meet its mandate to foster cooperation for economic and social development. The result, however, can be problems of duplication, inefficiency, and lack of coordination, as discussed in Chapter 2. The newer challenges of globalization and the persistence of poverty heighten the need for economic governance and for better coordination of the different parts of the UN system, yet they do not lessen the value of the UN's longtime role in the development of norms and ideas.

THE UN AND EVOLVING IDEAS ABOUT DEVELOPMENT

In contrast to issues of peace and security, as well as thinking about the role of the UN and its Secretariat more generally, traditional international relations theories for the most part do not help us understand what has shaped the UN system in dealing with development. For that, we turn to ideas rooted in economic liberalism. The institutions discussed above, including the Bretton Woods institutions and most of the specialized agencies, were heavily shaped by development thinking in the immediate post–World War II period, particularly in Western Europe and North America, and, hence, by economic liberalism.

Economic Liberalism

Based on ideas from Adam Smith to contemporary thinkers, **economic liberalism** asserts that human beings are rational and acquisitive and will seek to improve their condition in the most expeditious manner possible. Markets develop to ensure that individuals are able to carry out the necessary transactions to improve their well-being. To maximize economic welfare and efficiency and to stimulate individual (and therefore collective) economic growth, markets must operate freely, economics and politics must be separated as much as possible, and governments must permit the free flow of trade and economic intercourse. If they do not interfere in the efficient allocation of resources provided by markets, the increasing interdependence between domestic economies will lead to greater cooperation and aggregate economic development.

Since multinational corporations expanded dramatically beginning in the 1960s, liberals have viewed them as key engines of growth. Economic development, it was thought, could best be achieved through open markets for goods and capital, with international agencies providing limited amounts of assistance in order for development to get off the ground. The private sector would be the engine of development. Yet very quickly, it was recognized that economic development did not just happen; planning was important, as was the development of needed skills, education, health, hygiene, and national administrative services. These were the roots of the initial UN technical assistance programs to develop states' capacity for growth. The Bretton Woods agencies would provide capital for specific infrastructure, address short-term balance-of-payments problems, and provide a forum to negotiate freer trade. FAO programs would be designed to enhance agricultural productivity. Enhanced productivity would lead to surpluses used to invest in growth opportunities across all sectors. But from shortly after the founding of the Bretton Woods system and the establishment of the

UN, these liberal economic ideas were challenged by some groups and programs within the UN itself.

Challenges to Economic Liberalism

Belief in the capacity of economic liberalism to meet development challenges was first questioned in the ECLA in the early 1950s and then in UNCTAD in the 1970s. Both in the UN Secretariat and ECLA, academic economists from Latin America argued that development could not take place without fundamental changes in international economic relations to redress the inequalities of power and wealth. Their position was embedded in Marxist thinking: that is, capitalist economic systems are inherently deterministic and expansionary, and they require new resources and the colonization of less developed regions to generate necessary profits. These economists saw the need for radical change in the distribution of international political and economic power if the disadvantaged position of developing countries was to be altered.[17] This view, known as dependency theory, posits that the capitalist international system divides states into two groups: those on the periphery and those at the core. Those on the periphery are locked into a permanent state of dependency. This dependency stems from the observation that the prices of primary commodity exports from the developing world do not keep pace with the prices of manufactured goods imported by the same countries. This inequality was perceived to be relatively permanent, irrespective of the domestic policies pursued or external assistance they received. Multinational corporations with extensive operations within such peripheral states were criticized for exacerbating the dependency, making these companies targets for nationalization.

In essence, dependency theory has argued that development could not take place without fundamental changes in international economic relations to redress the inequalities of power and wealth. These views had strong appeal and came to undergird much of the agenda of developing countries in the UN in the 1960s and 1970s.

The Debate over the New International Economic Order. During 1973 and 1974, the G-77, impatient with the slow progress toward development and bolstered by support from OPEC members—whom the developing countries admired for their challenge to the major oil companies and the developed world—increased its pressure for restructuring international economic relations. In two successive special sessions of the UN General Assembly in 1974–1975, in global conferences on food, population, and women, as well as in UNCTAD, the G-77 used its wide majority and strong solidarity to secure the adoption of the Declaration on the Establishment of a New International Economic Order and the Charter of Economic Rights and Duties of States. The

1975 Seventh Special Session of the UN General Assembly marked the peak of confrontation between developed North and developing South that dominated not only UNCTAD but much of the UN system, including the specialized agencies, in the 1970s.

Through the proposed NIEO, the G-77 sought changes in six major areas of international economic relations with the goal of altering the relationship of dependency between the developed and the developing countries. It sought changes in international trade, including adjustment in the **terms of trade**, to stabilize the prices of such commodities as coffee, cocoa, bauxite, tin, and sugar, and to link those prices with the price of finished products imported from developed countries. The G-77 also demanded greater authority over natural resources and foreign investment in developing countries, particularly through the regulation of MNCs. It wanted improved means of technology transfer to make it cheaper and more appropriate for the local needs. To propel development, the South also demanded increased foreign aid and improved terms and conditions.

Although the G-77 won adoption of the Generalized System of Preferences (GSP) in GATT in 1967, waiving the nondiscrimination rule, GSP schemes were applied unilaterally by the European Community, the United States, and others. They could be withdrawn at any time. Still, this was a step toward establishing the principle of preferential treatment for developing-country exports. The G-77 also won more favorable terms for commodity-price stabilization. On most other issues, however, the North refused to negotiate. No common fund was established to stabilize commodity prices. No regulations on MNCs were concluded. There were no dramatic increases in development assistance. In fact, by the late 1980s, "donor fatigue" had set in, and levels of official development assistance had steadily decreased.

Two other issues pushed by the G-77 remain on the agenda today—restructuring the international financial institutions and debt relief. As discussed above, changes in voting power in the World Bank and IMF were approved in 2010 but blocked by the US Congress until late 2015; in the WTO, emerging countries have become much more skilled at exercising leverage. For example, before the Doha Round of trade negotiations stalled, rich countries agreed to major concessions eliminating all tariffs and quotas on 97 percent of goods from the fifty poorest countries.

Debt Reduction. The issue of excessive debt in developing countries has also been much debated since the early 1970s. It has led some developing countries to spend as much as four times more on debt servicing than on social services or education. When repayment crowds out opportunities for investment in the economy, sectors such as infrastructure, health care, and education suffer. Poverty increases. The debt burden has increased the dependence of developing countries on foreign creditors and on the international financial institutions as well as reduced the ability of their citizens to control their own development policies.

Almost twenty years after the NIEO debate dominated UN agendas, a popular movement known as Jubilee 2000—a coalition of development-oriented NGOs, church groups, and labor groups—launched a campaign advocating debt cancellation. To overcome injustice and poverty, "Breaking the Chains of Debt" became its rallying cry. The movement attracted a broad following, with more than sixty national Jubilee campaigns. They demonstrated, sponsored forums, and lobbied UN regional groups, simplifying a complex issue and spurring action.

In 1996, the IMF and World Bank undertook a major policy shift called the Heavily Indebted Poor Countries Initiative (HIPC), an initiative that was accelerated in 1999 and in 2005, permitting 100 percent debt relief from the IMF and World Bank, among others. States seeking relief are required to submit a Poverty Reduction Strategy Paper and implement it. To be developed in consultation with groups from civil society and UN agencies such as UNDP, UNICEF, and WFP, the plan details how the debt relief funds will be channeled to social spending and how management reforms will be implemented to avoid future debt crises. By the middle of 2015, thirty-six states had received complete debt relief (out of thirty-nine eligible), thirty of them in Africa. About 44 percent of the funding comes from the IMF and other multilateral institutions, with the rest from bilateral creditors. The bank and fund rely on moral suasion to encourage creditors to cooperate. The Jubilee movement itself splintered after 2000, with its position vindicated by the HIPC.

The founding of UNCTAD coming out of dependency theory and subsequent actions by the G-77 coalescing in the NIEO provided a fundamental, sustained challenge to the dominant liberal economic thinking. More than four decades after the NIEO was first proposed and many of its key elements rejected, some elements such as debt relief and trade preferences for developing countries have been implemented. This has occurred despite the fact that there is now even wider acceptance (some say triumph) of economic liberalism. Yet there have also been modifications of liberalism to incorporate changes in development thinking.

Modifying Economic Liberalism

While NIEO proponents were challenging the fundamental tenets of liberal economic development, some UN agencies recognized the need to modify economic liberalism in view of its perceived failure to eliminate poverty, hunger, illiteracy, and growing income inequality. Collaboration between development scholars and various UN agencies, including the World Bank, produced new approaches oriented to basic human needs and the redistribution of income from growth to the needs of the poorest and to groups left out of the development process. As discussed above, sustainable human development and poverty alleviation have subsequently become the primary focus for UN development programs.

Women and Development. UN agencies and liberal economic theorists had long believed that as development occurred, women's economic status would inevitably improve. During the early years of the UN, the Commission on the Status of Women, one of the original six functional commissions of ECOSOC, focused on ensuring that women had the right to vote, hold office, and enjoy equal legal rights. There was no special reason to target women as actors in the development process, it was thought, as all groups would benefit as economic development occurred.

In the 1970s, Esther Boserup, an activist, academic, and UN consultant, found otherwise. In her landmark book, *Women's Role in Economic Development*, she argued that as technology improves, men benefit economically, but women become increasingly marginalized economically.[18] Thus, by 1975, when the UN-sponsored International Women's Year was launched with the first World Conference on Women in Mexico City, the idea emerged that women needed special attention if they were to become participants and active agents in development. Programs should be designed to reduce women's traditional activities and to expand new activities into economically productive roles for them in agriculture, small business, and industry.

The women-in-development agenda, the International Decade for Women, and the first three UN women's conferences in 1975, 1980, and 1985 were all heavily affected by the North-South conflict of that period and by debates over the proposed NIEO. But with governments in the lead at the UN-sponsored conferences, and women's groups working only from the sidelines of parallel NGO meetings, the central issues of women's economic roles and social status were often lost in the process.

Following the approval in 1979 of the Convention on the Elimination of All Forms of Discrimination Against Women (CEDAW), the UN in 1982 established the International Research and Training Institute for the Advancement of Women (INSTRAW) to implement the women-in-development agenda. Funded by voluntary contributions, INSTRAW provided training to integrate and mobilize women in the development process and acted as a catalyst in promoting the role of women. The UN Development Fund for Women, established in 1975, has supported projects run by women. The World Bank established the post of adviser on women in 1977. And now virtually all of the UN specialized agencies have integrated women's concerns into their programs.

That integration has been bolstered by the activities of women's groups and by the global conferences on the environment, population, human rights, social development, and, of course, women. Women's NGOs pushed for language in the conference declarations and programs of action affirming the centrality of women's roles in sustainable development.[19] For example, the 1994 Cairo Conference on Population and Development declared that the key to population growth and economic development lies in the empowerment of women through education and economic opportunity. It enshrined a new concept of population that gives women more control over their lives by promoting education for girls, a range of choices for family planning and health care, and greater involvement of women in development planning.

Three global women's conferences and the publication in 1990 of *The World's Women*, discussed above, contributed to a major attitudinal shift within the UN system that linked the social status and political empowerment of women to poverty, violence, the environment, sustainable development, and population control. The Platform for Action unanimously approved by the 1995 Fourth World Conference on Women in Beijing reaffirmed this connection by calling for the "empowerment of all women" through ensuring "women's equal access to economic resources including land, credit, science and technology, vocational training, information, communication, and markets."[20] This was reiterated at the "Beijing Plus Five," "Beijing Plus Ten," and "Beijing Plus Twenty" meetings in 2000, 2005, and 2015.

The MDGs also called for promoting gender equality and empowering women through promoting women's education and improving the health status of women and children. Those goals were needed, for, as Devaki Jain noted in 2005, "the situation on the ground for many women, especially those living in poverty and in conflict-ridden situations, seems to have worsened, despite the fact that it has been addressed specifically by both the UN and development thought."[21]

In 2010, in an effort to improve the effectiveness of women's programs, the UN General Assembly created UN Women, the United Nations Entity for Gender Equality and the Empowerment of Women. The goal was to merge and build on the work of the different parts of the UN, including INSTRAW, UNIFEM, the Division for the Advancement of Women, and the Office of the Special Adviser on Gender Issues and Advancement of Women. UN Women brings together the human rights dimension (gender equality as a basic human right), the political (underrepresentation in political decisionmaking), and the economic (empowering women fuels thriving economies, spurring productivity and growth). It is designed to help UN bodies formulate policy and standards, advise states with technical and financial support, and monitor the progress of each. Michelle Bachelet, the former president of Chile, was named the first undersecretary-general and executive director. Current director Phumzile Mlambo-Ngcuka is in charge of the forty-one-member board and the annual budget of about $690 million. UN Women has provided more than $95 million in grant funds to 132 countries between 2010 and 2015. According to one scholar, it has significantly bolstered the UN's approach to promoting gender equality and holding the UN itself accountable to gender equality and gender mainstreaming. Much of the organization's growing impact lies with effective data collection and raising awareness. The most significant contribution of UN Women, according to one observer, is progress on the reduction of violence toward women.[22]

In July 2015, the UN hosted the Third International Conference on Financing for Development, which highlighted gender equality as one of the key elements of sustainable development. In addition to the focus on women's needs in policy goals, women themselves were an integral part of the negotiations, and their advocacy produced the Action Plan on Transformative Financing for Gender Equality and Women's Empowerment.[23] In September 2015, the "Beijing Plus Twenty" meeting (otherwise known as the Global Leaders' Meeting on Gender Equality and Women's Empowerment: A Commitment to Action) committed to the Planet 50-50 by 2030 initiative to establish equal economic opportunities for women and eliminate gender gaps by the year 2030. In advance of the meeting, a record 167 countries participated in national reviews of gaps and progress since the 1995 Beijing conference. "The highest leaders in the land are taking personal responsibility for their commitment to gender equality and the empowerment of women," emphasized Mlambo-Ngcuka. "Now the world looks up to them to lead the game-changing actions that secure and sustain implementation."[24]

The issue of women and development illustrates the ways in which NGOs, UN-sponsored global conferences, and studies by the UN Secretariat—in short, all three UNs—have contributed to reshaping thinking about development and the roles of women, with an impact throughout the UN system, including the World Bank and IMF. It also influenced the human development–centered thinking that emerged in the 1990s along with the concept of **sustainable development**, two other modifications of liberal economic thinking.

The Reconceptualization of Development: Sustainability and Human Development. Another modification of economic liberalism emerged out of the recognition that development defined as economic growth was too narrowly construed, leading to unintended and unanticipated side effects, including the marginalization of women. But what if development as conventionally practiced also led to environmental degradation or growth that was unsustainable into the future?

In 1980, the UN General Assembly adopted the World Conservation Strategy, advocating the new but poorly defined concept of sustainable development. In 1983, the assembly established the World Commission on Environment and Development (WCED), headed by Norwegian prime minister Gro Harlem Brundtland and composed of eminent individuals from many parts of the world.

WCED's task was to formulate a new development approach around the concept of sustainable development. This approach proved politically astute because it recognized that dealing with environmental problems would be ineffective if global poverty and economic inequalities were not addressed. The 1987 Brundtland Commission Report, titled *Our Common Future*, called for "development that meets the needs of the present without compromising the ability of future generations to meet their own needs."[25] It sought to balance ecological concerns with the economic growth necessary to reduce poverty. (That idea and its implementation are examined further in Chapter 7.) The evolution of the idea of sustainable development provides another example of the major role that the UN has had in the promotion of ideas. It also represents an important modification of liberal economic theory concerning development by linking the management and use of natural resources to their economic, social, and environmental consequences. The concept of sustainable development also created a way to link population and environmental problems.

A further modification occurred in the 1990s with UNDP's introduction of the concept of human development and the annual *Human Development Report* and HDI, as discussed earlier in this chapter. By putting "people at the centre of development," the concept provided "an integrated intellectual framework for catalyzing a new system-wide approach to economic and social development."[26] UNDP's motivation had much to do with the Bretton Woods institutions' harsh structural adjustment policies in the 1980s and the adverse effects on people in many developing countries. Thus, the concept of human development provided an alternative to neoliberal economic policies and a new paradigm.

Two distinguished economists from South Asian countries conceived of the idea and of the *Human Development Report*—Mahbub ul Haq and Amartya Sen. In the first report, human development was defined as "a process of enlarging people's choices. The most critical of these wide-ranging choices are to live a long and healthy life, to be educated and to have access to resources needed for a decent standard of living. Additional choices include political freedom, guaranteed human rights and personal self-respect."[27] Subsequent reports, all issued by individual authors, refined and expanded these ideas, adding among other things the notion of strengthening capabilities. Thus, the concept of human development underscores a point made in the first UN Development Decade: that state economic growth and prosperity measured by GNP and GNP per capita do not automatically translate into human advancement. Studies have in fact shown that countries may make progress on human development even with slow economic growth.

In sum, the importance of human development is that it has provided a framework for integrating activities across the UN system. Together with the outcomes of the global conferences of the 1970s, 1980s, and 1990s, it provided the basis for the MDGs and the springboard for the SDGs in 2015.

Creating a Comprehensive Approach to Development Through Goal-Setting: The Millennium Development Goals and the Sustainable Development Goals

As discussed earlier, the UN has been a major source of innovative ideas about development, namely, that it does not happen automatically, that economic growth does not necessarily result in equity among different socioeconomic groups, that technical skills are necessary and cannot always be found domestically, and that development must be reoriented to human and sustainable development. The UN has also set a series of goals for the development community, beginning with the designation of the 1960s as the "United Nations Development Decade." In 2000, it set two successive sets of ambitious goals accompanied by various targets for each goal, measures to be used, and reporting requirements. We look first at the MDGs and then at their successor, the SDGs. Underlying both goal-setting exercises is the hope that they will facilitate the marshaling of the necessary political will and resources among the UN's member states and a wide array of public and private partners to make significant, measurable progress toward the goals.

The Millennium Declaration adopted at the UN's Millennium Summit in September 2000 incorporated the set of eight Millennium Development Goals. These represent a conceptual convergence, or what the *Human Development Report 2003* calls a "compact among nations," about reducing poverty and promoting sustainable human development in response to globalization. The mutually reinforcing and intertwined MDGs included halving world poverty and hunger by 2015 (a goal that was achieved in 2010), reducing infant mortality by two-thirds, and achieving universal primary education. The eighth goal dealt with partnerships among UN agencies, governments, civil society organizations, and the private sector as a means to achieving the other seven goals. (See Box 5.1 for the complete list.) The goals were disaggregated into eighteen specific targets, specific time frames, and forty-eight performance indicators with an elaborate implementation plan involving ten global task forces, MDG report cards for each developing country, regular monitoring, and a public information campaign to keep pressure on governments and international agencies.

With the MDGs, "the UN had returned once again to make distinct and pioneering contributions," noted a group of scholars, "by organizing an unprecedented millennium consensus in defining global goals for poverty reduction and mobilizing commitments in support of those goals."[28] What is also most remarkable about the MDGs, John Ruggie noted at the time, is that "it is unprecedented for the UN and its agencies, let alone also the Bretton Woods institutions, to align their operational activities behind a unifying substantive framework."[29] The bank and fund produced the *Global Monitoring Report*, which focused on evaluating the progress of the MDGs.

But were the MDGs achieved? Data are now available to evaluate progress, although there are questions about the quality of some of the data. Box 5.1 outlines some of the results achieved as of 2015. Three key goals were met: the number of individuals living in extreme poverty (i.e., on less than $1.25 a day) and poverty rates have fallen in every developing region, including sub-Saharan Africa. The percentage of the population having completed primary education increased by 98 percent and infant mortality dropped by 50 percent between 1990 and 2015. Much of the improvement is attributed to major gains in China and India, while sub-Saharan Africa still lags on virtually every indicator. Several other goals came close. Universal primary education is also within reach, and the number of children not in school fell by an impressive 43 million between 2000 and 2015, even considering population growth (although again, sub-Saharan Africa and South Asia remained behind). The overall target for gender parity in completing primary school was met in South Asia, but many gaps remained in other areas. Likewise, globally, the maternal mortality ratio declined by 45 percent with the expansion of the number of skilled health care workers, with more than half of the deaths concentrated in six countries (the DRC, Ethiopia, India, Nigeria, Afghanistan, and Pakistan). Another advance came as the mortality rate for children under five declined by over 50 percent, with 43 deaths per 1,000 live births in 2015, down from 90 in 1990. Yet this did not meet the two-thirds reduction goal, with sub-Saharan Africa and South Asia falling short once again. Portions of Goal 7 were met, as 4.2 billion people had access to safe drinking water in 2015, rising from 2.3 billion people.

Yet challenges remain, and on other MDGs the assessment is not as positive. Targets were not reached in reducing hunger or in providing access to basic sanitation, areas that negatively affect health status. The spread of HIV and HIV-related deaths has begun to slow, but the number of people living with HIV/AIDS continues to rise, and mortality from malaria remains high, especially in Africa. In 2015, 1 billion people still lived on less than $1.25 a day and 600 million still lacked access to clean water.

Can the improvements in some categories be attributed to the MDGs? John McArthur points to the methodological problem that many of the improvements predated the MDGs, noting that "progress toward the Goals is not the same as progress because of the Goals."[30] Despite major improvements, the data have been widely questioned, and the MDGs were not without their critics. Some asked why specific MDGs were selected rather than other ones that might, in fact, be better choices. Why were uniform targets set for all countries rather than recognizing that some countries are more handicapped than others in meeting

---

BOX 5.1. **The Millennium Development Goals:
Results Achieved as of 2015**

Goal 1: *Eradicate extreme poverty and hunger: Halve proportion of people living on less than $1.25 a day and proportion who suffer chronic hunger.*
Results: 14% of people in developing countries live on $1.25 a day, down from 50% in 1990. Proportion of undernourished decreased from 24% to 15%, but progress slowed. Virtually all gains in China and Southeast Asia, not Africa.

Goal 2: *Achieve universal primary education: Ensure that all children complete full course of primary education.*
Results: 91% of children attending primary school, but progress stagnated since 2012. Many of the out-of-school children are in conflict zones.

Goal 3: *Promote gender equality and empower women: Eliminate gender disparity in primary, secondary, and tertiary education.*
Results: All regions achieved or near to closing gender gap in primary education. Gender disparity in higher levels of education and in labor market persists.

Goal 4: *Reduce child mortality: Reduce by two-thirds the mortality rate of children younger than five years.*
Results: Child mortality dropped by over 50%. Four out of five child deaths are in Africa.

Goal 5: *Improve maternal health: Reduce by three-quarters the maternal mortality rate by 2015.*
Results: Maternal mortality dropped 48% to 210 deaths per 100,000 live births. Africa saw a reduction from 990 to 510 deaths per 100,000 live births.

Goal 6: *Combat HIV/AIDS, malaria, and other diseases: Halt and reverse the spread of HIV/AIDS. Slow spread of malaria and other diseases.*
Results: 9.5 million people in developing countries have access to antiretrovirals. 6.2 million deaths from malaria averted. 37 million lives saved in fight against tuberculosis.

Goal 7: Ensure environmental sustainability: *Reverse the loss of environmental resources. Halve the proportion of people without sustainable access to safe drinking water and basic sanitation.*
Results: 13 million hectares of forest lost. 50% increase in CO_2 emissions. 89% of population have access to improved source of drinking water. 2 billion people have improved access to sanitation.

Goal 8: Develop a global partnership for development.
Results: In 2013 official development assistance was $135.2 billion, the highest ever recorded, but there was some shift away from aid to the poorest countries. Debt burden for developing countries was stable at 3% of revenue.

Source: United Nations, *The Millennium Development Goals Report 2014.*

targets for poverty reduction or other goals and that there are different ways of achieving targets?

As noted economist Jagdish Bhagwati points out, "A more serious problem with the MDG approach, however, is that the central task in development is not the specification of desirable targets but rather the specification of policy instruments that achieve these targets."[31] He and others were particularly critical of Goal 8, concerning partnerships, because partnerships often involve major corporations of which they are critics. Yet partnerships with corporations, think tanks, foundations, and other actors have become increasingly important, as discussed above, and were one of the reasons why the process of developing the SDGs was very different from that of the MDGs.

Even as work toward the MDGs continued, diplomats and experts began to hammer out the goals for the next fifteen years. The SDGs were designed to address some of the weaknesses of the MDGs, including insufficient focus on the poorest of the poor, lack of attention to conflict and good governance, and the absence of targets on sustainability. For more than two decades, the discussions about international development moved in different directions, one on economic development and one on sustainability. With the SDGs, these once separate strands came together. The goals adopted in 2015 aimed to be as inclusive as possible in terms of both the process of creating the goals and the final targets. The drafting process was described as the "most intense and inclusive consultation in history with businesses, civil society, and citizens across the globe."[32] The MDGs were largely the work of then Secretary-General Kofi Annan, while the SDG process was set in motion by the Rio+20 conference in 2012 and the creation of an Open Working Group. Overseeing the post-2015 development agenda was a high-level panel of eminent individuals that included stakeholders from civil society, the scientific community, and the UN system, plus a UN system task team composed of representatives from sixty UN agencies and other international organizations. The process also included both national consultations and a global conversation via MyWorld that invited users to select six priorities from a list of sixteen themes ranging from "honest and responsive government" to "action taken on climate change." As one diplomat described, "The tent is very large, and everyone is in it," yet "priorities differ, agendas differ. The willingness to take on commitments differs."[33] In September 2015, the General Assembly approved the final document. People are the center of the new commitments, which combine economic development goals with expanded pledges to foster social development and environmental protection by 2030. The new list aims to focus on "people, planet, prosperity, peace and partnership." The SDGs converge on several areas of UN concern and constitute a more holistic and inclusive agenda, albeit an ambitious one. In this regard, the SDGs highlight the connections between extreme poverty, gender equality, and environmental sustainability. The list includes seventeen goals and 169 targets with familiar themes such as ending poverty and hunger and ensuring education and gender equality, yet it adds new objectives such as promoting clean energy, securing peace and justice, and preserving marine resources (see Box 5.2). The new goals encourage a view that promotes social justice and moves away from the focus on the state and economic development per se.

Before the ink was dry and the goals formally adopted, critiques abounded. The process itself was controversial. As one observer notes, "Something for everyone has produced too much for anyone."[34] Each individual strand (such as economic development, social equality, and sustainability) is in itself extremely ambitious, and when they are taken together, implementation of the SDGs may not be feasible. The value of the MDGs was often described as raising awareness, motivating governments and publics, and providing an accessible focus for the UN's development agenda. With the SDGs, there are concerns that key target audiences will find the new goals unfocused, unobtainable, and even incomprehensible. The SDGs have also been condemned as too expensive and a distraction from work on the ground. Although they satisfy inclusiveness, there are too many indicators, and the parameters about measuring progress on many of the goals are vague.[35] *The Economist* complained, "Many are impossible to measure."[36] In addition, monitoring the long list of goals places a significant burden on states and a demand for substantial statistics (and manpower) that in the end may actually inhibit states from conducting accurate tracking. Still, observers point out that "the SDGs are part of an important shift in thinking about development that is making it both more ambitious and more realistic. . . . The main reason there are so many is that they were set by consensus rather than written by a few specialists, mostly from rich countries. This lessens the feeling that rich men from 'the north' are telling 'the south' how to do better."[37]

In conjunction with the MDGs and SDGs, the UN has increasingly interacted with other types of actors in addressing economic development issues. Historically, outside consultants and experts have been a primary source of research, advice, and some of the UN's most important ideas. Since the 1990s, MNCs, foundations, think tanks, and NGOs have formed a variety of partnerships with the UN. Two of the biggest contributors to meeting goals in the health and transparency areas, respectively, are the Bill and Melinda Gates Foundation and George Soros' Open Society Foundation. Think tanks have been important in monitoring and measuring the results of aid spending. The Children's Investment Fund Foundation, for example, has focused on improving children's lives and is an important player in efforts to measure the need for and impact of the SDGs' nutrition targets, recognizing that fewer than half of the UN's 193 member states have enough data to assess whether they are on track to meet those targets.[38] Likewise, partnerships between major corporations and the UN have

BOX 5.2. The Sustainable Development Goals

Goal 1: *End poverty in all its forms everywhere*

Goal 2: *End hunger, achieve food security and improved nutrition, and promote sustainable agriculture*

Goal 3: *Ensure healthy lives and promote well-being for all at all ages*

Goal 4: *Ensure inclusive and equitable quality education and promote lifelong learning opportunities for all*

Goal 5: *Achieve gender equality and empower all women and girls*

Goal 6: *Ensure availability and sustainable management of water and sanitation for all*

Goal 7: *Ensure access to affordable, reliable, sustainable, and modern energy for all*

Goal 8: *Promote sustained, inclusive, and sustainable economic growth, full and productive employment, and decent work for all*

Goal 9: *Build resilient infrastructure, promote inclusive and sustainable industrialization, and foster innovation*

Goal 10: *Reduce inequality within and among countries*

Goal 11: *Make cities and human settlements inclusive, safe, resilient, and sustainable*

Goal 12: *Ensure sustainable consumption and production patterns*

Goal 13: *Take urgent action to combat climate change and its impacts*

Goal 14: *Conserve and sustainably use the oceans, seas, and marine resources for sustainable development*

Goal 15: *Protect, restore, and promote sustainable use of terrestrial ecosystems, sustainably manage forests, combat desertification, halt and reverse land degradation, and halt biodiversity loss*

Goal 16: *Promote peaceful and inclusive societies for sustainable development, provide access to justice for all, and build effective, accountable, and inclusive institutions at all levels*

Goal 17: *Strengthen the means of implementation and revitalize the global partnership for sustainable development*

Note: The seventeen SDGs include 169 targets and more than 200 indicators.

made an important contribution both to achieving the MDGs and to addressing other needs. In short, one UN report noted that partnerships have become "the most significant funding trend in the recent past."[39]

THE UN AND OTHER ACTORS

MNCs and the Global Compact

As liberal economic theory predicts, private capital has played a key role in economic growth in many parts of the world, and this growth is a prerequisite for development. MNCs produce 25 percent of the world's wealth, and the top 1,000 produce 80 percent of the world's industrial output. Motivated by profit, they have the ability to raise enormous sums of capital and invest in projects around the world that offer employment, thus stimulating growth and raising standards of living.

Since the mid-1980s, capital flows to developing countries increased dramatically, reaching more than $1.06 trillion in 2010, while official development aid leveled off, illustrating the private sector's growing importance in development. Private international capital was essential to the success of the Asian "tigers," although statist policies were crucial in harnessing that capital and making it productive. Africa and Latin America have benefited from heavy Chinese investment in recent years through both official and private channels. Yet only about 20 percent of private international finance actually goes to the least developed countries, for which reliance on private capital is risky and potentially limiting. Also, most private investment goes to just a few countries, for example. In Africa, the most capital-poor region, it has been targeted most notably at South Africa and Nigeria, not at the least developed. Only since 2005 have a number of other African countries found themselves on the receiving end of significant private investment. Another problem is that private capital flows are highly volatile. After the 2010 peak in private international finance, the figure dropped to $775 billion two years later.

By the mid-1980s, under strong US influence, the World Bank and IMF included privatization and deregulation of business among conditions for lending in order to support private foreign investment. And with the growth of private investment, especially in Asia, as a source of development capital, UNDP in collaboration with major donors began to provide governments interested in attracting foreign investment with the support to do so by publishing investment guides.

Yet critics of the liberal economic model have long been dissatisfied with the role international private capital and especially multinational corporations play in economic affairs, believing that they occupy a position of preeminence without being subject to adequate international or national controls. Their goal has been to develop ways of regulating MNCs' activities, and in fact, such regulation was a goal of the NIEO, described above. The search within the UN for an international code of conduct officially terminated when the Commission on Transnational Corporations was eliminated in 1994. What remained of its work was integrated into UNCTAD.[40] Yet the pressure on MNCs from NGO-led grassroots campaigns has continued, leading many major corporations to implement their own codes of conduct and monitoring mechanisms. One recent campaign is the Extractive Industries Transparency Initiative, which targets corruption in the mining, oil, and gas industries; as of 2016, fifty-one governments and ninety big corporations have agreed to publicize payments and revenue.[41]

The break from the historical approach to MNCs within the UN, however, was solidified officially in 1999 when Secretary-General Kofi Annan proposed a global compact at the World Economic Forum in Davos, Switzerland. He hoped to join the UN, relevant UN agencies, research centers, corporations, environmental groups, human rights groups, and labor NGOs (represented by the International Confederation of Free Trade Unions) into a partnership committed to providing the social foundations of a sustainable global economy, encouraging private-sector investment in developing countries, and promoting good corporate practices.

The **Global Compact on Corporate Responsibility** revolves around nine principles that participating companies agree to uphold. These include adherence to international human rights law, rejection of child and forced labor, abolition of discrimination in employment, and promotion of greater environmental responsibility. Several of these principles reflect earlier work of both the ILO and the Office of the High Commissioner for Human Rights. More than 8,000 companies had signed the Global Compact by 2015 along with more than 4,000 non-businesses, with stakeholders in 170 countries. John Ruggie, the father of the Global Compact within the UN Secretariat, describes it as a set of nested networks where parties learn what works and what fails, enhancing corporate social responsibility.[42]

One 2010 empirical study of the effects of the Global Compact on MNC behavior found that firms that sign on will follow up by reporting on their activities. Some companies have actually made policy statements establishing better human rights practices. Over time, other studies have begun to notice more responsible MNC behavior. By participating in that exercise and practice, the reputation of particular MNCs has been enhanced.[43] Yet measuring what MNCs do compared to what they say is difficult. Some critics contend that joining is nothing more than a publicity ploy. Others, including many economists, doubt the effectiveness of voluntary mechanisms. Still others point to the fact that the approach does not include any remedies for MNC policies that run counter to the principles.

The Global Compact has not eliminated other efforts to regulate MNCs. UNCTAD still addresses issues of restrictive business practices. WHO has targeted specific MNCs and their marketing practices, most notably the tobacco and pharmaceutical companies. (These issues are addressed in Chapter 7.) Yet, in general, there has been a shift, with the UN seeking to work with MNCs, often in partnership arrangements with NGOs and states and, through those partnerships, to hold them accountable. Indeed, the UN now operates the UN-Business Action Hub (business.un.org)—"a platform where UN and business engage in dialogue and take action to advance UN objectives and the Sustainable Development Goals." It was initiated by the Global Compact, a Hong Kong-based NGO, and twenty UN agencies. As Catia Gregoratti notes, "The universe of UN-business partnerships is vast and expanding. Within it virtually every global development issue is seemingly addressed."[44] Although Northern corporations and corporate foundations dominated the partnerships initially, she notes, corporations and foundations based in China, Brazil, South Africa, and India have become increasingly involved. Yet these partnerships are not just about money; they also involve commercial activities (such as the retailer Macy's selling handcrafted items from developing countries) or mobilizing market expertise, as well as promoting principles of good conduct. And, not surprisingly, critics question whether the partnerships really work for both business and the poor: do they truly improve corporate conduct through setting standards and principles of conduct, or do they hide MNCs' efforts to avoid taxes, depriving poor countries of revenues?

NGOs and the Third UN

NGOs are a critical part of the development puzzle. Since the 1980s, they have participated in shaping the discourse and pushing for new approaches to development. During the 1990s, they lobbied for a voice in the global conferences that made the critical links between women and development, the environment and development, population and development, and, as shown in the next chapter, development and human rights. Their participation in drafting the SDGs is reflected in this comment: "The opportunity to rethink and redefine our global development pathway comes once in a generation. This is our opportunity and we must seize it."[45] And NGOs have increasingly taken on more responsibilities in terms of delivery of services funded by both states and multilateral donor organizations such as the UN and the World Bank.

Some NGOs acquired their expertise in development work by first responding to humanitarian emergencies. The complex emergencies in the 1990s in Somalia, Kosovo, Bosnia, the DRC, Liberia, Sudan, and Haiti drew NGOs in to provide humanitarian assistance, working with UN agencies such as the WFP and UNHCR. But as Save the Children, CARE, and World Vision increasingly recognized, their short-term relief work was becoming long-term. Recovering from humanitarian emergencies required supporting longer-term development objectives—stimulating agricultural development to curb food shortages, increasing forestation to enhance soil productivity, and improving local skills for village development. At the same time, states, the UN system, and even the World Bank realized that they could benefit from the local-level expertise of the NGOs, who often provide service delivery at a lower cost than the bank's high-cost professional staff. Such are the origins of the development partnerships (and subcontracting relationships) that are now an essential part of the development system, where NGOs implement UN and World Bank projects. In a few cases, such as Bangladesh, Somalia, or the Sudan, where weak states are either unable or unwilling to provide public services, NGOs are even performing services that governments generally perform.

As NGOs become the implementers of the programs of others, however, they risk losing the very advantages for which they are attractive. Like all organizations, they become agents of the funders, having to prove themselves with each contract, and thus less willing to risk taking new positions and trying new approaches.

LESSONS LEARNED

The United Nations and its specialized agencies have struggled to be relevant to major contemporary economic issues, including the imperative for economic development. The complexities of globalization, the strength of MNCs and volume of international private capital, the preeminence of the Bretton Woods institutions, the growth of emerging markets, and the activities of NGOs have made the UN institutions and programs just another set of actors among many. Still, the UN remains in the forefront of developing new ideas and thinking about economic development and serving as a forum for policy debates on the balance between economic growth and economic equity. The UN has played the role of critic, constructive to some and obstructionist to others. And now, we ask, what lessons have been learned along the way?

First, the UN, along with the rest of the development community, has learned that international involvement in countries should be based on individual countries' needs. Thus, for example, where countries have experienced lengthy periods of civil conflict, as in Namibia, Cambodia, and Mozambique, the UN's development cooperation activities are part of its wider engagement in political and humanitarian areas. The Peacebuilding Commission, as discussed in Chapter 4, is designed to support continuing engagement after conflict has ended. In other situations, the UN's activities are more limited to technical assistance. In countries in transition from socialist economies in the 1990s, the priorities were formalizing accountability and increasing transparency, as well as providing technical assistance for banking reforms and formulating property laws. The move by the IMF and World Bank away from the Washington Consensus and structural adjustment demonstrates their acknowledgment that one strategy cannot fit all. There are now special programs aimed at states emerging from conflict as well as at states at the lowest level of economic development.

Second, the value of coordinating efforts at the grassroots level has been recognized. To overcome what was often a fragmented approach by various UN programs and agencies, UNDP is now charged with playing a coordinating role within each recipient country, whether or not that involves a central location, a UN House, where the individual agencies and UNDP are located. The move to require that the Poverty Reduction Strategy Papers be a product of local NGOs as well as various UN agencies, the bank, and the fund provides another effort at wider coordination at the grassroots level. Yet as more actors, including bilateral and multilateral donors, participate, coordination becomes even more difficult. A country may have more than twenty-five different donors, each with its own preferences and procedures. Does such fragmentation promote diversity in approaches that may bring more effective results, or does fragmentation lead to chaos and ineffectiveness? That debate continues.

Third, at the substantive level, the UN has incorporated the liberal economic approach, the necessity of market-opening steps for expanding people's choices and ability to help themselves in a sustainable way. Thus, UNDP works with other donors and local officials to develop manuals for countries to use in attracting foreign investment. As part of that strategy, UNDP conducts surveys of what people in different countries want. The bank and fund increasingly listen to governments' desire to provide social safety nets or coordinate their own development policy.

Fourth, more than seventy years of UN development cooperation have shown that poverty is not reduced by general development and economic growth alone. For one thing, the World Bank's 2011 *World Development Report* shows that violence—civil war, ethnic conflict, and organized crime—has become the primary cause of poverty, creating not just a poverty trap but a violence trap that kills growth and from which countries have difficulty escaping. The legitimacy of government matters along with efforts to prevent violence and to build the conditions for stable peace over the long term. It is impossible, in short, to separate development, statebuilding, and peacebuilding. Bilateral and multilateral aid donors must work with the nonstate sector, including foreign direct investors, to promote poverty reduction and with the government to develop capacity for good governance. Aid workers must work with diplomats, peacekeepers, and human rights advocates. Hence, working in partnerships has become the norm. UNDP has learned also that "the value of educating and training many individuals will remain limited unless the overall policy and institutional environment within which these individuals live and work," along with the capacity of the country as a whole, is strengthened.[46] Hence, the UN and other development institutions are now more likely to critique government policies and make investment and aid contingent on meeting certain governance criteria. This represents a broader view of development, one that potentially infringes on state sovereignty.

Fifth, development is no longer seen as unidimensional. The concept of sustainable development has been firmly established, so development means attention to economic distribution, gender equity, and environmental concerns. Yet broadening the meaning of development and elucidating goals such as the MDGs, SDGs, and various governance indicators have not always produced the desired results. Financial and human resources, commitment, and follow-through by national policymakers and the UN are all essential if those goals are to be met.

THE PERSISTENT DILEMMAS

Dilemma 1: Expanding Needs Versus the UN's Limited Capacity
The UN has been an important advocate for the international economic issues that have proliferated in this era of globalization. It has shaped thinking about the requirements for development; introduced new issues to the international agenda; facilitated the mobilization of various constituencies, particularly through the global conferences of the 1970s and 1990s; and provided various institutional responses. The capacity of the UN, the specialized agencies, and the Bretton Woods institutions to respond to the UN Charter's broad mandate for economic and social cooperation has developed in fits and starts, often in an ad hoc and decentralized manner. New programs and agencies have created a largely unmanageable complex of organizations. With such proliferation inevitably come duplication, contradictory goals, and confusion for donors and recipients alike. Small wonder that coordination has long been an issue for UN economic and social activities and that ECOSOC has never been up to the task.

The main question for the twenty-first century is whether the UN is suited to meet these challenges. Can a decentralized, often redundant system that includes not only the various parts of the UN but also regional organizations, bilateral donors, specialized agencies, the Bretton Woods institutions, MNCs, private foundations, and NGOs become more cohesive? Can the current chaos of development aid lead to sustainable development? Several incremental changes have been made to further UN system coordination for sustainable development. For example, in 2002, the Administrative Committee on Coordination was reorganized into the UN Chief Executives Board for Coordination. This body provides a forum for twenty-eight heads of organizations and programs to meet, including the heads of the World Bank, IMF, WTO, WHO, WFP, UNEP, UNDP, FAO, UNIDO, and IAEA, among others, along with a permanent coordinating committee. This change did bring the Bretton Woods institutions together with other UN agencies and facilitated the global consensus on fighting poverty embodied in the MDGs and SDGs. But that has not changed the reality that leadership on economic issues resides largely outside the UN.

Dilemma 2: The Persistence of and Challenges to Sovereignty

Efforts by UN system institutions to address economic issues and developmental issues increasingly confront the dilemma of respecting state sovereignty versus intervention in the domestic affairs of states. IMF and World Bank structural adjustment programs clearly required that states adjust their economic and fiscal policies in return for assistance. Indeed, the IMF's power to shape the domestic economic policies of countries receiving aid borders on supranational authority and has been soundly criticized as such. Although the UN has been critical of such policies, UN programs, too, increasingly intrude into areas traditionally reserved for the state, pushing governments to accept a particular economic philosophy and condemning corruption among state officials. Providing technical assistance on issues such as creating a legal system, often with a view about how that system should be constructed, deeply impinges on an area traditionally reserved for states. Coupling economic assistance with calls for reforms of governance and critiques of sitting governments threatens state sovereignty. This is a trend that is likely to continue in the future. Because of that, the space between the international and the domestic will continue to be a contested one and the boundary between the two less clearly delineated.

Dilemma 3: The Need for Leadership

Unlike security issues, where the United States is still a dominant power, economic power is increasingly dispersed and the economic system multipolar, with China becoming an increasingly important but not entirely predictable player. Material resources count, but so do intellectual leadership and the strength of numbers in international economic relations. Japan, the EU, India, Brazil, and China are all economic powers whose involvement is critical for the success of development and trade efforts. The United States, for one, has been notably lukewarm on the MDGs, SDGs, and the Global Compact, with few US companies participating. Preoccupation since 2001 with the expanding threat posed by transnational terrorism, wars in Afghanistan and Iraq, and contentious domestic partisan politics have made the United States less likely to be a prime mover against global poverty. In a striking development following the 2008–2009 global financial crisis, developing countries for several years became the "engines of the world economy" and contributed most of the economic growth that took place, but that shifted by 2015, with big drops in the prices of most commodities, especially oil. Even China's booming economy was showing marked signs of slowing. Yet Chinese president Xi Jinping pledged $2 billion toward the implementation of the SDGs. This goes a long way toward explaining why the third dilemma, the need for leadership, is far more of a dilemma today than even five years ago.

As noted earlier, the World Bank and IMF have begun to accommodate these shifts. The emergence of the G-20 as a forum in international economic relations is yet another indicator. Even more striking is China's lead role in creating new development funding institutions—the New Development Bank and the AIIB. For meaningful change to occur in the leadership of UN development efforts, however, it is not just a matter of who the most powerful states are. Successful leadership in development also needs broad-based participation by people and grassroots organizations in decisionmaking as well as implementation at the lowest possible levels. Hence, there is greater recognition of the importance of nonstate actors, including NGOs, foundations, and MNCs, which speaks to the fourth dilemma—the need for more inclusiveness.

Dilemma 4: The Need for Inclusiveness

Inclusiveness is no longer considered a goal of development but rather is seen as a precondition. For example, where inequalities were once viewed as minor social issues, creating equal access for men and women is now considered an essential building block. This evolution was clear in the MDGs and now in the SDGs. Both the processes and targets are more inclusive, with women and nonstate actors part of the framing and drafting. For example, UN Women pushed for SDG 6, which prioritizes access to water. While this issue is not overtly gendered, by addressing access to water, UN Women helped establish opportunities for better education, jobs, and health for millions of women, as every year women in many sub-Saharan countries spend millions of hours collecting water. This takes them away from education and paid work and exposes them to increased health risks.[47]

Yet despite progress in both the inclusive targets and processes of creating policy within the UN itself, inequality persists—for women, for the very poor, for groups that experience discrimination and marginalization. On a global scale, in terms of financial parity, women tend to earn 24 percent less than men.[48] Women generally have unequal access to education, property rights, nutrition, sanitation, and basic social services despite many years of efforts by women's rights advocates. Progress has also met with retreat as several member states have pushed back on efforts to increase inclusiveness—both in terms of partnerships in development and gender equality. Like many other UN endeavors,

UN Women and other agencies that are focused on gender, human rights, and development face issues of funding, setting priorities, and fragmentation.

Development and human rights are now acknowledged as intricately connected. Both aspire to improve the human condition. The relationships between development, human rights, and environmental sustainability are explored further in Chapters 6 and 7.

NOTES

1. Thomas G. Weiss, David P. Forsythe, Roger A. Coate, and Kelly-Kate Pease, *The United Nations and Changing World Politics*, 6th ed. (Boulder, CO: Westview Press, 2010), 282.

2. Karen A. Mingst, "Decentralized, Often Disjointed: The UN and Regional Organizations in Economic Development," in *The United Nations: Past, Present, and Future: Proceedings of the 2007 Francis Marion University UN Symposium*, ed. Scott Kaufman and Alissa Warters (New York: Nova Science, 2009), 147–161.

3. For an extended discussion of the debate, see Richard Jolly et al., *UN Contributions to Development Thinking and Practice* (Bloomington: Indiana University Press, 2004), 66–83. This volume is invaluable for understanding the evolution of development thinking and the UN's contributions.

4. Craig N. Murphy, *The United Nations Development Programme: A Better Way?* (Cambridge: Cambridge University Press, 2006), 18.

5. Ibid., 242.

6. Mark Malloch Brown, quoted in Weiss et al., *The United Nations and Changing World Politics*, 285.

7. Yves Berthelot, "Unity and Diversity of Development: The Regional Commissions' Experience," in *Unity and Diversity in Development Ideas: Perspectives from the UN Regional Commissions*, ed. Yves Berthelot (Bloomington: Indiana University Press, 2004), 1, 13.

8. Michael Ward, *Quantifying the World: UN Contributions to Statistics* (Bloomington: Indiana University Press, 2004), 2.

9. United Nations, *The World's Women: Trends and Statistics, 1970–1990* (New York: United Nations, 1991).

10. Richard Jolly, Louis Emmerij, and Thomas G. Weiss, *UN Ideas That Changed the World* (Bloomington: Indiana University Press, 2009), 44.

11. Michelle Miller-Adams, *The World Bank: New Agendas in a Changing World* (London: Routledge, 1999).

12. See Michael Goldman, *Imperial Nature: The World Bank and Struggles for Social Justice in the Age of Globalization* (New Haven: Yale University Press, 2005); and Michel Chossudovky, *The Globalisation of Poverty: Impacts of IMF and World Bank Reforms* (London: Zed Books, 1997).

13. Joseph E. Stiglitz, *Globalization and Its Discontents* (New York: W. W. Norton, 2002); William Easterly, *The Elusive Quest for Growth: Economists' Adventures and Misadventures in the Tropics* (Cambridge, MA: MIT Press, 2001).

14. Nancy Birdsall and Francis Fukuyama, "The Post–Washington Consensus: Development After the Crisis," *Foreign Affairs* 90, no. 2 (2011): 45–53.

15. See Marc Williams, *Third World Cooperation: The Group of 77 in UNCTAD* (New York: St. Martin's Press, 1991); and Craig N. Murphy, *The Emergence of the NIEO Ideology* (Boulder, CO: Westview Press, 1984).

16. Jolly, Emmerij, and Weiss, *UN Ideas That Changed the World*, 46.

17. For early illustrations of the Latin American dependency approach, see Teotonio Dos Santos, "The Structure of Dependence," *American Economic Review* 60, no. 5 (1970): 235–246; and Celso Furtado, *Development and Underdevelopment: A Structural View of the Problems of Developed and Underdeveloped Countries* (Berkeley: University of California Press, 1964).

18. Esther Boserup, *Women's Role in Economic Development* (London: George Allen and Unwin, 1970).

19. See Elisabeth Jay Friedman, Kathryn Hochstetler, and Ann Marie Clark, *Sovereignty, Democracy, and Global Civil Society: State-Society Relations at UN World Conferences* (Albany: State University of New York Press, 2005).

20. "Platform for Action," in United Nations, *An Agenda for Women's Empowerment: Report of the Fourth World Conference on Women*, A/Conf.177/20, October 17, 1995. This report also contains the Beijing Declaration.

21. Devaki Jain, *Women, Development, and the UN: A Sixty-Year Quest for Equality and Justice* (Bloomington: Indiana University Press, 2005), 159.

22. Erin M. Stephens, "UN Women: Holistic Global Advocacy to Address Violence Against Women," in *Women, War, and Violence: Topography, Resistance, and Hope*, ed. Mariam M. Kurtz and Lester R. Kurtz (Santa Barbara, CA: Praeger, 2015), 475–490.

23. UN Women, "Addis Ababa Action Plan on Transformative Financing for Gender Equality and Women's Empowerment," www.unwomen.org/~/media/headquarters /attachments/sections/news/action%20plan%20on%20transformative%20financing%20 for%20gewe.pdf?v=1&d=20150715T215346.

24. UN Women, "World Leaders Agree: We Must Close the Gender Gap," press release, September 27, 2015. See www.unwomen.org/en/news/stories/2015/9/press-release-global-leaders-meeting#sthash.UbTXfmAg.dpuf.

25. World Commission on Environment and Development (Brundtland Commission Report), *Our Common Future* (Oxford: Oxford University Press, 1987), 8.

26. Jolly, Emmerij, and Weiss, *UN Ideas That Changed the World*, 186.

27. UNDP, *Human Development Report, 1990: Concept and Measurement of Human Development* (Oxford: Oxford University Press, 1990), 1.

28. Ibid., 299.

29. John Gerard Ruggie, "The United Nations and Globalization: Patterns and Limits of Institutional Adaptation," *Global Governance* 9, no. 3 (2003): 305.

30. John McArthur, "Seven Million Lives Saved: Under-5 Mortality Since the Launch of the Millennium Development Goals," Brookings Institution, September 2014, www .brookings.edu/research/papers/2014/09/under-five-child-mortality-mcarthur.

31. Jagdish Bhagwati, "Time for a Rethink," *Finance and Development* (September 2010): 15–16.

32. Homi Kharas, "Dispatch from UNGA: It's Done. The 2030 Agenda for Sustainable Development Has Been Approved," Brookings Institution, September 29, 2015, www

.brookings.edu/blogs/future-development/posts/2015/09/29-united-nations-sustainable-
-development-goals-kharas.

33. Eduardo Porter, "At the U.N., A Free-for-All on Setting Global Goals," *New York Times*, May 7, 2014.

34. "Unsustainable Goals," *The Economist*, March 28, 2015.

35. Maja Pleic, "The MDGs to SDGs Trade Off: What Has Been Lost and Gained for Global Equity?" PLOS Blog, October 5, 2015, http://blogs.plos.org/globalhealth/2015/10/the-mdgs-to-sdgs-trade-off-what-has-been-lost-and-gained-for-global-equity.

36. "Unsustainable Goals."

37. "The Sustainable Development Goals: Beyond Handouts," *The Economist*, September 19, 2015, 55.

38. Ibid., 56.

39. UN General Assembly, "Analysis of the Funding of Operational Activities for Development of the United Nations System for 2009, Report of the Secretary-General," 66th Session, Item 25(a), May 6, 2011, paragraphs 21 and 26.

40. For this history, see Tagi Sagafi-nejad with John Dunning, *The UN and Transnationals: From Code to Compact* (Bloomington: Indiana University Press, 2006).

41. EITI Countries, www.eiti.org/countries.

42. John Gerard Ruggie, "Global-governance.net: The Global Compact as Learning Network," *Global Governance* 7, no. 4 (2001): 371–378. For more of the story of creating the Global Compact, see John Gerard Ruggie, *Just Business: Multinational Corporations and Human Rights* (New York: Norton, 2013).

43. Patrick Bernhagen and Neil J. Mitchell, "The Private Provision of Public Goods: Corporate Commitments and the United Nations Global Compact," *International Studies Quarterly* 54, no. 4 (2010): 1175–1187.

44. Catia Gregoratti, "UN-Business Partnerships," in *International Organization and Global Governance*, ed. Thomas G. Weiss and Rorden Wilkinson (New York: Routledge, 2014), 311.

45. "Beyond 2015: Reaction to the Open Working Group's 'Focus Areas Document,'" March 2014, available at beyond2015.org. Cited in Arron Honniball and Otto Spijkers, "MDGs and SDGs: Lessons Learnt from Global Public Participation in the Drafting of the UN Development Goals," *German Review on the United Nations* 62, no. 6 (2014): 251–256.

46. UN Development Programme, "UNDP in Viet Nam: Some Lessons Learned in Supporting the Transition from Poverty to Prosperity," staff paper, September 1997, 18.

47. See more at UN Women, "SDG 6: Ensure Availability and Sustainable Management of Water and Sanitation for All," www.unwomen.org/en/news/in-focus/women-and-the-sdgs/sdg-6-clean-water-sanitation#sthash.BuIOmC2y.dpuf.

48. Saraswathi Menon, "UN Women: Prospects and Challenges," Future UN Development System Briefing No. 30, June 2015, www.futureun.org/media/archive1/briefings/FUNDS_Brief30_June2015_UN_Women.pdf.

6

⟋

Human Rights

The United Nations will fail in its duty to the world's peoples, who are the ultimate source of its authority, if it allows itself to be reduced to a mere static conference, whether on economic and social rights or on civil and political ones.

—*Former UN Secretary-General Kofi Annan (2014)*

Since the end of World War II, human rights have become a major issue in world politics and "the single most magnetic political idea of the contemporary time," in the words of Zbigniew Brzezinski, the former US national security adviser.[1] This trend is best explained not by realism or liberalism but by constructivism. With the spread of the idea that the protection of human rights knows no boundaries and the international community has an obligation to ensure that governments guarantee internationally recognized rights, state sovereignty has been diminished. The end of **apartheid** in South Africa, the recognition of women's rights as human rights, the spread of democracy, the emerging norm of responsibility to protect—all provide evidence of the trend. At the same time, news headlines regularly remind us that political, civil, social, and economic rights of individuals and groups are often violated, whether in Syria, the Sudan, Uganda, or China.

The UN has played an important role in the process of globalizing human rights. It has been central to establishing the norms, institutions, and activities for giving effect to this powerful idea that certain rights are universal. States have seldom been prime movers in this process, although their acceptance of the process and their support for human rights are critical. The international human rights movement—a network of human rights–oriented NGOs and dedicated

235

individuals—has been responsible for drafting much of the language of human rights conventions and for mounting transnational campaigns to promote human rights norms. The role of these groups and individuals and the processes by which they have persuaded policymakers to adopt human rights policies demonstrate the power of ideas to reshape definitions of national interests, consistent with constructivism.[2] Before we examine the UN and other actors' roles in this process, however, let us look at the historical antecedents in the League of Nations, the International Labour Organization, and key events.

FROM THE LEAGUE OF NATIONS TO THE UNITED NATIONS

Although the League of Nations Covenant made little mention of human rights as such, it nonetheless addressed rights-related issues and set important precedents. For example, it included specific provision for the protection of minorities and, through the Mandate System, for dependent peoples in colonies of the defeated powers of World War I (Turkey and Germany). A designated victor nation would administer the territory under the League's supervision and so provide a degree of protection from abuses. And although the Mandates Commission itself did not have rights to inspect, it did acquire a reputation for neutrality in administration. This reflected the growing sentiment that the international community had responsibilities over dependent peoples, the eventual goal being self-determination.

The 1919 Paris Peace Conference also produced five agreements, known as the Minority Treaties, that required beneficiaries of the peace settlement (such as Poland, Czechoslovakia, and Greece) to provide protection to all inhabitants regardless of nationality, language, race, or religion. Similar obligations for civil and political rights were imposed on the defeated states. Minority rights became a major agenda item for the League Council, Assembly, and committees, the admission of new members being contingent on a pledge to protect minority rights; special mechanisms were established for monitoring implementation. In addition, the League established principles on assisting refugees and the Refugee Organization. This step marked the first recognition that the international community has responsibility for protecting those forced to flee their homelands because of repression or war. The League also devoted attention to women's and children's rights, as well as the right to a minimum level of health. In the 1930s, the League's Assembly discussed the possibility of an international human rights document, but it took no action.

The ILO's mandate to work for the improvement of workers' living conditions, health, safety, and livelihood was consistent with the concepts of economic and social rights. Between 1919 and 1939, the ILO approved sixty-seven conventions that covered such issues as hours of work, maternity protection, minimum age, and old-age insurance; in 1926, it was the first IGO to introduce a procedure for supervising the standards established. This procedure provided an important model for the UN and continues to be a key part of the international human rights regime.

The precedents established by the League and ILO influenced the drafting of the UN Charter's provisions at the end of World War II. In addition, the drafters were influenced by wartime Allied goals, the Holocaust, and human rights advocates. First, US president Franklin D. Roosevelt's famous "Four Freedoms" speech in 1941 called for "a world founded upon four essential freedoms" and together with his vision of "the moral order" formed a normative base for the Allies in their fight against Germany and Japan.[3] The liberation of Nazi concentration camps in the closing weeks of World War II revealed the full extent of the Holocaust and the deaths of 6 million Jews, Gypsies, and other "undesirables." This was a second powerful impetus for seeing human rights as an international issue that required more than talk, though there is debate today over the impact that the Holocaust had on international human rights.[4] In addition, at the UN's founding conference in San Francisco in 1945, a broad spectrum of groups from churches to peace societies, along with delegates from various small states, pushed for the inclusion of human rights language in the Charter. Although they were more weakly worded than these advocates had hoped, seven references to human rights were scattered throughout the final document. Thus, the UN Charter placed the promotion of human rights among the central purposes of the new organization.[5] Over time, the UN's actions changed the public discourse, cemented the idea of human rights for all, and provided an arena for international action.[6]

UN CHARTER PRINCIPLES
AND ORGANIZATIONAL STRUCTURES

One of the primary purposes of the UN, as set forth in Chapter I, Article 1, is international cooperation in solving various international problems, including those of a "humanitarian character," and "in promoting and encouraging respect for human rights and for fundamental freedoms for all without distinction as to race, sex, language, or religion." Articles 55(c) and 56 amplify the UN's responsibility to promote "universal respect for, and observance of, human rights and fundamental freedoms for all" and the obligation of member states to "take joint and separate action in cooperation with the Organization for the achievement of the purposes set forth in Article 55."

These provisions did not define what was meant by "human rights and fundamental freedoms," but they established that human rights were a matter of

international concern and that states had assumed an as yet undefined international obligation relating to them. They also contradicted the Charter's affirmation of state sovereignty and the principle of nonintervention in the domestic
affairs of states contained in Article 2(7). They provided the UN with the legal
authority, however, to undertake the definition and codification of these rights.
The foundation for that effort was laid by the General Assembly's passage on
December 10, 1948, of the Universal Declaration of Human Rights to "serve as a
common standard of achievement for all peoples of all nations."[7] Taken together,
the UN Charter and the Universal Declaration of Human Rights represented
a watershed in the revolution that placed human rights at the center of world
politics.

The General Assembly

The General Assembly's broad mandate to discuss any issue within the scope of
the UN Charter led states to use this forum to raise specific human rights issues
almost from the beginning. Two of the assembly's main committees contribute
to the drafting of human rights treaties—the Social, Humanitarian, and Cultural (or Third) Committee and the Legal (or Sixth) Committee. The General
Assembly itself must then approve all UN human rights conventions. In its first
session in 1946, India and other countries introduced the issue of South Africa's
treatment of its sizable Indian population. Thus began the UN's longest-running
human rights issue: apartheid in South Africa. Debates concerning colonial issues, and particularly the right to self-determination of colonial and dependent
peoples, occupied a major share of General Assembly agendas in the 1950s and
1960s.[8] During the Cold War, some Western countries pushed issues such as
forced labor under Communism. Over the years, the General Assembly and almost every other UN body have been pressed by Arab states and their allies to
condemn Israel's treatment of the Palestinian people in the Occupied Territories. In 2000, for example, the assembly adopted more than twenty resolutions
on Israeli-related issues. In the late 1990s, the assembly repeatedly condemned
the Taliban government in Afghanistan for its appalling human rights record.
Among a number of human-rights related resolutions approved in 2014 was
one that condemned the "ongoing systematic, widespread and gross violations
of human rights" in North Korea following the release of a special commission
of inquiry's report (A/RES/69/188). In short, the General Assembly's attention
to human rights issues has reflected the majority at any given time. These debates have often spilled over into other organs and specialized agencies, leading
to charges of politicization. Yet because the assembly is the primary global forum, its debates and resolutions draw attention to issues and, in naming specific
states, may shame them into taking action.

The assembly's power under Article 13, section 1 "to conduct studies and make recommendations for the purpose of . . . assisting in the realizing of human rights and fundamental freedoms for all without distinction as to race, sex, language, or religion" has been used with respect to a variety of issues. Thus, for example, the General Assembly established the UN Decade for Women (1975–1985) and the UN Decade for Human Rights Education (1995–2005). It has approved rights-related declarations such as the 1959 Declaration on the Rights of the Child, the 1967 Declaration on the Elimination of Discrimination Against Women, the 1993 Declaration on the Elimination of Violence Against Women, and the 2007 Declaration on the Rights of Indigenous Peoples. These often form the basis for binding international conventions. In 2008, after contentious debate, the General Assembly approved a declaration seeking to decriminalize homosexuality, breaking the taboo on the subject of homosexual rights in UN bodies. Besides the assembly's own committees, two other types of bodies dealing with human rights report to the General Assembly. These include the ten treaty bodies established by the parties to select human rights treaties to monitor implementation. Their members are independent experts (see Figure 6.1). Also reporting to the assembly is the Human Rights Council (HRC), created in 2006 to replace the former Commission on Human Rights.

Human Rights Council. The forty-seven members of the Human Rights Council are selected in a secret ballot by a majority of the General Assembly's members for three-year renewable terms, with seats distributed among the five recognized regional groups. All council members' human rights records are subject to scrutiny, and the council can suspend members suspected of abuses with a two-thirds vote. The HRC meets for at least ten weeks throughout the year. It may also convene special sessions, as it has done on a number of occasions since 2006, including in 2011, when it condemned the Libyan government's attacks on its own people. Special sessions in 2014 addressed the human rights situation in Iraq in light of abuses committed by ISIS and the situation in Occupied Palestine; a special session in 2015 examined Boko Haram's terrorist attacks and human rights abuses.

The Human Rights Council replaced the Commission on Human Rights, which between 1946 and 2006 had been the hub of the UN system's human rights activity and reported to ECOSOC. The commission had drafted most of the major documents that elaborate and define human rights norms, including the Universal Declaration on Human Rights, the two international human rights covenants, and treaties on a range of issues from torture to the rights of the child and the rights of migrant workers. After 1970, its responsibilities had expanded to include procedures for investigating gross violations such as racism and

240

FIGURE 6.1. UN Human Rights Organizational Structure (Selected Bodies)

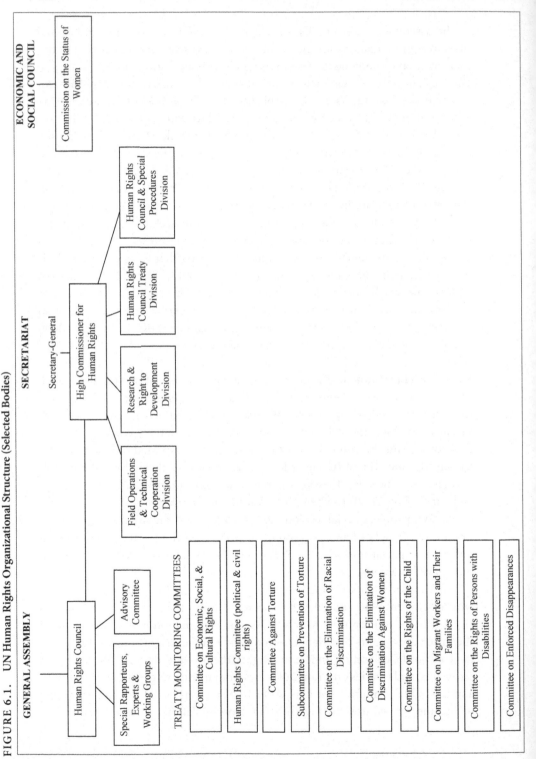

violations in Israeli-occupied Arab territories as well as individual complaints (through what are known as 1235 and 1503 procedures). An empirical study of the commission's actions from 1979 to 2001 found that "targeting and punishment were driven to a considerable degree by the actual human rights records of potential targets."[9] By the mid-1990s, some 60 percent of the more egregious violators had been examined by the commission, a finding that remained consistent in the 2002–2005 period. The commission was criticized, however, for singling out some human rights abuses and not others and for having among its elected members well-known abusers such as Sudan, Zimbabwe, Saudi Arabia, Pakistan, Cuba, Nepal, and Libya. Widespread public attention was drawn to the commission in 2001 when the United States lost its seat for the first time. Those who voted against the United States, including some of its allies, did so because of perceived US lack of support for the UN, its continued support of Israel, and its efforts to single out China and Cuba for their human rights abuses.

By creating the Human Rights Council, the General Assembly hoped to improve the credibility of the UN's primary human rights body. The fact that states such as Libya, Russia, China, Saudi Arabia, and Cuba have been elected to the council has caused many to question, however, whether the HRC is different. That question was only partially addressed in 2011 when the HRC denounced the armed attacks on civilians, killings, arrests, and detentions committed by the Libyan government and the General Assembly subsequently removed Libya from its seat on the HRC. Still, the failure to act earlier on Libya's human rights violations shows that the council has not improved its handling of rights violators. And the fact that membership is based on "equitable geographical distribution" means that the Global South holds the majority of seats and that political factors rather than human rights records tend to influence who gets elected.[10] One empirical study of four years of council decisions found that the most controversial and polarizing resolutions are, indeed, sponsored by countries with blemished human rights records, including most notably Cuba, Egypt, and Pakistan.[11]

The HRC has retained many of the same responsibilities and mechanisms as the commission, including the system of so-called **Special Procedures** whereby it can mandate a special rapporteur, a special representative of the secretary-general, or a working group of independent experts (usually five members, one from each region) to address specific country situations or thematic issues such as child soldiers or violence against women. These are discussed further in the section "From Articulating Human Rights Norms to Monitoring." The Office of the High Commissioner for Human Rights (discussed below) provides personnel, research, and logistical support for these HRC-appointed special rapporteurs and members of the working groups, who may serve no longer than six years, are unpaid, and operate independently of the HRC.

In 2008, the HRC established an Advisory Committee made up of eighteen human rights experts representing various regions who form a think tank for the council. They conduct studies and provide research-based advice at the request of the HRC, drawing on information from NGOs with ECOSOC consultative status, specialized agencies, other IGOs, member states, and national human rights institutions. The Advisory Committee is clearly intended to be more subordinate to the HRC than its predecessor, the former Sub-Commission on the Promotion and Protection of Human Rights. The council has four other subsidiary bodies (not shown in Figure 6.1): the Expert Mechanism on the Rights of Indigenous People, the Forum on Business and Human Rights, the Forum on Minority Issues, and the Social Forum.

An important HRC innovation is the Universal Periodic Review (UPR), where each member state is reviewed by three separate sources: the state itself, the Office of the High Commissioner for Human Rights with input from other UN bodies, and international human rights groups. The reviews along with the monitoring role of the treaty bodies are discussed below.

Some of the HRC's work has attracted public attention. In 2011, the council approved the "Guiding Principles on Business and Human Rights," a strong normative statement on how governments and businesses are expected to behave to protect human rights in a commercial setting, captured by the slogan "Protect, Respect, Remedy." The story of how that norm was created across various UN bodies and legitimated by the council is told by John Gerard Ruggie, one of the architects, in the book *Just Business: Multinational Corporations and Human Rights*.[12] In 2013, the council established the Commission of Inquiry on Human Rights in the Democratic People's Republic of Korea. With testimony from 80 witnesses and 240 confidential interviews, the commission's 2014 report cataloged evidence of systematic human rights abuses by the North Korean regime against its own citizens. North Korea vehemently denied the allegations. In late 2014, however, on a procedural vote where the P-5 veto did not apply, the Security Council added the subject of North Korea's human rights violations to its agenda along with the report's recommendation that the council refer the problem to the ICC. The issue was taken up again in late 2015. Whether or not the council acts, the very fact of putting the issue of human rights violations in North Korea on its agenda signifies how the Security Council has come to be involved in human rights issues.

The Security Council

The UN Charter left the Security Council free to define what constitutes a threat to international peace and security. Throughout the Cold War years, the council did not link security with human rights violations. Like the General Assembly, it did address issues such as the rights of colonial peoples to self-determination, the rights of the Palestinians in the Occupied Territories, and the rights of black majorities under apartheid in South Africa and in Southern Rhodesia, because these were seen as situations that threatened international peace and security. The Cold War's end, greater emphasis on human rights issues, and egregious human rights violations in various conflicts made it increasingly difficult to separate human rights abuses and threats to peace. And since Secretary-General Pérez de Cuéllar's 1991 report to the General Assembly, each secretary-general has urged the Security Council to address the links between human rights and security. Ethnic cleansing, genocide, and other crimes against humanity led it to create ad hoc war crimes tribunals for the former Yugoslavia, Rwanda, and Sierra Leone. Peacekeeping operations now regularly have protection of civilians as part of their mandates.

Since the end of the 1990s, the Security Council has routinely issued declarations on issues ranging from child soldiers to the role of women in promoting international peace and security. As discussed in Chapter 4, Resolution 1325 in 2000 mandated gender training in peacekeeping operations and urged stronger participation by women in field operations. In 2005, the council took the step of agreeing to hear a report from Secretary-General Kofi Annan on human rights violations in Myanmar. It also referred the situation in Darfur and Sudan to the ICC. Later in 2007, however, China and Russia vetoed a resolution on those violations, claiming that they had nothing to do with international peace and security. In 2008, the United States and others pushed the council to impose international sanctions on Zimbabwe for its government's human rights violations, but once again both China and Russia vetoed the action, explaining that the measure represented excessive interference in that country's domestic affairs. In 2011, the council referred Libya to the ICC on the grounds of the Qaddafi government's violent repression against its own people. North Korea's human rights abuses and the HRC's call for it to be referred to the ICC pose yet another challenge to the Security Council members. And in 2015, the ICC itself asked the council to take steps to enforce Sudan's compliance with the indictments against President Omar al-Bashir and three associates for war crimes and crimes against humanity in view of the failure of other UN member states to arrest them.

As discussed in Chapter 4, the Security Council has a mixed record in responding to complex humanitarian emergencies since the Cold War's end. Its actions in crises from Haiti to Bosnia, Somalia, the DRC, East Timor, Darfur, Libya, and Syria reflect mixtures of traditional concerns about threats to international peace and security, greater attention to human rights, and the evolving notion of human security, discussed in Chapter 7. Nevertheless, it is clear that the Security Council now plays a significant role within the UN system in efforts to address human rights violations.

ECOSOC

The Economic and Social Council was given authority under Article 62 to conduct studies, issue reports, and make recommendations "for the purpose of promoting respect for, and observance of, human rights and fundamental freedoms for all." It has used this authority to address a number of issues such as genocide, the protection of minorities, and, with the ILO, the prevention of forced labor. In addition, Article 68 gave ECOSOC the specific mandate of setting up commissions in the area of human rights, and in 1946 and 1947 it established the Commission on Human Rights, the Commission on the Status of Women, and the Sub-Commission on Prevention of Discrimination and Protection of Minorities (renamed the Sub-Commission on the Protection and Promotion of Human Rights in 1999, but replaced in 2008 by the HRC's Advisory Committee, as discussed earlier). Until the establishment of the Office of the High Commissioner for Human Rights (discussed below) and the Human Rights Council (discussed above), these commissions had borne the major responsibility for human rights activities in the UN system. With the creation of the HRC, ECOSOC clearly has much less involvement with human rights issues.

Secretariat: The UN High Commissioner for Human Rights

An important addition to the UN organizational structure relating to human rights is the Office of the High Commissioner for Human Rights (OHCHR), established in 1993. It provides a visible international advocate for human rights in the same way that the UN High Commissioner for Refugees focuses international attention on that problem. The office is responsible for promotion and coordination, for mainstreaming human rights into the UN system, and for furnishing information to and supporting the work of relevant UN bodies. It serves as the secretariat for the Human Rights Council and supports the work of Special Procedures—special rapporteurs, independent experts, and working groups—appointed by the HRC to monitor specific human rights situations and problems.

Increasingly, OHCHR has assumed an operational role, providing technical assistance to countries in the form of training courses for judges and prison officials, electoral assistance, and advisory services on constitutional and legislative reform, among other things.[13] With field offices in many countries, OHCHR is able not only to help strengthen domestic institutions but also to promote compliance with international human rights standards and to report directly to the high commissioner on abuses. The high commissioner sits on the UN Secretary-General's Senior Management Group, which effectively serves as a cabinet. The office, however, is handicapped by its small budget allocation (just over 3 percent of the total UN budget), which is supplemented by voluntary contributions from member states and institutional donors. Although the amount of funding from the UN's regular budget has increased gradually since 2005, more than two-thirds of OHCHR's funding still comes from voluntary contributions. OHCHR also oversees two trust funds that were established by the General Assembly to support activities advancing specific human rights issues: the Voluntary Fund for Victims of Torture and the Voluntary Trust Fund on Contemporary Forms of Slavery.

The effectiveness of the office depends in part on the legitimacy, personality, leadership skills, and initiative of the commissioner. Three of the seven commissioners to date have been women. Mary Robinson, former president of Ireland, and Louise Arbour, Canadian judge and former prosecutor for the Yugoslav and Rwandan ad hoc criminal tribunals, clearly elevated the effectiveness and prestige of the office. The appointment in 2008 of Navanethem (Navi) Pillay, former judge on the South African High Court, the Rwandan tribunal, and the International Criminal Court, also enhanced the credibility of the office. Her call for an independent investigation into human rights abuses in Sri Lanka after the end of that country's civil war in 2009 and her support for international protection of civilians in the 2011 Libyan conflict were evidence of a strong human rights voice. Zeid Ra'ad Al Hussein, the seventh high commissioner, was formerly Jordan's permanent representative to the UN and involved in the establishment of the ICC, serving as president of the Assembly of State Parties and overseeing the election of the ICC's first judges, prosecutor, and president.

The International Court of Justice

The ICJ's role in human rights has generally been minimal. It did confirm the principle of self-determination in the Western Sahara case (1975), and it concluded in a 1971 opinion that South Africa had violated its obligations toward South West Africa (Namibia) under the Universal Declaration of Human Rights. In 2007, the court ruled on the question of whether Serbia had committed genocide in Bosnia-Herzegovina. A similar case involving Croatia and Serbia was concluded in 2015.[14] The ICJ's lack of attention to human rights is due primarily to the fact that only states can bring contentious cases to the court, while the General Assembly and Security Council can seek advisory opinions. This tells us more about the limitations of the court itself than about the UN and human rights.

THE ROLE OF THE UN IN HUMAN RIGHTS

To see how the UN organs and bodies have addressed human rights issues, we focus first on how the UN has helped to set the norms, then examine how monitoring, promotional, and enforcement activities occur. Thereafter, we use a series of case studies to illustrate the UN's role.

PHOTOGRAPH 6.1. Eleanor Roosevelt holds the Universal Declaration of Human Rights, November 1949
Source: UN Photo 23783.

Defining Human Rights: Setting Standards and Norms

The UN's first step in setting human rights standards came with the General Assembly's unanimous approval of the Universal Declaration of Human Rights on December 9, 1948, and the passage one day earlier of the Convention on the Prevention and Punishment of the Crime of Genocide. Under the tireless leadership of Eleanor Roosevelt, the wife of the late US president Franklin D. Roosevelt and chair of the UN Commission on Human Rights, these documents articulated a far-reaching human rights agenda for the UN.

The Universal Declaration, called by some the most important document of the twentieth century, drew on ideas dating from the French and American revolutions and earlier bills of rights as well as principles of natural rights.[15] Among its catalog of thirty principles, it elucidated rights critical for the exercise of political freedom, rights essential for the preservation of a civil society, and the social and economic rights of individuals. The declaration listed those claims as a first step toward the articulation of international human rights standards. Since the declaration was only a General Assembly resolution, the expectation was that these rights would be set forth in a covenant (or treaty) that would bind states to respect them. It took until 1966 for the General Assembly to approve the International Covenant on Civil and Political Rights and the International Covenant on Economic, Social, and Cultural Rights, with both entering into force in 1976. Together with the Universal Declaration, they are known as the **International Bill of Rights**.

The two international covenants took so long to ratify because they reflected very different perspectives about which rights are deemed to be universal. The first covenant emerged from so-called **first-generation human rights**, those rights associated with political and civil liberties. They were the first rights to be incorporated into national constitutions and are "negative rights" in that they are intended to block government authorities from interfering with private individuals in civil society. Linked to Western liberalism, they include the right to free speech, the right to freedom of religion, the right to a free press, and the right to congregate at will. The second covenant encompasses **second-generation human rights**, building upon the socialist view that emphasizes economic and social rights such as the right to employment, the right to health care, and the right to social security. Referred to as "positive rights," these are the basic material benefits that the state must provide to individuals. While the Universal Declaration incorporated both sets of rights, conflict between Western and socialist views blocked conclusion of a single treaty and resulted ultimately in two treaties. The fact that the United States has yet to ratify the Covenant on Economic, Social, and Cultural Rights indicates that the difference in views persists.

Both prior to and following the approval of the covenants, the UN has brought into being an array of other human rights treaties that systematically define a variety of first- and second-generation rights. These include treaties on genocide, slavery and forced labor, refugees, torture, racial discrimination, and discrimination against women. Some of these evolved from the work of UN specialized agencies, particularly the ILO; most were drafted by the former Commission on Human Rights. More recent conventions include what many call **third-generation human rights** that protect designated groups, including children, the disabled, indigenous peoples, and migrant workers. Many human rights activists also advocate for collective rights to a safe environment, peace, democracy, and development, although these are more controversial. A list of selected UN human rights conventions is found in Table 6.1.

Just as the West has dominated international economic relations, it has dominated the setting of standards for human rights. Thus, the strongest global and regional human rights mechanisms protect civil and political rights (the first-generation human rights), with the other two generations receiving less attention. It is also far more difficult to establish standards of compliance for economic and social rights (second-generation rights) and politically far more difficult to secure agreement on third-generation rights, as the General Assembly's failure to approve the draft convention on indigenous peoples demonstrates.

TABLE 6.1. Selected UN Human Rights Conventions

Convention	Opened for ratification	Entered into force	Ratifications (as of 2015)
General Human Rights			
International Covenant on Civil and Political Rights	1966	1976	168
International Covenant on Economic, Social, and Cultural Rights	1966	1976	164
Racial Discrimination			
International Convention on the Elimination of All Forms of Racial Discrimination	1966	1969	177
International Convention on the Suppression and Punishment of the Crime of Apartheid	1973	1976	109
Rights of Women			
Convention on the Elimination of All Forms of Discrimination Against Women	1979	1981	189
Human Trafficking and Other Slave-like Practices			
UN Convention for the Suppression of the Traffic in Persons and of the Exploitation of the Prostitution of Others	1949	1951	82
Supplementary Convention on the Abolition of Slavery, the Slave Trade, and Institutions and Practices Similar to Slavery	1956	1957	123
ILO Convention Concerning the Prohibition and Immediate Action for the Elimination of the Worst Forms of Child Labor	1999	2000	180
UN Convention Against Transnational Organized Crime: Protocol to Prevent, Suppress and Punish Trafficking in Persons, Especially Women and Children	2000	2003	169
Refugees and Stateless Persons			
Convention Relating to the Status of Refugees	1951	1954	145
Protocol Relating to the Status of Refugees	1967	1967	146

(continues)

TABLE 6.1. Selected UN Human Rights Conventions *(continued)*

Convention	Opened for ratification	Entered into force	Ratifications (as of 2015)
Children			
Convention on the Rights of the Child	1989	1990	196
Optional Protocol to the Convention on the Rights of the Child on the Involvement of Children in Armed Conflict	2000	2002	162
Optional Protocol to the Convention on the Rights of the Child on the Sale of Children, Child Prostitution and Child Pornography	2000	2002	171
Other			
Convention on the Prevention and Punishment of the Crime of Genocide	1948	1951	147
Convention Against Torture and Other Cruel, Inhuman or Degrading Treatment or Punishment	1984	1987	158
Optional Protocol to the Convention Against Torture and Other Cruel, Inhuman or Degrading Treatment or Punishment	2002	2006	80
Convention Concerning Indigenous and Tribal Peoples in Independent Countries	1989	1991	20
International Convention on the Protection of the Rights of All Migrant Workers and Members of Their Families	1990	2003	48
Convention on the Rights of Persons with Disabilities	2007	2008	160
Optional Protocol for the Convention on the Rights of Persons with Disabilities	2008	2008	88
International Convention for the Protection of All Persons from Enforced Disappearance	2006	2010	51

SOURCES: International Labour Organization; University of Minnesota Human Rights Library; UN High Commissioner for Human Rights.

There is also lingering controversy over whether human rights are truly universal, applicable to all peoples in all states, religions, and cultures, or whether those rights depend on the cultural setting. In the 1990s, a number of Asian states argued that many of the human rights documents represented Western values and that the West was interfering in their internal affairs with its own definition of human rights. Particularly sensitive has been the debate relating to issues of religion, women's status, child protection, family planning, and practices such as female circumcision. As legal scholar and activist Abdullahi An-Na'im argues, "Detailed and credible knowledge of local culture is essential for the effective promotion and protection of human rights in any society."[16]

Despite this debate, the Final Declaration and Programme of Action of the 1993 Vienna World Conference on Human Rights stated: "All human rights are universal, indivisible and interdependent and interrelated." Regional arrangements, the declaration stated, "should reinforce universal human rights standards, as contained in international human rights instruments, and their protection." As former secretary-general Kofi Annan noted, "It was never the people who complained of the universality of human rights, nor did the people consider human rights as a Western or Northern imposition. It was often their leaders who did so."[17]

"Getting countries to toe the mark is only possible when there is a mark to toe."[18] Clearly, the UN has played a major role in establishing those marks. Yet setting standards is only the first step in protecting human rights norms. There must be effective actions by states. Thus, the UN has moved in bits and pieces from articulating norms to monitoring, promoting, and enforcing the standards.[19]

From Articulating Human Rights Norms to Monitoring

Monitoring the implementation of human rights norms requires procedures for receiving complaints of violations from affected individuals or interested groups as well as reports of state practice. It may also involve the power to comment on reports, make recommendations to states, appoint working groups or special rapporteurs, and vote on resolutions of condemnation. Publicity and public shaming are key tools of multilateral monitoring of state compliance.

The ILO was the first international organization to establish procedures for monitoring human rights within states—in this instance, workers' rights—beginning in 1926. Acclaimed as having the most effective monitoring system, the ILO compiles reports from governments about practices under various ILO conventions. ILO staff then prepares comments for the Committee of Experts using a variety of sources: direct contacts, reports of other UN bodies, and reports from employers' and workers' groups to supplement government reports. The findings of the Committee of Experts, while not binding on states, are conveyed to a conference committee for a final report. In some cases, the ILO actually investigates allegations of state noncompliance through its Commission of Inquiry. Although ILO procedures can lead to enforcement under Article 33 of the organization's constitution, the norm is not to utilize coercive measures, but to work with the country in question and offer technical assistance programs to facilitate compliance.

With only governments represented in the UN and in both the former Commission on Human Rights and the Human Rights Council, however, monitoring is much more problematic than standard setting. Nevertheless, developments in the 1970s outside of the UN provided a major impetus for the further evolution of international human rights protection. First, the number of human rights NGOs increased dramatically, emerging as a powerful political force, publicizing information on human rights violations, and pressing for action by governments, the UN, and regional organizations. Second, events in several parts of the world fueled activists' efforts. Among these were the repressive military regimes that came to power in Chile and Argentina, apartheid's deepening repressiveness in South Africa, and the 1975 Helsinki Accords between the Soviet Union, Eastern European countries, Western Europe, and the United States, which opened the Communist countries to scrutiny and pressure for political liberalization. Third, several countries, including the United States, introduced human rights into their foreign policies in the 1970s. President Jimmy Carter's public support for human rights provided a major boost. Fourth, a broad coalition of West, East, and nonaligned states helped bring much greater attention to UN human rights activities. Most states then found it impossible politically not to give at least some token support to international human rights efforts.

In 1967, the UN Commission on Human Rights was empowered for the first time to examine gross violations of human rights in South Africa and Southern Rhodesia. Further investigations against specific states followed, setting precedents for monitoring. In 1970, ECOSOC Resolution 1503 authorized the commission to undertake confidential investigations of individual complaints that suggest "a consistent pattern of gross and reliably attested violations." This 1503 procedure, however, only provided for examination of complaints in private and terminated with a report to the commission. Nonetheless, the commission significantly expanded its activities during the 1970s, creating working groups to study specific civil rights problems such as forced disappearances, torture, religious discrimination, and the situation in Chile after the 1973 coup.[20] The 1503 procedure was succeeded by a new complaint procedure in 2007. Although it can handle only a fraction of the complaints received each year, it does provide means for placing pressure on offending governments as well as encouraging dialogue to address the complaints.

In 2008, the Human Rights Council completed a review of the Special Procedures that had been established to monitor various human rights issues and situations, including all existing mandates for special rapporteurs and working groups. In 2015, there were forty-one thematic and fourteen country mandates, ranging from issues such as the Palestinian territories and involuntary detentions to torture, contemporary forms of slavery, and disappearances. The mandates typically call for the mandate holders (who serve voluntarily, without pay, in order to remain impartial) to examine, monitor, advise, and publicly report on the human rights situation in a given country or a major worldwide problem of violations. Special rapporteurs may respond to individual complaints, conduct studies, and make country visits to investigate the situation. The Universal Periodic Reviews initiated after the creation of the HRC are another major means of monitoring UN members' human rights records. A 2013 study of the P-5 and the first round of the UPRs showed that all participated, but France, Great Britain, the United States, and Russia all received many negative comments, while China got primarily positive ones.[21] As transparent as the process was, the balance of comments clearly suggests a degree of politicization in the HRC, as discussed earlier.

The other primary mode for UN monitoring is through the ten treaty bodies created in connection with specific human rights treaties (see Figure 6.1).[22] Two are linked to the two covenants: the Human Rights Committee, provided for by the Covenant on Civil and Political Rights, and the Committee on Economic, Social, and Cultural Rights. Others are linked to eight specific conventions. Each requires states to submit periodic reports of their progress toward implementation of the treaty. Committees of independent experts elected by the parties to each treaty review the reports, engage in dialogue with governments, and issue concluding comments. Human rights NGOs frequently prepare their own "shadow reports," which provide the committees with an independent assessment of whether governments are fulfilling their commitments and put additional pressure on governments. National human rights institutions (and in some cases, such as the disabilities convention, subnational institutions) also have opportunities to participate in providing reports independent of national delegations.[23] Other UN agencies (such as UNICEF in the case of the Committee on the Rights of the Child) may also be important sources of information, while the OHCHR assists with follow-up and regional meetings for each treaty body to assist with the cumbersome reporting processes.

The human rights treaties vary in their provision for individual or group petitions and complaints. Even where there is such a provision, states themselves are generally reluctant to accept it. For example, only about one-third of the states that are party to the International Covenant on Civil and Political Rights have accepted the optional provision that allows individual petitions;

the same is true for the Convention Against Torture. The record is even worse with respect to the Convention on the Elimination of Racial Discrimination: only a dozen of the parties permit petitions, and of those only a few are African states. No Asian states have accepted this provision. A further problem arises from the limited number of petitions that can be handled in a given year. Of the thousands of complaints relating to civil and political rights filed with the secretary-general each year, only a small fraction can be considered by the Human Rights Committee. Nonetheless, the committee does conduct open meetings that expose states' practices and publishes its conclusions, thereby making its work transparent.

Most scholars agree that further reforms are needed. The treaty bodies are overburdened with work, making effective follow-up impossible. States are bogged down by multiple reporting requirements; late and incomplete reports remain a persistent problem. And even if reports are adequate, many of the UN monitoring systems lack the mandate and capacity to push implementation to the next level. Following a review process begun in 2009, the General Assembly approved a series of steps in 2014 to improve the treaty body system; these include a capacity-building program to assist states in fulfilling their treaty obligations and measures to make the bodies' public sessions and documentation more accessible. Both were scheduled to be implemented beginning in 2015.

This leads us to ask whether UN investigations, reports, and resolutions make a difference. One argument contends that, over time, repeated condemnations (often referred to as "naming and shaming") can produce change; this was true to some extent in South Africa, as discussed below. Yet in that case, the repeated condemnations were subsequently coupled with more coercive sanctions. Another point of view holds that public condemnations can antagonize states and harden their position—the opposite of the intended effect. For example, sixteen years of General Assembly resolutions linking Zionism with racism only antagonized Israel and the United States, and had no effect on the rights of Palestinians in Israel or the Occupied Territories.

So do human rights standards and treaties change state behavior? The evidence is mixed. One study found that if issues within the treaties are taken up by civil society groups, then the state's actual human rights practices are improved. In other words, NGO mobilization can effectively pressure governments.[24] Another study of the effectiveness of monitoring by the UN, NGOs, and the media between 1975 and 2000, however, found that "governments put in the global spotlight for violations often adopt better protections for political rights afterward, but they rarely stop or appear to lessen acts of terror. Worse, terror sometimes increases after publicity."[25] The same study also found that when NGOs subsequently took up those human rights issues, the state's human rights practices improved.

In short, although UN human rights monitoring has increased, its measurable impact is limited. Changes in procedures do not necessarily result in changes in states' attitudes and behavior. The case of China illustrates the difficulties. Following the 1989 Tiananmen Square massacre in China, the UN Sub-Commission on the Prevention of Discrimination approved resolutions criticizing human rights in China—the first condemnations against a P-5 member. China fought back, challenging the aggressive monitoring actions and drawing support from many developing countries. Together, they challenged the extent of NGO involvement, the independence of the subcommission members, the open proceedings, and the secret voting. Beginning in 1993, China successfully blocked all action on US-introduced resolutions dealing with its human rights situation.[26] Only in 2005, after ten years of effort, did the special rapporteur on torture, for example, secure China's agreement for an official visit. He found abuse "still widespread" and accused the Chinese authorities of obstructing his work.[27] China, in turn, attempted to get the rapporteur to alter the report. China files regular reports to the treaty bodies but continues to block efforts to examine its human rights record outside the UPR. NGOs and other states have used that process to target China's actions in Tibet and against Muslim Uighurs in western China, as well as its restrictions on freedom of expression.[28] China vigorously objected to a 2015 report by the UN Committee Against Torture on its failure to reduce the use of torture since a previous review in 2008, its continuing use of secret prisons, its "unprecedented detention and interrogation" of more than 200 lawyers in 2015, and its failure to produce requested information.[29] Similar to China's attempt to prevent damaging reports from being published, Rwanda attempted unsuccessfully to suppress the publication in 2010 of a report ordered by OHCHR that implicated it in genocide in the Democratic Republic of the Congo.[30] If states believed that such reports did not have an impact, they would not object to publication of the findings.

Translating norms and rhetoric into actions that go beyond stopping violations to change long-term attitudes and behavior is the challenge of promoting human rights. Efforts in this sphere have been scattered throughout the UN system.

From Monitoring to Promotion

Monitoring activities and evaluating successes and failures over time are not enough in themselves. There are various ways in which efforts are made through the UN system to promote the implementation and observance of international human rights norms. The OHCHR, as the secretariat for the Human Rights Council, plays a key role in the process and is considered one of the main focal points for promotional activities. As part of their mandates, special rapporteurs, independent experts, and working groups may provide technical assistance to governments and local groups and issue urgent appeals to governments. In December 2015, the Special Procedures collectively launched a campaign to promote full ratification of the two human rights covenants by the time of their fiftieth anniversary in December 2016, stating, "The Covenants have spurred considerable normative developments and institutional building at the international level, which have been matched by developments at national and local levels. Around the world, courts and tribunals, national human rights institutions, civil society activism and increasing public awareness have all contributed to making human rights a major legitimacy test for public and private policies and practices. We call for their universal ratification."[31]

The Universal Periodic Reviews also provide an opportunity for promoting human rights norms. To ensure equal treatment for all, every member state participates in evaluating the strengths and weaknesses of its human rights record every four years. The reviews are conducted by the UPR Working Group (the forty-seven council members) and any other state that wishes to participate. The group reviews national reports compiled by the state under review, information from independent human rights groups and experts within the UN system compiled by OHCHR, and information provided by other stakeholders, namely, national human rights institutions and nongovernmental organizations. During a three-hour interactive dialogue, states participate and stakeholders can attend, but the latter can speak only when the HRC convenes in regular session. The ultimate goal of the exercise is to design activities and programs to support and expand the promotion of human rights in member countries. States themselves are responsible for implementing the recommendations and are held accountable for progress when reviewed four years later.

A key OHCHR responsibility is to promote mainstreaming of human rights throughout the UN system. Since the early 1990s, the language of second- and third-generation human rights has been linked to development activities and programs across the entire UN system. Secretary-General Boutros-Ghali's *Agenda for Development* (1995) helped to make this connection through its emphasis on the right to development that had been endorsed by the General Assembly in 1986 (A/41/128). Similarly, the World Bank's promotion of "good governance" (including political and civil rights) among its aid recipients has provided added impetus, as have the empowerment of women and participation by civil society. UNDP's annual *Human Development Report* includes numerous indexes that measure gender empowerment, life expectancy, literacy, well-being, and other variables linked to human development. The Millennium Development Goals and now the Sustainable Development Goals discussed in Chapter 5 join all three generations of rights to the goals of eradicating poverty; promoting human dignity; achieving peace, democracy, and environmental sustainability; and involving people in decisions affecting them and their communities.

The shift in UNICEF's activities since the 1980s illustrates how the incorporation of rights-based language has been influential. UNICEF was pressured by NGOs who saw the ethical and pragmatic justification for rights-based language protecting children. The bureaucracy recognized that such an approach was in its interest as it moved into new activities such as its program on "children in especially difficult circumstances," that is, children in natural disasters, in wars, or generally at risk. UNICEF became an active participant in the writing of the Convention on the Rights of the Child, then mobilized to promote its adoption. The convention has since served as a motivator for UNICEF programming under both its traditional activities (education, medical care, and nutrition for children) and its newer activities (promoting political and civil rights for children, opposing child trafficking, and working against abuse). As one scholar notes, "UNICEF consistently argues that it now takes a more 'holistic' approach to children in need, looking at all their needs, rather than narrowly focusing on survival and basic development."[32]

Rights-based approaches and programming have also infused the UN's work in promoting democracy. Since the end of the 1980s, the UN has promoted democratization through its electoral assistance programs in conjunction with peacebuilding missions such as those in Namibia, Cambodia, Kosovo, East Timor, Iraq, and Afghanistan. Many of these missions have also involved drafting constitutional, judicial, and security reforms consistent with democratic systems, as well as protection of civilians and human rights.

The UN Electoral Assistance Division, created in 1992, plays a key role in promoting political and civil rights and democracy by providing technical assistance regarding political rights and democratization. More than one hundred member states have requested assistance on the legal, technical, administrative, and human rights aspects of organizing and conducting democratic elections since 1991. The role the UN plays varies according to the wishes of the state. Sometimes that activity entails certifying electoral processes, as it did in the contested Côte d'Ivoire election in 2010. At other times, it involves expert monitoring and reporting back to the secretary-general, using personnel from the UN as well as regional organizations such as the Organization for Security and Cooperation in Europe (OSCE) and the Organization of American States (OAS), and from NGOs such as the Carter Center and the National Endowment for Democracy. In a few cases, the UN has been fully in charge of organizing elections (Cambodia in 1992–1993 and East Timor in 2001–2002) or has shared that responsibility with states (Afghanistan in 2004–2005, 2009, and 2014, Iraq in 2005, and South Sudan in 2011). In Afghanistan's 2014 presidential election, the UN was responsible for overseeing a recount of all the votes.

From Promotion to Enforcement

As discussed in Chapters 2 and 4, the foundation for UN enforcement actions is found in the Charter's Chapter VII. On the two occasions during the Cold War when the council authorized enforcement, it was in response to the persistent gross violations of the rights of black majorities by white minority governments, first in the breakaway British colony of Southern Rhodesia (1966–1980) and then in South Africa (1978–1993). In neither case did the council make an explicit linkage between human rights violations and security threats. Since 1989, however, the UN's member states have been much more willing to link international peace and security with human rights and to authorize enforcement action.

When the Security Council authorized a US-led peacekeeping operation to restore the democratically elected government of Haiti in 1993, it signaled a willingness to enforce the emerging right to democracy—one of the third-generation rights. Famine and state collapse in Somalia, ethnic cleansing in Bosnia, genocide in Rwanda and Darfur, sectarian violence in the Central African Republic, systematic rape and chaos in the DRC, and the Qaddafi government's deliberate targeting of civilians in Libya in 2011 have been among the human rights and humanitarian crises that have led the Security Council to authorize peace operations with mandates to use military force. Likewise, the debates over R2P and POC, discussed in Chapter 4, clearly signal the linkage of human rights violations and threats to peace and security.

The Security Council has been less inclined to institute sanctions against governments responsible for gross violations of human rights. For example, since 2000, the regime of Robert Mugabe in Zimbabwe has engaged in systematic human rights abuses against its citizens and undermined democratic processes. In 2008, the United States and the EU proposed targeted UN sanctions against Mugabe and other officials, but Russia and China vetoed the draft resolution. The same sequence of events occurred in 2007 when the council debated a proposal to impose sanctions on senior officials in Myanmar for that government's gross violations of human rights.

Since the mid-1990s, the work of the ad hoc international criminal tribunals for the former Yugoslavia and Rwanda along with that of the International Criminal Court has provided a new approach to human rights enforcement involving individuals. Because these judicial processes link directly to cases of genocide, war crimes, and crimes against humanity, they are discussed below as part of the case study of those issues.

THE ROLE OF NONGOVERNMENTAL ORGANIZATIONS

We cannot understand the UN's roles in setting standards and in monitoring, promoting, and even enforcing human rights in specific cases, however, without taking a look first at the roles of NGOs involved in human rights and humanitarian activities. It was the increasingly influential activity of NGOs more than political events that produced the shift in UN responses from the 1970s to the 1990s.

Much of the UN's success in defining human rights norms, monitoring respect for human rights, and promoting human rights, in fact, has depended on the activities of the large networks of international human rights NGOs—the third UN. They perform a variety of functions and roles: providing information and expertise in drafting human rights conventions, monitoring violations, implementing human rights norms, mobilizing public support within countries for changes in national policies, mounting publicity campaigns and protests, lobbying, and bringing petitions before international bodies. Human rights advocates have been instrumental in getting governments to incorporate human rights norms into their concepts of national interest. Networks of advocates, and the NGOs of which they are a part, have gotten international responses to human rights violations by motivating governments to cooperate. Humanitarian NGOs not only perform similar roles in calling attention to humanitarian crises but also deliver relief aid to refugees and victims.

Many human rights NGOs were established in the late 1970s after the two international covenants went into effect and after the 1975 Helsinki Accords were signed. The Helsinki Accords gave Western governments and NGOs a basis for monitoring human rights in Eastern Europe and the Soviet Union. This helped weaken Communist regimes in those states and contributed to political and social liberalization. Similarly, the large number of disappearances and other human rights abuses under dictatorships in Chile, Argentina, and other Latin American countries in the 1970s spurred the growth of human rights NGOs. This converged with a greater interest among members of the US Congress in linking human rights with US foreign policy, including foreign economic assistance. They, in turn, relied on NGOs for expertise and information. In the late 1970s and 1980s, many of those same NGOs gained experience in mobilizing and lobbying when they sought to change US policies in Central America. Today there are literally thousands of human rights groups at the international, national, subnational, and grassroots levels. Over time, discrete human rights NGOs have together forged the international human rights movement, due in part to the rise of investigative journalism and the attention it has brought to human rights issues.[33] The information revolution has facilitated the movement's ability to transmit such information across borders.

NGOs' activities range from mere reporting and publicizing violations to promotion, supervisory, and enforcement activities. Although the larger and better-known of the human rights NGOs have ECOSOC consultative status, that status no longer provides the sole avenue of access. As discussed in Chapter 3, NGOs increasingly utilize other formal and informal opportunities, drawing on their expertise, information, and grassroots connections to legitimize their participation within the UN system, such as in the UPR and treaty bodies, as discussed above. As one UN official noted, "Eighty-five percent of our information came from NGOs. We did not have the resources or staff to collect information ourselves."[34] The relationships between NGOs and the treaty bodies vary, however. The Committee on the Rights of the Child enjoys the closest working relationship with NGOs, which regularly review state reports, maintain dialogue with local NGOs, and disseminate information. The Committee Against Torture, however, calls upon concerned NGOs only on an ad hoc basis. So while NGOs have a unique capacity to engage in monitoring, their ability to carry out this function depends on the political space provided by each separate treaty body.

NGOs provided much of the momentum for the 1993 World Conference on Human Rights in Vienna and the 1995 Fourth World Conference on Women in Beijing. Their activities were directed at both shaping the official conference outcomes and organizing the parallel NGO conferences. NGOs provided information for official delegates, lobbied governments and international policymakers, and networked with delegates and other NGOs. Some NGOs were also represented on official delegations. Yet because human rights NGOs, like groups in other issue areas, have traditionally been diverse and diffuse in their efforts, coordinated initiatives were difficult.

The best-known international human rights NGO is Amnesty International (AI), founded in 1961. AI gained attention for identifying specific political prisoners in countries without respect to political ideology and for conducting publicity and letter-writing campaigns to pressure governments on their behalf. It earned a reputation for scrupulous neutrality by investigating and censuring governments of all types. It has subsequently moved to support campaigns on broader cross-national issues, such as torture, the death penalty, violence against women, and discrimination based on sexual orientation. In these situations, AI has acted strategically, finding issues and states where there is reasonable likelihood of success for its campaigns, based on dissemination of information.[35] Criticisms have been leveled against AI, however, for concentrating on powerful countries such as China, Russia, and the United States, while some of the most repressive states, including Afghanistan, Somalia, and Myanmar, receive considerably less attention.[36]

Other key human rights NGOs include the International Commission of Jurists and Human Rights Watch (HRW). It was Aryeh Neier, executive director of Human Rights Watch, who in 1992 proposed creating the ad hoc war crimes tribunal for Yugoslavia. Without his initiative, supported by a number of other NGOs, the tribunal never would have been established. Many human rights NGOs are dedicated to specific issues such as indigenous peoples or India's

Dalits. Others are grouped in coalitions such as the International Lesbian, Gay, Bisexual, Trans, and Intersex Association (ILGA), which is the umbrella for hundreds of **LGBT** groups, and the Coalition for the International Criminal Court.

Humanitarian NGOs are concerned traditionally not with rights but with alleviating human suffering, such as by providing food during famines, as in Niger or Mozambique, aiding innocent victims of war, as in Syria and South Sudan, and leading relief efforts following natural disasters, such as the 2010 earthquake in Haiti. They are distinguished from human rights groups because they often deliberately refrain from advocacy roles. Their neutrality permits them to take a variety of actions that may be unavailable to governments.

The first humanitarian organization to gain recognition in the nineteenth century was the ICRC (and its affiliated Red Crescent Societies in predominantly Muslim states). Working closely with governments during conflicts, the ICRC is known for its neutrality, which has facilitated its work behind the scenes to ensure that prisoners of war receive fair treatment and to assist victims of war by providing medical care, clothing, shelter, and food. Following the 2003 Iraq War, for example, the ICRC inspected facilities where prisoners of war were being held by American authorities, quietly pressured the US government to follow the Geneva Conventions, and, when they were unable to effect changes in prisoner treatment, leaked reports of prisoner abuses to the international press.[37] Other prominent humanitarian NGOs include Oxfam, Save the Children, Doctors Without Borders (Médecins Sans Frontières, or MSF), and CARE. All the major humanitarian relief groups have been active in providing aid for victims of genocide in Darfur, and in the ongoing conflicts and humanitarian crises in the DRC, Afghanistan, Syria, Central African Republic, South Sudan, Yemen, and elsewhere.

NGOs are also active in the promotion and enforcement areas. They have provided education on human rights in Central America, Cambodia, Afghanistan, and other postconflict areas. During the 1992–1995 war in Bosnia-Herzegovina, AI issued three reports on widespread human rights abuses and ethnic cleansing between October 1992 and January 1993, and it was among the NGOs that pressed the Security Council to establish the war crimes tribunal for the former Yugoslavia in 1994. An umbrella group of more than a thousand NGOs, the Coalition for the International Criminal Court, helped mobilize international support in 1997 and 1998 to create the International Criminal Court, then pushed for ratification and now its usage. Save Darfur was the most prominent NGO advocating action in Darfur, while the International Rescue Committee took on the task of compiling data on casualties in the DRC, including victims of rape.

NGOs, therefore, through monitoring and promoting human rights and humanitarian norms, are major actors within and alongside the UN system in the human rights area. Yet NGOs (and concerned individuals and states) are frequently frustrated when governments fail to act, or when they limit access to official UN meetings to protect nation-state prerogatives and interests.

CASE STUDIES OF THE UN SYSTEM IN ACTION

In all four case studies of human rights issues that follow, the UN has provided a forum for getting the issue onto the international agenda and for setting and monitoring standards. In one case, it undertook enforcement. In another, it is now promoting implementation of norms. In each case, NGOs have played key roles, working both within and outside the UN system.

The Campaign Against Apartheid

One of the major human rights issues faced by the UN from 1946 to the early 1990s was the apartheid policy of the Republic of South Africa. A political and economic policy supporting the legal "separateness" of the races, apartheid was embodied in a series of South African laws dating from 1948 that enveloped the country's black majority population as well as other people of color in increasingly restrictive regulations that violated all human rights standards. To quell domestic opposition, the government used detention, torture, and state-sanctioned murder.

These gross violations of human rights directed against the black majority by the white minority provoked an international campaign against apartheid that was conducted inside and outside the UN by Third World states and NGOs. The UN General Assembly, the main forum for the campaign, passed its first resolution on the subject in December 1946. Led by India, the assembly approved annual resolutions rejecting South Africa's claims that the Charter's human rights provisions constituted no special obligations for member states and that there was no widely accepted definition of these rights and freedoms.

After South African troops fired on demonstrators in the Sharpeville massacre of 1960, twenty-six newly independent African countries, along with other countries, called for members to break diplomatic ties with South Africa and impose economic sanctions. This marked an acceptance by a majority of the UN's members that enforcement was necessary. In 1963, the Security Council adopted a voluntary embargo on military sales to South Africa. Other General Assembly resolutions called for sanctions against oil, trade, investment, and IMF credits, as well as diplomatic and cultural isolation. The Commission on Human Rights created the first monitoring body, the Ad Hoc Working Group on Southern Africa, and after ECOSOC agreed to allow the commission to examine gross violations of human rights in 1967 (Resolution 1235), the practice of apartheid was the focus of investigation.

From 1974 to 1994, South Africa was prohibited from taking its seat in the General Assembly, and the assembly granted observer status to two opposition groups—the African National Congress (ANC) and the Pan African Congress. Pressure mounted for enforcement action by the Security Council. In 1976, the International Convention on the Suppression and Punishment of the Crime of Apartheid went into effect, establishing apartheid as an international crime. In 1977, after a series of particularly egregious actions by the South African government, a mandatory arms embargo was approved by the Security Council under Chapter VII. Pressure for economic sanctions continued, and the General Assembly declared 1982 the International Year of Mobilization for Sanctions Against Apartheid. Yet the three Western P-5 members—the United States, Great Britain, and France—had economic and security interests at stake, and thwarted further Security Council action.

The international campaign against apartheid included other actions, some orchestrated by the General Assembly's Special Committee on Apartheid.[38] Virtually every meeting held under UN auspices singled out apartheid for examination. The WHO scrutinized health care for blacks; the ILO probed labor practices. South Africa's sports teams were also banned from international competition and its cultural activities boycotted. The campaign included NGOs such as the World Council of Churches, World Peace Council, International Confederation of Free Trade Unions, and International League for Human Rights. Numerous national and subnational NGOs, including university students and women's and civil rights groups, supported the cause, employing a variety of tactics.[39] The UN and NGOs also provided aid to groups resisting apartheid and were instrumental in publicizing and educating the world about apartheid. This support enabled the exiled South African opponents of apartheid to survive decades of severe repression.[40]

In the 1980s, the campaign against apartheid inside and outside the UN grew stronger as apartheid itself became more repressive. Media coverage of violence in South Africa increased public awareness of the problem. High-profile black leaders in South Africa who were not imprisoned, such as Bishop Desmond Tutu, the winner of the 1985 Nobel Peace Prize, actively advocated economic sanctions. In the United States, public pressure and a campaign of civil disobedience by prominent politicians and civil rights activists led Congress to approve the Comprehensive Anti-Apartheid Act, including sanctions, over a presidential veto. Britain followed suit in imposing sanctions. This was one instance where grassroots pressure and the strength of moral condemnation mattered.

In 1990, the South African regime announced a political opening that led to black majority rule and the dismantling of apartheid. Nelson Mandela, the ANC leader, was freed from prison after twenty-seven years. Open elections were held in 1994, and a black-majority government has governed South Africa since then.

Apartheid laws were eliminated, sanctions and the country's diplomatic isolation ended, and although racism and inequality persist in South Africa, the long process of promoting human rights among blacks and whites continues.

What role did the UN play in this change? For one, the UN General Assembly and other UN bodies where majority voting was the rule were crucial forums for sustained criticism of South Africa over almost forty years, for isolating the apartheid government diplomatically, and for giving the domestic opposition and exiles visibility, legitimacy, and material aid. The Western P-5 members, however, used their veto power to block Third World proposals for comprehensive sanctions, approving only the 1978 arms embargo. The imposition of sanctions by Britain and the United States in the 1980s was a morale boost for the campaign against apartheid as well as a means to inflict pain on the South African business community and, through them, on the government. Enlightened white leaders realized that internal opposition could no longer be suppressed and that sanctions were having a damaging effect on the economy.[41] In testimony to the UN's role in delegitimizing and defeating apartheid, Nelson Mandela made one of his earliest public speeches after being freed to the UN General Assembly, thanking members for their support.

In some sense, apartheid might be considered an "easy" case. The discrimination was systematic and egregious, and the campaign against apartheid found early and widespread support for which the UN provided an important forum.

Women's Rights as Human Rights

Women face various forms of discrimination in virtually every country and culture. In the 1940s, however, women's rights were viewed as separate and different from human rights, even though Article 2 of the Universal Declaration of Human Rights states that "rights and freedoms set forth in this Declaration" must be given "without distinction as to race, color, sex, or language." It was a long process within and outside the UN system before women's rights were recognized as human rights.

Initially, the political status of women appeared on the UN agenda because the Western liberal democracies and the socialist states agreed on the importance of granting women political rights. The Commission on the Status of Women had primary responsibility for ensuring women's right to vote, hold office, and enjoy various legal rights. Beginning in 1952, ECOSOC drafted the Conventions on the Political Rights of Women (1952), Nationality of Married Women (1957), and Consent to Marriage (1962). During the 1960s and 1970s, more attention was given to elevating the status of women as economic actors through the women-in-development initiatives discussed in Chapter 5.

During the 1980s and 1990s, women's issues were increasingly viewed within the rubric of universal human rights.[42] The shift began with the 1979 Convention on the Elimination of All Forms of Discrimination Against Women, which set the standard for states "to modify the social and cultural patterns of conduct of men and women, with a view to achieving the elimination of prejudices and customary and all other practices which are based on the idea of inferiority or the superiority of either of the sexes or on stereotyped roles for men and women" (Article 5[a]) and "to eliminate discrimination against women in the political and public life of the country" (Article 7). CEDAW did not establish a system for reviewing complaints of violations of women's rights, but in 2000 the Optional Protocol to CEDAW provided procedures for individual and group complaints.

Ratifications of CEDAW have often been accompanied by reservations and understandings that show major differences in treaty interpretation. For example, Algeria declares reservations about articles that contradict the Algerian Family Code; Egypt's reservations are in areas that conflict with Muslim sharia law; and Israel expresses reservations about articles that conflict with laws on personal status binding on its various religious communities. Those differences point to the question of whether human rights are applicable universally or not. The preamble to the 1995 Beijing declaration attempted to put that to rest by affirming: "While the significance of national and regional particularities and various historical, cultural and religious backgrounds must be borne in mind, it is the duty of states, regardless of the political, economic and cultural systems, to promote and protect all human rights and fundamental freedoms." Still, the issue is not dead.

The four successive UN-sponsored World Conferences on Women—in Mexico City (1975), Copenhagen (1980), Nairobi (1985), and Beijing (1995)—raised awareness of women's rights and mobilized action at new levels. They greatly expanded women's international NGOs and led to new networks, representing every hue in the ideological rainbow, from secular to religious, radical to conservative, grassroots to elite. They also led to coalitions around issues affecting women, such as population, the environment, and development. Over time, as the NGOs gained experience with UN procedures, they became more effective in their lobbying efforts, organizing participation in preparatory meetings, developing strategies to push selected issues, gathering information, and monitoring governments' positions. Ninety human rights and women's NGOs joined in the Global Campaign for Women's Human Rights prior to the 1993 Vienna World Conference on Human Rights and succeeded in linking women's rights to human rights.[43]

UN Women, discussed in Chapter 5, now provides an institutional home for coordinating UN system work on gender equality and empowerment, including human rights, development, humanitarian action, and peace and security. One of the major issues it has taken up is gender-based violence, an age-old problem long hidden in the private sphere of the family and communal life. Forced marriages at a young age; physical abuse by spouses, including disfigurement and rape; crippling dowry payments; female genital mutilation; and honor killings all occur within the home and family. A gendered division of labor often forces women into sweatshop labor, prostitution, and trafficking in their bodies; in wars, women are raped, tortured, and forced into providing sexual services for troops.

NGOs played a major role in bringing attention to the issue of violence against women after the 1975 UN Conference on Women failed to address it. In 1976, activists organized the International Tribunal on Crimes Against Women, which heard testimonials of women who had experienced domestic or community violence. The tribunal provided impetus for networking, building alliances, and agenda setting and contributed to CEDAW in 1979, even though that treaty did not address violence against women.

Among those working in the UN system, violence against women became recognized as a criminalized activity during the 1980s as a result of intergovernmental meetings of experts from multiple UN agencies, including the Division for the Advancement of Women and the Crime Prevention and Criminal Justice Division of the UN Department of International Economic and Social Affairs. The first UN survey on violence against women was published in 1989. And, in conjunction with the 1993 Vienna Conference on Human Rights, women's NGOs organized another tribunal, with international judges hearing testimony from victims that put a human face on domestic violence, torture, political persecution, and denial of economic rights.

The joint efforts of women's and human rights groups produced Article 18 of the Vienna Declaration and Programme of Action, which declared: "The human rights of women and of the girl-child are an inalienable, integral and indivisible part of universal human rights. . . . The human rights of women should form an integral part of the United Nations human rights activities, including the promotion of all human rights instruments relating to women." Violence against women and other abuses in situations of war, peace, and domestic family life, including sexual harassment, were also identified as breaches of both human rights and humanitarian norms. The declaration called for their elimination through national and international legal means. Later in 1993, the General Assembly approved the Declaration on the Elimination of Violence Against Women and called for states to take steps to combat violence in accordance with provisions of that declaration.[44] It also called for a special rapporteur on violence against women. Although still "soft" law, the declaration makes states responsible for providing and enforcing human rights guarantees to women not only in public life but also in private life in the sanctity of the home, a responsibility that many states have so far failed to uphold.

The use of rape as a tool of war is not new, but recognition of it is, and while it is not used only against women, they have been the primary victims. The war in Bosnia in the 1990s and the genocide in Rwanda brought widespread recognition of its systematic use. A decision by the International Criminal Tribunal for Rwanda (ICTR) brought the first conviction of rape as a crime against humanity and a means of perpetrating genocide. Almost half of those convicted by the International Criminal Tribunal for the Former Yugoslavia (ICTY) were found guilty of crimes involving sexual violence. ICTY was also the first to convict individuals of sexual enslavement as a crime against humanity and rape as a form of torture. In 2008, the Security Council unanimously adopted Resolution 1820, declaring rape to be a "tactic of war to humiliate, dominate, instill fear in, disperse and/or forcibly relocate civilian members of a community or ethnic group" and a threat to international security.

Sexual violence has been a major problem in the Democratic Republic of the Congo, as discussed in Chapter 4, despite the size of (and because of) the UN peacekeeping force there. In early 2010, the secretary-general responded by appointing a special representative on sexual violence in conflict, with emphasis on the DRC. In September 2010, the Security Council admitted that the UN's actions were inadequate, "resulting in unacceptable brutalization of the population." An investigation into UN failures followed, but as discussed in Chapter 4, the problem of peacekeepers in a number of operations either committing gender violence or failing to halt it persists.

Various UN agencies support programs to stop the violence and to help the victims. Efforts have been made to improve training. The inclusion of more women in UN peacekeeping missions is designed to enhance sensitivity to the issue, and gender advisers work with both peacekeepers and local women who are victims or at risk. UNICEF supports a mobile clinic for survivors of sexual violence, and OHCHR, with funding from UN Women, is sponsoring projects to improve women's ability to earn income after being violated. Numerous NGOs offer assorted services. Still, the violence continues, and the UN's failure to protect the population is a black mark on its peacekeepers' record.

Human Trafficking: The Modern Form of Slavery

Violence against women is part of the larger problems of human trafficking and other slave-like practices that victimize not only women and children but also men. While institutionalized slavery disappeared at the end of the nineteenth century due to the tireless efforts of antislavery groups, who were the first human rights advocates, slavelike practices of forced labor and trafficking in persons within and across national borders continue today. The scope of human trafficking owes much to the rapid pace of globalization following the dissolution of the Soviet Union, which opened doors not only to the free flow of ideas, capital, and people but also to illicit industries such as human trafficking. Many of those trafficked are women and children who are tricked with promises of education, work, and a better life; are held against their will once they discover what has happened; work long hours with no breaks; often suffer beatings and other abuse; and are denied contact with their families.

In 2015, the ILO estimated that approximately 21 million people worldwide were "enslaved" in forced labor, which includes debt bondage and trafficking, and approximately one-fifth of those (4.5 million) were victims of forced sexual exploitation, including many more women than men. An estimated 5.5 million (26 percent) victims of forced labor were below eighteen years of age.[45] The difficulty of establishing firmer figures has to do both with varying definitions of what constitutes trafficking and with the often clandestine nature of the problem. It has been framed as both a human rights issue and a transnational crime, with profits estimated at more than $100 billion annually. This dual framing of human trafficking has produced two separate lines of action within the UN system.

Human rights framing means setting standards and securing victims' rights to legal and rehabilitative remedies. The UN system has long been actively involved in establishing norms against slavelike practices. The Universal Declaration on Human Rights included the right to be free from slavery or servitude. The 1951 Convention for the Suppression of Traffic in Persons prohibited trafficking in human beings for the explicit purpose of prostitution (even with their consent). In 1956, the General Assembly explicitly identified contemporary practices that were considered "slavelike," among them serfdom, forced marriage, child labor, debt bondage, and trafficking in human beings, when it approved the Supplementary Convention on the Abolition of Slavery, Slave Trade, and Institutions and Practices Similar to Slavery. The ILO banned forced labor in a 1957 convention, addressed abuses of migrant workers in a 1975 convention, and approved a Protocol to the Forced Labour Convention in 2014. Other related UN actions include the conventions on women (CEDAW), children, and migrant workers; the Optional Protocols on Children in Armed Conflict and on the Sale of Children, Child Prostitution, and Child Pornography (2002); and the use of Special Procedures on several aspects of the problem. (See Table 6.1.)

Framing policy under the rationale and language of criminal justice means focusing on ensuring aggressive prevention and prosecution of traffickers. Because of this, the General Assembly established the Commission on Crime Prevention and Criminal Justice under ECOSOC in 1992. In 1994 the commission convened a global conference on transnational crime, which produced a formal action plan against transnational organized crime. Subsequently, ECOSOC proposed drafting a new convention, which the General Assembly then authorized in 1997.

Early in the drafting of the Convention Against Transnational Organized Crime, work began on a separate protocol on trafficking in persons. The drafting process lasted from late 1998 through 2000, was highly contentious, and drew active NGO advocacy. The most heated tug-of-war concerned the definition of sex trafficking. One camp, supported prominently by the Coalition Against Trafficking in Women, insisted that prostitution in all its forms was exploitative and should qualify for global criminalization. The opposing view, advanced by the Human Rights Caucus, posited that noncoerced, consensual migrant sex work should not be prohibited by the protocol. The debate hinged on the definition of sex trafficking and "force" as a required element as well as on whether "consent" should serve as a delineating concept between noncoerced sex work and sex trafficking or whether the coerced consent of victims would allow traffickers to escape prosecution. Both camps sought to influence the delegates directly as well as national governments.[46] The final language maintains a distinction between consensual sex work and sex trafficking, but it does not permit the consent of victims to be used as a shield for prosecution if other elements of exploitation are apparent.

The Convention Against Transnational Organized Crime, with the additional protocol for trafficking in persons as well as protocols for migrant smuggling and arms trafficking, was adopted by the General Assembly in 2000 and entered into force in 2003. All four are often referred to as the Palermo Convention and Protocols. The trafficking protocol defines trafficking in persons as

> the recruitment, transportation, transfer, harbouring or receipt of persons, by means of the threat or use of force or other forms of coercion, of abduction, of fraud, of deception, of the abuse of power or of a position of vulnerability or of the giving or receiving of payments or benefits to achieve the consent of a person having control over another person, for the purpose of exploitation. Exploitation shall include, at a minimum, the exploitation of the prostitution of others or other forms of sexual exploitation, forced labour or services, slavery or practices similar to slavery, servitude or the removal of organs.[47]

As of 2016, 169 states had become party to the trafficking protocol. Because of its link to the transnational crime convention, this protocol uses the language of criminal law rather than of human rights. This means that the focus of implementation is not so much monitoring and promotion as law enforcement. The UN Office of Drugs and Crime (UNODC) works to combat trafficking under the convention and both protocols; assists signatory states in crafting comprehensive policies against human trafficking; and provides training resources, primarily for law enforcement officials and lawmakers. Notably excluded from its antitrafficking initiatives are resources and assistance for other "first responders" to human trafficking such as health care professionals, victims' advocates, or social service providers.

The Geneva-based UN human rights organs have continued their antitrafficking work. As of 2015, there were special rapporteurs for contemporary forms of slavery as well as for trafficking in persons, and for the sale of children, child prostitution, and child pornography. As discussed above, these Special Procedures are a primary means of monitoring as well as promoting specific human rights by conducting country visits, receiving complaints from individuals, issuing reports to the HRC and General Assembly, and communicating with governments concerning violations. There is also an SRSG on children in armed conflict who addresses the problem of child soldiers. Among the treaty-based bodies, the Committee on the Rights of the Child in recent reports to the General Assembly, for example, has taken note of the special vulnerabilities of children to human trafficking.

Other trafficking-related activities across the UN system have included the UN General Assembly declaration of 2004 as the International Year to Commemorate the Struggle Against Slavery and Its Abolition along with sponsorship of programs, exhibits, and educational programs. In 2009, UNODC appointed Academy Award–winning actress Mira Sorvino as its first Goodwill Ambassador for the Global Fight Against Human Trafficking to help bring visibility to the problem and efforts to address it. In 2010, the General Assembly approved a Global Plan of Action, one of whose outcomes was to task UNODC with data collection and biennial reporting on patterns and flows at the global, regional, and national levels. The first of these reports was published in 2012. A high-level meeting of the General Assembly in 2013 then reviewed efforts to combat trafficking over the previous decade, noting the significant increase in the number of states with antitrafficking legislation, the ongoing challenges of data collection, the low conviction rates, and inadequate support for victims. Forced labor and human trafficking are among the priority areas for the ILO, which undertook major studies in 2001 and 2005 of forced labor, including human trafficking, calling for a broad effort to eliminate forced labor within ten years.[48] Both reports linked human trafficking with globalization and the ways it promotes forced labor, such as the pressure to cut costs, the surplus of migrant workers, and the deregulation of labor markets.

In 2010, the General Assembly also established the UN Voluntary Trust Fund on Contemporary Forms of Slavery to provide financial assistance to individuals who are victims as well as to NGOs dealing with these issues. The aid to individuals is based on needs for security, education, independence, and reintegration and can include safe housing, legal aid, medical care, vocational training, and psychosocial support. In its second grant cycle (2014–2017), the Voluntary Fund is providing grants to nineteen NGOs for aid to victims.

A second source of assistance between 2007 and 2015 for all stakeholders dealing with human trafficking, including governments, businesses, academics, civil society, and the media, was the United Nations Global Initiative to Fight Human Trafficking, better known as UN.GIFT. It was established by the ILO, OHCHR, UNICEF, UNODC, OSCE, and the International Organization for Migration, with funding from the United Arab Emirates, a number of other states, UNIFEM, UNDP, and public donations. UN.GIFT's primary focus was on eradicating trafficking by supporting partnerships for joint action, promoting effective rights-based actions, and building the capacity of state and nonstate stakeholders. It ceased to exist, however, at the end of 2014.

A particularly striking element of the efforts to deal with human trafficking has been the absence of a single dominant NGO coalition such as those formed to deal with violence against women or with slavery itself, or to push for the International Criminal Court. The two coalitions active during the drafting of the Palermo trafficking protocol have not formed a single network to coordinate and facilitate antitrafficking efforts. Anti-Slavery International includes human trafficking among its activities and works to raise awareness and lobby countries to ratify conventions and strengthen their antitrafficking efforts. Yet many NGOs continue to prefer to operate independently and often see other NGOs as competitors for funding and attention. For example, the Coalition Against Trafficking in Women International focuses on women, while other NGOs focus on children, and some address both women and children; still others address all victims and forms of trafficking.

Despite all of the human rights–oriented and crime-oriented activities within the UN system (and by other IGOs) as well as by NGOs and governments, human trafficking remains a growing and highly lucrative form of transnational organized crime. Lack of public awareness of the problem in countries where trafficking originates (more than half originates from countries in the Asia-Pacific region) as well as in destination countries, including the United States, continues to be an obstacle to antitrafficking efforts. Furthermore, the migration crisis of 2015, discussed in Chapter 7, has been abetted by human traffickers. Hence, antitrafficking efforts inside and outside the UN system must continue to raise awareness of the problem and seek solutions. Setting standards, monitoring, promotion, and even enforcement are not enough.

Genocide, Crimes Against Humanity, and War Crimes

During the twentieth century, millions were victims of genocide, ethnic cleansing, other crimes against humanity, and war crimes. The Holocaust is often singled out for the deaths of some 6 million Jews, Gypsies, and other "undesirables" under the Nazi German regime, but there were other incidents of what is now called **genocide** before World War II as well as several since. The post–World

War II trials of war criminals held in Nuremburg, Germany, and Tokyo, Japan, organized by the victors, made it painfully obvious that there was no international law prohibiting genocide. In fact, prior to 1944, the term *genocide* did not exist. It was coined by a Polish lawyer, Raphael Lemkin, who, along with Chilean and Greek jurists, was largely responsible for drafting the genocide convention as part of the Ad Hoc Committee on Genocide created by ECOSOC. Some countries believed that such a convention was worthless because it could never be enforced. In 1948, however, the General Assembly unanimously adopted the Convention on the Prevention and Punishment of Genocide. The treaty defines the crime of genocide and lists acts that are prohibited. It calls for persons committing genocide to be punished, for states to enact legislation, and for persons charged to be tried either in the state where the crimes were committed or by an international tribunal. (See Box 6.1 for key provisions.)

The Genocide Convention was rapidly signed and ratified and widely recognized as a major advance in international human rights law. Yet it contained ambiguities that can create problems with interpretation and enforcement. For example, it does not specify how many people have to be killed for the incident to be considered genocide, but only addresses the intention on the part of the perpetrators to destroy a group of people "in whole or in part." In contrast to later human rights treaties, the convention created no permanent body to monitor situations or provide early warnings of impending or actual genocide. And for many years, it seemed to have little effect. In Cambodia, Sudan, China, and the former East Pakistan (now Bangladesh), millions of people were killed or forced to flee their homelands as a result of war or deliberate government actions in the 1960s and 1970s. The international community paid little attention. Still, the norm had been established.

Along with the legal prohibition against genocide came the codification of other **crimes against humanity** and crimes committed during warfare, albeit outside the UN system. These norms are contained in four 1949 Geneva Conventions, two additional protocols concluded in 1977, and related treaties dealing with use of specific weapons. They are designed to protect civilians, prisoners of war, and wounded soldiers, as well as to ban particular methods of war (e.g., bombing hospitals) and certain weapons that cause unnecessary suffering (e.g., poisonous gases). Together these form the foundations of **international humanitarian law** and establish the legal basis for **war crimes**. International human rights law—including the Universal Declaration of Human Rights, the Covenant on Political and Civil Rights, and the conventions on torture, genocide, refugees, and children—and the fundamental principle of nondiscrimination between peoples enshrined in Article 1 of the UN Charter establish the basis for crimes against humanity. These are all now incorporated in Article 8 of the International Criminal Court Statute (see Box 6.2).

BOX 6.1. The Genocide Convention

Article I . . . genocide, whether committed in time of peace or in time of war, is a crime under international law which they undertake to prevent and punish.

Article II . . . genocide means any of the following acts committed with intent to destroy, in whole or in part, a national, ethnical, racial or religious group, as such:

    (a) Killing members of the group;
    (b) Causing serious bodily or mental harm to members of the group;
    (c) Deliberately inflicting on the group conditions of life calculated to bring about its physical destruction in whole or in part;
    (d) Imposing measures intended to prevent births within the group;
    (e) Forcibly transferring children of the group to another group.

Article III . . . The following acts shall be punishable:

    (a) Genocide;
    (b) Conspiracy to commit genocide;
    (c) Direct and public incitement to commit genocide;
    (d) Attempt to commit genocide;
    (e) Complicity in genocide.

Article IV . . . Persons committing genocide or any of the other acts enumerated in article III shall be punished, whether they are constitutionally responsible rulers, public officials or private individuals.

Article V . . . The Contracting Parties undertake to enact . . . the necessary legislation to give effect to the provisions of the present Convention and to provide effective penalties for persons guilty of genocide or any of the other acts enumerated in article III.

The enforcement of these norms against genocide, crimes against humanity, and war crimes has, however, proven problematic. Only in the 1990s, with the humanitarian crises in the former Yugoslavia, Rwanda, and Sierra Leone, did the international community begin to pay attention to evidence of ethnic cleansing, genocide, and other crimes and demand action, although too late to prevent atrocities. Only then were mechanisms created for prosecuting those accused of crimes against humanity and of war crimes, initially on an ad hoc basis and then through the ICC.

Three post–Cold War cases, Bosnia, Rwanda, and Darfur, illustrate the dilemmas associated with application of the conventions against genocide, crimes

---

BOX 6.2. Crimes Against Humanity

- Attack against or any effort to exterminate a civilian population
- Enslavement
- Deportation or forcible transfer of population
- Imprisonment or other severe deprivation of physical liberty
- Torture
- Rape, sexual slavery, forced prostitution, pregnancy, and sterilization
- Persecution of any group or collectivity based upon political, racial, national, ethnic, cultural, religious, or gender grounds
- Enforced disappearance of persons

---

against humanity, and war crimes. Did these cases constitute genocide, with a systematic attempt by one group to exterminate another group or were they just brutal civil wars? If a situation is determined to constitute genocide, the parties to the convention are obligated to respond under Article I of the Genocide Convention, but proving genocide is problematic. Few perpetrators provide conclusive evidence of intent to commit it. In all three of the cases, as discussed in Chapter 4, UN member states failed to act decisively to stop the killing.

During the Yugoslav civil war, the term "ethnic cleansing" was coined to refer to systematic efforts by Croatia, Serbia (the rump of the former Yugoslavia), and Bosnian Serbs to remove peoples of another group from their territory, but not necessarily to wipe out the entire group, or part of it, as specified in the Genocide Convention. In Bosnia, Bosnian Muslims were forced by Bosnian Serb troops to flee ethnically mixed towns for Muslim areas within Bosnia or for neighboring countries. Some were deported to neighboring Macedonia; others were placed in concentration camps. An estimated sixty thousand Bosnian women were raped by Serb forces. Croatia expelled Serbs from its territory, and Serbia expelled Albanian Kosovars from Kosovo.

Investigators from the UN Commission on Human Rights, beginning in 1992, reported "massive and grave violations of human rights." Several months later, another report concluded that Bosnian Muslims were the principal victims and were being threatened with extermination. In 1992, the General Assembly condemned Serbia's ethnic cleansing of Bosnia's Muslims as a form of genocide and condemned its actions. In 1993, the ICJ issued a unanimous order to Serbia to follow the Genocide Convention, and, prompted by the World Conference on Human Rights in Vienna, the Security Council created a Commission of Experts to conduct further investigations. The latter heard hundreds of hours of taped testimony and sifted through intelligence information, concluding that although all sides were committing war crimes, only the Serbs were conducting a systematic campaign of genocide. Even before its report was issued and well before the notorious Srebrenica massacre in 1995, the council created the International Criminal Tribunal for the Former Yugoslavia, imposed an arms embargo on all parties, and imposed trade sanctions on Serbia, condemning it for human rights violations. By the time the Dayton Peace Accords were signed in 1995, the war had resulted in 200,000 deaths and millions of homeless, missing, or internally displaced persons.

Was ethnic cleansing in Bosnia equivalent to genocide? The UN Commission of Experts and the Commission on Human Rights both said that Serbia had a policy of systematic genocide. Some states and NGOs, such as Doctors Without Borders, disagreed. Still others maintained that all sides were guilty. Only in 2007, after procedural delays, did the ICJ rule on the merits, concluding that although Serbia failed to prevent the 1995 Srebrenica genocide, the state did not commit genocide, did not conspire to commit genocide, and was not complicit in the act of genocide. The judges pointed to insufficient proof of intentionality to destroy the Bosnian Muslims as a whole or in part.[49] In 1999, however, Croatia filed a second suit against Serbia over the genocide claims, and Serbia filed a countersuit in 2010. The decision in 2015 was that neither Croatia nor Serbia had committed genocide against each other's populations during the wars that followed Yugoslavia's disintegration in the early 1990s. Crimes were committed by both countries, but the intent to commit genocide had not been proven against either, the court concluded.[50] As for those individuals prosecuted for war crimes and crimes against humanity, the record of the ICTY is discussed below.

The evidence of genocide was much clearer in the case of Rwanda, where more than 800,000 people were killed in a ten-week period in the spring of 1994 out of a total Rwandan population of 7 million. There were radio broadcasts of Hutu extremists' calls to slaughter the minority Tutsis. Even before the April 1994 plane crash that killed the Rwandan and Burundian presidents, reports from NGOs and UN peacekeepers warned that there were plans to target the Tutsi population. General Roméo Dallaire warned of an impending genocide in a communication to UN headquarters in New York. Samantha Power has documented the evidence of US officials' failure to heed the evidence of something more than "random tribal slaughter" in Rwanda and avoidance of using the term "genocide," knowing full well that if it was invoked, they would be forced by the terms of the Genocide Convention to take action.[51] Other scholars place blame on the UN Secretariat, and some have suggested that because the genocide occurred so fast and began in outlying areas, the world could not have reliably known enough or had the time to prevent it. Still, as evidence mounted of the systematic slaughtering of the minority Tutsis by Hutu extremists, both the P-5 and the UN Secretariat ignored the evidence and never used the word

CARTOON 6.1. "Darfur Genocide Charges," by Dave Granlund, January 27, 2009

"genocide."[52] As in the case of the former Yugoslavia, the Security Council created an ad hoc International Criminal Tribunal, which has prosecuted many of those accused of war crimes and crimes against humanity, as discussed below.

More recently, despite affirmations of "never again," the response was too little and too late for victims of violence in the western region of Darfur, Sudan, between 2003 and 2008, as discussed in Chapter 4. UN and other responses have never been sufficient to stop the violence and killing. In this instance, however, the UN Security Council took the unprecedented action of calling on the International Criminal Court to indict Sudan's president, Omar al-Bashir. The ICC's efforts to deal with the Darfur-related cases and to get UN member states who are parties to the Rome Statute to arrest President Bashir are discussed below.

The three cases of Bosnia, Rwanda, and Darfur demonstrate the UN's failure to enforce the norm prohibiting genocide, but they also demonstrate the practical limitations to taking action against massive human rights violations that may amount to genocide. Timing (close to the Somalia debacle) and flawed bureaucratic handling of information proved critical in the Rwanda case; remoteness was a factor in the Darfur case, as it has been in the cases of interethnic and sectarian violence bordering on genocide in the newly independent South

Sudan and the Central African Republic in 2014 and 2015. In all three cases, the UN Security Council's P-5 had competing priorities and therefore lacked the political will to act in a timely fashion. In the Bosnian and Rwandan cases, UN investigations and apologies by former Secretary-General Kofi Annan led to efforts at reform. In 2004, the UN Office of the Special Adviser on the Prevention of Genocide was established to provide early warning by collecting information on potential future genocides and making recommendations to the Security Council on actions to prevent or halt genocide.

There are many other cases involving alleged war crimes and crimes against humanity associated with conflicts in different parts of the world. One in particular illustrates the political sensitivity of such investigations, namely, the report on human rights violations during the Gaza war of 2008–2009. In this conflict between Israel and Hamas, more than 1,400 Gazans and 13 Israelis were killed in a three-week period, and both sides were accused of deliberately targeting civilians. The fact-finding mission appointed by the Human Rights Council found evidence of potential war crimes and crimes against humanity by both Hamas and Israel, calling for both to investigate their own actions. The mission was chaired by Judge Richard Goldstone, a South African jurist who was well known for judgments in South Africa that helped to undermine apartheid and for his involvement in the international tribunals for both the former Yugoslavia and Rwanda. Israel refused to cooperate with the mission, but later launched its own investigation and found no evidence of deliberate targeting of civilians. As a result, although the Goldstone Report was initially hailed as evidence of Israel's violations and the HRC's own neutrality, Goldstone later wrote, "If I had known then what I know now, the Goldstone Report would have been a different document." He added that the report marked the first time that illegal acts of terrorism were investigated and condemned by the UN, giving him some hope that the mission would begin "a new era of evenhandedness at the U.N. Human Rights Council, whose history of bias against Israel cannot be doubted." Goldstone went on to note that the Palestinian Authority had initiated an independent inquiry into the mission's allegations concerning abuses by Fatah in the West Bank against members of Hamas, but there had been no such effort by Hamas.[53] Other members of the commission stood by their findings, setting off a storm of controversy, indicative of states' sensitivity to charges of genocide and war crimes.

Although UN members have failed to completely stop, let alone prevent, genocide, ethnic cleansing, and crimes against humanity or war crimes, the idea of individual responsibility for such crimes has now been firmly established by the work of ad hoc and hybrid international tribunals as well as that of the ICC. And, as discussed in Chapter 4, while international efforts through the UN to do more to protect civilians during conflicts and to respond to potential genocides have been inconsistent, the steps that have been taken, although small, do represent forward movement.

Ad Hoc International War Crimes Tribunals. To bring those responsible for crimes during interstate or civil wars to justice, the UN Security Council used its Chapter VII authority to establish the International Criminal Tribunal for the Former Yugoslavia in 1993, followed in 1994 by the International Criminal Tribunal for Rwanda. Initially, these ad hoc, temporary courts lacked established structures and procedures, as well as actual criminals in custody. Yet they recruited prosecutors, investigators, administrators, and judges; devised rules of procedure and evidence; and worked to gain the cooperation of states to carry out their tasks. Deciding whom to indict, arresting those individuals, and trying them in a timely fashion have been ongoing challenges.

Employing sixteen judges and three separate proceedings, as well as more than 1,200 staff members from around the world, the ICTY developed answers to questions of authority, jurisdiction, evidence, sentencing, and imprisonment that have aided other tribunals. By the end of 2015, 161 individuals had been indicted. Of those cases, 80 resulted in sentencing, 13 were transferred to local courts, 36 were terminated for different reasons (the most well-known defendant, former Serbian president Slobodan Milošević, died in custody in 2006 before the conclusion of his trial), and 18 resulted in acquittal. In March 2016, Radovan Karadžić, the wartime leader of the Bosnian Serbs, was convicted of genocide in the area of Srebrenica, as well as of crimes against humanity and war crimes, and sentenced to forty years in prison. Twelve trials continue, the most famous being that of General Ratko Mladić, who was also indicted for genocide in the killing of almost 8,000 Bosnian Muslim men and boys in Srebrenica in 1995. Altogether, the ICTY by the end of 2015 had heard more than 4,650 witnesses, had 10,800 trial days, and produced 2.5 million pages of transcripts. Its work is not expected to be completed until at least 2017, due in part to health problems among some indictees.

One scholar wrote, "The real success of the ICTY lies in the fact that . . . it is a functioning international criminal court that is providing a forum for victims to accuse those who violated civilized norms of behavior . . . stigmatizing persons . . . and forcing them to relinquish any official power . . . and generating a body of jurisprudence that will undoubtedly continue to build over time."[54] The ICTY's judgments have elaborated on the Geneva Conventions, for example, by defining sexual violence including rape as a war crime; the elements of crimes of genocide and torture; and the application of international humanitarian law to internal armed conflicts. The court has considered fairness and impartiality of paramount importance, so while the largest number of cases dealt with Serbs and Bosnian Serbs, the court has also convicted Croats, Bosnian Muslims, and Albanian Kosovars for crimes against Serbs and others.

The Rwandan tribunal has had significant problems securing cooperation in arresting suspects and was also slow in processing cases. It concluded its work at the end of 2015, having issued 93 indictments, 61 sentences, and 14 acquittals, but seven fugitives remain at large (an eighth was captured in the DRC in December 2015). Its last action upheld the guilty verdicts on six individuals, including the sole woman to be tried—Pauline Nyiramasuhuko, Rwanda's minister for family and women's development at the time of the genocide. The ICTR's most important contributions to international criminal law are the convictions of Jean Kambanda, the former prime minister of Rwanda, for the crime of genocide— the first such conviction of a head of government—and of four former military officers for conspiracy to commit genocide. As of late 2015, there were still more than 400 outstanding indictments issued by the Rwandan government for individuals accused of involvement in the genocide. Residual functions of the ICTR are being assumed by the Mechanism for International Criminal Tribunals, which will take on the same functions for the ICTY once its work is completed.

In addition to these two ad hoc tribunals, two courts employing national and international law, procedures, and jurists were established by agreements between the UN and the governments of Sierra Leone and Cambodia in 2002 and 2008 to judge individual criminal responsibility for crimes against humanity and war crimes in those two countries. Of these so-called hybrid courts, the Special Court for Sierra Leone tried ten individuals, the most well-known of whom was former Liberian president Charles Taylor. He was convicted in 2012 of terrorism, participation in a joint criminal enterprise, planning attacks on three cities, war crimes, and crimes against humanity. He was the first former head of state to be found guilty by an international criminal tribunal. His trial was held in The Hague, and he is serving his sentence in a UK prison. The tribunal concluded its work at the end of 2013. The Khmer Rouge Tribunal (Extraordinary Chambers in the Courts of Cambodia) has faced significant difficulties in carrying out its work because of the length of time that has passed since the crimes were committed between 1975 and 1979. The Cambodian government has also tried to obstruct the court proceedings. There are a number of other hybrid, mixed, or internationalized courts now that vary in makeup and procedures as well as in how they link national and international law. These include programs in Kosovo, Lebanon, and Timor-Leste.

The International Criminal Court. In 1998, in light of the ad hoc nature of the Yugoslav and Rwandan tribunals, and in response to a long-standing movement to create a permanent international criminal court, UN members concluded the Rome Statute for the International Criminal Court, which sets out the legal status and rules of procedure for the court as well as the crimes within its jurisdiction. The statute had been drafted by the International Law Commission over several years at the request of the General Assembly. The Coalition for the ICC (a group of more than 1,000 NGOs) played an important role in mobilizing international support for the ICC and continues to promote ratification and implementation. The ICC is officially independent of the UN system, but reports its activities to the UN; it has observer status in the General Assembly and access to UN conference and other services. Under Article 13 of the Rome Statute, the Security Council may refer situations to the ICC, as it has done with two as of 2015—those of Darfur/Sudan and Libya—even though neither Sudan nor Libya is a party to the statute.

In contrast to the ICJ, the ICC has not only compulsory jurisdiction but also jurisdiction over individuals. Called "the most ambitious initiative in the history of modern international law," the court has jurisdiction over only "serious" war crimes that represent a "policy or plan" rather than just random acts in wartime.[55] They must also have been "systematic or widespread," not single abuses. Four types of crimes are covered: genocide, crimes against humanity, war crimes, and crimes of aggression. The last of these were left undefined in the Rome Statute, but at the 2010 Review Conference, a major step was taken toward adopting a definition that would preserve the Security Council's primacy in determining when aggression has taken place. No individuals (save those younger than eighteen) are immune from ICC jurisdiction, including heads of state and military leaders. The ICC functions as a court of last resort and hears cases only when national courts are unwilling or unable to deal with grave atrocities. Prosecution is forbidden for crimes committed before July 1, 2002, when the court came into being, and defendants must be present during trial. Furthermore, the ICC may act only in cases where the state on whose territory the crime was committed, or whose nationals are accused, has ratified the Rome Statute. Anyone—an individual, a government, a group, or the UN Security Council—can bring a case before the ICC. The court became operational in 2003. By the end of 2015, 139 states had signed the Rome Statute, and 124 states had ratified it. Among those who had not signed were the United States, China, and India, while Russia had signed but not ratified.

Although the United States has historically supported international accountability for war crimes, there has been strong opposition within the United States to the ICC, with President George W. Bush taking the unprecedented action of unsigning the Rome Statute in 2001, three years after the United States had signed under the administration of his predecessor, President Bill Clinton. One major concern is the possibility that the ICC might prosecute US military personnel or even the president without American approval. More generally, the United States has asserted that the ICC infringes on its sovereignty and that, as a world power, it has a unique role to play in international relations. For this reason, the United States would have preferred an international court whose powers depended upon approval by the UN Security Council and are thus subject to veto.

To protect itself, the United States negotiated bilateral immunity agreements with more than 100 states that promised not to turn over indicted US nationals, as permitted under Article 98 of the ICC statute. US economic aid to countries not signing such agreements can be suspended. The 2003 American Service-Members Protection Act offers another measure of protection, prohibiting the United States from assisting the ICC in any way and prohibiting military aid to countries who are ICC members but have not signed Article 98 waivers, with some key exceptions.

In reality, the United States has ended up taking a more pragmatic approach to the ICC. In 2005, it abstained on the Security Council resolution referring Darfur/Sudan to the court, and in 2011, it voted in favor of referring Libya. It has sent US troops to help capture indicted Ugandan rebel leader Joseph Kony, who has been hiding in remote areas of the DRC and CAR. The United States and France also pushed a Security Council draft resolution to refer the situation in Syria to the court in 2014, knowing Russia would veto it.

It is significant, however, that the ICC came into being in spite of American objections. Its establishment moved international adjudication and international law far more in the direction of accepting individuals and nonstate entities such as terrorist and criminal groups as subjects of international law, where only states historically have enjoyed such status.

The ICC initiated its first trials in 2009 after almost seven years of preparatory work ranging from selection of initial judges and appointment of the chief prosecutor to developing the processes for investigations and selecting cases, establishing court regulations, and evaluating issues of jurisdiction and admissibility. For the two ad hoc tribunals with much clearer missions, these processes had taken about two years. At the end of 2015, the ICC had twenty-three cases on its docket in nine situations in eight different countries, with nine preliminary examinations under way. It had issued three verdicts, two of which convicted Congolese warlords charged with war crimes, crimes against humanity, and recruiting child soldiers. The court had indicted thirty-nine other individuals, including Joseph Kony, Sudanese president Omar al-Bashir, Kenyan president Uhuru Kenyatta as well as his deputy prime minister, and former Ivorian president Laurent Gbagbo. The case against Kenyatta, initiated by the Kenyan government following interethnic violence during the 2007 elections, was dropped in late 2014 for lack of evidence and cooperation. In March 2016, the ICC convicted Congolese politician and militia leader Jean-Pierre Bemba Gombo of war crimes and crimes against humanity, including a campaign of rape, murder, and torture by his militia in the Central African Republic in 2002 and 2003. This was the ICC's first conviction for rape as a war crime and a crime against humanity; it was also the first conviction based on the principle of command or superior responsibility, as Bemba was found guilty of having "failed to prevent" crimes committed by his subordinates.

The Darfur situation was the first to be referred by the Security Council to the ICC, an important precedent. Six individuals have been indicted, including President al-Bashir, who is accused of genocide, war crimes, and crimes against humanity for what the court calls his "essential role" in the murder, rape, torture, and pillage of civilians. He has openly defied the court with the support of the Arab League and African Union. The court suspended investigations in late 2014 because no arrests had been made in a decade, and it called for the Security Council to take steps to enforce compliance. The unwillingness of other states, especially African states party to the Rome Statute, to arrest him when he traveled outside Sudan demonstrated a significant weakness of the ICC. As one commentator noted, the ICC "was set up in such a way that the world's most powerful countries were able to keep themselves—and often their allies—out of its reach. That . . . has allowed African leaders to assert that they have been unfairly and disproportionately targeted by the court."[56]

In addition to these indictments and referrals, the ICC has received almost 9,000 communications from more than 140 countries, the majority from individuals in the United States, Great Britain, Germany, Russia, and France. These referrals and communications are reviewed to see if they meet the statutory threshold; the vast majority are declared outside of the court's jurisdiction.

The prevalence of African cases at the ICC and the high-profile cases of Presidents al-Bashir and Kenyatta have sparked a strong backlash against the court in Africa. The AU, OIC, and Arab League have all accused the court of racism and neocolonialism, and some African leaders have mounted a campaign to get African states to withdraw from the ICC. A countermovement has also been launched by an international advocacy group, Avaaz, calling on African leaders to stay in the ICC.

Even Western advocates for the ICC, however, are increasingly disillusioned by the high costs the ICC has incurred. Is $1 billion for just two convictions worth the price? Is the annual budget of $166 million justified? Others note that the nature of international criminal proceedings, especially in multiple countries where conflicts and violence may still be present, is inherently time-consuming and expensive if justice is to be served. There is also the tension between peace and justice. The jurisdiction of the ICC involves crimes committed during times of war and violence. Yet seeking to hold key individuals responsible for those crimes may jeopardize the possibility of securing long-term peace. The indictment of President al-Bashir and his defiance of the ICC have contributed to the failure of efforts to secure peaceful resolution of the Darfur conflict, and thousands of civilians in the region have suffered still more as the government expelled humanitarian aid agencies in 2009 and 2010 in retaliation for the arrest warrant. Is it more critical to try individuals for wrongdoing or to ensure a peace?

In sum, the UN has been central to efforts to codify standards relating to genocide, crimes against humanity, and war crimes. It has also been instrumental in more recent efforts to apply those standards in preventing these egregious crimes and to establishing judicial bodies to try those accused of committing them. Much as there are questions about the work of the ICC, so too are there different points of view on what the UN has and has not accomplished with regard to achieving greater respect for human rights norms.

EVALUATING THE UN'S HUMAN RIGHTS RECORD

The four case studies above illustrate the variations in the UN's role with respect to human rights issues. They also show the complex processes by which human rights norms have gained acceptance as well as the challenges of promoting their application and enforcement. The UN's inability to prevent the well-publicized human rights tragedies in Bosnia, Rwanda, and Sudan in the 1990s and 2000s called into question the organization's human rights record, just as did its earlier inability to put a prompt end to apartheid in South Africa. Unquestionably, the UN has failed to address many egregious human rights violations. When it has cataloged abuses, its follow-up activities have too often been weak and ineffectual. The monitoring mechanisms may be too diverse and state-dominated to be effective. The funds allocated for these activities are limited. But this harsh indictment does not tell the whole story.

The UN has played a central role in institutionalizing human rights norms in world politics. In 1948, only slavery, genocide, and abuses against aliens were legally proscribed. By 2015, that list had expanded to include extensive protection for individuals as well as women, children, minorities, indigenous peoples, the disappeared, migrant workers, and persons with disabilities. The expansion of these protections is an ongoing process; for example, the General Assembly in 2008 broke the taboo on the subject of homosexual rights in major UN bodies by approving a declaration seeking to decriminalize homosexuality. In 2010, Secretary-General Ban Ki-moon began to speak out publicly, affirming, "Where there is a tension between cultural attitudes and universal human rights, universal rights must carry the day."[57] In 2011, the Human Rights Council adopted the first UN resolution (Resolution 17/19) on sexual orientation and in 2012 became the first UN body to hold a formal debate on the subject of LGBT rights. The vast majority of states have ratified not only the two international covenants but also many of the other human rights conventions, as Table 6.1 demonstrates. It is broadly recognized that human rights are internationally protected and universally applicable, even if enforcement still lags.

The UN itself has moved a long way from the time when mere reporting by states themselves was the only mechanism of monitoring and enforcement. NGOs have played a key role in this process, providing independent monitoring of human rights activities, filing petitions on behalf of victims, publicizing gross violations in a way that the UN cannot, promoting ratification of human rights treaties, and mounting international campaigns against gross violators, including boycotts and sanctions. Moreover, human rights NGOs have been increasingly integrated into the work of the various UN bodies. In this respect, there is a partnership between the first and second UNs and the third UN.

In late 2013, Secretary-General Ban Ki-moon launched the Human Rights Up Front initiative—a major effort to foster a more activist organizational culture within the UN itself and ensure that the UN takes early, effective action to prevent or respond to large-scale violations of human rights or international humanitarian law. The initiative seeks to galvanize the second UN to take an activist, principled stand and to see protection of civilians and human rights as a systemwide responsibility. The initiative was prompted by an independent UN Internal Review Panel's 2012 report that described a "systemic failure" of the UN during the last stages of the conflict in Sri Lanka in 2009.[58] A 2015 examination of the initiative's results describes the "greater vigor" of UN officials engaging with governments on crises such as that in South Sudan and broaching situations of concern in Security Council briefings. Still, the author noted, "it will take effort beyond the term of the current UN leadership in order for a new organizational culture to take root."[59]

The UN's activities on human rights have been complemented by the even more extensive development of human rights norms and institutions at the regional level. By far the most developed is the human rights regime in Europe, where governments are held accountable for actions against their citizens through the European Court of Human Rights. The inter-American human rights regime, including the Inter-American Court of Human Rights, is also well developed, but human rights regimes are weak in Africa and Southeast Asia and nonexistent in the Middle East.

UN and other international efforts to address human rights issues confront challenges relating to our four dilemmas because states traditionally were free to treat their own citizens however they chose. And although liberalism provides a basis for explaining the UN's role and the expansion of international human rights law, it is constructivism that provides the framework for understanding how new norms emerge and become widely accepted.

Dilemma 1: Expanding Needs for Governance Versus the UN's Limited Capacity

With the expansion of democracy and the communication revolution, there is much greater knowledge about violations of human rights in different areas of the world and demands for international action by victims and human rights advocates. Those demands for action, however, face the reality that the UN's monitoring and enforcement mechanisms are weak instruments. The UN has been even less successful in enforcement, precisely because enforcement offends the states that are its constituents. Thus, the UN has been slow to use the "naming and shaming" approach that human rights NGOs frequently employ. The 1990s marked a major shift in this regard, but it is still a relatively small number of violators that get singled out for action, especially by the Security Council. The increasing visibility of the high commissioner, pressures from NGOs and human rights advocates, the expansion of Special Procedures, Secretary-General Ban Ki-moon's Human Rights Up Front initiative, and even the still politicized Human Rights Council will bring shame on errant states and continue the work of advancing respect for human rights.

Dilemma 2: Human Rights at the Nexus of State Sovereignty

Attempts to protect individuals and groups from human rights abuses occurring within the borders of states directly challenge traditional interpretations of state sovereignty and Article 2(7) of the UN Charter, which proscribes intervention in matters within the domestic jurisdiction of states. Thus, key to the increased UN attention to human rights has been a shift in the understanding of what states are free to do and an evolving interpretation of what the international community through the UN can and ought to do. Through its role as a forum for bringing human rights into the center of world affairs, the UN has sharpened the sovereignty dilemma.

States still assert the principle of noninterference in internal affairs, especially on human rights issues. China, a strong proponent of the sovereignty argument, for example, expends enormous amounts of diplomatic capital to defend itself and to avert public criticism. Rwanda's attempt to keep reports of its atrocities in the DRC quiet and Israel's vehement defense of its record in light of the Goldstone Report confirm that state sovereignty is not a dead issue. Likewise, Sudanese president Omar al-Bashir's defiance of the ICC arrest warrant, along with the support of other states for that defiance and Kenya's request to withdraw the case against Kenyatta once he became president, further demonstrate the tension between sovereignty and the expansion of international criminal justice.

Dilemma 3: The Need for Leadership
Versus the Dominance of a Sole Superpower

The establishment of the ICC over the active objections of the United States clearly demonstrated the unwillingness of many states to allow the world's sole superpower to prevent the advance of international criminal law. In fact, historically, no major power has played a leading role in promoting human rights through the UN. The United States has a poor record of signing but not ratifying human rights conventions despite its rhetorical support for democracy and human rights. So, too, do China and Russia. Instead, leadership has come from the Netherlands, Norway, India, Canada, Costa Rica, and a handful of other states. NGOs such as Amnesty International, Human Rights Watch, and Anti-Slavery International have been prime movers, and grassroots groups of all stripes are important sources of information and advocacy. Thus, human rights is an area where leadership has not depended on traditional sources of power and where the powerless have made a difference.

Dilemma 4: The Need for Inclusiveness Versus
Deep-seated Prejudices, Cultural Habits, and Inequalities

The expansion of international human rights norms through the UN has been closely tied to the push for inclusiveness—inclusion of women, of disabled persons, of indigenous persons, of LGBT persons. That inclusiveness extends to access for NGOs and civil society groups to the various parts of the UN system— access that has been central to their roles in setting standards and promoting, monitoring, and pushing for enforcement of human rights. The dilemma between the need for inclusiveness and the persistence of traditional religious and social structures is particularly well illustrated with respect to the issue of LGBT rights. Although LGBT groups have had successes in Europe, some South American countries, Canada, the United States, India, and South Africa, advocates face much greater challenges in developing countries and especially in the Islamic world and Africa, where laws criminalizing homosexuality are still common and harassment, assault, and murder of gays and lesbians continue to be widespread. In 2014, ten countries made homosexuality punishable by death or life imprisonment. Change will come only slowly, if at all, in many parts of the world.

It is also because of the evolution of international human rights and humanitarian norms that new conceptions of security have emerged. These conceptions reject the idea that security applies only to states and embrace the notion that poverty, disease, gross violations of human rights, and environmental degradation threaten the security and well-being of human beings.

NOTES

1. Zbigniew Brzezinski, *The Grand Failure: The Birth and Death of Communism in the Twentieth Century* (New York: Charles Scribner's Sons, 1989), 256.

2. Kathryn Sikkink, "Transnational Politics, International Relations Theory, and Human Rights," *PS: Political Science and Politics* 31, no. 3 (1998): 517–521.

3. Franklin D. Roosevelt, Annual Message to Congress, January 6, 1941, *Congressional Record* 44 (1941): 46–47.

4. See Samuel Moyn, *The Last Utopia: Human Rights in History* (Cambridge, MA: Belknap Press, 2010).

5. The seven references appear in Articles 1, 13 (section 1), 55, 56, 62, 68, and 76.

6. See Sarah Zaidi and Roger Normand, *The UN and Human Rights Ideas: The Unfinished Revolution* (Bloomington: Indiana University Press, 2006).

7. Mrs. Franklin D. Roosevelt, "General Assembly Adopts Declaration of Human Rights," statement before the General Assembly, December 9, 1948, *Department of State Bulletin*, December 19, 1948, 751.

8. On the UN and colonialism, see Rupert Emerson, *From Empire to Nation: The Rise to Self-Assertion of Asian and African People* (Cambridge, MA: Harvard University Press, 1960); and Harold K. Jacobson, "The United Nations and Colonialism: A Tentative Appraisal," *International Organization* 16 (Winter 1962): 27–56.

9. James H. Lebovic and Eric Voeten, "The Politics of Shame: The Condemnation of Country Human Rights Practices in the UNHCHR," *International Studies Quarterly* 50, no. 4 (2006): 863.

10. Rosa Freedman, *The United Nations Human Rights Council: A Critique and Early Assessment* (New York: Routledge, 2013), 67–69.

11. Simon Hug and Richard Lukacs, "Preferences or Blocs? Voting in the United Nations Human Rights Council," *Review of International Organizations* 9, no. 1 (2014): 83–106.

12. John Gerard Ruggie, *Just Business: Multinational Corporations and Human Rights* (New York: Norton, 2013).

13. Julie Mertus, *The United Nations and Human Rights: A Guide for a New Era*, 2nd ed. (New York: Routledge, 2009), chap. 2.

14. For details, see the International Court of Justice, Advisory Opinions on Western Sahara (*Spain v. Morocco*) (1975) and Legal Consequences for States of the Continued Presence of South Africa in Namibia (1971); and the contentious cases *Bosnia and Herzegovina v. Yugoslavia* [Serbia and Montenegro] (2007) and *Croatia v. Serbia* (2015).

15. Louis Henkin, "The Universal Declaration and the U.S. Constitution," *PS: Political Science and Politics* 31, no. 3 (1998): 512.

16. Abdullahi A. An-Na'im, "The Cultural Mediation of Human Rights: The Al-Arqum Case in Malaysia," in *The East Asian Challenge for Human Rights*, ed. Joanne R. Bauer and Daniel A. Bell (Cambridge: Cambridge University Press, 1999), 147. This volume is an excellent set of critical essays on the Asian-values debate.

17. Quoted on the Web site for the UN High Commissioner for Human Rights, www .unhchr.ch.

18. David Weissbrodt, "Do Human Rights Treaties Make Things Worse?" *Foreign Policy* 134 (2003): 89.

19. On this evolution, see Paul Gordon Lauren, *The Evolution of International Human Rights: Visions Seen*, 3rd ed. (Philadelphia: University of Pennsylvania Press, 2011), chaps. 8–9.

20. See Howard Tolley Jr., *The UN Commission on Human Rights* (Boulder, CO: Westview Press, 1987); and Mertus, *The United Nations and Human Rights*, 56–64.

21. Rhona Smith, "'To See Themselves as Others See Them': The Five Permanent Members of the Security Council and the Human Rights Council's Universal Periodic Review," *Human Rights Quarterly* 35, no. 1 (2013): 13–14, 25.

22. For extensive discussion of the treaty bodies, see Mertus, *The United Nations and Human Rights*, chap. 4.

23. Andrew Wolman, "Welcoming a New International Human Rights Actor? The Participation of Subnational Human Rights Institutions at the UN," *Global Governance* 20, no. 3 (2014): 445–446.

24. Emilie Hafner-Burton and Kiyoteru Tsutsui, "Human Rights in a Globalized World: The Paradox of Empty Promises," *American Journal of Sociology* 110, no. 5 (2005): 706.

25. Emilie Hafner-Burton, "Sticks and Stones: Naming and Shaming the Human Rights Enforcement Problem," *International Organization* 62, no. 4 (2008): 706.

26. Ann Kent, "China and the International Human Rights Regime: A Case Study of Multilateral Monitoring, 1989–1994," *Human Rights Quarterly* 17 (1995): 1–47.

27. "UN: China Torture Still Widespread," www.cbsnews.com/stories/2005/12/02/world /main1093457.shtm.

28. Smith, "'To See Themselves as Others See Them,'" 16.

29. Nick Cumming-Bruce, "Chinese Justice System Relies on Torture, U.N. Panel Finds," *New York Times*, December 10, 2015.

30. UN Office of the High Commissioner for Human Rights, *The Democratic Republic of Congo, 1993–2003: Report of the Mapping Exercise*, August 2010, www.ohchr.org/Documents /Countries/ZR/DRC_MAPPING_REPORT_FINAL_EN.pdf. Rwanda's reactions are documented in numerous reports in August and October 2010.

31. See Office of the UN High Commissioner for Human Rights, "'As the Covenants Turn 50, It Is Time to Turn Norms into Action'—UN Experts," news release, December 9, 2015, www.ohchr.org/EN/NewsEvents/Pages/DisplayNews.aspx?NewsID=16861&LangID= E#sthash.MxlFdqEf.dpuf.

32. Joel E. Oestreich, *Power and Principle: Human Rights Programming in International Organizations* (Washington, DC: Georgetown University Press, 2007), 35. This book contains a detailed description of the process.

33. Aryeh Neier, *The International Human Rights Movement: A History* (Princeton: Princeton University Press, 2012), 5.

34. Margaret E. Keck and Kathryn Sikkink, *Activists Beyond Borders: Advocacy Networks in International Politics* (Ithaca, NY: Cornell University Press, 1998), 96.

35. On Amnesty International, see Stephen Hopgood, *Keepers of the Flame: Understanding Amnesty International* (Ithaca, NY: Cornell University Press, 2006); Ann Marie Clark, *Diplomacy of Conscience: Amnesty International and Changing Human Rights Norms* (Princeton: Princeton University Press, 2001); and for Amnesty's own voluminous publications, see www.amnesty.org.

36. James Ron, Howard Ramos, and Kathleen Rodgers, "Transnational Information Politics: NGO Human Rights Reporting, 1986–2000," *International Studies Quarterly* 49, no. 3 (2005): 557–587.

37. David Forsythe, *The Humanitarians: The International Committee of the Red Cross* (Cambridge: Cambridge University Press, 2005).

38. See Audie Klotz, *Norms in International Relations: The Struggle Against Apartheid* (Ithaca, NY: Cornell University Press, 1995).

39. For a comprehensive treatment of the actions of international, national, and local NGOs, see Janice Love, *The U.S. Anti-Apartheid Movement: Local Activism in Global Politics* (New York: Praeger, 1985).

40. Klotz, *Norms in International Relations*, 53.

41. For an analysis of the role sanctions played in the end of apartheid, see ibid., chap. 9.

42. See Charlotte Bunch, "Women's Rights as Human Rights: Toward a Re-Vision of Human Rights," *Human Rights Quarterly* 12, no. 4 (1990): 486–498; and Radhika Coomaraswamy, *Reinventing International Law: Women's Rights as Human Rights in the International Community* (Cambridge, MA: Harvard Law School Human Rights Program, 1997).

43. Donna J. Sullivan, "Women's Human Rights and the 1993 World Conference on Human Rights," *American Journal of International Law* 88 (1994): 152.

44. See Jutta Joachim, *Agenda Setting, the UN, and NGOs: Gender Violence and Reproductive Rights* (Washington, DC: Georgetown University Press, 2007).

45. ILO, "Statistics and Indicators on Forced Labour and Trafficking," www.ilo.org/global/topics/forced-labour/policy-areas/statistics/lang--en/index.htm.

46. Philip Shenon, "Feminist Coalition Protests U.S. Stance on Sex Trafficking Treaty," *New York Times*, January 13, 2000.

47. Protocol to Prevent, Suppress, and Punish Trafficking in Persons, Especially Women and Children, to the Convention on Transnational Organized Crime,.

48. International Labour Organization, *A Global Alliance Against Forced Labour: Report of the Director-General* (Geneva: International Labour Office, 2005), www.ilo.org/public/english/standards/relm/ilc/ilc93/pdf/rep-i-b.pdf.

49. International Court of Justice, Case Concerning Application of Convention on the Prevention and Punishment of the Crime of Genocide (*Bosnia and Herzegovina v. Serbia and Montenegro*) (2007).

50. International Court of Justice, Application of the Convention on the Prevention and Punishment of the Crime of Genocide (*Croatia v. Serbia*) (2015).

51. Samantha Power, *"A Problem from Hell": America and the Age of Genocide* (New York: Basic Books, 2002).

52. There are many good sources on the failure of international responses to genocide; in addition to Power, "A Problem from Hell," see Michael Barnett, *Eyewitness to a Genocide: The United Nations and Rwanda* (Ithaca, NY: Cornell University Press, 2002); Philip Gourevitch, *We Wish to Inform You That Tomorrow We Will Be Killed with Our Families: Stories from Rwanda* (New York: Farrar, Straus, and Giroux, 1998); and Alan J. Kuperman, *The Limits of Humanitarian Intervention: Genocide in Rwanda* (Washington, DC: Brookings Institution, 2001).

53. Richard Goldstone, "Reconsidering the Goldstone Report on Israel and War Crimes," *Washington Post*, April 1, 2011.

54. Sean D. Murphy, "Progress and Jurisprudence of the International Criminal Tribunal for the Former Yugoslavia," *American Journal of International Law* 93, no. 1 (1999): 96–97.

55. Marlise Simons, "World Court for Crimes of War Opens in The Hague," *New York Times*, March 12, 2003.

56. Somini Sengupta, "Bashir Case Shows Criminal Court's Limits," *New York Times*, June 17, 2015.

57. Ban Ki-moon, "Confront Prejudice, Speak Out Against Violence, Secretary-General Says at Event on Ending Sanctions Based on Sexual Orientation, Gender Identity," UN press release, December 10, 2010, www.un.org/press/en/2010/sgsm13311.doc.htm.

58. Report of the Secretary-General's Internal Review Panel on United Nations Action in Sri Lanka, November 2012, www.un.org/News/dh/infocus/Sri_Lanka/The_Internal_Review _Panel_report_on_Sri_Lanka.pdf.

59. Gerrit Kurtz, "With Courage and Coherence: The Human Rights Up Front Initiative of the United Nations," Global Public Policy Institute Policy Paper, July 2015, www.gppi .net/publications/peace-security/article/with-courage-and-coherence.

7

⟋⟍

Human Security:
The Environment, Health,
and Migration

The concept of security must change—from an exclusive stress on national security to a much greater stress on people's security, from security through armaments to security through human development, from territorial security to food, employment, and environmental security.

—1993 Human Development Report

Traditionally, international peace and security has meant states' security and the defense of states' territorial integrity from external threats or attack. Yet out of the people-oriented concept of sustainable human development, articulated in the early 1990s, and the evolution of international human rights norms has come the broader concept of human security. "Making human beings secure," it is argued, "means more than protecting them from armed violence and alleviating their suffering."[1] This conceptualization has major implications not only for how the UN and its member states think about security but also for how the UN and other multilateral institutions are organized and conduct their work, for a human security–oriented approach cuts across traditional divisions between peace and security issues and economic and social issues. This more inclusive view of human security comes at a time when the security of both people and the planet are increasingly threatened. As evidence of these growing threats, the UN Office for the Coordination of Humanitarian Affairs estimated it would need a record $20 billion in funds (double the amount from five years earlier) to provide emergency humanitarian assistance to more than 87 million people who were likely to be displaced as a result of violence or natural disaster in 2016.[2] In addition to increased funding, there are serious concerns about the UN's capacity to meet the challenges of climate change and human security.

AN EXPANDED VIEW OF SECURITY

Some scholars have argued that the concept of human security lacks precision and is too expansive.[3] Nevertheless, it has been increasingly accepted within the UN system as a useful way to conceptualize a variety of threats that affect states, vulnerable groups such as women and children, and individuals—threats that go beyond physical violence. In 2000, for example, the Millennium Declaration set the goal of attaining "freedom from fear" and "freedom from want" for all people. In 2004, the High-Level Panel on Threats, Challenges, and Change incorporated many ideas relating to human security in its report, including poverty, infectious diseases, environmental degradation, civil war, genocide, terrorism, and transnational organized crime. A decade later, UN deputy secretary-general Jan Eliasson, in discussing the SDGs, noted, "It is clear that the principles enshrined in human security, including the right of people to live in freedom and dignity, can help us in our efforts to achieve peace and security."[4] This evolution in thinking about security "has recognized the security needs of individuals and the responsibilities of states and organizations in attending to those needs."[5] An important part of that evolution involves the roles of nonstate actors—NGOs, civil society, private corporations, scientists, foundations, think tanks, and IGOs—in empowering individuals and communities to act on their own behalf. "Correspondingly," two members of the Commission on Human Security noted, "human security requires strong and stable states."[6]

Viewed in this way, human security has already been addressed in the previous three chapters through the examination of threats to peace and security, including humanitarian crises and the R2P norm, nuclear nonproliferation, terrorism, and the Security Council's initiatives on women in conflict, child soldiers, and civilians at risk; through the UN's efforts to eradicate poverty, reduce economic inequalities, and promote human and sustainable development; and through the UN's role in promoting greater respect for human rights. In this chapter, the focus is on protecting the environment, on human health, and on the growing crisis of forced displacement of people. None of these issues is new on the UN's agenda; indeed, health is one of the oldest areas of functional cooperation. What has changed is recognition that failure to address environmental degradation, major threats to health, or the growing refugee and migration flows has a fundamental impact on human security. As illustrated by the 2015 Syria refugee crisis and the 2014 Ebola outbreak in West Africa, these issues can also have "a direct impact on peace and stability within and between states."[7] In short, issues once perceived as "merely environmental" or "merely social" have far-reaching security implications when people rather than states become the primary concern.

PROTECTION OF THE ENVIRONMENT

The desire to protect the environment dates from the nineteenth century, when neighboring states established commissions to coordinate cross-border environmental issues (such as the United States and Canada on the Great Lakes and interstate river commissions in Europe). NGOs also formed to protect specific species (for example, the Society for the Protection of Birds in 1898) or to promote general environmental awareness (the Sierra Club in 1892). In the twenty-first century, the threat posed by major environmental degradation is much greater. As one scholar noted, "Climate change, land degradation and desertification, the largest wave of species extinctions since the dinosaurs, and multifarious pollutants are real and growing sources of insecurity."[8] Added to these are the rapid increase in the melting of polar ice caps, rising sea levels, the destruction of forests, declining fresh water supplies, and intense storms. International cooperation in pursuit of environmental security has also grown, especially with the proliferation of environmental treaties. At the forefront have been NGOs, industries, scientists, the UN, and other IGOs. Much of this activity has taken place since the early 1970s, with the UN playing a major role in promoting new thinking about the economic, social, and environmental aspects of resource management, the global commons, and the links between environment and development, but the need for global cooperation and management of the environment for the sake of human security has reached a critical point now. Although some states and a few NGOs recognized the need for environmental protection at the time, neither the League of Nations Covenant nor the UN Charter contained specific provisions to that effect. This is not surprising, because environmental issues did not emerge on most states' agendas until the late 1960s. Inspired by works such as Rachel Carson's *Silent Spring* and Garrett Hardin's essay "Tragedy of the Commons," as well as photographs of the earth taken by Apollo 11 astronauts in 1969, an entirely new image of the planet as a single ecosystem began to emerge.[9] Concerns about the consequences of economic growth on the earth's environment and on human health grew. Responding to this growing environmental consciousness, the UN played a key part in the emergence of an international environmental agenda. This included developing a global policymaking framework through UN-sponsored global conferences, the articulation of new norms, and the drafting of environmental conventions. NGOs, industries, and major scientific and professional groups have all had important inputs along with developed and developing states. From the beginning, divisions between developed and developing countries have marked the politics of environmental issues.

In response to scientists' growing concerns about the biosphere, the UN Educational, Scientific, and Cultural Organization sponsored the first international environmental conference in 1968. In that same year, Sweden offered to host a larger UN conference. The 1972 UN Conference on the Human Environment (UNCHE), or Stockholm Conference, was the first UN-sponsored conference on an issue of global concern. At this time, there was little recognition that environmental degradation might become so severe that it would lead to conflict between states and among groups for precious resources, let alone threaten human security and lead to large-scale movement of people.

The Genesis of an Idea: The Stockholm Conference

The Stockholm Conference put environmental issues on the UN and global agendas, as well as on many national governments' agendas, initiating a process that has led to the piecemeal construction of international environmental institutions, expansion of the global environmental agenda, increasing acceptance by states of international environmental standards and monitoring regimes, and extensive involvement of both NGOs and scientific and technical groups in policymaking efforts. Linking environmental issues to development was also an innovation as important as peacekeeping was to the UN's role in maintaining international peace and security.

During the preparatory meetings for the 1972 conference, UNCHE secretary-general Maurice Strong provided leadership for attempts to bridge the divergent interests of North and South. The developed countries saw environmental issues as stemming from the population explosion in the less developed countries, putting greater pressures on natural resource utilization and greater strains on the environment. In contrast, the developing countries blamed environmental problems on the overutilization of natural resources and the pollution caused by the consumption excesses of the developed countries, and they feared that environmental regulation could hamper their economic growth and divert resources from economic development. Many developing countries were reluctant even to attend the Stockholm Conference and had to be persuaded that environmental problems were neither a concern simply of developed, industrialized countries nor a plot to keep developing countries underdeveloped. It was incumbent on Strong and others to forge conceptual links between development and the environment.

The Stockholm Declaration introduced such a conceptual link: the principle that it is states' obligation to protect the environment and their responsibility not to cause damage to the environment of other states or areas beyond their national jurisdiction. Delegates also endorsed the principle that environmental policies should enhance developing countries' development potential and not hamper the attainment of better living conditions for all. Environmental concerns are not to be used to justify discriminatory trade practices or as a way to restrict access to domestic markets. Finally, the conference called for the creation of a new UN body, the UN Environment Programme, to coordinate environmental activities and promote intergovernmental cooperation.

The Stockholm Conference also inaugurated the important practice of holding a parallel forum of NGO representatives, run simultaneously with the official conference. This has proved critical over the years for generating new ideas and involving a key set of actors. The almost two hundred groups that participated in the NGO forum at Stockholm set important precedents for similar forums at various UN-sponsored global conferences.

Solidification of an Idea: Sustainable Development

The ideas generated at Stockholm on integrating the environment and development continued to be challenged over the next two decades. Other UN-sponsored global conferences dealt with specific issues such as food, population, desertification, water, human settlements, and climate (see Box 2.2). The tension between developed and developing countries led the UN General Assembly in 1983 to establish the Brundtland Commission, discussed in Chapter 5, whose report *Our Common Future* introduced the concept of sustainable development by making the link between economic development and the necessity of balancing environmental concerns. It underscored that developing countries could not follow the path of the industrialized countries in exploiting resources in view of the degradation of global life support systems.

The Brundtland Commission's approach was adopted in 1987 by the UN General Assembly, UNEP, and later the World Bank, NGOs, and many national development agencies; it became the rallying cry of the environmental movement, including activists, government officials, and leading scientists. The commission acknowledged that poverty is a critical source of environmental degradation; it called on people to think about links among agriculture, trade, transportation, energy, and the environment; and it drew attention to the long-term view. This growing movement led to the convening of a second global environmental conference twenty years after Stockholm.

The Rio Conference and Sustainability. The 1992 UN Conference on the Environment and Development (UNCED), or Earth Summit, in Rio de Janeiro and its extensive preparatory process were major outgrowths of the debate over the necessity of balancing economic growth with preserving the environment. The Rio Conference and its preparatory process were also influenced, like Stockholm before it, by important scientific findings during the 1980s such as the discovery of the ozone hole over Antarctica; the growing evidence of global warming, or climate change; and the accumulating data on loss of biodiversity and depletion of fisheries. Rio was further influenced by three agreements dealing with ozone depletion: the 1985 Vienna Convention for Protection of the Ozone Layer, the 1987 Montreal Protocol on Substances That Deplete the Ozone Layer, and the 1990 London amended protocol phasing out ozone-depleting chemicals. The largest developing countries, most notably China, India, Brazil, and Indonesia, were successful in bargaining with the industrialized countries for unprecedented guarantees of technology and resource transfers and for additional financing—a major victory for the developing world. This was a crucial step in getting the developed and developing world working together to address environmental issues—specifically ozone depletion—without lessening the shared commitment to promoting economic growth and greater well-being for rich and poor.

The 1992 Rio Earth Summit was the largest of the UN-sponsored global conferences in the number of participants and in the scope of the agenda. As with other conferences, a series of preparatory meetings were used to articulate positions, hammer out basic issues, and negotiate the text for all conference documents. NGOs played significant roles in the preparatory process as well as in the conference. Although the environmental movement continued to be dominated by Northern NGOs, UNCED provided even further impetus for global spread through opportunities for networking among the participating NGOs. The 1,400 accredited environmental organizations included not only traditional, large, well-financed Northern NGOs, such as the World Wide Fund for Nature and the International Union for the Conservation of Nature, but also many new groups pursuing grassroots activities in developing countries; typically these newer groups were poorly financed and had few previous transnational linkages.

The Rio Earth Summit is credited with integrating environmental and development policies worldwide by demonstrating the interconnections between various human activities such as industry, agriculture, and consumption patterns and the environment. Outputs included the Rio Declaration of Twenty-Seven Principles, Agenda 21, the UN Convention on Biological Diversity, and the UN Framework Convention on Climate Change. Broader issues of global economic reform such as debt, structural adjustment, and commodities were incorporated into Agenda 21 (Chapters 2, 3, 4, and 12), with provisions for cost evaluations along with human resource development and capacity-building. While the principle of sovereignty over natural resources was reaffirmed, states also accepted that deforestation, the degradation of water supplies, atmospheric pollution, and desertification were threats to global security and that states were responsible for exercising control over environmentally damaging activities within their boundaries.

Rio also marked acceptance of NGO participation in dealing with environmental issues, as sustainable development depends not only on governments, businesses, and IGOs but also on ordinary people whose interests NGOs often purport to represent. Although the member states excluded NGOs from negotiating the final documents, Section II (Chapter 4) of Agenda 21 recognized the unique capabilities of NGOs and recommended that they participate at all levels, from decisionmaking to implementation. What began as a parallel informal process of participation within the UN system thus evolved into a more formal role—a high point for NGOs and the international environmental movement. For the small grassroots organizations from the developing world, participation in Rio and in the UN system was viewed as a significant breakthrough, making the UN more representative of the "peoples of the world."

Finally, just as Stockholm led to the establishment of UNEP, Rio led to the creation of the Commission on Sustainable Development (CSD) in 1993 as the body to encourage and monitor the implementation of Agenda 21. One observer concluded, "Institutionalization of sustainable Third World development within the UN system may be the most important consequence of Rio for the less industrialized world."[10]

Beyond Rio: The Challenges of Implementing Sustainable Development. Moving from promises and commitments to implementing sustainable development as articulated in the Rio documents has proved difficult. Additional international environmental conventions have been concluded, such as the UN Convention to Combat Desertification and the UN Fish Stocks Agreement. Other UN conferences that followed Rio, including the 1994 International Conference on Population and Development in Cairo, the 1995 Social Summit in Copenhagen, the 1995 Fourth Women's Conference in Beijing, and the 1996 Habitat II Conference in Istanbul, reinforced the discourse of sustainable development. The Millennium Declaration and the Millennium Development Goals represented yet another effort to bring together outcomes from these various conferences and to integrate environmental concerns with other threats to human security (see Box 5.1). In particular, MDG 7 called for ensuring environmental sustainability by integrating principles of sustainable development into country policies and programs.

Rio Plus 10, officially known as the UN World Summit on Sustainable Development, convened in Johannesburg, South Africa, in 2002. Its purpose was to build on the ambitious yet poorly executed agenda of Rio. Participants hoped to stem the rising toll of poverty and curb pollution, and wanted more aid for economic growth. The Europeans wanted targets and timetables, while the

United States thought targets were unnecessary. The divisions were profound and, compared to previous meetings, the outcome was disappointing. Among the regional groups, only the European Union had held adequate preparatory meetings. Although the gathering was large (10,000 delegates and almost 1,000 NGOs), NGOs could not fully participate. The summit's Plan of Implementation included some targets, such as access to clean water and proper sanitation, but on other issues, including restoration of fisheries, reversing biodiversity loss, and more use of renewable energy, no specific targets or plans were set. The goals were to be achieved through partnerships among governments, citizen groups, and business (called action coalitions). One observer wrote, "Partnering is a legitimation strategy for UN agencies to maintain their relevance and mission in an era when multilateralism relies on collaboration between state, market, and civil society actors."[11]

By the time the Johannesburg Summit convened in 2002, there was increasing disillusionment with the notion of sustainable development. The term was perceived as a "buzzword largely devoid of content," and some officials, especially in the developing world, had begun to argue that "sustainable" referred to continuity of economic growth without even acknowledging the term's environmental dimension.[12] Ironically, just as disillusionment set in during the early 2000s, there was growing recognition that environmental degradation can cause conflicts between states. The degradation of water resources was exacerbating conflict between Israel and Jordan and among states around the shrinking Caspian and Aral Seas. A widely read book, *Collapse*, argued that environmental degradation and the ensuing struggle for scarce resources had led not only to the collapse of states and empires in the past but also to state failure in Rwanda and Haiti.[13] And, as the Indian Ocean tsunami (2004), Hurricane Katrina in the United States (2005), and the major earthquakes in Haiti (2010), Chile (2010), and Japan (2011) have shown, humans living in environmentally fragile zones are vulnerable to natural disasters, some of which may be linked to global climate change.

Rio Plus 20 in 2012 hardly yielded more positive results than had Rio Plus 10, at least in part because of the economic downturn caused by the global financial crisis beginning in 2008. The UN Commission on Sustainable Development invited contributions by all the stakeholders and submitted a detailed road map leading to the 2012 meetings. Focusing on two issues—the green economy in the context of sustainable development and poverty eradication, and a reexamination of the institutional framework—the goal was to produce more tangible outcomes at Rio Plus 20. The gathering was dubbed the "mega-summit," with 50,000 participants, 192 member states represented by more than 100 heads of state and government, and many companies including Microsoft and the Italian oil company Eni. This reflected an inclusive approach, as thousands of private sector participants joined the discussions.

The conference focus was twofold. The first priority was building a "green economy" with a goal of sustainable development. The second goal was reducing poverty and advancing social equity. Secretary-General Ban Ki-moon explained, "Rio+20 has given us a solid platform to build on. And it has given us the tools to build with. The work starts now."[14] The Rio Plus 20 outcome document titled "The Future We Want" provided a foundation for the SDGs adopted in 2015 (discussed in Chapter 5), and it combined the goal of reducing poverty with changing patterns of consumption, and the goal of protecting biodiversity with prioritizing food security. Another innovative component was Local Agenda 21, which highlighted connections between the global and the local in fostering sustainable development. Still, as Maria Ivanova describes, the final document "offers no targets, timelines, or specific objectives . . . it does not prioritize any areas or express a particular sense of urgency. Its most important achievement . . . was simply that it did not regress."[15]

Appraisals of Rio Plus 20 vary. Many were critical of both the process and the outcome of the conference. Even with the engagement of the private sector and the NGO community, some found that much of the work was done prior to the conference without the involvement of the NGO community and others. Some were uneasy with the inclusion of private corporations who may be looking to brand themselves as "sustainable" yet continue exploitative and unsustainable practices. Others found the process lacked credibility because member states "conveniently removed any assessment of the (lack of) progress in implementing previous global commitments."[16] One chief executive of a leading NGO proclaimed, "Rio will go down as the hoax summit. They came, they talked, but they failed to act."[17] A less pessimistic view was that while the meeting did not produce the concrete action plan many had hoped for, it continued to move the process forward and was "an extraordinary trade fair of political, social, technological and commercial ideas. . . . A new generation of business and political leaders has started to connect company success with social and environmental issues that were previously the concern only of NGOs."[18] Although questions remain on whether such global conferences are still useful, they are now an ingrained part of the UN's approach to addressing human security issues.

The Institutional Framework for Environmental Protection

The creation of international environmental institutions, including new organizations and a large number of environmental treaties, has been a permanent legacy of UN-sponsored activities since the early 1970s. These have set standards and contributed to the evolution of key ideas. The organizations coordinate initiatives; encourage and support treaty negotiations; monitor state compliance; aid member states, NGOs, and other IGOs in the promotion of environmental standards; and, occasionally, enforce environmental norms. One scholar put it this way: "The clearest evidence for the ecological turn in world politics is the astonishing array of recent treaties on a host of environmental problems, including marine pollution, acid rain, stratospheric ozone depletion, loss of biodiversity, and the export of toxic waste to developing countries."[19] (See Table 7.1.) While some of the conferences discussed above have been more productive than others, they have led not only to new organizations and treaties but also to General Assembly resolutions, intergovernmental negotiating committees, meetings and conferences of treaty parties, and decisionmaking by consensus.

United Nations Environment Programme. The United Nations Environment Programme was the chief product of Stockholm and was established by the General Assembly in 1972. With Maurice Strong as its first executive director, UNEP became the champion of the emerging environmental agenda, and, by establishing its headquarters in Nairobi, Kenya, it became the first UN agency based in a developing country. With a relatively small professional staff and a small budget that relies heavily on states' voluntary contributions, its mandate is to promote international cooperation in the field of the environment, serve as an "early warning system" to alert the international community to environmental dangers, provide guidance for the direction of environmental programs in the UN system, and review implementation of these programs. Its responsibilities are both "normative and catalytic."[20] To strengthen UNEP as an organization, its original Governing Council of fifty-eight members was upgraded to become the United Nations Environment Assembly in 2013. As executive director Achim Steiner commented, "Universal membership establishes a new, fully representative platform to strengthen the environmental dimension of sustainable development, and provides all governments with an equal voice on the decisions and action needed to support the global environment, and ensure a fairer share of the world's resources for all."[21] UNEP's secretariat is organized around its various programs, such as early warning and environmental assessment, environmental policy implementation, and supporting existing environmental conventions. As one scholar notes, "The UNEP secretariat is the hub of global environmental information." Its strongest source of influence is its expertise on the state of the environment and on international environmental law.[22]

UNEP has four major responsibilities.[23] First, it plays a key role in negotiating international environmental agreements and in providing the secretariat and oversight for more than a dozen treaty bodies. In a number of instances, it has been a catalyst for negotiations. For example, in the mid-1980s, UNEP executive director Mustafa Tolba provided leadership for the negotiation of the Montreal

TABLE 7.1. Selected UN Environmental Agreements

Treaty	Year Opened for Ratification	Year Entered into Force	Number of Ratifications, Accessions (2015)
Convention on Wetlands of International Importance Especially as Waterfowl Habitat	1971	1975	169
Convention for the Protection of the World Cultural and Natural Heritage	1972	1975	191
Convention on the Prevention of Marine Pollution by the Dumping of Wastes and Other Matter	1972	1975	87
Convention on the International Trade in Endangered Species of Wild Fauna and Flora (CITES)	1973	1975	181
Convention on Long-Range Transboundary Air Pollution	1979	1983	51
Vienna Convention for the Protection of the Ozone Layer	1985	1988	197
Montreal Protocol on Substances that Deplete the Ozone Layer	1987	1989	197
Convention on the Control of Transboundary Movements of Hazardous Wastes and Their Disposal	1989	1992	193
UN Convention on Biological Diversity	1992	1993	196
UN Framework Convention on Climate Change	1992	1994	196
UN Convention to Combat Desertification in Those Countries Experiencing Serious Drought and/or Desertification, Particularly in Africa	1994	1996	195
Kyoto Protocol to UN Framework Convention on Climate Change	1997	2005	192
UN Fish Stocks Agreement	1995	2001	82
Convention on Persistent Organic Pollutants	2001	2004	179
International Treaty on Plant Genetic Resources for Food and Agriculture	2001	2004	136
International Convention for the Control and Management of Ships' Ballast Water and Sediments	2004	pending	44
International Tropical Timber Agreement	2006	2011	72
Minamata Convention on Mercury	2013	pending	19

Note: For additional information, see International Environmental Agreements Database Project, http://iea.uoregon.edu.

Protocol on Substances That Deplete the Ozone Layer and the 1990 London Amendment, which further tightened states' agreement to phase out ozone-depleting chemicals. In this process, Tolba mobilized an international constituency and initiated consultations with key governments, private interest groups, and international organizations. He argued for flexibility, applied pressure, floated his own proposals as a stimulus to participants, and managed the negotiating process expeditiously.[24] Senior UNEP officials have played similar leadership roles in negotiations that led to the Mediterranean Action Plan, the 1992 UN Convention on Biological Diversity, the 1989 Basel Convention on Hazardous Waste Substances and Their Disposal, and the 2001 Stockholm Convention on Persistent Organic Pollutants. UNEP provides secretariat support for all of these.

Second, UNEP is charged with monitoring the international environment, drawing on a variety of sources. For actual research, it commissions outside experts. Together with the World Meteorological Organization, it monitors atmospheric quality and, in 1988, initiated the Intergovernmental Panel on Climate Change (IPCC). UNEP shares ocean-quality monitoring with the International Oceanographic Council and, together with the FAO and WHO, it conducts studies of freshwater quality. The monitoring and assessments enable UNEP to play an agenda-setting role on particular issues such as chemical pollutants, hazardous wastes, and marine pollution.[25]

Third, UNEP oversees the Regional Seas Programme to protect thirteen regional seas. The program was an expansion of UNEP's success with the Mediterranean Action Plan. Although the program is often seen as one of UNEP's major successes, the plans for various seas have faced a number of difficult problems, including contentious political relationships among participating states.

Fourth, UNEP manages the multi-stakeholder Dams and Development Project, which builds on the work of the World Commission on Dams in the late 1990s in setting guidelines for large dam projects. The project is designed to improve decisionmaking, planning, and operation of dams so that dams are built and operated in an environmentally sustainable fashion.

Although UNEP is often given credit for its role in the ozone "solution," it is not an implementing agency as such except in its role of building states' capacity in environmental law. As a result, it collaborates with a number of other UN agencies. In this respect, it is handicapped by its limited leverage over the UN specialized agencies and national governments, as well as by its location in Nairobi, far removed from other UN centers; its limited budget ($631 million in 2014–2015); the multiplicity of issues and institutions under its purview; and its inability to coordinate international environmental action, provide for greater harmonization of reporting requirements for various conventions, or help states enhance national environmental capacity. UNEP is not a funding agency, but it disburses small amounts from a number of funds, including the Environment

Fund and trust funds linked to particular environmental issues such as organic pollutants and ozone depletion.

UNEP was designed as a program within the UN system, not a specialized agency or world environment organization. This contributes to its shortcomings, just as its location in Africa hampers its activities and makes it difficult to hire expert personnel. UNEP, like many UN agencies and programs, has long been a venue for North-South confrontation over the need to square environmental concerns with development priorities. Developed countries and UNEP need the cooperation of developing countries to address environmental problems and strengthen international environmental governance. Yet the developed countries have often feared that UNEP was too heavily influenced by LDC interests and have been reluctant to support a strong, more independent UNEP bureaucracy.

From the Commission on Sustainable Development to the High-Level Political Forum. The Commission on Sustainable Development was created following the 1992 Rio Conference to encourage and monitor implementation of Agenda 21, review reports from states, and coordinate sustainable development activities within the UN system, overlapping in part with UNEP. After it first convened in 1993, an important task for the CSD was strengthening the participation of major societal groups, including NGOs, indigenous peoples, local governments, workers, businesses, women, and the young, in decision-making. Located in New York and reporting to ECOSOC, the commission, with fifty-three members elected by ECOSOC for three-year terms, served for twenty years as the venue for discussing issues related to sustainable development. As part of its monitoring role, the CSD was supposed to review national reports and information from other UN programs on actions relating to Agenda 21 recommendations. It was also charged with preparations for the follow-ups to Rio—the Rio Plus 5 special session of the General Assembly, the 2002 Johannesburg Summit (Rio Plus 10), and the Rio Plus 20 conference in 2012. One analyst noted, "It is difficult to determine what the influence of this institution has been. It is not charged with creating any new obligations for states and has no legal authority to compel states to act. Its primary impact is in the generation of information, the creation of norms, and the development of capacity." She adds, however, that we should not entirely dismiss the CSD, since it has played a valuable role in bringing nonstate actors into discussions and increasing their access within the UN.[26]

The 2012 Rio Plus 20 Summit made the decision to replace the CSD with the High-Level Political Forum on Sustainable Development, which convenes annually under ECOSOC and every four years at the heads-of-state level under the General Assembly. The hope is that the forum will prove more capable of meeting the challenges of sustainable development, given the role of high-level officials in reviewing progress and suggesting an actionable agenda.[27]

Global Environmental Facility. Established in 1991, the Global Environmental Facility (GEF) is the most prominent international funder of environmental projects in low- and middle-income countries. The World Bank serves as the trustee of the funding facility and provides administrative services. UNEP provides scientific oversight and helps in selecting priorities, and UNDP coordinates with other bilateral donors. NGOs are involved in the planning and execution of projects. The GEF has emerged as a useful complement to other sources of financial assistance for environmental projects in developing countries.

GEF funds are designed to induce the developing countries to take environmental actions, with the fund covering the cost differential between a project initiated with environmental objectives and an alternative project undertaken without attention to global environmental concerns. Most important, however, GEF funds help leverage other funding for projects. By late 2015, it had disbursed some $14.5 billion in grants, supplemented by $75 billion in cofinancing. In addition, through a series of small grants ($50,000–$250,000 each), GEF subsidizes grassroots groups, thereby building on its commitment to NGO participation.

GEF's priorities include financing the commitments under the UN Convention on Biological Diversity, the UN Framework Convention on Climate Change, and the Kyoto Protocol, with almost 90 percent of its funding aimed at these areas. GEF grants also support projects on land degradation, protection of international waters, and persistent organic pollutants. Most ozone-related funding is handled through the Montreal Protocol Multilateral Fund, not the GEF.

GEF's Council is composed of thirty-two states, with sixteen from developing countries, fourteen from developed countries, and two from the former Soviet bloc. It meets twice a year to approve work programs and projects. Generally decisions are taken by consensus; if a formal vote is needed, decisions are taken by a double weighted majority including a 60 percent majority of all participants and a 60 percent majority of the developed-country funders. Every three years, GEF's assembly, composed of all member countries (183), along with representatives from implementing agencies and the conventions that use the GEF, reviews general policies and approves any changes to the GEF agreement. Funds are replenished by donors every four years, and programmatic initiatives have become more cohesive. NGOs enjoy an open invitation to participate, a unique privilege not often found in other international institutions. One criticism of the GEF is that it does not work closely enough with state-level and civil society actors to reflect priorities.

The World Bank. Because the World Bank is the largest multilateral donor for economic development, it has come under pressure for more than twenty-five years to make its economic development policies compatible with environmental sustainability. Yet its record has been a mixed one. It was, in fact, major World

Bank development projects and their harm to the environment that fueled transnational environmental advocacy networks in the 1960s and 1970s—projects such as Brazil's Amazon basin development, dams in India, and Indonesia's relocation of population from Java to neighboring islands. The bank was slow to respond, although in the 1970s it began to appoint environmental advisers. Only in the late 1980s did the bank begin to work more closely with environmental NGOs. In 1993, it increased its lending for environmental programs and established the independent Inspection Panel to investigate citizen claims of harm from specific projects. The number of staff addressing sustainable development and environmental issues has expanded, and the bank has published ten social and environmental safeguard policies, showing how it promotes sustainable development. The annual *World Development Report* now includes considerable coverage of environmental issues in the context of sustainable development.

Catherine Weaver asks whether the bank has become "green" or has just been "greenwashed." She and others have questioned the depth of the World Bank's commitment to environmental sustainability, pointing to the "incongruence of sustainable development goals with the intellectual and operational cultures of the Bank."[28] One of the harshest critics argues that the bank has actually hastened environmental destruction.[29] An evaluation of 274 World Bank environmental projects using the bank's own evaluation process found that the projects that addressed local priorities (namely, water and sanitation projects) were more successful than those that addressed global issues (such as climate change or biodiversity), because the former were subject to greater accountability from local constituencies.[30]

Regional development banks, as discussed in Chapter 5, have followed the World Bank's lead in adopting environmental agendas, safeguards, and implementing mechanisms. In some cases, this process has lagged; in others, such as that of the African Development Bank, it has gained urgency as the effects of climate change have become apparent. The AfDB also serves as the implementing agency for the GEF in Africa, and it has "green growth" as a central part of its 2013 strategy to build resilience to climate shocks with infrastructure and natural resource protection.

Since the 1970s, the creation and functioning of these institutions within the UN system have represented one of the UN's main accomplishments in this issue area. Multilateral and bilateral financial resources have been marshaled, though not nearly enough to meet the demands. Global successes have included reducing the threat to the ozone layer caused by chlorofluorocarbons, cleaning up international waters, developing standards to decrease the prevalence and malevolent effects of persistent organic pollutants, and creating fruitful partnerships with state and local institutions to mitigate soil erosion and plant emissions.

Case Study: Comparing UN System Initiatives on
Ozone Depletion and Climate Change

Given the relatively rapid success beginning in the 1980s of efforts to address the problem of ozone depletion and the prolonged and only marginal success to date in addressing climate change, it is instructive to compare UN system initiatives on these two issues. The general approaches to both issues have been similar—several General Assembly resolutions, conclusion of a framework convention followed by a protocol, creation of various institutional structures, meetings and conferences of the parties, and consensus as the decisionmaking mode. Yet in contrast to the rapid progress in addressing the problem of ozone in the mid-1980s and repeated refinements of the legal commitments through subsequent agreements since then, there have been almost thirty years of diplomacy surrounding climate change to date. Each round has been protracted, yielding relatively few hard commitments, continuing disputes about the nature of the problem, and confrontations between developed and developing countries about who should do what.

Six lessons stand out. First, there must be agreement on the nature of the environmental problem itself. Ozone depletion was thrust onto the international agenda in 1975 when two American scientists submitted a report attributing the depletion of the ozone layer to use of chlorofluorocarbons (CFCs). The correlation between use of CFCs and ozone depletion was contested for several years among scientists, but in a little less than a decade following publication of data confirming a widening ozone hole over Antarctica, most states and scientific experts acknowledged the problem. In contrast, the acknowledgment of global climate change has proved more contested. In 2007, after almost twenty years of debates over the scientific data, the IPCC, an independent network of experts in the physical and natural sciences, engineering, social sciences, public policy, and management, released its fourth assessment, which concluded that the evidence of global warming was "unequivocal" and that human activity was very likely (more than 90 percent likely) to be responsible. Most greenhouse gas emissions come from automobile emissions and from the use of fossil fuels for power generation in the industrialized Northern countries and, increasingly, from China, India, and other emerging economies. Despite corroboration in other studies, there remains a very public and politically charged debate, particularly in the United States, over whether there is human-induced (anthropogenic) global climate change taking place. The IPCC's fifth assessment report, in 2013, was still more definitive in the degree of confidence experts felt regarding the evidence of human influence, calling it "extremely likely" that human activity is the dominant cause of increased greenhouse gas concentrations; observed warming; changes in global water cycles; reductions in snow, ice, glaciers, and Arctic sea ice; mean sea level rise; and some climate extremes.[31] Without consensus on the nature and magnitude of the problem, mustering the political support for actions by both developed and developing countries has been difficult. Furthermore, climate change is a multifaceted problem—far more complex and with more far-reaching implications, and potential winners and losers, than is the case with ozone depletion.

The second lesson is that key states need to support action, and leadership from the UNEP executive director can make a difference in the outcome of negotiations. In the 1980s, the United States and European states were not only the major producers of CFCs but also the major consumers, although usage in the new industrializing economies of India, China, Brazil, and Mexico was rising by about 10 percent annually. US, Canadian, and Norwegian leadership was critical to success in negotiating the Montreal Protocol and subsequent amendments. The support of those countries rested on a mobilized public and on supportive NGOs. The US government was particularly active, and the two important American-based MNCs that produced CFCs, Dow Chemical and DuPont, found suitable substitutes for most uses at an acceptable price and, hence, did not oppose phasing them out. Furthermore, UNEP executive director Mustafa Tolba is credited with leadership in mobilizing an international constituency and facilitating the negotiations in a number of ways, as discussed earlier.[32] The successive agreements on ozone following the Montreal Protocol further tightened states' commitments to phase out ozone-depleting chemicals. Over time, states agreed to permanent, quantitative emission limits on almost a hundred ozone-depleting substances, with some provision for international trading in entitlements.

For many years, key European states provided leadership on climate change, while the United States was either absent or obstructionist, and developing countries argued that climate change was a problem caused by the developed countries for which they should not be obliged to sacrifice their own economic growth. The issue was first addressed in the 1992 UN Framework Convention on Climate Change (UNFCCC), but the convention contained no legally binding obligation to reduce carbon dioxide emissions. It was supplemented by the 1997 Kyoto Protocol, which aimed to stabilize the concentration of greenhouse gases and required developed countries to reduce their overall greenhouse gas emissions to at least 5 percent below 1990 levels by 2010. The United States, however, raised major objections to both the Kyoto Protocol and UNFCCC and refused to support any international agreement calling for specific mandated cutbacks in emissions, believing that the costs of compliance would be too high and that the US economy would be adversely affected. The United States also objected to the fact that countries such as China and India were excluded from Kyoto's emission limits, a concern that grew after China surpassed the United States as the largest carbon emitter in 2009. Nevertheless, the Kyoto Protocol came into force in early

2005 with 156 parties, accounting for 55 percent of greenhouse gas emissions. Absent US participation and in the face of flagging European commitment, the goals were not attained.

The Kyoto agreement was intended as a relatively short-term step in the process of addressing climate change and was scheduled to expire in 2012. Consequently, the UN convened a series of conferences beginning in 2007 with the goal first of extending Kyoto and later of reaching a new agreement under the UNFCCC regime by the end of 2015. Each of the conferences focused on a particular issue or set of issues. In Bali in 2007, for example, there was agreement that China and India should be included in a follow-on agreement. The 2008 meetings agreed that states should be given credit for saving forests and agreed to expand a fund to help poorer countries adapt to climate change. The 2009 Copenhagen conference resulted in 140 parties (80 percent of global emissions) agreeing to provide both technology and financing to decrease emissions and mitigate the effects of climate change. The 2010 Cancun conference built on pledges for mitigation for the developing countries. In the 2014 Lima meeting, there was agreement that every country—rich or poor—must take steps to reduce the burning of oil, gas, and coal by some amount and announce its pledge of cuts by mid-2015. The series of meetings showed that the ozone example, where major powers agreed to take significant measures relatively quickly, was unworkable for addressing climate change.

Climate change diplomacy under the UN, in fact, has a twenty-year reputation for being dysfunctional, with procedural issues often taking precedence over substantive ones, problems of framing and poor management, and a pattern of last-minute—if any—breakthroughs.[33] The negotiations over Kyoto's successor show that "most of the important work will be driven outside the U.N. process."[34] The accumulating evidence of climate change, however, along with shifts in key countries' positions, did produce different results in the 2015 Paris conference, as discussed below. And there is some evidence that UNSG Ban Ki-moon provided leadership for negotiations at critical points in the process, as discussed below.

The third lesson to be drawn from the two cases is how differences in the nature of the environmental problems and the politics surrounding them can influence the institutional structures established to facilitate implementation of the conventions and protocols. For ozone, UNEP's secretariat is at the center of the implementation process, including ongoing research and data gathering, and the ozone secretariat is part of UNEP. Other components of the ozone regime include a working group of the parties, a variety of expert panels, and the Multilateral Implementation Fund. The secretariat is the hub of a network of more than a hundred national ozone units that provide services to developing countries' ministries as well as draft amendments and adjustments to the

Montreal Protocol. Over time it has acquired a reputation for its technical expertise, transparency, strong diplomatic skills, and "balance between being an active player behind the scenes and being perceived as a neutral and 'passive' tool from the viewpoint of governments."[35] The scientific and legal staff of this small secretariat assists parties to the Vienna Convention and Montreal Protocol. The administration of resources for enhancing developing countries' technical and financial capabilities is, however, handled by the Multilateral Fund and GEF. The ozone secretariat is small and has a small budget (under $1 million), but the reputation and expertise of its staff have given it considerable influence in ozone politics, and for more than thirty years it has played an important role in keeping the problem of ozone depletion visible.[36]

In contrast, the UN Climate Change Secretariat is separate from UNEP and located in Bonn, Germany, where there are no other international agencies or diplomatic missions. It plays no role in generating new knowledge about climate change, keeping the problem on the agenda, or shaping discourse about it. Its functions are largely administrative and technical in conjunction with meetings and conferences of the parties, although it may make recommendations on the conduct of negotiations. States do not want a strong, independent secretariat, and the secretariat's own culture is averse to a more active role. Ironically, the climate secretariat, with 500 staff members, is among the larger environmental treaty secretariats and its budget is relatively large ($26.7 million in 2015). A separate executive board manages the Clean Development Mechanism, established under the Kyoto Protocol. Developed states and private companies can use this to meet domestic emission targets under the protocol by financing projects in developing countries such as the installation of solar panels for rural electrification. Projects are assigned one carbon emission credit for every ton of greenhouse gas saved. These credits may be sold on the international carbon exchanges, of which there were six in 2015. The mechanism stimulates emission reductions and gives industrialized countries some flexibility in meeting their emission reduction or limitation targets. These transfers are validated by the UNFCCC secretariat.

The fourth lesson is that pledges of funding from developed countries to aid developing countries with the incremental costs of compliance are key to securing agreement. During the negotiations that produced the Montreal Protocol, for example, the industrialized countries agreed to create the Multilateral Fund for the Implementation of the Montreal Protocol. The GEF has provided financial assistance to Central and Eastern European countries. Since 1991, the Multilateral Fund has supported more than $3.0 billion in activities including industrial conversion, technical assistance, training, and capacity-building.

Unlike the ozone case, where affordable substitutes were found in relatively short order, climate change demands long-term major changes in the use of fossil fuels and major funding for mitigation of effects already being experienced. There are a number of funds that have been created to aid developing countries in adapting to climate change, starting with the funding mechanism called for in the UNFCCC and including the Adaptation Fund, the Special Climate Change Fund, and the Least Developed Countries Fund, the last two of which are managed by GEF. In 2010–2012, these disbursed about $600 million and were supplemented by funding from other multilateral funds, official development assistance, and other public and private sources, including the World Bank, which in 2011 signed an agreement with mayors from forty of the world's largest cities to fund climate change–reduction projects. The Green Climate Fund, established in 2013 to invest in technology, raised $6.5 billion in 2015, and in that same year GEF announced it had raised $250 million in new funding for the least developed countries. Given the scale and scope of anticipated needs in conjunction with a new climate change agreement and the inadequacy of funding pledges to date, however, it is not surprising that funding has been one of the major stumbling blocks to a new climate agreement.

The fifth lesson is that international environmental agreements need flexibility—a way to change standards when new scientific information becomes available—without renegotiating the entire treaty. The Montreal Protocol is a flexible instrument that can and has been made more restrictive, as the scientific evidence warranted, through a series of four amendments; its provisions could also be relaxed should the ozone problem become less severe.

The Kyoto Protocol provides flexibility primarily through the Clean Development Mechanism. The core disagreement, however, comes from the overarching "principle of common but differentiated responsibilities." Must all states take responsibility? Do some states have more responsibility than others? Do developing states have time to catch up in terms of economic development? If a new global agreement is to be reached, how will it reconcile the principle with the need for flexibility? As Robert Keohane and David Victor note, "Both political reality and the need for flexibility and diversity suggest that it is preferable to work for a loosely linked but effective regime complex for climate change."[37] For this reason, they and others have described the climate change regime complex as "a loosely coupled system of institutions with no clear hierarchy or core . . . [its] elements are loosely linked to one another." The UNFCCC and Kyoto Protocol form one part; other parts include climate change initiatives taken by the **Group of Eight (G-8)**, the G-20, the EU, and World Bank; the Nuclear Suppliers Group; regional pollution control institutions; the US Climate Action Partnership (an alliance of firms and NGOs); and a wide array of national and subnational activities.

Finally, what can be learned from the outcomes of efforts to address ozone and climate change? There is evidence showing that improvement in the ozone layer has occurred as a result of states' compliance with the protocol and its amendments. Worldwide consumption of ozone-depleting substances has declined more than 75 percent since the Montreal Protocol came into force in the late 1980s, even while production has grown slightly in the developing world. In 2014, UNEP scientists concluded that Earth's ozone layer was "well on the way to recovery" thanks to actions against the ozone-depleting substances. They also reported that the protocol has made a large contribution to the reduction of greenhouse gases— which constitute some 90 percent of the emissions linked to ozone-depleting substances.[38] Although demand for products using CFC-like compounds increases as growing middle classes in China, India, and other developing countries demand refrigerators and air conditioners, research on substitutes has also been promising. The jury is still out on whether the change is permanent.

The Kyoto Protocol has not reduced the emissions of greenhouse gases, even though some countries have met their targets, and the IPCC's 2013 report showed that the rate of climate change is accelerating. The long-term effects of the trend have become widespread: glaciers and sea ice melting, oceans becoming acidified, hurricanes and typhoons strengthening, more extreme weather patterns affecting land use in many parts of the world. Given current global dependence on oil and gas as major sources of energy to sustain global economic growth, the issue of climate change is clearly too complex and politically charged to be addressed in a single treaty regime such as that for ozone. It is with this in mind that we turn to the 2015 UN-sponsored Paris Conference and examine what was and was not accomplished.

Before doing so, however, it is important to call attention to the fact that climate change, more than any other environmental issue, is now widely seen as a threat to security—to human security and to the security of at least some states, including small island states such as the Marshall Islands, Tuvalu, and Kiribati, where the land may be only six feet above sea level and whose very existence is threatened by rising sea levels. As a result, beginning in 2005, the UN Security Council began to consider its possible role in addressing the problem. It has convened two thematic debates on the relationship between climate change and security issues, the first in 2007 and the second in 2011. Not surprisingly, it was some of the small island states that particularly pressed their concerns. Russia, China, and the G-77 opposed Security Council consideration of the issue; the United Kingdom, France, and Germany all supported it. In 2007, the United States opposed action, but in 2011 US ambassador Susan Rice declared, "It is past time for the Security Council to come into the 21st century and assume our core responsibilities."[39] Eventually, many African states and others broke from the G-77 on the grounds that desertification and heat waves were creating economic and social disruption, including contributing to the growth of radical terrorism.[40]

CARTOON 7.1. "UN Climate Change Conference 2015 in Paris," by Marian Kemesky, Slovakia, November 28, 2015

The 2015 Paris Conference: "There Is No Planet B." In December 2015, after nine years of intermittent negotiations, the leaders of 195 nations were joined by thousands of other officials, environmental activists, scientists, and support staff in Paris, France, with the goal of concluding a new, legally binding agreement that would compel states to cut their carbon emissions and reduce climate change.[41] As the UNFCCC's Conference of Parties (COP21) convened, the effects of climate change had become even more evident. Several island states had already experienced erosion of their coastlines, salination of the soil with repeated flooding (which destroys crops), and contamination of wells (which increases disease). Tony A. deBrum, the foreign minister of the Marshall Islands, explained, "We see the damage occurring now. We're trying to beat back the sea."[42] The small island states, in fact, had a significant voice in Paris. Reflecting more than just their concerns, however, French president François Hollande noted in opening the conference, "Never have the stakes been so high because this is about the future of the planet, the future of life."[43] In short, there was a greater sense of urgency, creating a shift in the geopolitics of climate change and in the perception of global warming as an immediate threat. Declining prices for renewable sources of energy also created more economically viable alternatives to coal, oil, and gas.

Several other important factors contributed to the agreement reached after two weeks of negotiations. The first was leadership from U.S. president Barack Obama and Chinese president Xi Jinping. President Obama's approval of stringent environmental regulations on coal-fired power plants in 2014 "fundamentally altered the perception of the United States in international climate talks." China's awareness that its heavy use of coal was causing major air pollution in its cities led to a shift in its views on climate change. As a result, in late 2014, the two presidents announced that they would work jointly to pursue emission cuts—a major breakthrough and an example to others.[44] Getting India—the third-largest carbon emitter—on board was also important, but India dragged its feet on making a commitment to cuts and, along with China, opposed proposals for requiring more stringent pledges every five years and for an outside monitoring system for emissions until very late in the negotiations.[45] A second key factor was the agreement that emission cuts would be binding on all parties. No longer would developing countries be exempted, as they were in the Kyoto Protocol. In contrast to earlier top-down efforts to impose targets on parties, all were expected to announce voluntary pledges to cut emissions in advance of the conference, which 186 did, representing 90 percent of the world economy. Third, agreement in Paris was facilitated by public-private partnerships, with twenty governments pledging to double spending on clean energy research and development over the next five years and a coalition of business leaders led by Bill Gates, billionaire founder of Microsoft, pledging to invest billions in a green energy fund for clean-energy start-ups. Fourth, from the outset of his first term as UNSG, Ban Ki-moon had made climate change a priority. He created a Climate Change Support Team within his office and regularly engaged with heads of state and government both at summits (2007, 2009, 2014, 2015) and in bilateral meetings to get them to provide overall direction to the negotiation process. The presence of 150 leaders on the first day of the Paris Conference can be attributed at least in part to his efforts. A final factor was the role of the French government itself in facilitating the successful outcome through careful preparations and gracious hosting.[46]

The Paris conference faced multiple challenges. The first was creating consensus about the binding nature of an agreement. This process was highly political, as developing nations such as Brazil were called upon to cease the lucrative harvesting of timber in the Amazon rain forest to preserve an essential global "carbon sink." The persistent tensions between rich and poor countries also had to be resolved over poor countries' demand that rich industrialized countries provide financial assistance to support their adaption to climate change; the small island states in particular pushed for funding to minimize and address

---

BOX 7.1. Key Provisions of the 2015 Paris Agreement

Temperature increase: *Keep global warming below 2°C with effort to contain temperature increase to 1.5°C*

Abandon fossil fuels by midcentury: *Reach global peak of greenhouse gas emissions as soon as possible and reach carbon neutrality by 2050*

Preservation of forests: *Reduce deforestation and enhance forests that serve as carbon sinks*

"Ratcheting up": *Come together every five years to set more ambitious targets as required by science*

Transparency and accountability: *Monitor and report to each other and the public on how well they are doing to implement their targets (with built-in flexibility for countries' different capacities)—a "name-and-shame" approach*

Funding: *Developed countries expected to take the lead and raise $100 billion per year (both public and private funds) until 2025, when a new collective goal will be set (not binding)*

Support: *Developed countries to support developing countries' efforts to mitigate climate change and foster greener economies*

Loss and damage: *Recognizes the importance of averting, minimizing and addressing loss and damage associated with adverse effects of climate change*

Source: Coral Davenport, Justin Gillis, Sewell Chan, and Melissa Eddy, "Inside the Paris Climate Deal," *New York Times*, December 12, 2015.

---

loss and damage associated with adverse effects such as rising sea levels and salination of arable lands. The conference also faced challenges in creating a robust and transparent process to hold states accountable for the commitments they made—a major US condition. In addition, it faced the task of ratcheting up those commitments over time. During the conference a "high-ambition coalition" emerged that included, among others, the United States, the EU, Brazil, and several island nations.

The Paris agreement was called "a rare victory for global multilateral deal making," with one observer claiming, "The UN should take a victory lap."[47] (See Box 7.1.) UN secretary-general Ban Ki-moon called it "truly a historic moment. . . . For the first time, we have a truly universal agreement on climate change, one of the most crucial problems on earth."[48] One hundred and eighty-eight parties both rich and poor did set individual voluntary goals to reduce greenhouse gas emissions and agreed to further reductions every five years. The agreement calls for a $100 billion climate fund and accepts the need to address loss and damage. Pieces that had yet to be worked out included details on transparency measures and compensation for climate change damages.

Despite the diplomatic success, the agreement faced hurdles at the domestic level in many parliaments and legislatures as well as with finance ministers and regulatory agencies. First, it must be signed by at least fifty-five countries representing at least 55 percent of total greenhouse gas emissions—a goal that was surpassed with more than 177 signatories in April 2016. The UN must get the remaining parties to submit emissions-reduction pledges, and rich countries must make good on funding pledges. The agreement will not be considered a treaty under American law but rather will be classified as an extension of the UNFCCC, which the US Senate ratified in 1992; given US domestic divisions on the issue of climate change, there was no possibility of securing Senate ratification for a new treaty. Much of the success of the agreement depends on global peer pressure on countries to meet their emissions reduction commitments. For this reason, some in the scientific community claimed that the language in places allowed for too much interpretation and not enough enforcement; they called instead for zero greenhouse gas emissions by 2050.[49] Most scientists, in fact, remained pessimistic, warning that if countries did not cut their greenhouse gas emissions still more, the planet would face a breaking point, where climate change would become catastrophic.

One of the major challenges in addressing environmental threats to human security such as climate change is the long time lag before major effects may be felt. Changes made now may take a generation or more to show their effects. This stands in contrast to infectious diseases and health threats, where short-term actions can have immediate effects.

HEALTH AND HUMAN SECURITY

Public health and disease are hardly new issues, but globalization has had a dramatic effect on the transmission, incidence, and vulnerability of individuals and communities to disease through migration, air transport, trade, and troop movements. Intensified human mobility poses major problems for containing outbreaks of cholera, influenza, HIV/AIDS, tuberculosis, West Nile virus, severe acute respiratory syndrome (SARS), avian (bird) influenza, H1N1 flu virus (a form of swine flu), Ebola, and other diseases that can be carried in a matter of hours from one part of the globe to another long before symptoms may appear. Globalization has thus exacerbated the urgency and the scope of the threats that infectious diseases can pose to human security. The issue is not only vulnerability to large-scale loss of life, however; it is also one of disease impeding development and weakening societies, as the WHO-appointed Commission on

Macroeconomics and Health has argued.[50] There is significant need to fortify what Ban Ki-moon has described as "collective global health security."

Rudimentary international rules to prevent the spread of epidemics, including procedures for instituting quarantines, date back hundreds of years, and institutionalized collaboration can be traced to 1851. With the HIV/AIDS epidemic and recent outbreaks of SARS and avian flu, there has been a substantial strengthening of global health governance, in which the World Health Organization is a central actor. The 2014–2015 Ebola outbreak in West Africa prompted even further examination of WHO's capacity for managing responses to epidemics. The linkage of health and human security was first made by the UN Security Council in a special session in January 2000 devoted to the challenge of HIV/AIDS. Three of the MDGs dealt with health, and MDG 6 specifically targeted HIV/AIDS, malaria, and other diseases. Several of the SDGs also deal with health, although SDG 3 ("Ensure healthy lives and promote well-being for all at all ages") is the only one that specifically targets health. Among the targets (3.3) is "By 2030, end the epidemics of AIDS, tuberculosis, malaria and neglected tropical diseases and combat hepatitis, water-borne diseases and other communicable diseases."[51]

Developing International Responses to Health Issues

Between 1851 and 1903, a series of eleven international conferences developed procedures to prevent the spread of contagious and infectious diseases. In 1907, the Office International d'Hygiène Publique (OIHP) was created with a mandate to disseminate information on communicable diseases such as cholera, plague, and yellow fever. More than a decade later, at the request of the League of Nations Council, the International Health Conference met to prepare for a permanent International Health Organization, but the OIHP did not become part of this new health organization. Following the UN's creation, in 1948, the World Health Organization came into being and became a UN specialized agency. In membership, staff, and budget, it is one of the largest agencies. With six regional offices, one located on every inhabited continent, it is also one of the more decentralized functional organizations. The WHO secretariat, located in Geneva, is highly technical, as the director-general, other secretariat officials, and many delegates are medical doctors. The medical and allied health communities form a strong epistemic community based on their technical expertise and training.

The main decisionmaking body is the World Health Assembly (WHA), composed of three delegates from each member state, including delegates from the scientific, professional, and nongovernmental communities. Each country, however, has one vote, unlike in the ILO, where representatives of each functional group have a separate vote. The executive board is a smaller group of thirty-four members elected by the WHA. By a "gentlemen's agreement," at least three of the Security Council P-5 members are supposed to be represented.

WHO Initiatives. WHO's activities have historically included three major areas.[52] The first area, building on the work of predecessor organizations, is containing the spread of communicable diseases. In 1951, WHO passed the International Health Regulations (IHR), requiring states to report outbreaks of four communicable diseases (yellow fever, cholera, plague, and smallpox) and take appropriate measures without interrupting international commerce. Those regulations covered only a few diseases, they were not legally binding, and only governments received reports, which they could block, fearing adverse economic consequences such as loss of tourism.

Globalization has had a dramatic effect, however, on the transmission, incidence, and vulnerability of individuals and communities to disease through migration, air transport, trade, and troop movements, including of UN peacekeepers. During the 1980s and 1990s, new communicable diseases emerged that were not covered under the IHR, including Ebola, West Nile virus, HIV/AIDS, and avian flu. Older diseases thought to be under control, such as tuberculosis, reemerged in different, often drug-resistant forms. New threats to health arose with incidents of bioterrorism, such as the Tokyo sarin gas attack in 1995 and the US anthrax scare in 2001. At the same time, the Internet, cell phones, social media, and other technologies have facilitated faster and better information about outbreaks that states might once have been able to hide. As a result, revised International Health Regulations took effect in 2007 after ten years of work. These brought changes to WHO and committed states to notify the WHO Strategic Health Operations Centre of any emerging global health threat within twenty-four hours. In turn, WHO can also now utilize the Internet to publicize potential problems, regardless of state objections. This was intended to resolve the problems encountered during the SARS outbreak in 2002–2003, when China initially suppressed information on the outbreak, was slow to permit WHO officials to visit potentially affected areas, and failed to undertake preventive measures for several months. Although the epidemic killed fewer than 1,000 individuals, the potential for a global pandemic was widely recognized, and the economic repercussions for the most-affected countries—China, Vietnam, Singapore, and Canada—were significant.

The second area of WHO activity is eradication programs for certain diseases and working with state health authorities to improve health infrastructure. The current malaria and polio eradication campaigns are examples. They followed the widely acclaimed and successful eradication of smallpox in the 1970s. With the support of Rotary International, the Bill and Melinda Gates Foundation, and other groups, the goal of polio eradication was close to realization in 2006;

then local resistance to vaccination in Nigeria led to outbreaks that subsequently spread in neighboring countries, South Asia, and most recently Syria. The World Bank is providing major funding for the global effort to recontain the disease. After years of stagnation, the campaign against malaria is now showing improvement, thanks in part to an increase in funding for mosquito control and for provision of insecticide-treated bed nets that have been effective in protecting the young.

The third area of WHO activity includes interaction with the pharmaceutical industry. Developing countries have been concerned about the quality of imported drugs and have sought technical assistance in monitoring quality control. WHO approved guidelines for drug-manufacturing quality control in 1970, covering such issues as labeling, self-inspection, and reporting adverse reactions. WHO also has dealt with the pharmaceutical industry on the issue of pricing AIDS drugs in poor countries and on the potential for an Ebola vaccine. In several cases, it touched on the contentious issue of MNC regulation, such as following the WHA's adoption in 1981 of the Code of Marketing for Breast-Milk Substitutes. This called for states to adopt regulations banning marketing and advertising of infant formula that discouraged breast-feeding, while acknowledging a "legitimate market" for breast-milk substitutes. The issue of the accessibility, quality, and affordability of drugs in developing countries remains on WHO's agenda.

In recent years, WHO has taken up a number of lifestyle-related health issues—a new fourth area of focus. Key among them is its campaign against tobacco. When the issue first appeared in the World Health Assembly, the large tobacco companies mounted stiff opposition, as did the United States and some other key states. Yet in 2003, member states approved the Framework Convention on Tobacco Control, which bans advertising of tobacco products, requires health warnings on packages, and mandates broader liability for manufacturers. The convention took effect in 2005 and had been ratified by 180 state parties as of 2015 (but not the United States). Implementation has been slow, however. Smoking rates continue to rise in developing countries, and the marketing restrictions have not been implemented. There has been a loss of momentum on the issue. With these expanding mandates, WHO has been criticized for overextending itself, particularly after the problems it encountered in the 2014 Ebola crisis.

Case Study: WHO, Ebola, and Crisis Management for Human Security

In contrast to the HIV/AIDS epidemic that began in the 1980s and where UN system responses evolved over many years, the speed with which Ebola spread in West Africa beginning in 2014 tested WHO's ability to manage a major crisis. The Ebola outbreak revealed many of the challenges facing the global management of "problems without borders." On one hand, the relevance of the UN and the need for a global response were highlighted, as global resources and coordination were essential for stopping the epidemic. On the other hand, the crisis also revealed the limits of a UN agency's capacities, the weight of an overextended bureaucracy, and the problems of a state-centered agenda.

In March 2014, the World Health Organization was notified of an outbreak of Ebola virus in Guinea. By the end of that month, cross-border transmission was first reported. Not until five months later, in August, did WHO declare the situation an epidemic and a "public health emergency of international concern" under the IHR, which provide guidelines for preventing the spread of infectious disease. The three countries most affected by the epidemic were Guinea, Liberia, and Sierra Leone, with isolated cases in neighboring countries and among international health care workers returning to Europe and the United States. With weak public health systems, persistent unemployment rates of close to 80 percent, literacy rates below 50 percent, and a chronic lack of medical personnel and hospitals, the three West African countries needed outside help. In Liberia, there were fewer than two doctors for every 100,000 Liberians (by contrast, in the United States there are 245 physicians for every 100,000 Americans). All three countries were also still recovering from civil wars in the 1990s, and there was still a UN peacekeeping mission (UNMIL) in Liberia. The lack of adequate health care systems contributed to the rapid transmission of the virus, and training about treating Ebola and its containment protocols was essential to containment. The movement of people between the densely populated national capitals and rural areas contributed to the rapid transmission rate, as did reluctance of local villagers to speak with international aid workers. Families often kept transmissions and deaths secret, and it was difficult to track the disease in remote areas. Cultural traditions surrounding human interactions and death conflicted with the fact that Ebola is transmitted by contact with bodily fluids of infected individuals, meaning that those who care for the sick and deceased are most vulnerable.

The disease spread exponentially throughout 2014 with an initial death rate of 80 to 90 percent among those infected. People were dying in the streets for lack of hospital beds and treatment centers. Panic set in, along with fear that the overwhelmed countries themselves would collapse: food supplies had dropped, there were riots and attacks on health care workers, all commercial air service between the countries had been stopped, and much economic activity had halted. By the end of 2015, when the epidemic was declared over in all three countries, almost 30,000 cases of Ebola had been reported, with more than 11,300 deaths.

With broken health care systems unable to contain the outbreak and WHO's African regional center and Geneva headquarters not responding for months, the NGO Doctors Without Borders (MSF) found itself the primary international medical group organizing assistance on the ground. It benefited from having well-organized stockpiles of protective gear and well-trained personnel available immediately, but in June 2014, it declared the epidemic "totally out of control." At that point, the situation was still seen as a health crisis, however, not a security issue.

Shortly after WHO declared the epidemic a public health emergency in August, UN secretary-general Ban Ki-moon appointed a senior UN system coordinator for Ebola and in early September activated the UN Crisis Response Mechanism, recognizing that he had no confidence in WHO's ability to handle the crisis. In mid-September, the epidemic finally gained global attention. For only the third time, the Security Council passed a resolution on a health issue. Resolution 2177 declared Ebola a threat to international peace and security due to the "unprecedented extent of the epidemic in Africa." It called on member states to facilitate assistance, to communicate and implement established safety and health protocols, and to provide deployable medical capabilities as well as to lift travel and border restrictions that some had begun to impose. The resolution set a record for cosponsors, with 134 states adding their names. The council meeting raised the profile of the crisis and galvanized responses. Within weeks, for example, the United States, United Kingdom, China, and other countries deployed medical personnel and hospital units to West Africa. Ban Ki-moon also announced his plan to create the first-ever UN emergency health mission, the United Nations Mission for Ebola Emergency Response (UNMEER), which was promptly endorsed unanimously by the General Assembly (Resolution 69/1). The two UN resolutions marked a shift toward what is now termed the "securitization" of global health.[53]

UNMEER was tasked with overall planning and coordination of UN agencies, national governments, and other humanitarian actors, operating jointly under WHO and the UN Secretariat. It focused heavily on contact tracing, safe burials, and community education. The senior UN system coordinator for Ebola worked with the World Bank president and others to raise funds to meet the estimated cost of stopping the epidemic, almost $1 billion. WHO was able to bring together representatives from Ebola-affected countries with development partners, civil society, regulatory agencies, and pharmaceutical companies as well as funding agencies to discuss fast-track testing of vaccines for Ebola.[54] It also worked to provide key information to states that were considering imposing travel bans to and from countries with infected patients.

In July 2015, the UN secretary-general convened the International Ebola Recovery Conference to focus attention on the need for targeted investments in the three affected countries following the epidemic, to build medical infrastructure and ensure a "sustainable recovery." Also in July 2015, having achieved its core goals and with significant declines in transmission rates, UNMEER was disbanded.

There have been multiple reviews inside and outside WHO of its shortcomings in responding to the crisis. Among the factors cited are budget and staff cuts that had gutted the Global Outbreak and Response Network in particular, incompetent staff in the African regional office who issued overly optimistic reports for months, the absence of a culture of rapid decisionmaking and proactive reaction to emergencies, preoccupation of Geneva staff with the annual WHA meeting scheduled in May 2014, an executive director inclined to defer to national governments and regional offices, advisers who told headquarters that Ebola was a "small problem" compared to the three countries' other health needs, and others who advised that invoking the IHR by declaring a public health emergency might be seen as "a hostile act . . . and may hamper collaboration between WHO and the affected countries."[55] One observer described WHO's response as "fumbling."[56]

In January 2015, WHO's Executive Board delivered its own harsh assessment, stating that there was "a clear gap in the WHO's mission and structure . . . no clear lines of decision-making or dedicated funding in place [leading to] a slow, uncoordinated response to the Ebola outbreak." It criticized the failure to prevent countries from taking steps in violation of the IHR (such as halting air transport, trade, and insurance coverage for air rescue services).[57] The board called for long-overdue reforms to bolster WHO's rapid-response capacity, including the creation of a reserve of global health emergency workers to be supported by a $100 million contingency fund. Most critics called for the organization to focus on its core competencies to reestablish its role as the "guardian of global public health" and to create a basis for future rapid action. Some have suggested that WHO can never be a crisis manager but fail to suggest an alternative agency. Others have urged WHO to focus on basic public health programs that would be more capable of coping with an outbreak such as Ebola. Still others argue that future epidemics are inevitable and the world must be prepared to deal with them effectively.[58] Indeed, the outbreak of the Zika virus in 2016 quickly tested WHO's emergency response capability again.

HUMAN SECURITY: THE REFUGEE
AND MIGRATION CRISIS

In the latter half of 2015, the media were filled with images of people on the move from Africa and the Middle East to Europe—at times as many as 10,000 people a day crossing the Mediterranean in flimsy boats or walking miles upon miles northward through the Balkans—desperate to reach safe places to resettle and rebuild their lives. Many were refugees from the wars in Syria, Afghanistan, and Iraq; many more were pushed or pulled by a variety of other factors. Arguably the current refugee and migration crisis, alongside climate change, is one of the greatest challenges for international cooperation and human security for the foreseeable future. Fueled on an unprecedented scale by violent conflicts, civil unrest, persecution, human rights abuses, economic disparities, natural disasters, and environmental degradation, the numbers alone barely begin to tell the story (and can be very difficult to pin down). The problems are greatest in the Middle East and Africa, yet hardly any part of the globe is untouched. Furthermore, the long-standing distinction between refugees and migrants is becoming blurred, creating a "protection gap" for those who do not meet the strict legal definition of a refugee at the same time that the sheer numbers of those in need of humanitarian assistance are overwhelming the capacity of the UN system and other humanitarian agencies.

As António Guterres, UN High Commissioner for Refugees, has noted, "We are witnessing a paradigm change, an unchecked slide into an era in which the scale of global forced displacement as well as the response required is now clearly dwarfing anything seen before."[59] The scale and complexity of the crisis challenge the institutions created over the last seventy years to deal with displacement and migration that occurred on a smaller scale and at a slower pace.

Once thought to be a temporary problem at the end of World War II, the refugee problem worldwide has increased dramatically, with multiple conflicts and humanitarian crises occurring simultaneously. At the end of 2015, UNHCR, the UN agency that has had primary responsibility for refugees since 1950, noted that there were more than 60 million "persons of concern"—the highest number since the end of World War II. This figure included 15.1 million **refugees** and 42.4 million **internally displaced persons (IDPs)**.[60] There were also 5.1 million Palestinians under the care of the UN Relief and Works Agency (UNRWA), created in 1949 specifically to serve their needs. The largest numbers of refugees were from Syria, Afghanistan, Somalia, Sudan, and South Sudan; 80 percent of them were hosted by developing and least-developed countries, which bear the brunt of the burden of assistance. Women and children made up the vast majority of the refugees and IDPs. Yet while the number of those needing resettlement increased by 50 percent between 2012 and 2015, only 126,800 refugees returned to their countries of origin during 2014, and a mere 74,000 were resettled in more than seventy countries, illustrating what has become a problem of protracted displacement. It is compounded by a crisis of asylum, as states, including many in the EU, have adopted restrictive asylum policies in the face of the scale of the refugee and migrant flows in 2015.

UNHCR and the 1951 Convention Relating to the Status of Refugees, supplemented by the 1967 protocol, plus UNRWA, constitute the primary institutions defining who is a refugee and organizing assistance to those who are forcibly displaced across borders. According to the convention, a refugee is a person who, because of a "well-founded fear of being persecuted for reasons of race, religion, nationality, membership of a particular social group or political opinion, is outside the country of his nationality and is unable or, owing to such fear, is unwilling to avail himself of the protection of that country." The UNHCR's responsibility is to protect people who are certified as refugees by providing temporary refuge until another state grants them asylum or they can return home. The most significant right of a refugee is **non-refoulement**—the principle that refugees cannot be forced to return to their country of origin. Therefore, UNHCR provides administrative assistance and identity papers, and protects refugees from forced repatriation and from exploitation in the host state. This legal protection mandate has become increasingly difficult to implement as the numbers have surged.

Originally, the 1951 convention applied only to Europe, but it was made universal by the 1967 protocol. The definition of refugee was broadened through regional agreements to include those displaced by internal conflicts. These regional documents correspond more to the actual causes of flight now and to the reality that it is "often impossible for asylum seekers to generate documented evidence of individual persecution required by the 1951 Convention . . . [since] most contemporary mass exoduses occur when political violence is of a generalized nature rather than a direct individual threat."[61] Thus, UNHCR has adapted its own mandate to address this reality, shifting from legal protection to providing assistance to refugees in camps.

Internally displaced persons—people forced to move or relocate within their own country due to violence, human rights violations, development projects, or natural disasters (but not poverty or unemployment)—are not considered refugees under the convention. They present particular challenges since they remain within the boundaries of ostensibly sovereign states and, hence, are subject to domestic jurisdiction. The largest numbers of IDPs are found in Syria, Colombia, Iraq, Sudan, and the DRC, with more than 2 million in each state. Their numbers have increased dramatically because of changes in the nature of warfare, ethnic cleansing, and more accurate data. There was a surge of 4.2 million in the first half of 2015 alone as a result of increased armed conflict in Yemen, Ukraine, Nigeria, and elsewhere.[62]

Until the late 1990s, there was no international legal basis for providing assistance to IDPs. As a result of the work of two individuals, Roberta Cohen and Francis Deng, in framing the idea of protection for IDPs and bringing attention to the issue, the 2005 World Summit endorsed the Guiding Principles on Internal Displacement, which affirm that national governments have primary responsibility for protection and assistance but that international assistance to IDPs is not to be considered interference in a state's internal affairs.[63]

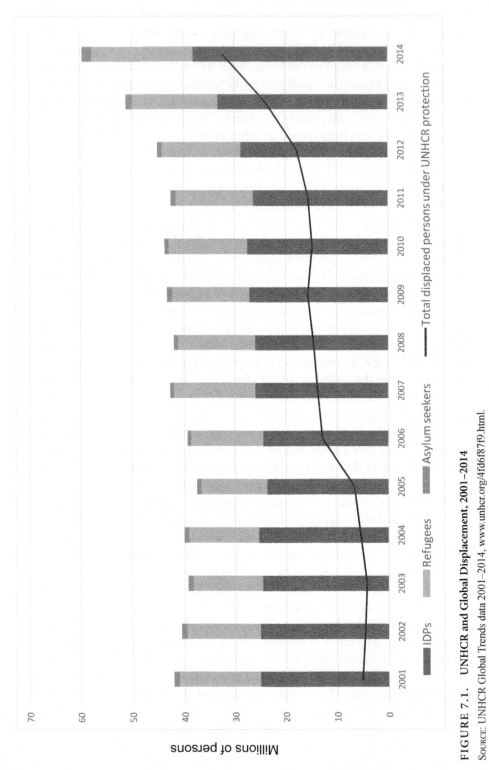

FIGURE 7.1.   UNHCR and Global Displacement, 2001–2014

Source: UNHCR Global Trends data 2001–2014, www.unhcr.org/4fd6f87f9.html.

Even before 2005, however, UNHCR had gradually taken on responsibility for assisting a significant portion of IDPs worldwide and the UN had established a system of appointing different UN agencies, including the WFP, UNICEF, and UNESCO, as leads in various areas of humanitarian action such as supplying food, schooling for children, housing, and health care. UNHCR retains the overall responsibility because of its role in registering all refugees and displaced persons. There are also a number of NGOs such as the ICRC and Doctors Without Borders that are active in serving refugees, IDPs, and other migrants. The funding, however, for all UN humanitarian agencies and most NGOs dealing with the current crisis falls well short of needs, leading the WFP to cut food rations to 1.6 million Syrian refugees in late 2015, for example.

The total number of migrants in the world is estimated to be over 200 million, dwarfing the numbers of refugees and IDPs. Currently, there is "no formal or coherent multilateral institutional framework regulating states' responses to international migration" beyond the 1951 refugee convention and its 1967 protocol; "there is no UN Migration Organization and no international migration regime."[64] There is the International Organization for Migration (IOM), but it is not part of the UN system. It was established in 1949 to facilitate settlement of the displaced in Europe after World War II and now operates in various parts of the world providing a range of services in refugee, migrant, and disaster relief camps and tracking migration trends. There is no treaty, convention, or statute, however, to give it a clear, normative mandate.

Many factors can prompt people to migrate. A major challenge going forward will be dealing with those who are environmental migrants—forced or choosing to move from their places of origin due to multiple sudden or long-term changes to their local ecosystems, such as disruption of seasonal weather patterns, sea level rise, drought, and desertification. Climate-related migration threatens the economic stability, security, and social stability of both rural and urban areas and of low-lying island states worldwide. The complex interconnectedness between climatic variables, violence, and conflict has contributed to the massive increase in migrants of all types, including refugees and IDPs. A 2015 study, for example, cited drought worsened by climate change as a contributing factor in the Syrian civil war.[65]

In short, environmental change constitutes a significant threat to human security and is expected to become a significant driver of human migration, according to the IPCC's fifth assessment report, published in 2014.[66] Estimates of the number of persons who will be displaced as a result of climate change–induced disasters over the next twenty-five years range from 20 million to 1 billion.[67] Human beings have proven able to adapt to environmental changes throughout history. Yet climate change disproportionately affects those in the poorest regions of the world.

The term "environmental refugee" was first coined by Lester Brown in 1976 and has been used loosely since then, but it has no legal standing.[68] Referring to the 1951 convention's definition of a refugee, Robert McLeman notes, "The environment does not persecute; only humans are capable of this and so people made stateless by MSLR [mean sea-level rise] or by any other effects of climate change are by definition *not* refugees under international law."[69] He further notes that the Guiding Principles on Internal Displacement do make reference to persons displaced by "natural or human-made disasters" in describing those who have a right to protection and assistance, although there is no legal obligation imposed by the document.[70] The legal status of citizens of small island nations that become uninhabitable as a result of sea-level rise, he adds, does not necessarily render them stateless (there are currently 10 million stateless persons, including the Rohingya in Myanmar, who are denied citizenship despite having resided there for generations), but it does create a new way of becoming stateless. In short, it is not always possible to distinguish forced migration from voluntary migration. There is also no agreement whether environmental migration should be considered a form of forced displacement.

From the outset of the IPCC's work in the late 1980s and the UNFCCC's conclusion in the early 1990s, migration has been treated as one of the possible outcomes of climatic events and changes. The 2010 Cancun Agreement by the UNFCCC Conference of Parties further mentions migration and displacement in the context of adaptation and calls for "measures to enhance understanding, coordination and cooperation . . . at the national, regional and international levels."[71] The 2015 COP21 final agreement merely acknowledged the adverse impact climate change will have on migration patterns and called for international advisory groups to recommend ways "to avert, minimize and address" such displacement.[72] But as McLeman notes, "Just as cultural, economic, environmental, political, and social factors operating at macro-, meso-, and micro-scales affect migration options, decisions, and behavior . . . they also affect adaptation options, decisions, and behavior."[73] Some adaptive measures have been taken by small island states, some by urban coastal cities and regional authorities, and others by individuals and groups, but very limited attention has been paid within the UN system to these issues.

In 2015, UNHCR has more than 9,300 staff operating in 123 countries to provide protection and assistance to refugees, returnees, internally displaced persons, and stateless persons. The handling of the situation is different in each country; UNHCR works with many partners, including other UN agencies and IGOs, NGOs, and local groups, but generally it serves as the lead agency because of its responsibility for registering all persons. In many refugee and IDP situations, UNHCR has constructed and maintains refugee camps (more than twenty, for example, in Turkey alone to handle Syrian refugees, yet these serve only about 30 percent of the refugees). In addition to the registration of refugees, the tasks include the provision of shelter, food, education, health care, clean water, sanitation, translation, security, social activities, assistance and advice on asylum applications, and counseling. Long-term refugee camps such as Dadaab in Kenya, founded in 1992 to serve refugees fleeing Somalia's civil war, tend to become small (and not-so-small) cities, with residents creating small businesses, rudimentary governance, radio stations, and hospitals. Some countries such as Lebanon, however, have refused to permit the construction of camps, forcing all refugees to shelter with family or friends, or wherever else they can find accommodation. UNHCR also assists people who return home, arranging transport and giving returnees assistance packages. It is involved in local integration or reintegration programs as well. With the current crisis, funding is a critical issue, as voluntary contributions supported only 40 percent of the 2015 budget.[74]

Well before the current crisis, there was recognition within the UN of the need for a better international institutional framework for governing migration, including refugees. The issue was raised at the 1994 International Conference on Population and Development in Cairo, following which Secretary-General Kofi Annan invited Michael Doyle to examine the then existing institutions. Doyle's 2002 report led to the creation of the Global Commission on International Migration, which in turn led to the appointment of an SRSG on Migration and Development and the Global Forum on Migration and Development, which includes seventeen UN agencies plus the IOM. A crisis such as that in 2015, however, demands quick responses, and as the inability of the EU member states to agree on cooperative action demonstrated, IGOs are rarely good at being flexible and nimble even when the lives and security of thousands of human beings are at stake, and especially when cooperation requires opening states' borders and communities to welcome refugees, asylum seekers, and migrants.

DILEMMAS IN HUMAN SECURITY

Environmental degradation, pandemics, and natural disasters are only three of many human security issues. Extreme poverty, physical insecurity, and weak states are among other threats to human security. The growth in numbers of refugees and migrants worldwide is just a reflection of these various causes of human insecurity. The disparities evident in a country such as Haiti, for example, have critical ramifications, as a UN panel warned several months before the September 11, 2001, attacks: "In the global village, someone else's poverty very soon becomes one's own problem: of lack of markets for one's products, illegal immigration, pollution, contagious disease, insecurity, fanaticism, terrorism."[75] Because they represent new needs for governance that cut across traditional ways of defining issues, challenge state sovereignty, and require leadership, human security issues pose major dilemmas for the United Nations system.

Dilemma 1: Needs for Governance Versus the UN's Weakness

Human security issues are now widely accepted as a permanent part of the UN's agenda, though framing environmental degradation and health as human security issues has occurred only since the mid-1990s. Institutionalization, however, has tended to be ad hoc and piecemeal, often with little thought to how coordination was to occur. There is a perennial shortage of funds to tackle the governance challenges posed by human security issues. Should there be greater centralization of these international activities under UN authority, or is a more decentralized approach more effective? How much emphasis should be put on public-private partnerships, which are now filling part of the gap between inadequate member country contributions and funding needs?

The debate over environmental governance exemplifies this dilemma. On one side are those who argue for the greater centralization of environmental institutions through a world or global environmental organization. They note that often there are multiple institutions within a given issue area, addressing different aspects of a problem or different types of solutions. The result is overlapping mandates, too many meetings, and competition for scarce resources. They see a single global organization also as a remedy for UNEP's weak mandate, insufficient powers, and inadequate resources.[76] On the other side are those who suggest that restructuring or creating a new architecture will divert attention from the major institutional and policy issues, including confusion over the norm of sustainable development and the challenge of integrating nonstate actors and civil society into the governance process. In all likelihood, the only suitable approach to international environmental issues is a multilevel one with a wide variety of partnerships.[77] On the issue of global warming, clearly the latter approach is ascendant.

The UN and various specialized agencies play valuable roles in dealing with human security issues, but their weaknesses as institutions mean they may not be able to accomplish the tasks they are mandated to address, as WHO's slow response to the Ebola epidemic illustrates. And in a case such as migration, there may be no UN agency. Whether the issue is the environment, health, or the multiple human security issues illustrated by the refugee and migration crisis, decentralized approaches and partnerships among global, regional, national, and local entities, both public and private, with or without the UN, are the modus operandi for global governance in the future.

Dilemma 2: Sovereignty Versus Challenges to Sovereignty

Human security issues are boundary-spanning issues because epidemics, people, and pollution do not stop at state borders. As a result, these issues and responses to them challenge state sovereignty. That challenge is just as fundamental as it is with human rights issues and humanitarian intervention. States, quite predictably, continue to be wary of such challenges, just as they have resisted interference in their domestic affairs on other issues. Although the hard shell of sovereignty has been breached to some extent, it has not yet been fully broken, and the tension remains. The Ebola epidemic illustrates the necessity of gathering all possible information on infectious disease despite the reluctance of governments to admit there is a problem or to cooperate with WHO to provide data. Ozone depletion and climate change illustrate the potential for cooperation when there is shared recognition of a problem and a willingness to deal with it, including providing assistance to developing countries in making necessary adjustments. Climate change also illustrates the difficulties of coming to an agreement on addressing a problem whose effects take a long time to be felt and whose causes are linked to the very foundations of economic growth. The refugee and migration crisis challenges states' authority to define citizenship and control who enters and may reside in their territory. Solutions to the crisis will require enhancing existing international law and securing states' cooperation in accepting refugees and migrants. These cases also illustrate the variety of factors, including a powerful state, that can block action. And in places where state capacity is weak, such as Liberia, Sierra Leone, and Guinea, UN agencies, international donors, and NGOs have to work to strengthen it if the threats to human security are to be addressed.

Dilemma 3: The Need for Leadership

For action to occur, leaders must seize an issue, publicize it, mobilize constituencies, forge potential solutions, and work for implementation. On human security issues, this has often come from among the handful of states such as Japan and Canada that have made human security an integral part of their foreign policy or from a group of states such as those that ratified the Kyoto Protocol and forged ahead with its implementation even without the participation of the United States. It can come from major powers such as the United States and China agreeing to take steps to curb carbon emissions, thereby setting an example for both developed and developing nations. Leadership can also come (or fail to come) from the UN secretary-general, the executive director of UNEP, the director-general of WHO, an ambassador such as Richard Holbrooke, who convened the first UN Security Council session on the threat of HIV/AIDS, or even prominent individuals such as Bill Gates, who helped form a coalition of wealthy business leaders to fund green energy.

Given the wide recognition of threats to the environment and human security now, no one state or one international organization (even the UN) is apt to be in the lead on all issues. Nonstate actors of various kinds are important partners in addressing these issues. Commitments of governmental funding are important, but private foundations such as the Bill and Melinda Gates Foundation have shown how much can be done with private initiative.

Dilemma 4: The Need for Inclusiveness

In 2013 Ban Ki-moon declared, "You cannot end poverty without empowering women and girls." He went on to call for a broader level of participation: "We need traditional partners, like governments and non-governmental organizations. But we also need academics, businesses, philanthropists and others to help end poverty, promote development and establish peace." Many groups are not included in UN policy processes, however, and continue to be marginalized. These claims were prominent in the Rio Plus 20 conference as well as at the Paris conference in 2015. Generally, women are underrepresented at all levels of decisionmaking on climate change, which limits their ability to contribute and implement solutions.[78] Yet at the same time that many argue for greater participation, there are those who find that too much inclusiveness may actually dilute progress and weaken policy commitments. The challenge for the UN is to maintain legitimacy and access for civil society, NGOs, and the marginalized in its processes and, at the same time, not alienate key states and centers of power that are essential to promoting human security. For, despite all its shortcomings, the UN remains central to these efforts.

The challenges posed by human security issues reinforce what we have seen with respect to peace and security issues, economic development, and human rights, namely, that reform of the UN system is imperative. When has the UN been successful? When has it failed? What can we learn from those experiences? It is to that topic we now turn.

NOTES

1. Thomas G. Weiss, David P. Forsythe, and Roger A. Coate, *The United Nations and Changing World Politics*, 4th ed. (Boulder, CO: Westview Press, 2004), 278.

2. Mark Leon Goldberg, "El Nino + ISIS: Why the UN Is Preparing for the Toughest Year Ever," *UN Dispatch*, December 8, 2015.

3. See, for example, Roland Paris, "Human Security: Paradigm Shift or Hot Air?" *International Security* 26, no. 2 (2001): 87–102.

4. See International Institute for Sustainable Development, "UNGA Debates Role of Human Security in Post-2015 Agenda," June 18, 2014, http://sd.iisd.org/news/unga-debates -role-of-human-security-in-post-2015-agenda.

5. Richard Jolly, Louis Emmerij, and Thomas G. Weiss, *The Power of UN Ideas: Lessons from the First 60 Years* (New York: United Nations Intellectual History Project, 2005), 34.

6. Sadako Ogata and Johan Cels, "Human Security: Protecting and Empowering the People," *Global Governance* 9, no. 3 (2003): 275. Sadako Ogata was cochair of the Commission on Human Security and former UN high commissioner for refugees. Johan Cels was the commission's project coordinator for conflict.

7. Edward Newman, "Human Security and Constructivism," *International Studies Perspectives* 2, no. 3 (2001): 241. For a somewhat different approach to the link between environmental degradation and state security, see Thomas Homer-Dixon, *Environment, Scarcity, and Violence*, 2nd ed. (Princeton: Princeton University Press, 1999). Also see Michael T. Klare, *The New Landscape of Global Conflict* (New York: Metropolitan/Owl Books, 2001).

8. Karen T. Litfin, "Constructing Environmental Security and Ecological Interdependence," *Global Governance* 5, no. 3 (1999): 364.

9. See Rachel Carson, *Silent Spring* (Boston: Houghton Mifflin, 1962); and Garrett Hardin, "The Tragedy of the Commons," *Science* 162 (December 13, 1968): 1243–1248.

10. Craig N. Murphy, "The United Nations Capacity to Promote Sustainable Development: The Lessons of a Year That 'Eludes All Facile Judgment,'" in *The State of the United Nations: 1992*, ed. Albert Legault, Craig N. Murphy, and W. B. Ofuatey-Kodjoe, ACUNS Reports and Papers no. 3 (Academic Council on the United Nations System, 1993), 60.

11. Karin Bäckstrand and Mikael Kylsäter, "Old Wine in New Bottles? The Legitimation and Delegitimation of UN Public-Private Partnerships for Sustainable Development from the Johannesburg Summit to the Rio+20 Summit," *Globalizations* 11, no. 3 (2014): 331.

12. Daniel C. Esty, "A Term's Limits," *Foreign Policy* 126 (September–October 2001): 74.

13. Jared Diamond, *Collapse: How Societies Choose to Fail or Collapse* (New York: Penguin, 2005).

14. "Statement at Closing of Rio+20, UN Conference on Sustainable Development," UN News Center, 22 June 2012. http://www.un.org/apps/news/infocus/sgspeeches/search_full .asp?statID=1584

15. Maria Ivanova, "The Contested Legacy of Rio + 20," *Global Environmental Politics* 13, no. 4 (2013): 4.

16. Tom Bigg, "Five Things We've Learnt from Rio+20," IIED, July 3, 2012, www.iied.org /five-things-we-ve-learnt-rio20?utm.

17. Brendan Montague, "Analysis: Rio+20—Epic Failure," June 22, 2012, www.thebureau investigates.com/2012/06/22/analysis-rio-20-epic-fail.

18. John Vidal, "Rio+20: Reasons to Be Cheerful," *The Guardian*, June 27, 2012.

19. Litfin, "Constructing Environmental Security and Ecological Interdependence," 367.

20. Maria Ivanova, "UNEP in Global Environmental Governance: Design, Leadership, and Location," *Global Environmental Politics* 10, no. 1 (2010): 30–59.

21. UNEP, "United Nations Environment Programme Upgraded to Universal Membership Following Rio+20 Summit," www.unep.org/newscentre/default.aspx?Document ID+2700&ArticleID=9363.

22. Steffen Bauer, "The Secretariat of the United Nations Environment Programme: Tangled Up in Blue," in *Managers of Global Change: The Influence of International Environmental*

Bureaucracies, ed. Frank Biermann and Bernd Siebenhüner (Cambridge, MA: MIT Press, 2009), 185.

23. Elizabeth R. DeSombre, *Global Environmental Institutions* (London: Routledge, 2006), 14–20.

24. Richard Elliot Benedick, *Ozone Diplomacy: New Directions in Safeguarding the Planet,* enlarged ed. (Cambridge, MA: Harvard University Press, 1998).

25. See Bauer, "The Secretariat of the United Nations Environment Programme."

26. DeSombre, *Global Environmental Institutions,* 34.

27. Ivanova, "The Contested Legacy of Rio+20."

28. Catherine E. Weaver, *Hypocrisy Trap: The World Bank and the Poverty of Reform* (Princeton: Princeton University Press, 2008), 21, 24.

29. Bruce Rich, *Foreclosing the Future: The World Bank and the Politics of Environmental Destruction* (Washington, DC: Island Press, 2013).

30. Mark T. Buntaine and Bradley C. Parks, "When Do Environmentally Focused Assistance Projects Achieve Their Objectives? Evidence from World Bank Post-Project Evaluations," *Global Environmental Politics* 13, no. 2 (2013): 77.

31. Intergovernmental Panel on Climate Change, *Climate Change 2013: The Physical Science Basis, Working Group I Contribution to the Fifth Assessment Report, Summary for Policymakers,* ed. Thomas Stocker et al., www.climatechange2013.org.

32. Benedick, *Ozone Diplomacy.*

33. See Lorraine Elliott, "Climate Diplomacy: Two Steps Forward, One Step Back," in *The Oxford Handbook of Modern Diplomacy,* ed. Andrew Cooper, Jorge Heine, and Ramesh Thakur (New York: Oxford University Press, 2013), 848.

34. Michael A. Levi, quoted in John M. Broder, "Climate Talks End with Modest Deal on Emissions," *New York Times,* December 11, 2010.

35. Steffen Bauer, "Does Bureaucracy Really Matter? The Authority of Intergovernmental Treaty Secretariats in Global Environmental Politics," *Global Environmental Politics* 6, no. 1 (2006): 43–44.

36. Steffen Bauer, "The Ozone Secretariat: The Good Shephard of Ozone Politics," in *Managers of Global Change: The Influence of International Environmental Bureaucracies,* ed. Frank Biermann and Bernd Siebenhüner (Cambridge, MA: MIT Press, 2009), 225–241.

37. Robert O. Keohane and David G. Victor, "The Regime Complex for Climate Change," *Perspectives on Politics* 9, no. 1 (2011): 20.

38. UNEP, "Ozone Layer on Track to Recovery: Success Story Should Encourage Action on Climate," www.unep.org/newscentre/default.aspx?Document ID=2796&ArticleID=10978.

39. Quoted in Dane Warren, "Climate Change and International Peace and Security: Possible Roles for the U.N. Security Council in Addressing Climate Change," Columbia Law School, Sabin Center for Climate Change Law, July 2015.

40. Ibid.

41. The phrase "There is no Planet B" was used by US secretary of state John Kerry in remarks in February 2015, but has also been used by UNSG Ban Ki-moon and many others for much longer.

42. Coral Davenport, "The Marshall Islands Are Disappearing," *New York Times,* December 1, 2015.

43. Cited in Ben Brumfield and Michael Pearson, "COP21 Climate Change Summit: 'Never Have the Stakes Been So High,'" CNN.com, November 30, 2015.

44. Ibid.

45. Coral Davenport, "Climate Negotiators Face Hurdles on Key Issues as Deadline Looms," *New York Times*, December 9, 2015.

46. Davenport, "Stung by Failure," A8.

47. Bruce Jones and Adele Morris, "Beyond the Paris Agreement," *PlanetPolicy* blog, The Brookings Institution, December 14, 2015.

48. Coral Davenport, "In France, Consensus on a Need to Lower Carbon Emissions," *New York Times*, December 13, 2015.

49. Chris Mooney, "Scientists Criticize Draft Climate Agreement," *Washington Post*, December 12, 2015.

50. World Health Organization, *Macroeconomics and Health: Investing in Health for Economic Development, Report of the Commission on Macroeconomics and Health* (Geneva: World Health Organization, 2001), www.who.int/macrohealth/documents/en. For an extended treatment on health and security, see Andrew T. Price-Smith, *Contagion and Chaos: Disease, Ecology, and National Security in the Era of Globalization* (Cambridge, MA: MIT Press, 2009).

51. See "Goal 3: Ensure Healthy Lives and Promote Well-Being for All at All Ages," UN Sustainable Development Goals, www.un.org/sustainabledevelopment/health.

52. See Mark W. Zacher and Tania J. Keefe, *The Politics of Global Health Governance: United by Contagion* (New York: Palgrave Macmillan, 2008).

53. Gian Luca Burci and Jakob Quirin, "Ebola, WHO, and the United Nations: Convergence of Global Public Health and International Peace and Security," *ASIL Insights* 18, no. 25 (November 14, 2014).

54. WHO, "WHO Convenes Industry Leaders and Key Partners to Discuss Trials and Production of Ebola Vaccine," news release, October 24, 2014, www.who.int/mediacentre/news/releases/2014/ebola-vaccines-production/en.

55. Laurie Garrett, "Ebola's Lessons," *Foreign Affairs* 94, no. 5 (2015): 97.

56. Ibid., 80–107.

57. Ibid., 104.

58. Ibid., 102–107. Among various reports, see Suerie Moon et al., "Will Ebola Change the Game? Ten Essential Reforms Before the Next Pandemic. The Report of the Harvard-LSHTM Independent Panel on the Global Response to Ebola," *The Lancet* 386, no. 10009 (2015): 2204–2221; World Health Organization, "Report of the Ebola Interim Assessment Panel," July 2015, 5, www.who.int/csr/resources/publications/ebola/report-by-panel.pdf?ua=1.

59. UNHCR, *World at War: UNHCR Global Trends: Forced Displacement in 2014* (2015), www.unhcr.org/cgi-bin/texis/vtx/home/opendocPDFViewer.html?docid=556725e69.

60. A valuable source of information on UNHCR is Gil Loescher, Alexander Betts, and James Milner, *The United Nations High Commission for Refugees (UNHCR): The Politics and Practice of Refugee Protection into the Twenty-First Century* (New York: Routledge, 2008).

61. Gil Loescher and James Milner, "UNHCR and the Global Governance of Refugees," in *Global Migration Governance*, ed. Alexander Betts (Oxford: Oxford University Press, 2011), 191–192.

62. Internal Displacement Monitoring Centre, www.internal-displacement.org/global -figures.

63. See Khalid Koser, "Internally Displaced Persons," in *Global Migration Governance*, ed. Alexander Betts (Oxford: Oxford University Press, 2011), 210–223.

64. Alexander Betts, "Introduction: Global Migration Governance," in *Global Migration Governance*, ed. Alexander Betts (Oxford: Oxford University Press, 2011), 1–33.

65. Henry Fountain, "Researchers Link Syrian Conflict to a Drought Made Worse by Climate Change," *New York Times*, March 2, 2015.

66. Intergovernmental Panel on Climate Change, *Climate Change 2013: The Physical Science Basis, Working Group I Contribution to the Fifth Assessment Report, Summary for Policymakers*, www.ipcc.ch/pdf/assessment-report/ar5/wg1/WGIAR5_SPM_brochure_en.pdf.

67. Franck Laczko and Christine Aghazarm, eds., *Migration, Environment, and Climate Change: Assessing the Evidence* (Geneva: International Organization on Migration, 2009), 9.

68. Lester Brown, P. McGrath, and B. Stokes, "Twenty-Two Dimensions of the Population Problem," Worldwatch Paper no. 5, Worldwatch Institute, Washington, DC, 1976.

69. Robert A. McLeman, *Climate and Human Migration: Past Experiences, Future Challenges* (New York: Cambridge University Press, 2014), 204.

70. Ibid., 196.

71. UNFCCC Conference of Parties, Cancun II (2010), Section II, quoted in McLeman, *Climate and Human Migration*, 53.

72. Sewell Chan, "Global Warming's Role in Mass Migration Is Addressed," *New York Times*, December 13, 2015.

73. McLeman, *Climate and Human Migration*, 59.

74. See UNHCR, "Needs and Funding Requirements, 2015–2016," www.unhcr.org/564 da0e20.html.

75. United Nations General Assembly, *Report of the High-Level Panel on Financing for Development Appointed by the United Nations Secretary-General*, 55th Session, Agenda Item 101, June 26, 2001, A/55/1000, 3, www.un.org/esa/ffd/a55-1000.pdf.

76. Frank Biermann, "The Case for a World Environment Organization," *Environment* 42, no. 9 (2000): 22–31. See also Frank Biermann and Steffen Bauer, ed., *A World Environment Organization* (Aldershot, UK: Ashgate, 2005).

77. See Adil Najam, "The Case Against a New International Environmental Organization," *Global Governance* 9, no. 3 (2003): 367–384.

78. United Nations Framework on Climate Change, "Gender and Climate Change," available at http://unfccc.int/gender_and_climate_change/items/7537txt.php#connection.

8

〜

Is There a Future for the United Nations?

The United Nations today leads what seems at times like a double life. Pundits criticize it for not solving all the world's ills, yet people around the world are asking it to do more, in more places, than ever before.

—*Secretary-General Ban Ki-moon,*
Sydney Morning Herald, *December 31, 2010*

Secretary-General Ban Ki-moon's words echo a refrain often heard from supporters of the UN: "If the UN did not exist, a similar institution would have to be created." In this final chapter, we explore some of the ways in which the UN has made a difference over more than seventy years and identify areas where it has failed. We examine factors that have shaped its successes and failures and the question of whether, in fact, the UN can be reformed to play an even more vigorous role in global governance.

As former UN secretary-general Kofi Annan wrote in reflecting on his experience, "To say the world is interdependent had become the worst kind of cliché. . . . True in the literal sense, but unable to generate the kinds of multilateral engagement befitting a world where no threat was limited to one country or region."[1] The UN may have more reach than any other IGO, but that has never meant that it has had the resources, authority, competence, and coordination capabilities needed to address the many challenges it has faced.

DOES THE UN MAKE A DIFFERENCE?

You might imagine in a book on the UN that the automatic, unequivocal answer to this question would be "of course." If you were to pick up literature from the UN's Department of Public Information, you would find it filled with a list of UN achievements over the years, including the positioning of peacekeepers along fragile borders in the Middle East and Cyprus, energizing the voices of newly independent colonies on behalf of self-determination and economic development, pushing an international human rights agenda for marginalized peoples, and improving global health through the WHO's eradication of smallpox and UNAIDS partnerships. Some books that dwell on the UN's achievements also note its shortcomings, much as we have. Still others are critiques of the UN or even polemics that emphasize that the institution is overtly politicized, criticizing states such as Israel and not others or responding to threats to the peace emanating from smaller states while neglecting those posed by the P-5. These critics point to the UN's failures: its inability to halt genocides, to stop weapons proliferation, and to close the gap between the rich and the poor. For some American pundits, the only logical response is for the United States to pull out and withdraw its support.

In weighing these questions of success and failure, it is important to acknowledge that the world of the twenty-first century is very different from the world of 1945. The scale and nature of today's problems go far beyond those envisioned by the UN's founders. The speed of changes, from the growing effects of climate change and numbers of refugees and migrants flooding into Europe in 2015 to the rapid spread of Ebola and the sudden emergence of ISIS in 2014, demand new ways of thinking as well as timely action. UN agencies, like bureaucracies everywhere, are not geared to handling rapid change and generating new thinking. They tend to be "silos"—created to deal with a particular category of problems, but now operating in a world of interconnected and interdependent problems with far fewer resources at hand.

Yet before examining what the UN can and cannot do, we must return to the notion that there is not just one UN but three UNs, each of which plays and has played a role in shaping what the UN does. As three experts put it, there is "the UN of governments, the UN of staff members, and the UN of closely associated NGOs, experts, and consultants."[2] It is the third UN that has been most neglected by scholars, diplomats, and governments because of the long-standing state-centric focus of international relations. And it is the third UN that has grown immensely in recent years, with NGOs and civil society organizations taking active roles in shaping new norms and policies and challenging notions of representation, accountability, and legitimacy; with for-profit corporations being drawn into UN activities with the establishment of the UN Global Compact;

and with foundations such as the Gates Foundation now funding a significant portion of global health needs. All three UNs have influenced what the UN has and has not been able to do over the years, although it is admittedly difficult to differentiate between them in the area of one of the UN's major accomplishments, the development of new ideas.

Developing New Ideas

Over the decade 1999–2009, the United Nations Intellectual History Project (UNIHP) produced fifteen books and seventy-nine in-depth oral history interviews that trace and document the history of key ideas and concepts about security and economic and social development within the UN system. Thanks to UNIHP, we have important insights into those areas where the UN has had a major impact. The final volume, *UN Ideas That Changed the World*, brings together the wealth of insights that emerged from the project. The authors conclude that ideas are among the most significant contributions the UN has made to the world and to human progress. And all three UNs have played various roles "collectively . . . sometimes in isolation and sometimes together or in parallel" in generating ideas, providing a forum for debate, giving ideas legitimacy, promoting adoption of ideas for policy, implementing or testing ideas and policies at the country level, generating resources for implementing ideas, monitoring their progress, and sometimes burying them.[3]

In the area of peace and security, the UN has advanced an idea that has proven to be of tactical importance to the UN's own role and has shown itself as flexible enough over time to encompass a variety of tasks. *Peacekeeping*—the idea that military personnel, police, and civilians from states acting on behalf of the international community, wearing the UN's blue berets, could insert themselves into conflict situations—represents an institutional innovation that was not explicit in the UN Charter. Peacekeepers can separate, disarm, and demobilize combatants; police cease-fires; and, in limited circumstances, even use more coercive measures under Chapter VII mandates to preserve international peace and security. They can protect aid workers, monitor human rights violations, undertake security sector reform, repatriate refugees, and provide interim civil administration. The idea has been implemented on six continents, using small to large contingents, some with pronounced effect and others deemed as mixed successes or even failures. Peacekeeping has become an integral part of the UN's approaches to addressing threats to peace and security, along with mediation, preventive diplomacy, and enforcement. As discussed in Chapter 4, however, the UN has now encountered serious problems of sexual abuse by some peacekeeping contingents that are jeopardizing the UN's and peacekeeping's reputations; this is compounded by the failure of the UN to take responsibility for the cholera epidemic in Haiti that has been traced to peacekeepers from Nepal.

The UN has also been instrumental in expanding the very concept of security from state security to *human security*. Humans, too, need to be secure in their own person, protected from violence, economic deprivation, poverty, infectious diseases, human rights violations by states, and environmental degradation. While it is governments' responsibility to provide for security within the state, some states may need assistance in controlling cross-border arms, human trafficking, and drug trafficking, and may need funding for economic development, monitoring disease, and adaptations to reverse or protect against environmental threats. In implementing the idea of human security, then, the UN can help states protect individuals and carry out the responsibilities of sovereignty.

Following from this, the UN legitimized the norm of states' *responsibility to protect* their own citizens, particularly from war crimes or crimes against humanity. This particular idea introduced a new interpretation of both state sovereignty and the obligations of the international community. As Edward Luck, the first assistant secretary-general for R2P (2008–2012), notes, "For all its ups and downs in practice, in political and normative terms the progress of R2P has been remarkably rapid, especially compared to other human rights and human protection norms. Among the member states, there are still questions about implementation—as well there should be—but not about the validity and legitimacy of the prevention and protection principles that lie at the heart of R2P. The level of understanding, not just acceptance, today is much deeper and much wider." But, Luck cautions, "knowing that we need to protect and knowing how to protect are two different things. . . . The credibility of norms can be gained only in the field and in the lives of the vulnerable."[4]

In the area of economic development, the UN has benefited from the creativity of innovative economists who have at one time or another been employed by the UN or served as consultants and who have contributed to key UN ideas. *Sustainability*, as enunciated in the Brundtland Report, clearly showed that economic development cannot occur without consideration of the future, resources cannot be exploited without assurance that there are not detrimental side effects, and resource uses need to be managed with an eye to future generations. As a result, the UN and other development institutions have attempted to weigh development needs against environmental imperatives. And with the approval of the SDGs in 2015, sustainability figures in the majority of the goals that are intended to serve as the focus of UN development-related operations until 2030.

Development has also been reconceived as *human development*. Introduced in the 1990s, this idea represented a sea change in thinking from traditional economic theory that measured development in terms of growth in a state's GNP over time and in comparison to that of other states. Instead, UNDP and some of the specialized agencies began to think of development in terms of how it affected people: their health, educational level, income, and overall well-being, and the differential effects of gender. Thinking about human development led to the MDGs, then the SDGs, and to concerted action to eliminate extreme poverty and improve human well-being.

Universalizing *human rights for all* represents a key normative idea where all three UNs share credit. NGOs, in particular, were instrumental in getting human rights provisions into the UN Charter, and they continue to play critical roles in the promotion and monitoring of human rights. As one noted scholar has said, "Among the most improbable developments of the previous hundred years or so is the spectacular rise of human rights to a position of prominence in world politics. This rise cuts across the grain of both the structure of world order and the 'realist' outlook of most political leaders acting on behalf of sovereign states."[5]

And in human rights, as well as in peace and security and development, new categories of individuals as well as groups have been recognized as needing protection, including the disappeared, migrants, indigenous peoples, and lesbian, gay, bisexual, and transgender (LGBT) persons. The UN system has devoted particular attention to enhancing the status and role of women, but the UN itself did not initiate these efforts—key states and NGOs played that role—and the League of Nations provided the first international forum for promoting women's rights. But as the founding director of UNIFEM has said, "The global women's movement would be lost or at least much weaker without the UN."[6] Indeed, the four UN-sponsored world women's conferences played a major role in the creation of the global women's movement. And countless UN resolutions "have forced . . . governments to be more accountable . . . showing that this is the way that governments should behave, or corporations should behave, or men should behave."[7] Another major achievement on the long road for gender equality was the creation of UN Women in 2010.

Developing ideas is, therefore, an important way in which the UN has made a difference, but ideas alone are inadequate. Furthermore, some ideas took hold, while others did not. The UN itself sometimes implemented ideas, sometimes buried them. What, then, are other ways in which the UN has made a difference?

Filling Knowledge Gaps, Gathering Data

In the early years, the UN played a key role in helping states gather basic data and measure outcomes. That data collection largely reflected the perspective and methods of liberal economists and dominant states. But as new ideas emerged, the data collected had to change. Just as critical as monitoring deaths and refugee flows from interstate wars is knowing death rates and displacements during civil wars and monitoring flows of those forcibly displaced by climate change. Did economic development projects really benefit everyone, as liberal economists anticipated? We did not know the answer until data were collected comparing women and men on various development indicators. We now have a variety of indicators and data that help us to provide numbers to assess the impact of new ideas, and also help us to set goals, another key UN contribution. Data gathering and reporting have been core elements of the MDG process, as they will be in the SDG process now under way.

Setting, Promoting, and Monitoring Goals

The UN is often criticized as a forum for empty rhetoric and hot air, for resolutions and declarations that make no difference. One of the surprising conclusions from the UNIHP is the importance of goal setting; indeed, setting targets for economic and social development is seen as a "singular UN achievement."[8] More than fifty economic and social goals in all, beginning with the First Development Decade in 1960 and including the most recent ones—the MDGs for poverty reduction and the SDGs—have been set, promoted, and monitored. Despite concerns, for example, that many of the MDGs would not be met by the deadline in 2015, as noted in Chapter 5, the final report showed that the proportion of people in dire poverty worldwide was more than halved ahead of the target year. The long list of human rights treaties negotiated under UN auspices established the normative foundation for global human rights and, hence, a set of goals of rights for all. The UN has established international machinery for their promotion through the OHCHR, as well as the Universal Periodic Review mechanism and treaty review processes for monitoring states' human rights records and the implementation of the various treaties. In the areas of arms control and counterterrorism, the UN has also set goals and provided assistance for both state and international monitoring. The IAEA plays a central role in the nuclear nonproliferation regime monitoring processes, as does the OPCW for chemical weapons. With the 2015 Paris climate change agreement, states agreed to five-year review cycles for their emission reduction targets. In short, "goals have also served over the years as a focus for mobilizing interests, especially the interests of NGOs, and for generating pressures for action."[9]

Agenda Setting: The UN's Value as a Forum

The value of the UN as a general forum, and particularly the General Assembly as a voice of the "peoples of the world," means that member states have used it to raise and act on new issues, thereby setting agendas for the UN itself, for other IGOs, for NGOs, and for states themselves. No one doubts the forum's value over time for promoting self-determination and decolonization in the 1950s and 1960s, calling attention to apartheid and pressuring South Africa to change over more than forty years, negotiating the comprehensive UN Convention on the Law of the Sea over nine years in the 1970s, recognizing the unique position of small island states in the climate change debate, or putting on the agenda the rights of the disabled, migrant workers, LGBT persons, and indigenous peoples. For more than forty years, the Palestinians have used the General Assembly and other UN agencies as forums to gain recognition of their existence and rights. In 2011, Palestine was admitted as a member of UNESCO, and in 2012, it was granted nonmember observer state status by the General Assembly—a de facto recognition of sovereignty. To be sure, in the eyes of some, the forum has been abused, as when it was used to repeatedly link Zionism with racism in General Assembly resolutions over many years. Still, it is valuable for the international community to have a place where issues can be raised, resolutions can be put forward, and consensus can be built or votes taken, both as a way to set agendas and to let off steam. The General Assembly's vote in 2015 calling for a more transparent process for selecting the next secretary-general illustrates well the frustration of a majority of UN member states with the stalled process of UN reform.

Partnerships

The UN's various organs, programs, and agencies increasingly work with a variety of partners to accomplish their objectives, making partnerships an important modus operandi. UN specialized agencies and programs not only work in tandem but also work with NGOs, local community groups, corporations, and foundations. The UN Joint Programme on HIV/AIDS, established in 1996, is a partnership of seven UN specialized agencies along with UNDP, WFP, national governments, corporations, religious organizations, grassroots groups, and NGOs to meet the multifaceted challenges of HIV/AIDS. It tracks the epidemic, monitors responses, distributes strategic information, mobilizes resources, and reaches out to diverse groups. It also illustrates that not all UN partnerships are effective: while it continues its work, it is supplemented by the independent Global Fund to Fight AIDS, Tuberculosis, and Malaria. And it underscores how the UN increasingly works with the private sector, including in improving labor and environmental policies (UN Global Compact, Green Energy Fund) and in tackling specific health threats (pharmaceutical companies and the Gates Foundation). Partnerships are essential for augmenting financial resources and marshaling expertise for global problem solving, for providing broader participation from donors, and for improving buy-in and, hence, legitimacy for recipient states and individuals.

Former UN secretary-general Kofi Annan, who initiated the Global Compact with corporations, asks, "Can it [the UN] confine itself, in the twenty-first century, to the role of coordinating action by States? . . . Is it not obliged, in order to fulfill the purposes of the Charter, to form partnerships with all these different actors? To listen to them, to guide them, and to urge them on?" As Thomas Weiss notes, "Such partnerships represent a new way to govern the world . . . that is underresearched and poorly understood, especially the role of transnational business."[10] In peace operations, the UN has also undertaken partnerships with regional and subregional organizations, especially the African Union, ECOWAS, the EU, and NATO, as well as with coalitions of the willing.

Yet as much as the UN has demonstrated how it has made a difference, history has also made evident what the UN cannot do. Identifying these lessons is critical to considering what changes are needed in UN operations and in the expectations of member states and UN supporters.

LESSONS ABOUT WHAT THE UN CANNOT DO

At its core, the UN remains a product of the state system, an IGO whose member states retain sovereignty and whose policy outcomes must reflect state agreement. As John Ruggie reminds us, "International organizations remain anchored in the state system. . . . Their role in actual enforcement remains tightly constrained by states."[11]

Enforcement

Referring to the UN, Thomas Weiss and Ramesh Thakur acknowledge that "no ways exist to enforce decisions and no mechanisms exist to compel states to comply with decisions."[12] Although that may sound extreme, the fact is most UN bodies can only make recommendations. Hence, as the same authors explain, "One of the main tactics used in the face of these constraints has been to embarrass those who do not comply. This tactic is used when UN secretariats or NGOs generate and publicize information and data about noncompliance."[13] In the human rights area, this tactic has been successful *if* it is accompanied by strong domestic measures for compliance, particularly in the form of NGO pressure. On other issues, however, publicly naming and shaming states for noncompliance may not yield the desired results. The practice will be tested in the years ahead with the implementation of the 2015 Paris climate change agreement.

The UN Security Council, under Chapter VII, can clearly authorize sanctions and direct, coercive military action if the P-5 concur (or do not exercise their vetoes). Although sanctions have been extensively used since the Cold War's end, there have been a number of key lessons learned, as discussed in Chapter 4. For one, comprehensive sanctions are not effective. Sanctions must be carefully targeted based on knowledge about the targeted country, key individuals, and groups; they must also be monitored and adjusted over time, and sanctions violators must be held accountable. It is also clear that each sanctions case is unique and prior experience is not necessarily a predictor of future outcomes. UN sanctions on Iran do appear to have been a factor in securing the 2015 agreement on its nuclear program, but sanctions have not worked with North Korea.

Military enforcement action is still rare, despite the greater use of Chapter VII authority in mandates for peace operations. Even if there is consensus on some type of enforcement, it may be for a relatively brief period of time, and member states may not back up that commitment with sufficient resources to ensure success. A clear lesson is that the UN must rely on major powers, a coalition of the willing, or NATO with its alliance capabilities for joint action. States are unwilling to provide the UN with the types of military resources necessary for major coercive action. And, as the Syrian civil war has tragically demonstrated, member states are also often reluctant to see the UN intervene in some situations. This particular failure has clearly damaged the UN's reputation and especially that of the Security Council. Too little attention has been given to precedents that may be set with UN authorized enforcement actions in the DRC and Mali that threaten to put peacekeepers at further risk and compromise the UN's ability to serve as an impartial broker, as discussed in Chapter 4.

Responding to Crises

As illustrated by the Ebola outbreak and the refugee/migration crisis, the UN system does not have a good track record in recent years in responding to emergencies. WHO has shown itself not to be the global health responder that it needs to be, and it is hobbled by bureaucratic and structural problems. UNHCR, WFP, and other parts of the UN humanitarian aid system are woefully underfunded to meet current needs, and there is no agency within the UN system (or outside) with a mandate to address larger migration issues.

Similarly, despite numerous calls over the years for the UN to create a rapid-reaction force to prevent the outbreak of armed conflict or secure an end to fighting pending deployment of a regular peacekeeping force, member states have failed to act on this except for where individual states have earmarked peacekeeping contingents. Multilateral military interventions, be they organized under the UN, NATO, or the EU, require time: time to get the consent of the P-5 in the case of the UN; time to organize the military units from member states; time to transport troops and equipment to the crisis area. A small UN rapid-reaction force could be designed for quick deployment, pending organization of a larger force. Boosting the UN's early-warning, intelligence-gathering, and analysis capabilities has long been promoted as a way of strengthening its ability to anticipate crises and undertake timely preventive diplomatic or other actions. Yet member states have been reluctant to permit this. So as Luck asserts, despite the UN's extensive field presence, "the United Nations has never been structured to do the kind of dynamic, candid, detailed, and layered cross-sectoral analysis of developments in states under stress that is needed to craft effective policy responses to early signs of trouble."[14]

Coordinating the Activities of a Variety of Agencies

As numerous UN staff and NGOs have remarked, "Everyone is for coordination, but nobody wants to be coordinated."[15] This has been a chronic problem, as seen in ECOSOC's coordination or lack of coordination of the multiple overlapping economic and social programs and agencies. It can also be seen in the problems of uncoordinated responses to complex humanitarian crises or the late and feeble responses to HIV/AIDS and Ebola. Weiss refers to the "spaghetti junction" of the UN organizational chart (see Figure 2.1) and suggests that it creates either "productive clashes over institutional turf and competition for resources, or paralysis. Both are less-than-optimal outcomes resulting from the structure of decentralized silos instead of more integrated, mutually reinforcing, and collaborative partnerships among the various moving parts of the United Nations."[16] Further evidence of the problems of coordination within the UN system come from looking at UN operations in developing countries, where there may be twenty or more different UN organizations with separate offices and staff—a problem that has been remedied only in a handful of cases by the creation of a single country representative, office, program, and fund. One small, encouraging sign came with the creation of UN Women, when four entities were merged—a rare occurrence at the UN.

Yet if the UN cannot coordinate itself, how can it participate effectively in broader partnerships involving regional organizations, NGOs, or the private sector that are requisite for addressing the challenges of the twenty-first century? Will it be able to form the partnerships so necessary to address the refugee/migration crisis or to achieve the SDGs? With these lessons of what the UN cannot do, is it possible to judge success and failure?

FACTORS IN UN SUCCESS AND FAILURE

How can we judge success and failure of the UN (or of any institution)? What criteria can be employed? What measures can be used? Did the UN meet the objectives of the founders as reflected in the Charter? Is the UN meeting the demands of the second decade of the twenty-first century? What frame of reference should we use—an individual program or a particular period of time? And for whom has the UN been a success or a failure—for dominant states, small states, or certain groups or individuals? For an institution with many moving parts, can we really measure success or failure as a whole, or should we evaluate particular parts? Although it is not up to us to set evaluation criteria, we can set forth some generalizations about the probability of success and failure.

First, if the UN's actions reflect consensus among member states and have financial backing from key donor states, corporations, or private foundations, then they have a greater likelihood of success. Second, if the relevant UN program or agency takes responsibility and seizes the initiative for an action, then there is a greater probability of success. Third, endorsement and support of professionals, outside experts, scholars, and NGOs—that is, the third UN—will increase the probability of success even more. Yet, given the size of the UN's diverse membership of sovereign member states, getting these conditions right is rare.

The UN's actions are more likely to lead to failure when they try to tackle an issue that, by institutional design, the founders did not intend. That includes having a strong role in international economic relations. If major powers oppose UN action, it will likely fail, as the case of Syria has so tragically demonstrated. Barring Security Council reform, P-5 power is ensured. Barring finding independent sources of funding, economically strong states will wield the power of the purse, leading to greater likelihood that their policies will be followed. If member states turn to new institutions and programs that bypass the UN, this will marginalize the UN and undermine its legitimacy as the primary global institution. States may do this because they do not approve of UN actions, because they anticipate weak UN performance, or because of the effects of the changing distribution of power. Or other global institutions will replace the UN because the demands of the twenty-first century may really outrun the capacity of the UN in any form.

CAN THE UN BE REFORMED?

Because the UN has rarely lived up to the full expectations of all member governments, its own staff, and its supporters as well as critics, the topic of reform has been what Mark Malloch Brown, former deputy secretary-general under Kofi Annan and former administrator of UNDP, calls "an occupational obsession."[17] This has been particularly true with regard to Security Council reform and the perception for many years that the council's makeup reflects a world long gone. As we discussed in Chapter 2, however, Security Council reform is only a small part of the puzzle, and although there has been no change in its makeup, there have been other changes in the Security Council's operation and many types of changes in the Secretariat and other parts of the first and second UN. There have been a host of reforms in peacekeeping since the early 1990s as well as in human rights institutions, as noted in earlier chapters.

To make more substantial reforms, Brown asserts, there is no alternative "to a real commitment by member states to a better UN. . . . Real reforms will require major concessions from powerful and weak countries alike. The intergovernmental gridlock between the big contributors and the rest of the membership concerning governance and voting is the core dysfunction. To overcome it, both sides would have to rise above their own current sense of entrenched rights and privileges and find a grand bargain to allow a new, more realistic governance model for the UN."[18]

What will it take to break the deadlock and change the political equation for a major overhaul of the UN? Will it take some type of international crisis? In Brown's view: "When politicians reach for a solution for climate change or a war and cannot find it, this absence will build the case for a better UN."[19] Indeed, it took the outbreak of World War II to make possible the creation of the UN as a replacement for the League of Nations—a stronger League, if you will. Brown adds, "Until the sense of crisis at the UN is strong enough to make governments let go of their own agendas, there cannot be the kind of cathartic recommitment and renewal of the UN proper that is required."[20] So what might such a crisis look like? The expansion of ISIS as a protostate controlling territory in North, East, and West Africa in addition to the Middle East? An environmental catastrophe? A global recession or depression greater than the financial meltdown in 2008? The outbreak of war in the Middle East involving Iran, Israel, Saudi Arabia, Turkey, Russia, the United States, and others, or perhaps a war in Northeast Asia involving North and South Korea, Japan, the United States, and China?

To undertake major reform of the UN will require member states—both powerful and weak—to be willing to make major concessions. They will need to create a new system of representation in the Security Council and other bodies that not only accommodates today's emerging powers but also is flexible enough to adjust to future power shifts. They will have to overcome their reluctance to bring modern management principles and procedures into the UN Secretariat, empower the secretary-general to exercise more authority, and establish a more open, competitive process for selecting the secretary-general. They will need to devise a means for the third UN—civil society, NGOs, the private sector—to be involved in the work of the organization, recognizing the major contributions (including financial resources) to be gained and the value of inclusiveness. Or, one might ask, will they scrap the UN itself and create an entirely new institution for global governance?

LINKING THE UN TO GLOBAL GOVERNANCE

The fact is that the UN must reform to meet the demands for governance and the challenges of diminished sovereignty, to find states and coalitions able and willing to lead, and to establish partnerships that provide the human and financial resources required to address contemporary global problems. Unless those dilemmas are addressed, the UN will become increasingly irrelevant. Global governance—rather, pieces of global governance to manage a wide variety of international issues and problems—is a reality, with many different actors, including the UN, having authority, resources, and processes in place. Yet none of these other actors, be they regional security organizations, the G-20, NGOs, various types of networks, public-private partnerships, MNCs, or even powerful states, can begin to replace the UN in its entirety. The real question for the UN is whether it will be a central player or a marginal one in global governance in the twenty-first century.

NOTES

1. Kofi Annan, *Interventions: A Life in War and Peace* (New York: Penguin, 2012), 144.

2. Richard Jolly, Louis Emmerij, and Thomas G. Weiss, *UN Ideas That Changed the World* (Bloomington: Indiana University Press, 2009), 32–33.

3. Ibid., 34–35.

4. Edward C. Luck, "R2P at Ten: A New Mindset for a New Era?" *Global Governance* 21, no. 4 (2015): 500–501.

5. Quoted in Thomas G. Weiss, "The John W. Holmes Lecture: Reinvigorating the International Civil Service," *Global Governance* 16, no. 1 (2010): 52.

6. Jolly, Emmerij, and Weiss, *UN Ideas That Changed the World,* 73.

7. Ibid., 75.

8. Ibid., 43.

9. Ibid., 44.

10. Thomas G. Weiss, *Governing the World? Addressing "Problems Without Passports"* (Boulder, CO: Paradigm, 2014), 85.

11. John Gerard Ruggie, foreword to *Global Governance and the UN: An Unfinished Journey,* by Thomas G. Weiss and Ramesh Thakur (Bloomington: Indiana University Press, 2010), xvii.

12. Weiss and Thakur, *Global Governance and the UN,* 21.

13. Ibid.

14. Luck, "R2P at Ten," 502.

15. Quoted in Thomas G. Weiss, *What's Wrong with the United Nations and How to Fix It,* 2nd ed. (Malden, MA: Polity Press, 2012), 14.

16. Ibid., 14.

17. Mark Malloch Brown, "The John W. Holmes Lecture: Can the UN Be Reformed?" *Global Governance* 14, no. 1 (2008): 1.

18. Ibid., 6.

19. Ibid., 7.

20. Ibid., 11.

Appendix

Charter of the United Nations (Selected Sections)

The Charter of the United Nations was signed on 26 June 1945, in San Francisco, at the conclusion of the UN Conference on International Organization, and it came into force on 24 October 1945. The Statute of the International Court of Justice is an integral part of the Charter.

Amendments to Articles 23, 27, and 61 were adopted by the General Assembly on 17 December 1963 and came into force on 31 August 1965. A further amendment to Article 61 was adopted by the General Assembly on 20 December 1971 and came into force on 24 September 1973. An amendment to Article 109, adopted by the General Assembly on 20 December 1965, came into force on 12 June 1968.

PREAMBLE TO THE CHARTER OF THE UNITED NATIONS

WE THE PEOPLES OF THE UNITED NATIONS DETERMINED

to save succeeding generations from the scourge of war, which twice in our lifetime has brought untold sorrow to mankind, and

to reaffirm faith in fundamental human rights, in the dignity and worth of the human person, in the equal rights of men and women and of nations large and small, and

to establish conditions under which justice and respect for the obligations arising from treaties and other sources of international law can be maintained, and

to promote social progress and better standards of life in larger freedom,

AND FOR THESE ENDS

to practice tolerance and live together in peace with one another as good neighbours, and

to unite our strength to maintain international peace and security, and

to ensure, by the acceptance of principles and the institution of methods, that armed force shall not be used, save in the common interest, and

to employ international machinery for the promotion of the economic and social advancement of all peoples,

HAVE RESOLVED TO COMBINE OUR EFFORTS TO ACCOMPLISH THESE AIMS.

Accordingly, our respective Governments, through representatives assembled in the city of San Francisco, who have exhibited their full powers found to be in good and due form, have agreed to the present Charter of the United Nations and do hereby establish an international organization to be known as the United Nations.

CHAPTER I

PURPOSES AND PRINCIPLES

Article 1

The Purposes of the United Nations are:

1. To maintain international peace and security, and to that end: to take effective collective measures for the prevention and removal of threats to the peace, and for the suppression of acts of aggression or other breaches of the peace, and to bring about by peaceful means, and in conformity with the principles of justice and international law, adjustment or settlement of international disputes or situations which might lead to a breach of the peace;

2. To develop friendly relations among nations based on respect for the principle of equal rights and self-determination of peoples, and to take other appropriate measures to strengthen universal peace;

3. To achieve international co-operation in solving international problems of an economic, social, cultural, or humanitarian character, and in promoting and encouraging respect for human rights and for fundamental freedoms for all without distinction as to race, sex, language, or religion; and

4. To be a centre for harmonizing the actions of nations in the attainment of these common ends.

Article 2

The Organization and its Members, in pursuit of the Purposes stated in Article 1, shall act in accordance with the following Principles.

1. The Organization is based on the principle of the sovereign equality of all its Members.

2. All Members, in order to ensure to all of them the rights and benefits resulting from membership, shall fulfill in good faith the obligations assumed by them in accordance with the present Charter.

3. All Members shall settle their international disputes by peaceful means in such a manner that international peace and security, and justice, are not endangered.

4. All Members shall refrain in their international relations from the threat or use of force against the territorial integrity or political independence of any state, or in any other manner inconsistent with the Purposes of the United Nations.

5. All Members shall give the United Nations every assistance in any action it takes in accordance with the present Charter, and shall refrain from giving assistance to any state against which the United Nations is taking preventive or enforcement action.

6. The Organization shall ensure that states which are not Members of the United Nations act in accordance with these Principles so far as may be necessary for the maintenance of international peace and security.

7. Nothing contained in the present Charter shall authorize the United Nations to intervene in matters which are essentially within the domestic jurisdiction of any state or shall require the Members to submit such matters to settlement under the present Charter; but this principle shall not prejudice the application of enforcement measures under Chapter VII.

CHAPTER II

MEMBERSHIP

Article 3

The original Members of the United Nations shall be the states which, having participated in the United Nations Conference on International Organization at San Francisco, or having previously signed the Declaration by United Nations of 1 January 1942, sign the present Charter and ratify it in accordance with Article 110.

Article 4

1. Membership in the United Nations is open to all other peace-loving states which accept the obligations contained in the present

Charter and, in the judgment of the Organization, are able and willing to carry out these obligations.

2. The admission of any such state to membership in the United Nations will be effected by a decision of the General Assembly upon the recommendation of the Security Council.

Article 5

A Member of the United Nations against which preventive or enforcement action has been taken by the Security Council may be suspended from the exercise of the rights and privileges of membership by the General Assembly upon the recommendation of the Security Council. The exercise of these rights and privileges may be restored by the Security Council.

Article 6

A Member of the United Nations which has persistently violated the Principles contained in the present Charter may be expelled from the Organization by the General Assembly upon the recommendation of the Security Council.

CHAPTER III

ORGANS

Article 7

1. There are established as the principal organs of the United Nations: a General Assembly, a Security Council, an Economic and Social Council, a Trusteeship Council, an International Court of Justice, and a Secretariat.

2. Such subsidiary organs as may be found necessary may be established in accordance with the present Charter.

Article 8

The United Nations shall place no restrictions on the eligibility of men and women to participate in any capacity and under conditions of equality in its principal and subsidiary organs.

CHAPTER IV

THE GENERAL ASSEMBLY

Composition

Article 9

1. The General Assembly shall consist of all the Members of the United Nations.

2. Each Member shall have not more than five representatives in the General Assembly.

Functions and Powers

Article 10

The General Assembly may discuss any questions or any matters within the scope of the present Charter or relating to the powers and functions of any organs provided for in the present Charter, and, except as provided in Article 12, may make recommendations to the Members of the United Nations or to the Security Council or to both on any such questions or matters.

Article 11

1. The General Assembly may consider the general principles of co-operation in the maintenance of international peace and security, including the principles governing disarmament and the regulation of armaments, and may make recommendations with regard to such principles to the Members or to the Security Council or to both.

2. The General Assembly may discuss any questions relating to the maintenance of international peace and security brought before it by any Member of the United Nations, or by the Security Council, or by a state which is not a Member of the United Nations in accordance with Article 35, paragraph 2, and, except as provided in Article 12, may

make recommendations with regard to any such questions to the state or states concerned or to the Security Council or to both. Any such question on which action is necessary shall be referred to the Security Council by the General Assembly either before or after discussion.

3. The General Assembly may call the attention of the Security Council to situations which are likely to endanger international peace and security.

4. The powers of the General Assembly set forth in this Article shall not limit the general scope of Article 10.

Article 12

1. While the Security Council is exercising in respect of any dispute or situation the functions assigned to it in the present Charter, the General Assembly shall not make any recommendation with regard to that dispute or situation unless the Security Council so requests.

2. The Secretary-General, with the consent of the Security Council, shall notify the General Assembly at each session of any matters relative to the maintenance of international peace and security which are being dealt with by the Security Council and shall similarly notify the General Assembly, or the Members of the United Nations if the General Assembly is not in session, immediately the Security Council ceases to deal with such matters.

Article 13

1. The General Assembly shall initiate studies and make recommendations for the purpose of:

a. promoting international co-operation in the political field and encouraging the progressive development of international law and its codification;

b. promoting international co-operation in the economic, social, cultural, educational, and health fields, and assisting in the realization of human rights and fundamental freedoms for all without distinction as to race, sex, language, or religion.

2. The further responsibilities, functions, and powers of the General Assembly with respect to matters mentioned in paragraph 1(b) above are set forth in Chapters IX and X.

Article 14

Subject to the provisions of Article 12, the General Assembly may recommend measures for the peaceful adjustment of any situation, regardless of origin, which it deems likely to impair the general welfare or friendly relations among nations, including situations resulting from a violation of the provisions of the present Charter setting forth the Purposes and Principles of the United Nations.

Article 15

1. The General Assembly shall receive and consider annual and special reports from the Security Council; these reports shall include an account of the measures that the Security Council has decided upon or taken to maintain international peace and security.

2. The General Assembly shall receive and consider reports from the other organs of the United Nations.

Article 16

The General Assembly shall perform such functions with respect to the international trusteeship system as are assigned to it under Chapters XII and XIII, including the approval of the trusteeship agreements for areas not designated as strategic.

Article 17

1. The General Assembly shall consider and approve the budget of the Organization.

2. The expenses of the Organization shall be borne by the Members as apportioned by the General Assembly.

3. The General Assembly shall consider and approve any financial and budgetary arrangements with specialized agencies referred

to in Article 57 and shall examine the administrative budgets of such specialized agencies with a view to making recommendations to the agencies concerned.

Voting

Article 18

1. Each member of the General Assembly shall have one vote.

2. Decisions of the General Assembly on important questions shall be made by a two-thirds majority of the members present and voting. These questions shall include: recommendations with respect to the maintenance of international peace and security, the election of the non-permanent members of the Security Council, the election of the members of the Economic and Social Council, the election of members of the Trusteeship Council in accordance with paragraph 1(c) of Article 86, the admission of new Members to the United Nations, the suspension of the rights and privileges of membership, the expulsion of Members, questions relating to the operation of the trusteeship system, and budgetary questions.

3. Decisions on other questions, including the determination of additional categories of questions to be decided by a two-thirds majority, shall be made by a majority of the members present and voting.

Article 19

A Member of the United Nations which is in arrears in the payment of its financial contributions to the Organization shall have no vote in the General Assembly if the amount of its arrears equals or exceeds the amount of the contributions due from it for the preceding two full years. The General Assembly may, nevertheless, permit such a Member to vote if it is satisfied that the failure to pay is due to conditions beyond the control of the Member.

Procedure

Article 20

The General Assembly shall meet in regular annual sessions and in such special sessions as occasion may require. Special sessions shall be convoked by the Secretary-General at the request of the Security Council or of a majority of the Members of the United Nations.

Article 21

The General Assembly shall adopt its own rules of procedure. It shall elect its President for each session.

Article 22

The General Assembly may establish such subsidiary organs as it deems necessary for the performance of its functions.

CHAPTER V

THE SECURITY COUNCIL

Composition

Article 23

1. The Security Council shall consist of fifteen Members of the United Nations. The Republic of China, France, the Union of Soviet Socialist Republics, the United Kingdom of Great Britain and Northern Ireland, and the United States of America shall be permanent members of the Security Council. The General Assembly shall elect ten other Members of the United Nations to be non-permanent members of the Security Council, due regard being specially paid, in the first instance to the contribution of Members of the United Nations to the maintenance of international peace and security and to the

other purposes of the Organization, and also to equitable geographical distribution.

2. The non-permanent members of the Security Council shall be elected for a term of two years. In the first election of the non-permanent members after the increase of the membership of the Security Council from eleven to fifteen, two of the four additional members shall be chosen for a term of one year. A retiring member shall not be eligible for immediate re-election.

3. Each member of the Security Council shall have one representative.

Functions and Powers

Article 24

1. In order to ensure prompt and effective action by the United Nations, its Members confer on the Security Council primary responsibility for the maintenance of international peace and security, and agree that in carrying out its duties under this responsibility the Security Council acts on their behalf.

2. In discharging these duties the Security Council shall act in accordance with the Purposes and Principles of the United Nations. The specific powers granted to the Security Council for the discharge of these duties are laid down in Chapters VI, VII, VIII, and XII.

3. The Security Council shall submit annual and, when necessary, special reports to the General Assembly for its consideration.

Article 25

The Members of the United Nations agree to accept and carry out the decisions of the Security Council in accordance with the present Charter.

Article 26

In order to promote the establishment and maintenance of international peace and security with the least diversion for armaments of the world's human and economic resources, the Security Council shall be responsible for formulating, with the assistance of the Military Staff Committee referred to in Article 47, plans to be submitted to the Members of the United Nations for the establishment of a system for the regulation of armaments.

Voting

Article 27

1. Each member of the Security Council shall have one vote.

2. Decisions of the Security Council on procedural matters shall be made by an affirmative vote of nine members.

3. Decisions of the Security Council on all other matters shall be made by an affirmative vote of nine members including the concurring votes of the permanent members; provided that, in decisions under Chapter VI, and under paragraph 3 of Article 52, a party to a dispute shall abstain from voting.

Procedure

Article 28

1. The Security Council shall be so organized as to be able to function continuously. Each member of the Security Council shall for this purpose be represented at all times at the seat of the Organization.

2. The Security Council shall hold periodic meetings at which each of its members may, if it so desires, be represented by a member of the government or by some other specially designated representative.

3. The Security Council may hold meetings at such places other than the seat of the Organization as in its judgment will best facilitate its work.

Article 29

The Security Council may establish such subsidiary organs as it deems necessary for the performance of its functions.

Article 30

The Security Council shall adopt its own rules of procedure, including the method of selecting its President.

Article 31

Any Member of the United Nations which is not a member of the Security Council may participate, without vote, in the discussion of any question brought before the Security Council whenever the latter considers that the interests of that Member are specially affected.

Article 32

Any Member of the United Nations which is not a member of the Security Council or any state which is not a Member of the United Nations, if it is a party to a dispute under consideration by the Security Council, shall be invited to participate, without vote, in the discussion relating to the dispute. The Security Council shall lay down such conditions as it deems just for the participation of a state which is not a Member of the United Nations.

CHAPTER VI

PACIFIC SETTLEMENT OF DISPUTES

Article 33

1. The parties to any dispute, the continuance of which is likely to endanger the maintenance of international peace and security, shall, first of all, seek a solution by negotiation, enquiry, mediation, conciliation, arbitration, judicial settlement, resort to regional agencies or arrangements, or other peaceful means of their own choice.

2. The Security Council shall, when it deems necessary, call upon the parties to settle their dispute by such means.

Article 34

The Security Council may investigate any dispute, or any situation which might lead to international friction or give rise to a dispute, in order to determine whether the continuance of the dispute or situation is likely to endanger the maintenance of international peace and security.

Article 35

1. Any Member of the United Nations may bring any dispute, or any situation of the nature referred to in Article 34, to the attention of the Security Council or of the General Assembly.

2. A state which is not a Member of the United Nations may bring to the attention of the Security Council or of the General Assembly any dispute to which it is a party if it accepts in advance, for the purposes of the dispute, the obligations of pacific settlement provided in the present Charter.

3. The proceedings of the General Assembly in respect of matters brought to its attention under this Article will be subject to the provisions of Articles 11 and 12.

Article 36

1. The Security Council may, at any stage of a dispute of the nature referred to in Article 33 or of a situation of like nature, recommend appropriate procedures or methods of adjustment.

2. The Security Council should take into consideration any procedures for the settlement of the dispute which have already been adopted by the parties.

3. In making recommendations under this Article the Security Council should also take into consideration that legal disputes should as a general rule be referred by the parties to the International Court of Justice in accordance with the provisions of the Statute of the Court.

Article 37

1. Should the parties to a dispute of the nature referred to in Article 33 fail to settle it

by the means indicated in that Article, they shall refer it to the Security Council.

2. If the Security Council deems that the continuance of the dispute is in fact likely to endanger the maintenance of international peace and security, it shall decide whether to take action under Article 36 or to recommend such terms of settlement as it may consider appropriate.

Article 38

Without prejudice to the provisions of Articles 33 to 37, the Security Council may, if all the parties to any dispute so request, make recommendations to the parties with a view to a pacific settlement of the dispute.

CHAPTER VII

Action with Respect to Threats to the Peace, Breaches of the Peace, and Acts of Aggression

Article 39

The Security Council shall determine the existence of any threat to the peace, breach of the peace, or act of aggression and shall make recommendations, or decide what measures shall be taken in accordance with Articles 41 and 42, to maintain or restore international peace and security.

Article 40

In order to prevent an aggravation of the situation, the Security Council may, before making the recommendations or deciding upon the measures provided for in Article 39, call upon the parties concerned to comply with such provisional measures as it deems necessary or desirable. Such provisional measures shall be without prejudice to the rights, claims, or position of the parties concerned. The Security Council shall duly take account of failure to comply with such provisional measures.

Article 41

The Security Council may decide what measures not involving the use of armed force are to be employed to give effect to its decisions, and it may call upon the Members of the United Nations to apply such measures. These may include complete or partial interruption of economic relations and of rail, sea, air, postal, telegraphic, radio, and other means of communication, and the severance of diplomatic relations.

Article 42

Should the Security Council consider that measures provided for in Article 41 would be inadequate or have proved to be inadequate, it may take such action by air, sea, or land forces as may be necessary to maintain or restore international peace and security. Such action may include demonstrations, blockade, and other operations by air, sea, or land forces of Members of the United Nations.

Article 43

1. All Members of the United Nations, in order to contribute to the maintenance of international peace and security, undertake to make available to the Security Council, on its call and in accordance with a special agreement or agreements, armed forces, assistance, and facilities, including rights of passage, necessary for the purpose of maintaining international peace and security.

2. Such agreement or agreements shall govern the numbers and types of forces, their degree of readiness and general location, and the nature of the facilities and assistance to be provided.

3. The agreement or agreements shall be negotiated as soon as possible on the initiative of the Security Council. They shall be concluded between the Security Council and Members or between the Security Council and groups of Members and shall be subject to ratification by the signatory states in

accordance with their respective constitutional processes.

Article 44

When the Security Council has decided to use force it shall, before calling upon a Member not represented on it to provide armed forces in fulfilment of the obligations assumed under Article 43, invite that Member, if the Member so desires, to participate in the decisions of the Security Council concerning the employment of contingents of that Member's armed forces.

Article 45

In order to enable the United Nations to take urgent military measures, Members shall hold immediately available national air-force contingents for combined international enforcement action. The strength and degree of readiness of these contingents and plans for their combined action shall be determined within the limits laid down in the special agreement or agreements referred to in Article 43, by the Security Council with the assistance of the Military Staff Committee.

Article 46

Plans for the application of armed force shall be made by the Security Council with the assistance of the Military Staff Committee.

Article 48

1. The action required to carry out the decisions of the Security Council for the maintenance of international peace and security shall be taken by all the Members of the United Nations or by some of them, as the Security Council may determine.

2. Such decisions shall be carried out by the Members of the United Nations directly and through their action in the appropriate international agencies of which they are members.

Article 49

The Members of the United Nations shall join in affording mutual assistance in carrying out the measures decided upon by the Security Council.

Article 50

If preventive or enforcement measures against any state are taken by the Security Council, any other state, whether a Member of the United Nations or not, which finds itself confronted with special economic problems arising from the carrying out of those measures shall have the right to consult the Security Council with regard to a solution of those problems.

Article 51

Nothing in the present Charter shall impair the inherent right of individual or collective self-defence if an armed attack occurs against a Member of the United Nations, until the Security Council has taken measures necessary to maintain international peace and security. Measures taken by Members in the exercise of this right of self-defence shall be immediately reported to the Security Council and shall not in any way affect the authority and responsibility of the Security Council under the present Charter to take at any time such action as it deems necessary in order to maintain or restore international peace and security.

CHAPTER VIII
REGIONAL ARRANGEMENTS

Article 52

1. Nothing in the present Charter precludes the existence of regional arrangements or agencies for dealing with such matters relating to the maintenance of international peace and security as are appropriate for

regional action provided that such arrangements or agencies and their activities are consistent with the Purposes and Principles of the United Nations.

2. The Members of the United Nations entering into such arrangements or constituting such agencies shall make every effort to achieve pacific settlement of local disputes through such regional arrangements or by such regional agencies before referring them to the Security Council.

3. The Security Council shall encourage the development of pacific settlement of local disputes through such regional arrangements or by such regional agencies either on the initiative of the states concerned or by reference from the Security Council.

4. This Article in no way impairs the application of Articles 34 and 35.

Article 53

1. The Security Council shall, where appropriate, utilize such regional arrangements or agencies for enforcement action under its authority. But no enforcement action shall be taken under regional arrangements or by regional agencies without the authorization of the Security Council, with the exception of measures against any enemy state, as defined in paragraph 2 of this Article, provided for pursuant to Article 107 or in regional arrangements directed against renewal of aggressive policy on the part of any such state, until such time as the Organization may, on request of the Governments concerned, be charged with the responsibility for preventing further aggression by such a state.

2. The term "enemy state" as used in paragraph 1 of this Article applies to any state which during the Second World War has been an enemy of any signatory of the present Charter.

Article 54

The Security Council shall at all times be kept fully informed of activities undertaken or in contemplation under regional arrangements or by regional agencies for the maintenance of international peace and security.

CHAPTER IX

INTERNATIONAL ECONOMIC AND SOCIAL COOPERATION

Article 55

With a view to the creation of conditions of stability and well-being which are necessary for peaceful and friendly relations among nations based on respect for the principle of equal rights and self-determination of peoples, the United Nations shall promote:

a. higher standards of living, full employment, and conditions of economic and social progress and development;

b. solutions of international economic, social, health, and related problems; and international cultural and educational cooperation; and

c. universal respect for, and observance of, human rights and fundamental freedoms for all without distinction as to race, sex, language, or religion.

Article 56

All Members pledge themselves to take joint and separate action in cooperation with the Organization for the achievement of the purposes set forth in Article 55.

Article 57

1. The various specialized agencies, established by intergovernmental agreement and having wide international responsibilities, as defined in their basic instruments, in economic, social, cultural, educational, health, and related fields, shall be brought into relationship with the United Nations in accordance with the provisions of Article 63.

2. Such agencies thus brought into relationship with the United Nations are hereinafter referred to as "specialized agencies."

Article 58

The Organization shall make recommendations for the co-ordination of the policies and activities of the specialized agencies.

Article 59

The Organization shall, where appropriate, initiate negotiations among the states concerned for the creation of any new specialized agencies required for the accomplishment of the purposes set forth in Article 55.

Article 60

Responsibility for the discharge of the functions of the Organization set forth in this Chapter shall be vested in the General Assembly and, under the authority of the General Assembly, in the Economic and Social Council, which shall have for this purpose the powers set forth in Chapter X.

CHAPTER X

THE ECONOMIC AND SOCIAL COUNCIL

Composition

Article 61

1. The Economic and Social Council shall consist of fifty-four Members of the United Nations elected by the General Assembly.

2. Subject to the provisions of paragraph 3, eighteen members of the Economic and Social Council shall be elected each year for a term of three years. A retiring member shall be eligible for immediate re-election.

3. At the first election after the increase in the membership of the Economic and Social Council from twenty-seven to fifty-four members, in addition to the members

elected in place of the nine members whose term of office expires at the end of that year, twenty-seven additional members shall be elected. Of these twenty-seven additional members, the term of office of nine members so elected shall expire at the end of one year, and of nine other members at the end of two years, in accordance with arrangements made by the General Assembly.

4. Each member of the Economic and Social Council shall have one representative.

Functions and Powers

Article 62

1. The Economic and Social Council may make or initiate studies and reports with respect to international economic, social, cultural, educational, health, and related matters and may make recommendations with respect to any such matters to the General Assembly, to the Members of the United Nations, and to the specialized agencies concerned.

2. It may make recommendations for the purpose of promoting respect for, and observance of, human rights and fundamental freedoms for all.

3. It may prepare draft conventions for submission to the General Assembly, with respect to matters falling within its competence.

4. It may call, in accordance with the rules prescribed by the United Nations, international conferences on matters falling within its competence.

Article 63

1. The Economic and Social Council may enter into agreements with any of the agencies referred to in Article 57, defining the terms on which the agency concerned shall be brought into relationship with the United Nations. Such agreements shall be subject to approval by the General Assembly.

2. It may co-ordinate the activities of the specialized agencies through consultation with and recommendations to such agencies

and through recommendations to the General Assembly and to the Members of the United Nations.

Article 64

1. The Economic and Social Council may take appropriate steps to obtain regular reports from the specialized agencies. It may make arrangements with the Members of the United Nations and with the specialized agencies to obtain reports on the steps taken to give effect to its own recommendations and to recommendations on matters falling within its competence made by the General Assembly.

2. It may communicate its observations on these reports to the General Assembly.

Article 65

The Economic and Social Council may furnish information to the Security Council and shall assist the Security Council upon its request.

Article 66

1. The Economic and Social Council shall perform such functions as fall within its competence in connection with the carrying out of the recommendations of the General Assembly.

2. It may, with the approval of the General Assembly, perform services at the request of Members of the United Nations and at the request of specialized agencies.

3. It shall perform such other functions as are specified elsewhere in the present Charter or as may be assigned to it by the General Assembly.

Voting

Article 67

1. Each member of the Economic and Social Council shall have one vote.

2. Decisions of the Economic and Social Council shall be made by a majority of the members present and voting.

Procedure

Article 68

The Economic and Social Council shall set up commissions in economic and social fields and for the promotion of human rights, and such other commissions as may be required for the performance of its functions.

Article 69

The Economic and Social Council shall invite any Member of the United Nations to participate, without vote, in its deliberations on any matter of particular concern to that Member.

Article 70

The Economic and Social Council may make arrangements for representatives of the specialized agencies to participate, without vote, in its deliberations and in those of the commissions established by it, and for its representatives to participate in the deliberations of the specialized agencies.

Article 71

The Economic and Social Council may make suitable arrangements for consultation with non-governmental organizations which are concerned with matters within its competence. Such arrangements may be made with international organizations and, where appropriate, with national organizations after consultation with the Member of the United Nations concerned.

Article 72

1. The Economic and Social Council shall adopt its own rules of procedure, including the method of selecting its President.

2. The Economic and Social Council shall meet as required in accordance with its rules,

which shall include provision for the convening of meetings on the request of a majority of its members.

Chapter XIV

The International Court of Justice

Article 92

The International Court of Justice shall be the principal judicial organ of the United Nations. It shall function in accordance with the annexed Statute, which is based upon the Statute of the Permanent Court of International Justice and forms an integral part of the present Charter.

Article 93

1. All Members of the United Nations are ipso facto parties to the Statute of the International Court of Justice.

2. A state which is not a Member of the United Nations may become a party to the Statute of the International Court of Justice on conditions to be determined in each case by the General Assembly upon the recommendation of the Security Council.

Article 94

1. Each Member of the United Nations undertakes to comply with the decision of the International Court of Justice in any case to which it is a party.

2. If any party to a case fails to perform the obligations incumbent upon it under a judgment rendered by the Court, the other party may have recourse to the Security Council, which may, if it deems necessary, make recommendations or decide upon measures to be taken to give effect to the judgment.

Article 95

Nothing in the present Charter shall prevent Members of the United Nations from

entrusting the solution of their differences to other tribunals by virtue of agreements already in existence or which may be concluded in the future.

Article 96

1. The General Assembly or the Security Council may request the International Court of Justice to give an advisory opinion on any legal question.

2. Other organs of the United Nations and specialized agencies, which may at any time be so authorized by the General Assembly, may also request advisory opinions of the Court on legal questions arising within the scope of their activities.

Chapter XV

The Secretariat

Article 97

The Secretariat shall comprise a Secretary-General and such staff as the Organization may require. The Secretary-General shall be appointed by the General Assembly upon the recommendation of the Security Council. He shall be the chief administrative officer of the Organization.

Article 98

The Secretary-General shall act in that capacity in all meetings of the General Assembly, of the Security Council, of the Economic and Social Council, and of the Trusteeship Council, and shall perform such other functions as are entrusted to him by these organs. The Secretary-General shall make an annual report to the General Assembly on the work of the Organization.

Article 99

The Secretary-General may bring to the attention of the Security Council any matter which in his opinion may threaten the maintenance of international peace and security.

Article 100

1. In the performance of their duties the Secretary-General and the staff shall not seek or receive instructions from any government or from any other authority external to the Organization. They shall refrain from any action which might reflect on their position as international officials responsible only to the Organization.

2. Each Member of the United Nations undertakes to respect the exclusively international character of the responsibilities of the Secretary-General and the staff and not to seek to influence them in the discharge of their responsibilities.

Article 101

1. The staff shall be appointed by the Secretary-General under regulations established by the General Assembly.

2. Appropriate staffs shall be permanently assigned to the Economic and Social Council, the Trusteeship Council, and, as required, to other organs of the United Nations. These staffs shall form a part of the Secretariat.

3. The paramount consideration in the employment of the staff and in the determination of the conditions of service shall be the necessity of securing the highest standards of efficiency, competence, and integrity. Due regard shall be paid to the importance of recruiting the staff on as wide a geographical basis as possible.

General Assembly and ratified in accordance with their respective constitutional processes by two-thirds of the Members of the United Nations, including all the permanent members of the Security Council.

Article 109

1. A General Conference of the Members of the United Nations for the purpose of reviewing the present Charter may be held at a date and place to be fixed by a two-thirds vote of the members of the General Assembly and by a vote of any nine members of the Security Council. Each Member of the United Nations shall have one vote in the conference.

2. Any alteration of the present Charter recommended by a two-thirds vote of the conference shall take effect when ratified in accordance with their respective constitutional processes by two-thirds of the Members of the United Nations including all the permanent members of the Security Council.

3. If such a conference has not been held before the tenth annual session of the General Assembly following the coming into force of the present Charter, the proposal to call such a conference shall be placed on the agenda of that session of the General Assembly, and the conference shall be held if so decided by a majority vote of the members of the General Assembly and by a vote of any seven members of the Security Council.

CHAPTER XVIII

AMENDMENTS

Article 108

Amendments to the present Charter shall come into force for all Members of the United Nations when they have been adopted by a vote of two-thirds of the members of the

Glossary

Advisory opinion An opinion issued by the International Court of Justice based on a request by an international organization for advice on a general question of international law.

Apartheid An Afrikaans term meaning "separateness"; the policy in South Africa from the 1950s to 1992 of official discrimination touching all aspects of public and private life, designed to keep the different races separate.

Arms control and disarmament Efforts to induce states to limit, reduce, or eliminate specific types of weapons and armaments.

Arrearages Unpaid assessed contributions to an international organization.

Balance of payments The flow of money into and out of a country from trade, tourism, foreign aid, sale of services, profits, and so on.

Basic human needs Proposals in the development community to shift from emphasizing economic growth to progress in meeting the population's basic needs, including better health care, education, and water supplies.

Bretton Woods institutions The international economic institutions—the World Bank and the International Monetary Fund—created in 1944 to promote global monetary stability and economic growth. Also includes the trade procedures established under the General Agreement on Tariffs and Trade (GATT), now the World Trade Organization (WTO).

BRICS Brazil, Russia, India, China, and South Africa. An informal group of emerging economic powers.

Civil society Organizations and associations that are independent of government and business, including advocacy groups, religious groups, ethnic associations, professional associations, and sporting associations.

Coalition of the willing An ad hoc group of states that volunteer to carry out a peace enforcement or humanitarian mission with or without Security Council authorization.

Collective legitimation The garnering of votes at the UN in support of a particular state's policy or a new international norm.

Collective security The concept behind the League of Nations and the United Nations, namely, that aggression by one state is aggression against all and should be defeated collectively.

Concert of Europe, or Concert system The nineteenth-century practice of multilateral meetings of leaders of major European powers to settle problems.

Conference of parties Governing body comprising all states that have ratified an international convention or treaty.

Constructivism An approach to the study of international relations that examines how shared beliefs, rules, norms, organizations, and cultural practices shape state and individual behavior.

Crimes against humanity International crimes that include murder, enslavement, forcible transfer of populations, ethnic cleansing, and torture.

Democratization The process whereby states become increasingly democratic; that is, citizens vote for representatives who rule on their behalf, and the political system is marked by the rule of law.

Dependency theory Derived from Marxism, an explanation of poverty and underdevelopment in less developed countries based on their historical dependence on and domination by rich countries.

Economic liberalism The theory that the free interplay of market forces leads to a more efficient allocation of resources, to the benefit of the majority.

Enforcement actions The use of direct actions—economic sanctions, withdrawal of aid, or military force—by the UN to ensure compliance with Security Council directives.

Exceptionalism Belief held in the United States that because of its tradition of democracy and adherence to human rights norms it has a unique role to play in international relations and is not subject to the same constraints as others.

First-generation human rights, or negative rights The civil or political rights of citizens that prevent governmental authority from interfering with private individuals in civil society.

Functionalism The belief that cooperation in solving social and economic issues can be separated from politics but will ultimately contribute to peace. UN specialized agencies are functionalist organizations.

Genocide The systematic killing or harming of a group of people based on racial, religious, or ethnic characteristics, with the intention of destroying the group.

Global Compact on Corporate Responsibility Voluntary principles that multinational corporations agree to accept and work toward in cooperation with the UN and NGOs.

Global governance The rules, norms, activities, and organizations designed to address the international problems that states alone cannot solve.

Globalization The idea that economies, social relations, and cultures are rapidly being linked by international market processes, international institutions, and NGOs in such a way that state sovereignty and distinctiveness are undermined; the internationalization of the capitalist economy in which states, markets, and civil society are restructured to facilitate the flow of capital.

Group of 7 (G-7) The major economic powers, who meet annually to address world economic problems.

Group of 20 (G-20) Group of developed and emerging powers who play an important role in international economic relations.

Group of 77 (G-77) A coalition of LDCs that pressed for reforms in economic relations between developing and developed countries; also referred to as "the South." Now includes 132 countries.

Human development The concept that economic growth alone does not ensure improvement in human standards of living, measured by such indicators as average life expectancy, infant mortality, adult literacy, and per capita nutritional level.

Human security The idea that security includes not only the security of the state and territory but also security of individuals from civil and economic turmoil and health and environmental threats.

Humanitarian intervention UN or individual states' actions to alleviate human suffering during violent conflicts without necessarily obtaining the consent of the host country.

Interdependence The sensitivity and vulnerability of states to each other's actions resulting from increased interactions generated by trade, monetary flows, telecommunications, and shared interests.

Internally displaced persons People who are forced to flee their homes in order to escape violence, natural disaster, or persecution but who remain within their country's borders.

International Bill of Rights A term for the three primary human rights documents: the Universal Declaration of Human Rights, the Covenant on International Civil and Political Rights, and the Covenant on Economic, Social, and Cultural Rights.

International humanitarian law International laws holding states and individuals accountable for actions during war, specifically including protection of and assistance to military and civilian victims of war.

International intergovernmental organization (IGO) International agency or body set up and controlled by member states to deal with areas of common interest.

Liberalism A theoretical perspective, based on the goodness of the individual and the value of political and legal institutions, holding that there are multiple actors in international politics and that the state has many different interests that sometimes conflict.

Militarized masculinity Term originating within critical analysis referring to a training process that dehumanizes opponents and women for the purpose of conducting warfare. This diminution of women may create an entitlement perspective that is conducive to violence against women.

Millennium Development Goals (MDGs) Eight goals agreed to by UN member states in 2000 to improve the economic and social conditions of people; included specific targets and a procedure for tracking progress toward attainment of the goals by 2015.

Multilateral diplomacy Diplomatic interactions involving three or more actors, whether states or nonstate actors, and the formation of coalitions for the purpose of pooling votes, resources, and power to secure desired outcomes in international bodies such as the UN.

Multilateralism The conduct of international activities by three or more states in accordance with shared general principles, often through international or multilateral institutions.

Multinational corporations (MNCs) Private enterprises with production facilities, sales, or activity in more than one country; also called transnational corporations.

New International Economic Order (NIEO) A list of demands by the G-77 in the 1970s to reform economic relations between the North and the South, that is, between the developed countries and the less developed countries.

Nonaligned Movement (NAM) Group of developing countries held together by principles of anticolonialism, opposition to racism, and neutrality toward the Cold War.

Noncompulsory jurisdiction When states are not obligated to bring disputes to a body such as the International Court of Justice for settlement.

Nongovernmental organizations (NGOs) Private associations of individuals or groups that engage in political activity, often across national borders.

Nonintervention The principle that obliges states and international organizations not to interfere in matters within the domestic jurisdiction of other sovereign states.

Non-refoulement A principle of international law prohibiting a state or international organization from returning a refugee or person seeking asylum back to the state of origin against his or her will if there is credible risk of persecution.

Peacebuilding Postconflict activities to strengthen and preserve peace settlements, such as development aid, civilian administration, and election and human rights monitoring.

Peaceful settlement Various techniques by which disputes are settled, including adjudication, arbitration, mediation, conciliation, and good offices.

Peacekeeping Use of multilateral forces to achieve different objectives: traditionally, observation of cease-fire lines and cease-fires and separation of forces; multidimensional complex operations may employ both military and civilian personnel and involve use of force to deliver humanitarian aid and promote law and order.

Politicization The linkage of different issues for political purposes, as in the introduction of a clearly political topic to an organization dealing with health problems.

Poverty alleviation Programs designed to improve food supply, nutrition, health, housing, and the standard of living for the poorest people, particularly in remote areas of developing countries and in minority groups whose poverty is not reduced by general economic growth and development.

Preventive diplomacy The practice of engaging in diplomatic actions to prevent the outbreak of conflict; the monitoring of hot spots before conflict erupts.

Privatization Belief held by economic liberals that economies function more efficiently if there is private ownership of industries and services.

Realist theory, or realism A theory of world politics that emphasizes states' interest in accumulating power to ensure security in an anarchic world.

Refugee As defined by the 1951 Refugee Convention, a person who, because of a "well-founded fear of being persecuted for reasons of race, religion, nationality, membership of a particular social group or political opinion, is outside the country of his nationality and is unable or, owing to such fear, is unwilling to avail himself of the protection of that country."

Regime The rules, norms, and decisionmaking procedures developed by states and international organizations to address common concerns and to organize common activities relating to specific issue areas or problems, such as human rights, trade, or nuclear proliferation.

Responsibility to protect (R2P) Emerging norm, in response to massive human rights abuses, that the international community has the responsibility to help individuals suffering at the hands of their own state or other states.

Second-generation human rights, or positive rights The social and economic rights that states are obligated to provide for their citizenry; may include the right to an education, the right to decent housing, and the right to medical care.

Self-determination The principle according to which nationalities and colonial peoples have the right to determine who will rule them; thought to minimize war for territorial expansion.

Sovereignty The authority of the state, based on recognition by other states and nonstate actors, to govern matters within its own borders that affect its people, economy, security, and form of government.

Special Procedures The system whereby the Human Rights Council can mandate a special rapporteur, a special respresentative of the UN secretary-general, or a working group of independent experts to address specific country siutations or thematic issues.

Special representative of the secretary-general Appointee of the UN Secretary-General who represents her/him in a conflict area, UN peace operation, or thematic area such as sexual violence in conflict, and who is empowered to negotiate and investigate on behalf of the United Nations.

Specialized agencies UN-related organizations established by separate agreements to deal with specific issues, such as health, working conditions, weather, air and sea transport, and education.

Statebuilding Activities taken by international actors to create, reform, or strengthen the governmental institutions of a state and their relationships to society.

Structural adjustment programs IMF policies and recommendations to guide countries out of payment deficits and economic crises through changes in domestic economic policies and practices.

Sustainable development An approach that tries to reconcile current economic growth and environmental protection with future needs and resource supplies.

Sustainable Development Goals (SDGs) Seventeen goals agreed to by UN member states in 2015 to build on the MDGs. They encompass a broad agenda, highlighting the connections between extreme poverty, gender inequality, and environmental sustainability.

Technical assistance The provision of human skills and resources necessary for economic development, including education, training, and expert advice.

Terms of trade The ratio of the price of imports to the price of exports. When import prices are greater than the value of exports, a state experiences adverse or declining terms of trade.

Third-generation human rights The collective rights of groups, such as the rights of children or indigenous people; includes the right to democracy and to development.

Third UN External experts, consultants, citizens, and NGOs who work with UN agencies and the Secretariat.

Trade preferences The granting of special trade arrangements, usually giving trade advantages to less developed countries.

Transnational terrorism Terrorist organizations that operate and recruit in multiple countries and whose political objectives and ambitions are regional or global.

United Nations system Includes not only the UN based in New York but also the specialized agencies and other autonomous organizations headquartered in different parts of the world.

Uniting for Peace Resolution The resolution that enables the General Assembly to assume responsibility for peace and security issues if the Security Council is deadlocked.

Veto A negative vote cast in the UN Security Council by one of the permanent members that effectively defeats a decision.

Voting blocs Groups of states voting together in the UN General Assembly or in other international bodies.

War crimes Illegal activities committed during war, including deliberately targeting civilians, abusing prisoners of war, and committing crimes such as torture and rape.

Weighted voting systems Systems in which states have unequal votes, based on financial contributions, population, or geographic representation. Used in the Bretton Woods institutions.

Index

ad hoc war crimes tribunals. *See*
war crimes tribunals
Adjudication, 48, 118, 280
advisory opinions (ICJ), 46, 47,
245
Afghanistan, 89, 119, 120, 173,
174, 176, 218, 256; human
rights, 238, 259, 260; Interim
Authority, 122–123; sanctions,
129–130 (table), 176; Security
Council endorsement of use
of force, 75, 122–123; Soviet
withdrawal from, 77, 118, 138;
See also Al Qaeda; Taliban
Africa. *See specific countries*
African-led International Support
Mission to Mali (AFISMA), 146
African National Congress
(ANC), 262
African Union (AU), 57, 58, 164;
and International Criminal
Court, 281; peacekeeping, 87,
116, 137, 162, 180, 342; Somalia,
38, 59, 141
African Union-United Nations
Hybrid Mission in Darfur
(UNAMID), 139 (table), 140,
163
agenda setting, 30, 265, 302,
340–341
aggression, 23, 26, 35, 116, 120,
181, 279
agriculture, 205, 207, 222,
295, 296; *See also* Food and
Agriculture Organization;
International Fund for
Agricultural Development
Ahlenius, Inga-Britt, 96
Ahtisaari, Martti, 98
AIDS. *See* HIV/AIDS
al-Bashir, Omar, 163, 243, 275,
280, 281–282, 284
Al Hussein, Zeid Ra'ad, 245
Al Nusra Front, 129–130 (table),
174

Al Qaeda, 75, 112, 122, 123,
171, 173, 174; sanctions, 126,
129–130 (table), 176
Al Qaeda in the Islamic Mahgreb
(AQIM), 89, 146, 174
Al Shabab, 89
Algeria, 264
American Service-Members
Protection Act (2003), 280
Amnesty International (AI), 13,
101, 259, 285
Angola, 89, 128, 129–130 (table),
138, 149
Annan, Kofi, 1, 15, 17, 44 (box),
95–96, 161, 163, 235, 243, 250,
335; Global Compact, 96, 105,
224, 341–342; High-level Panel
on Threats, Challenges and
Change, 104; humanitarian
intervention, 161–162, 166,
181; migration issue, 327;
Millennium Development
Goals, 220; Millennium
Summit, 7; Oil-for-Food
Programme, 64–65; UN
reforms, 52, 55–56, 57, 64, 96,
276; *We the Peoples*, 63
Anti-Slavery International, 270,
285
apartheid, 86, 235, 238, 243, 248
(table), 251, 282; campaign
against, 261–263, 340
Arab Human Development Report,
194–195
Arab-Israeli conflict, 87, 173. *See
also* Israeli-Palestinian conflict
Arab Spring, 124, 163, 172
arbitration, 22, 118
Arbour, Louise, 245
Argentina, 57, 85, 168, 254, 258
arms control, 3, 117, 138 (box),
154, 166–167, 172, 181, 340;
General Assembly role, 27,
167; Security Council role, 169;
See also chemical weapons;
disarmament; nuclear weapons

arms embargoes, 119, 128, 129
(table), 130
Arms Trade Treaty (2013), 30,
76, 167
arms trafficking, 171, 174, 268
arrearages, 63, 100
Arria, Diego, 36
Asian Infrastructure Investment
Bank (AIIB), 9, 82, 230
Association of Southeast Asian
Nations (ASEAN), 91 (box), 196
Atlantic Charter, 24
Atomic Energy Commission,
117, 167
Atoms for Peace (1954), 168
Australia, 16, 85, 86; East Timor,
86, 116, 150, 152
Avian flu, 316, 317

Bachelet, Michelle, 214
balance-of-payment issues, 198,
200, 209
balance-of-power politics, 114,
120
Ban Ki-moon, 15, 44 (box), 96,
97 (photo), 120, 174, 282, 299,
316, 330, 335; climate change
leadership, 7, 54, 308, 313,
314; ebola crisis, 320; Human
Rights Up Front Initiative, 283,
284; Syrian crisis, 39, 164; UN
reform, 56, 65, 136, 157
Bangladesh, 89, 134, 226
Barnett, Michael, 98, 99
basic human needs projects, 199,
212
Beijing Women's Conference
(1995). *See* Fourth World
Conference on Women
Belgium, 4, 21, 48, 143
Bhagwati, Jagdish, 220
Bill and Melinda Gates
Foundation, 14, 105, 106, 208,
221, 317, 330, 337, 341
Bin Laden, Osama, 173, 176

CPSIA information can be obtained
at www.ICGtesting.com
Printed in the USA
BVOW09s0419141017
497678BV00004B/5/P